Market Rules

AMERICAN BUSINESS, POLITICS, AND SOCIETY

Series Editors: Andrew Wender Cohen, Pamela Walker Laird,
Mark H. Rose, and Elizabeth Tandy Shermer

Books in the series American Business, Politics, and Society explore the relationships
over time between governmental institutions and the creation and performance of
markets, firms, and industries large and small. The central theme of this series is that
politics, law, and public policy—understood broadly to embrace not only lawmaking
but also the structuring presence of governmental institutions—has been fundamental
to the evolution of American business from the colonial era to the present. The series
aims to explore, in particular, developments that have enduring consequences.

A complete list of books in the series is available from the publisher.

MARKET RULES

Bankers, Presidents,
and the Origins
of the Great Recession

Mark H. Rose

PENN

UNIVERSITY OF PENNSYLVANIA PRESS

PHILADELPHIA

Published by
University of Pennsylvania Press
Philadelphia, Pennsylvania 19104-4112
www.upenn.edu/pennpress

Printed in the United States of America
on acid-free paper
1 3 5 7 9 10 8 6 4 2

A Cataloging-in-Publication record is
available from the Library of Congress
ISBN 978-0-8122-5102-9

For Andrew, Cara, Ari, and Levi, our grandchildren

CONTENTS

Preface   ix

Introduction. Politics and the Markets They Made   1

PART I. LAWMAKERS AND REGULATORS

Chapter 1. Deregulation Before Deregulation:
John Kennedy, Lyndon Johnson, and James Saxon   13

Chapter 2. Supermarket Banks: Richard Nixon and Donald Regan   39

PART II. BANKERS IN POLITICS

Chapter 3. Rescuing Banks Through Growth:
Walter Wriston and Citicorp   67

Chapter 4. A Marine in Banker's Clothing:
Hugh McColl and North Carolina National Bank   84

PART III. NEW REGIMES FOR BANKERS

Chapter 5. Full-Service Banks: Bill Clinton and Sandy Weill   105

Chapter 6. God's Work in Finance:
Ken Lewis, Charles Prince, Richard Fuld, and Henry Paulson   132

Chapter 7. Reregulating the Regulators:
Barack Obama and Timothy Geithner　　　　　　　　159

Epilogue. Another Round of Bank Politics　　　　　　180

Notes　　　　　　　　　　　　　　　　　　　197

Index　　　　　　　　　　　　　　　　　　　239

Acknowledgments　　　　　　　　　　　　　255

PREFACE

I grew up in Chicago during the 1950s and 1960s. Chicagoans have a place-name for every part of the city. We lived in West Rogers Park. At the time, I perceived banks and bankers through my parents' eyes. They had a mortgage with a savings and loan association (S&L) located near Devon and California, a half mile from our house. The S&L's senior officer sat in a room just beyond the doorway, where he greeted customers. I had a passbook saving's account at that S&L. No minimum balance was required for my child's account, which came with a desk bank for me to deposit coins at home.

Perhaps because S&Ls were not permitted to offer checking accounts, my father and uncle maintained a business checking account at a bank on Clark Street near their shop. My parents' financial arrangements had a neighborhood quality, now that I think about it. They did not have contact with the First National Bank of Chicago or with one of the other major banks in the city's famous Loop. Illinois law, I discovered years later, prohibited branch banking, even among the city and state's largest and most influential firms. My mother handled my father's bookkeeping as well as the household budget. For her to deposit cash at the First National would have required a fatiguing trip on public transit. And surely, my parents and uncle asked each other, would executives at a "downtown" bank approve loans to unincorporated partners in a drapery and slipcover shop who had a history of falling behind on payments during the off-season?

Other parts of our household finances were both local and personal. "Shelly," an insurance agent and my parents' friend, came to our house to collect premiums—and to recommend additions to existing policies. My mother paid Shelly in cash. He sometimes settled for less than the amount due, returning the following week to pick up the balance. The "off-season" permeated most aspects of our financial and domestic lives. Yet, my parents owned a home and paid the mortgage.

In 1967, when Marsha Lynn Shapiro and I married, we inherited those financial arrangements. We opened a checking account at a bank in Columbus, Ohio, across the street from The Ohio State University, where we were graduate students. The account was in my name. In 1974, members of Congress and President Gerald R. Ford passed the Equal Credit Opportunity Act, the terms of which prohibited bankers from including race, age, gender, and marital status in making determinations about account ownership and loans. In other respects, the organization of financial services remained as before. Marsha Lynn and I purchased renters and auto insurance at Allstate. They stationed agents in Sears, Roebuck's doorway at the mall. We had heard about Merrill Lynch's nationwide presence and its efforts to sell shares of stock to the middle class. We lacked the surplus funds and an ideological orientation toward investments. As a result, until the mid-1970s, our experience with financial institutions consisted of a checking account, two insurance policies, our Sears charge card, and a short-term loan with a finance company at the end of our block. Nor did I have reason to doubt that bank executives remained among the nation's most prestigious citizens, especially in rural America, where they ranked only a notch below the town doctor.

During the next ten years, I observed important changes taking place in still-distant financial realms. Federal law and regulators had capped interest rates that banks and S&Ls paid depositors. Those depositors in turn, I read in the daily newspaper, were moving savings and checking balances to money market and mutual funds, which paid higher rates of interest. In the early 1980s, a colleague told me about a money market fund paying some 18 percent, which presented a stark comparison with the more modest interest rate paid at our local bank and at our credit union located on campus. I also noticed that brokerage firms like Merrill Lynch "made a market" in the stocks they sold to retail customers. At the time, I was uncertain what that meant.

In the 1980s, the organization of financial services like banking and insurance remained divided, much as when I was a teenager. Insurance companies including Allstate and State Farm sold insurance, and S&Ls, like the one near my parents' house, wrote most home mortgages. Banks such as New York's mighty Chase Manhattan and Citibank made business loans and offered checking accounts, as did thousands of small banks in towns throughout the United States. Money market and other mutual funds, more recent to the scene, operated as independent actors, with no visible connections to banks or insurance firms. Equally normal, we thought, our bank in Upper

Michigan could not open a branch in Illinois or Wisconsin. To cash a check on visits to family in Chicago required multiple forms of identification. African American travelers could not bank on that privilege.

We were not alert to the tumultuous changes that had begun to roil the business of banking. Credit cards and the automated teller machines (ATMs) offered remarkable convenience. Starting in the late 1970s, bankers touted the ATM as evidence of their customer orientation and technology's unstoppable march toward nationwide customer service. The introduction of ATMs and credit cards like Visa, I learned years later, had only a little to do with technology and nearly everything to do with politics.

In 2003, Marsha Lynn and I secured a brief look at the changes in bank practices. Now, we resided in South Florida. We had a mortgage as well as checking and savings accounts at one of the largest banks in the United States. We sought to refinance our mortgage in order to pay our daughters' college bills. Bank officials not only approved our application, but also cheerfully offered a home equity line of credit and a new credit card. A bank officer brought in coffee and soft drinks while we completed the paperwork. Refreshments for teachers! We met in a conference room on an upper floor of a handsome downtown office building. The main banking room and phalanx of tellers, where customers cashed checks and made deposits, were located on the first floor. Customers like us transacted more business outside, at the ATM. The executive who greeted customers at my parents' S&L had disappeared generations earlier.

I could not discern each aspect of what was new about our transaction that afternoon. We had only to send our payments each month. In subsequent years, we had no reason to visit a bank branch office. Five years went by until I began to connect changes at our bank to my understanding of main themes in financial history and in American political development.

This study of bank politics began serendipitously. In 2008, I had the good fortune to serve as president of the Business History Conference. I needed a presidential address for June 2009. Then, in mid-September 2008, Lehman Brothers Holdings filed for bankruptcy. Massive financial and job losses followed. I would study how that financial calamity took place.

Early on in my study, I noticed that bankers and their publicists did a poor job explaining their past. They talked about how computers made interstate banking inevitable and how their dedication to customer service had virtually dictated legislative outcomes such as the lifting of restrictions on interstate branch banking. As I studied bankers, lawmakers, regulators, and presidents, I began to identify a far more sophisticated and nuanced story of social and political institutions that extended back to the 1960s.

Historians seek to answer large questions by looking for contexts and by pushing back in time. We also believe that people matter and that we need to allow those people to take the lead in our stories. I poked around the web and our university library. I began to read in the literature aimed at bankers, investors, and insurance agents. *American Banker*, for years delivered each day to most banks in the United States, emerged as a must read for understanding the ideas bankers relied on to lure depositors, evaluate loan applicants, and prepare strongly worded messages for their congressional representatives. Politics resided at the core of American banking, I learned.

My immersion in archives and in trade journals like *American Banker* suggested a large and previously unearthed series of stories about bankers' political behavior. During the period 1961 to 1999, I learned, everyone with a stake in the money business, such as S&L executives, insurance agents, and bankers, relied on courts, Congress, and regulators to advance their interests. Bankers and S&L executives, to identify only two sets of actors, had business organizations, income, an honored place in the business community, and long-established ways of life to protect and advance. Each president between John F. Kennedy and Bill Clinton also played an important part in fostering changes in the money business. To conclude my study in 1999 with congressional passage of important bank legislation would have created what historians describe as a natural periodization. That legislation overturned the remaining bank practices I had noticed growing up.

I decided, however, to study developments leading up to 2008, when the financial crisis started. And next, I wanted to understand the process by which lawmakers, regulators, bankers, and Treasury Secretary Timothy F. Geithner reached conclusions about how to prevent a similar catastrophe in the future. In 2010, Geithner and congressional leaders secured passage of the Dodd-Frank Act. By the time I completed that portion of my book, I detected the presence of yet another story that I wanted to tell. In this final phase, I studied leading figures in bank politics during the years between 2010 and early 2017. One of my key actors, Rep. Thomas Jeb Hensarling, sought to unravel the Dodd-Frank Act in theme and detail. Beginning in January 2017, President Donald J. Trump's aides worked with Hensarling to bring about new bank legislation and changed regulations that were supposed to accelerate the pace of economic growth.

Between 1961 and the first months of 2017, I had learned, every president wanted bankers to help speed the economy's pace. And yet, for presidents, bankers, or anyone else to foster their favored legislation required a steely outlook, long-term patience, and a willingness to engage in a grinding politics without end. That politics started with lofty symbols like freedom and prosperity but always included negative and even hostile views of opponents who, it was said, had set out to destroy the American economy.

INTRODUCTION

Politics and the Markets They Made

Contemporary Americans reside inside the myth of the marketplace. We imagine that the market governs the cost of merchandise at the mall, the wages awarded factory workers and executives, and the price we pay for our houses, home appliances, and automobiles. Meanwhile, we are able to attribute the prosperity many Americans enjoy to their hard work and their keen adaptation to the market's stern dictates. And, finally, we believe that corporate executives compete each day to identify new business and outdo competitors. By this reckoning, the entire world is a marketplace, or it ought to be. No wonder talk about how markets operate pervades nearly every aspect of American life. To simplify my discussion of this market mythmaking, I call it market talk.

No one should doubt the central place of the markets in American life. But market talk has often encouraged us to misunderstand how those markets were created and how they operated. The president of the United States was and remains a key actor in the organization of markets. And presidents had good reason to attend to their market-making responsibilities. Especially after 1945, Americans held presidents responsible to produce economic prosperity. Banks were and remain key actors in fashioning that prosperity. And at the same time, those banks, the largest and smallest, operated inside a complex set of rules about how and even where to conduct business. For all the market talk in which Americans engaged, the truth of the matter was that federal and state officials chartered banks, and those charters laid out rules about bank loans and about more complicated matters like the amount of capital that bankers needed to keep on hand. In other words, bankers in every decade operated in markets that government officials had created. Politics was present in banking from the outset. If presidents wanted bankers to help foster growth, then they would have to find a way to change bank rules.

Between 1961 and 2008, presidents helped put in place legislation and regulations that permitted bankers to create massive banks like Citigroup and Bank of America. Those large banks and their well-paid chief executives such as Charles O. Prince and Kenneth D. Lewis were deeply implicated in the Great Recession that began late in 2007. To appreciate the continued presence of politics and presidents in creating markets, and even market downturns, we must go back six decades to the earliest days of the John F. Kennedy administration and to James J. Saxon, an obscure yet influential figure in his administration. Kennedy charged Saxon to change bank rules. Saxon and his new bank rules created a number of enemies along the way.

Nearly every federal official disliked Saxon. Between 1961 and 1966, Saxon served as comptroller of the currency, the government's chief bank regulator. Members of Congress and small-town bankers wrote to Presidents Kennedy and Lyndon B. Johnson about Saxon's rules. Saxon's multiple critics described those rules as unfair, illegal, and certain to destroy small-town banking. Important congressional figures like Rep. Wright Patman (D-TX) demanded that Johnson fire Saxon on the spot. Basically, Comptroller Saxon challenged established law and precedent to permit bankers to merge firms, open branches, sell insurance, and underwrite revenue bonds. Saxon's ultimate goal was to create large, multipurpose banking firms that conducted business across the United States and that, in turn, would presumably hasten the nation's economic growth.

But Saxon's quest to remodel banking ran headfirst into federal law and into accustomed practice among a large number of bankers. Three decades earlier, members of Congress had approved the Banking Act of 1933. Bankers and journalists named that legislation the Glass-Steagall Act, after its principal authors' names. The Glass-Steagall Act, as every financial economist, regulator, and congressional leader had long known, forbade even the largest commercial banks such as David Rockefeller's Chase Manhattan from underwriting stock issues or offering additional financial products such as home and business insurance.

Saxon's ideas and his personality created enemies in and out of government. To start, no one to that point had demonstrated that larger banks providing a greater range of services would foster the national economic growth that Kennedy wanted to bring about. Quite the reverse, many Americans still associated big banks with the Depression's start; and were that perception not enough to harden dislike for Saxon's proposals, small-town bankers feared that a larger bank located in Chicago or New York would open a

branch and take away business they had serviced for decades. By this reasoning, moreover, bankers like Chase Manhattan's Rockefeller would replace
Main Street bankers among their town's most influential leaders. In plain
fact, moreover, Saxon was not an easy person with whom to work, and critics seized on his high-handed methods as another reason for Kennedy and
Johnson to replace him.

Presidents Kennedy and Johnson, it turned out, were Saxon's only supporters among federal officials. Kennedy and Johnson endured the tumult
that followed Saxon's innovative decisions on the hunch that larger banks
making more loans would bring about that much desired growth. And in
turn, Kennedy and Johnson brought legitimacy and political heft to the idea
that more big banks making larger loans would prove key actors in the economy's development.

Economic growth was among the most important ideas in postwar
American political life. And yet, Saxon's policies, if fully implemented, posed
a threat to the prestige, authority, and profits of every insurance agent, securities dealer, and small banker in the United States. Courts provided those
nervous actors with much needed protection. Securities dealers including
Merrill Lynch won a lawsuit that kept bankers out of their business. Insurance agents also triumphed in courts. In a nation ostensibly committed to
entrepreneurship at the hands of freewheeling executives, insurance agents
and securities dealers preferred to manage their firms within legal realms
that kept regulators like Saxon at a distance. Still more, Attorney General
Robert F. Kennedy, the president's brother, filed antitrust actions to block
several of the largest bank mergers and won many of those suits.

As I learned the contours of this story, I began to develop several themes.
First, I recognized that bankers had a turf and ways of conducting business to
protect. Next, I learned that not even the president of the United States possessed the authority to usher larger banks into existence. Nevertheless, each
president starting with Kennedy and Johnson in the 1960s and extending to
Bill Clinton during the 1990s made the creation of large, multipurpose
banks a central policy goal. The creation of big banks linked to faster economic growth was a presidential project that extended from the 1960s to
June 2017, when I completed work on this book. Starting in the 1970s, advocates described this new type of bank, with its proposed insurance and securities products, as similar to chain supermarkets like A&P that had been
replacing stand-alone butchers and independent grocers for decades. These
supermarket banks were actually an old idea, having appeared in Germany

during the nineteenth century and among a few American banks during the 1920s. In the 1960s, many in the United States described the supermarket bank idea as new and shocking.[1]

Comptroller Saxon did not initiate these changes in banking single-handedly. Starting in the late 1960s, several bankers joined this fledgling supermarket bank campaign. I focus on four of them. Between 1967 and 1984, Walter B. Wriston headed the gigantic Citicorp. Wriston was the nation's best-known banker. He gave speeches to business groups about the unfair regulations that kept his company penned into parts of New York State and out of the insurance and securities businesses. Wriston followed Saxon in announcing that federal rules put commercial banks like his Citicorp at a disadvantage compared to less regulated money market mutual funds or even Sears, Roebuck, with its successful credit card and insurance sales. Were this unfair situation to continue into the future, Wriston lamented, commercial banks would have to go out of business. Wriston brought each of these complaints to the heads of the Federal Reserve; and he hobnobbed with Presidents Richard M. Nixon and Ronald W. Reagan, who no doubt also had an opportunity to hear his laments—with which they concurred in theme and detail.

Donald T. Regan is the second banker I chose to study. Regan headed Merrill Lynch between 1971 and 1980. Merrill Lynch was not a commercial bank, like Wriston's Citicorp. As a consequence, Regan was able to underwrite stock issues, sell shares of stock to middle-income Americans, and offer money market and other mutual funds in branch offices located across the United States and overseas. In 1980, President Reagan asked Regan to serve as treasury secretary. Regan promptly got about the business of trying to secure congressional legislation to permit bankers to remodel their firms to look like his Merrill Lynch. Regan secured only modest changes in banking rules during four years in office.

Hugh L. McColl, Jr., is the third banker I write about in detail. In 1959, McColl completed his Marine Corps service and secured a trainee position at Charlotte's modest American Commercial Bank. Throughout his career, McColl made frequent reference to his beloved Marines. He rewarded successful employees at his renamed NationsBank with crystal grenades for desk display. McColl also spoke in profanities. News of his cursing preceded him into merger negotiations, where he sometimes lost coveted deals. Starting in 1992, however, McColl emerged as "the president's banker," an honorific that journalists conferred on bankers who were close to President Bill Clinton or to any president. In 1998, McColl merged his NationsBank with

California's BankAmerica, to create Bank of America located in Charlotte. The new behemoth featured 4,800 branch offices spread across twenty-seven states and thirty-eight countries. McColl recognized, as if by instinct, that the route to a supermarket bank ran through a wide swath of government agencies and top officials.

Sanford I. Weill, another dealmaker, rounds out my study of bankers' quests to preside over the assembly of supermarket banks. In 1985, Weill left American Express. The next year, he purchased a small company in Baltimore that made loans to lower-income Americans. Through a series of acquisitions, Weill took control of the Travelers Group, an insurance giant that also sold mutual funds and other financial products to middle-income Americans. Weill had shaped a supermarket financial firm that looked much like Donald Regan's Merrill Lynch. And identical to Merrill Lynch, Weill's firms reported to state insurance regulators and to the U.S. Securities and Exchange Commission rather than to the Federal Reserve or the comptroller. In 1998, Weill merged his Travelers Group with Citicorp. The new firm, renamed Citigroup, spanned the globe and offered both regular savings accounts and exotic financial instruments like asset-backed securities. By the late 1990s, Citigroup and Bank of America, with their multiple branches and product offerings, fulfilled President Kennedy and Comptroller Saxon's hesitant first steps toward creation of supermarket banks.

McColl and Weill were successful entrepreneurs. On the surface, they undertook large financial and political risks to assemble those megabanks. Along the way, they brought lawsuits and lobbied regulators and members of Congress. They enjoyed audiences with presidents starting with Nixon and extending to Clinton. As a matter of fact, Clinton invited McColl to talk about bank policy in the family's upstairs apartment at the White House. The once cursing, ex-marine had traveled a considerable social and political distance. And yet as I determine, McColl and other top bankers, acting alone and in concert, had not brought the supermarket bank to fruition. I organized Wriston, Regan, McColl, and Weill in successive chapters to underscore this singularly important point. To achieve success, these powerful bankers had to connect their corporate goals—to bestride the financial universe—to each president's legal obligation and political goal to accelerate economic growth.

Post–World War II presidents served as the nation's chief economic officers. They were responsible to make the economy work without inflation and at full employment. It was a tall order, and Congress had not handed them direct management tools.[2] In consequence, presidents as different in working style as John Kennedy, Ronald Reagan, Bill Clinton, and Donald J. Trump appointed bank regulators who would make decisions judged favorable to bank growth and the widespread economic advance each hoped would follow. As one example, Clinton appointed Eugene A. Ludwig comptroller of the currency. In symbolic fashion, Ludwig hung a painting of Saxon, Kennedy's innovative comptroller, behind his desk. Ludwig, acting on the basis of favorable litigation, permitted bankers to put their securities firms outside the bank and outside the comptroller's review. Those securities dealers, now deeply invested in the process of converting mortgages and credit card debt into asset-backed securities, could begin to operate in the same agile fashion as investment bankers at Merrill Lynch and Lehman Brothers. In turn, treasury secretaries Robert E. Rubin and Lawrence H. Summers insisted on putting Ludwig's legal innovations in the Gramm-Leach-Bliley Financial Services Modernization Act of 1999. That legislation, which key actors including securities dealers, insurance agents, and large and small bankers had argued about since the early 1960s, legalized supermarket banks across the nation at long last. Bankers like Wriston, McColl, and Weill played an important part in setting the stage for changed bank legislation and for promoting it tirelessly with regulators and lawmakers.

Most fundamentally, Gramm-Leach-Bliley represented the culmination of a nearly forty-year-long presidential campaign to bring supermarket banks into existence. Bank politics, as I noted, had a never-ending, grinding, and exhausting quality. In 1999, that grinding politics reached a temporary conclusion. Clinton, Weill, Senator Phil Gramm (R-TX), and others had coalesced around the time-honored idea of economic growth for nearly every American. Bank legislation for the new century was never that simple.

We should not think about Gramm-Leach-Bliley as bank deregulation and the abolition of rules. Instead, the bill's authors put a remodeled bank regime in place, one with new and old rules, but rules there were. Federal Reserve officials continued to monitor bank headquarters, known to financial personnel as the holding company. As before, the comptroller's seasoned examiners still checked on bank capital levels and looked at each bank's books to learn whether bad loans were piling up. Regulation did not end there, either. Banks like Weill's Citigroup that sold stocks and bonds and traded more complex, asset-backed securities also reported the results of those operations to the U.S. Securities and Exchange Commission. To be sure, regulators remained scattered, uncoordinated, and lacking the tools to understand how the financial system's multiple parts fit together. In contrast, those supermarket banks like Citigroup and Bank of America operated as one unit. Yet, for all the tools at their disposal and for all the senior executives who reported to them, top bank executives like McColl and Weill had not grasped their firms' many operations in detail. Similar to regulators at the Federal Reserve and comptroller's office, bankers such as McColl and Weill never probed how their firms' strengths, weaknesses, and ties to other banks might affect the financial system as a whole.

Despite those awkward features, the new bank system proved successful, at least for a few years. Banking innovations like the ATM and fancy new products like adjustable rate mortgages maintained the idea that bankers served financial markets automatically; and, it seemed, those bankers fostered prosperity in the form of millions of new mortgages for low-income Americans. The market, one might believe, had replaced government bureaucrats in building a more inclusive prosperity. That prosperity, moreover, rested in the hands of bank executives with decades of experience in building those nationwide banks.

Starting around 2000, a new generation of bank chiefs took over from McColl and others who had built and promoted supermarket banking. In making that changeover, those new bank leaders also maintained continuity with earlier personnel and their ideas. Each of the heads of the largest four banks had direct connections back to Wriston, McColl, or Weill.[3] Bank of America's Kenneth D. Lewis had worked with successful mentors like McColl to merge banks, open branches, and develop the business of cross-selling financial products. The idea underlying cross-selling was that a bank customer with a mortgage could be persuaded to open a checking account during one visit and take out a credit card and a home equity line of credit in the course of subsequent visits. Like their predecessors, Lewis and others who led large banks also assembled mortgages into securities marketed around the world. And again like their mentors, Lewis took short-term loans to finance those deals, at leverage ratios of $29 in borrowed money to $1 in his own capital and higher. Bank of America and Citigroup securities dealers emerged as investment bankers, with the same loose set of regulations about excessive debt. The system worked well, and the high ratio of borrowed money to invested capital magnified the banks' profitably, as long as homeowners continued to pay their mortgages.

Starting around 2006 and continuing for the next several years, large numbers of lower-income Americans could no longer afford to pay their mortgages. Those who failed to pay were frequently young, black, or brown. Most had sought to improve their lots and join their fellow citizens in the prospect of rising property values and the joy of a home of their own with improved schools for their children—a privilege denied their forebears.[4] Lower-income Americans of any color had not caused the financial crisis. The total of outstanding subprime mortgages, even if each had gone into default, was not large enough to cause the financial havoc that started in mid-2007.

Speaking directly, the bankruptcy of Lehman Brothers Holdings in September 2008, and the ensuing financial chaos, had their origins among those short-term $29-to-$1-and-higher overnight loans bankers made to one another. Bankers called those overnight loans by another name, repurchase agreements. By whatever name, however, banking systems ultimately rested first on a careful evaluation of the quality of collateral to back multimillion-dollar transactions and next on a fragile trust among bankers and securities traders who worked around the globe and had never met.[5] And as it turned out, not even the most experienced and probing bankers and regulators could understand and evaluate the vast networks of loans, mortgage-backed securities, and still other complex financial products that characterized standard and extremely lucrative practice at Lehman or Bank of America. (A mortgage-backed security is a type of asset-backed security.) This system, decades in the making, was largely invisible even to the best-trained regulators and most experienced bankers. Market talk—comments without end by business and political leaders to the effect that managers were only following the market's benign and always sovereign dictates—had a beguiling effect on everyone's ability to discern the large financial changes that were years in the making.

Starting in the 1970s, market talk pervaded every aspect of the American experience. Business executives, lawmakers, and publicists rendered nearly every human activity, including marriage choices, food shopping, or vacation destinations, as evidence of the market's invisible workings. Talk about markets was more congenial than talk about income redistribution, after all.

The bank supermarket ideal rested on more than talk. During several decades, bankers perfected methods for selling mortgages and credit card balances and having them appear a little while later as salable mortgage and other types of asset-backed securities. In taking on these immense transformations, bank executives removed debt from their books, thus reducing risk and at the same time making more fresh money available to loan. Here was a key part of the economic growth machine that treasury secretaries and comptrollers such as Regan and Ludwig and bankers like McColl had sought for so long. Treasury Secretary Rubin described Ludwig's regulatory innovations and the Gramm-Leach-Bliley Act as part of a financial architecture. The failure of that architecture to work as promised was a sad fact imposed on the millions whose homes disappeared to foreclosure orders.

Lehman's bankruptcy and the ensuing job and home losses forced most commentators to abandon market talk. Starting in 2009, lawmakers led by President Barack H. Obama refocused attention on efforts to tighten bank regulations. As yet another irony, government assumed a temporary prominence exactly at the moment that Americans lost confidence in financial experts and the political leaders who followed their advice.

I decided to follow this story through two additional turns in bank politics. In the first, I sought to understand the origins of the Dodd-Frank Act of 2010. Treasury Secretary Timothy F. Geithner and other authors of that legislation created complex rules for bankers dealing with matters like capital requirements. As part of that complexity, Dodd-Frank's authors added an idea first proposed by former Federal Reserve chair Paul A. Volcker. The Volcker Rule, as it was labeled, limited the ability of bankers to use bank funds to trade securities. Safety for bank funds and avoidance of another financial calamity served as the overriding symbols in securing the Volcker Rule's approval. Government, it appeared, was back in the saddle. Dispossessed homeowners were left to hope for an uptick in those much discussed markets.

In the second turn, I focus on Rep. Thomas Jeb Hensarling's efforts starting in 2010 to eliminate the Volcker Rule and the Dodd-Frank Act. I had never studied or written about a lawmaker like Hensarling. I found much to admire. Hensarling appeared charming, determined, and inexhaustible. He was, by my judgment, a superior phrasemaker. Hensarling's legislative priorities reminded me in part of those small bankers and their champion, Wright Patman. During the 1960s, he and his mostly small city banker allies fought the fight against Comptroller Saxon's efforts to mobilize big bankers to the prospect of developing large and threatening branch networks.

Hensarling, in the language of contemporary American politics, was a conservative. He detested large government, high taxes, and regulations that limited business owners' freedom of action. Hensarling aligned with President Donald J. Trump. Were the rules for supermarket and smaller bankers changed, each contended, the economy would boom once again. Trump, however, lacked Hensarling's ability to focus on important symbols like freedom and then marshal members of the U.S. Senate and House toward a legislative outcome. My study of bank politics is a study of the politics of economic growth.

During a period of more than fifty years, my key actors, including Saxon, Clinton, Weill, Geithner, and the others, sought a formula to hook supermarket banks to that much sought-after and talked-about growth. In 2017, bankers, lawmakers, and many others were still looking and still talking as if that one right growth formula resided just around the next policy corner. Every few years, political realignments presented opportunities to bankers and law-makers to shift legislative and regulatory attention a few degrees toward favored parts of the financial services field. To do so, Hensarling, Trump, and newly resurgent small bankers had to mobilize coalitions and link their proposals to time-honored symbols like economic growth and personal freedom. Whether in 1961, with Kennedy and Saxon, or in 2017, with Trump and Hensarling, bank politics had a grinding quality.[6] Among participants in this exhausting business, including Clinton, Weill, and Hensarling, the creation of networks among lawmakers, regulators, and bankers that would support a reframing of financial markets represented their highest form of political expression.

No one who had paid attention to banking since 1961 could have doubted that the federal government made markets.[7] And surely, no one could have doubted that success in bank politics required perseverance and luck. The biggest winners, including Walter Wriston, Sandy Weill, Bill Clinton, and Barack Obama, possessed the patience and skill to assemble large networks and appropriate venerated symbols like freedom and safety. Wriston, Weill, and Clinton, to take note only of those three among many supermarket bank enthusiasts, were willing to negotiate, litigate, and lobby across decades toward outcomes that were never certain and that were in turn likely to be promptly challenged and maybe overturned by leaders of other networks of bankers, lawmakers, and regulators. In1961, James J. Saxon helped launch the movement toward supermarket banks. Saxon launched that effort before Americans had heard of deregulation.[8]

PART I

Lawmakers and Regulators

CHAPTER 1

Deregulation Before Deregulation: John Kennedy, Lyndon Johnson, and James Saxon

On September 6, 1960, presidential candidate John F. Kennedy "pledge[d] . . . an administration that will get this Nation moving again." During his one thousand days in office, Kennedy's growth prescriptions included tax reductions, accelerated spending for the military and space exploration, and reorganization of federal agencies as diverse as the Interstate Commerce Commission and the Securities and Exchange Commission. As yet another economy-expanding idea, Kennedy wanted regulators to make it easier for commercial bankers to write more loans. In the early 1960s, however, few in Congress were prepared to risk careers to advocate for looser bank regulations. Just as much, most bankers expressed no interest in changing the rules that guided taking deposits and writing loans. Bank executives were often "plodding and unimaginative, with a pronounced tendency to be hereditary," a business historian later determined.[1] Kennedy, in other words, had few allies in his quest to change bank rules and speed economic growth.

Kennedy launched his quest to modify bank rules by appointing James J. Saxon to the post of comptroller of the currency. Although most Americans had never heard of the comptroller's office, Saxon and his small staff actually served as the federal government's principal bank regulator. The comptroller's rules governed every banker operating with a federal charter; and the comptroller decided who received those charters.

Appointing Saxon to the comptroller's post was only a modest first step in the long road to changing the way bankers operated. Nothing about Kennedy's initiatives and the subsequent changes in bank regulations took place easily, and they certainly were never automatic in nature. Beginning in the late 1960s, a few bank officers, led by the gigantic First National City

Bank's Walter B. Wriston, joined with Saxon's successors in the comptroller's office and with sitting presidents to press their case for fewer restrictions in the way government permitted them to conduct business. Still other bankers opposed those changes. Bankers, it turns out, were rarely united on policy questions. But, most important, every president of the United States after Kennedy—from Lyndon B. Johnson in the 1960s to Donald J. Trump in 2017—looked for legislative and administrative devices to foster bank growth and the economic development judged certain to follow.

Words and ideas surely mattered in the quest to change bankers' ways. In line with the favored words Americans used to talk about the economy, presidents and bankers like Wriston always cited abstractions such as a free market to describe the changes they wanted to bring about. But, in fact, the rules government officials and bankers put in place between 1961 and 2017 actually fixed the rules for those markets. Government made bankers' markets; and persuading lawmakers and regulators to make those bankers' markets still larger, faster, and then safer, it turns out, was a presidential project that endured across more than six decades. In order to understand the seeming paradox of bankers' and lawmakers' resistance to changes in the rules of the commercial banking that Saxon first brought into being, we first must understand the way that bankers conducted business at the start of the 1960s.

Conservative Bankers, Protective Lawmakers, and James J. Saxon

American bankers during the Kennedy era fashioned themselves both as the paragons of a capitalist economy and as sober evaluators of loan applications. Their loans allowed business owners and executives to purchase inventories, invest in new equipment, and meet payrolls. And in turn, bankers' loans to businesses served as an important factor in the prosperity that millions of Americans enjoyed daily in the form of suburban homes, new automobiles, home appliances, and maybe even tickets on jet airplanes for holidays in Miami, Hawaii, and Europe. By this way of thinking, bankers served as the bedrock for a dynamic capitalism. During the1960s, only a few like Saxon dared to question the business decisions of sensible and respected bankers.

But the plain truth was that commercial bankers operated in a rule-bound environment created during the Depression era. In 1933, as noted earlier, members of Congress and President Franklin D. Roosevelt approved the Glass-Steagall Act. Bankers were to stick to the business of taking deposits and making loans, and they were to stay out of riskier areas like underwriting stock issues. The Glass-Steagall Act also required large banks that offered both checking and securities services to break in two. The great J. P. Morgan & Co., for example, emerged as Morgan Stanley & Co., an investment bank prohibited from offering checking accounts, and as J. P. Morgan & Co., a commercial bank barred from underwriting securities issues.[2]

State lawmakers piled on more rules. Illinois law prohibited executives at Chicago's mighty First National Bank from opening branches in fast-expanding suburbs. Although sixteen states, including North Carolina and California, permitted in-state branching, legislatures and regulators in eighteen states, including Texas and Illinois, prohibited branch offices. First National Bank executives or executives at any bank operating under a federal charter also needed federal regulators' approval to merge with a bank located in that state or even up the street. In the early 1960s, some 13,500 commercial banks operated in the United States, but officers of no more than 100 competed for large corporate deposits in other states. Small banks, with limited capital, offered services in their towns and neighborhoods.

Additional rules fixed bank practice in considerable detail. Federal officials determined the interest rate bankers paid savers, which eliminated price competition among them. In short, law, regulation, and custom largely fixed bankers' way of conducting business. Those laws and customs in turn applied with equal force in the decisions of officers at the smallest, farm-belt banks as well as among executives at the nation's largest banks, such as San Francisco's Bank of America and New York's First National City Bank. (In 1976, Walter Wriston changed his firm's name to Citibank.)

Most bankers in turn endorsed those tight restrictions in theme and detail. Heads of the largest banks, including David Rockefeller at the storied Chase Manhattan Bank, participated willingly in a regulatory system that guided them toward steady growth, predictable profits, and security for capital. In 1960, the sixty-story Chase Manhattan headquarters opened across the street from the Federal Reserve Bank of New York, putting in concrete and spatial terms the mostly cooperative relationships between Chase's officers and powerful Federal Reserve officials. Again, whether among most bankers or public officials, to think about a substantial reworking of these time-honored rules about interest rates and nationwide branch banking was to think the unthinkable.

Congress was not the place to amend these rules. Congressional leaders had regularly pledged their support to the maintenance of these many regulations. Starting in 1929, as a critical example, Rep. Wright Patman (D-TX) kept a wary eye open for any effort to modify the rules that threatened his small-town bankers, local businessmen, and their farm customers. In 1933, Patman was among the members who approved the Glass-Steagall Act, forcing commercial and investment bankers to break their firms in two and stop doing business with each other. In 1956, members of Congress, including Patman, tightened bank rules again. To reinforce the protection that state boundaries offered bankers, members of Congress determined that a banker seeking business in another state would have to be invited in by the legislature, which would surely not prove an easy undertaking. "We have boarded up the big hole in the barn door," one of the congressional supporters announced.[3] The Glass-Steagall Act of 1933 and the 1956 legislation set the framework within which bankers operated when Kennedy took office. And yet, as one of the curious idioms of American life, bankers along with most Americans included banking as another example of their much-extolled system of free enterprise.

Kennedy inherited this rule-bound system. The new president, who had promised to speed up a sluggish economy, was not about to invest limited resources to launch a frontal assault on self-satisfied bankers, state lawmakers, and avid congressional watchdogs like Patman. Since World War II, the president was the economic commander in chief, but members of Congress had never created devices to enable the president to take a direct role in economic development. And besides, no one could say for certain—at least based on hard evidence—that loosening restrictions on bankers to merge and open branches would speed the economy's growth. During the late 1920s, the last time it was attempted, the nation fell into depression and millions lost their homes and savings. Three decades later, President Kennedy was willing to try out the idea of fewer restrictions once again. But he mostly had to go it alone. He chose to proceed slowly and carefully in the face of wide and deep opposition.

Kennedy selected a path of indirection to speed up banking and the larger economy. He would bring about changes in banking by making a key appointment. In November 1961, Kennedy invoked the mighty authority of the presidential office to appoint James J. Saxon as the nation's comptroller of the currency. Saxon was forty-seven years old. He had earned an undergraduate degree at St. John's College in Toledo, where he grew up. Later, Saxon graduated from Georgetown University's law school. Saxon also took graduate level courses in economics and finance at Catholic University. By 1966, according to a *New York Times* writer, the "pugnacious" Saxon had "shaken the financial world" during his term as comptroller.[4]

At quick glance, the comptroller's office was an unlikely place from which to launch a challenge to bank rules and bankers' habits built up since Glass-Steagall's passage nearly three decades earlier. In 1863, members of a Civil War Congress had created the Office of the Comptroller of the Currency to oversee the new system of national banks. The comptroller's office operated as a largely independent agency within the Department of the Treasury. A century later, the comptroller remained among the federal government's chief bank regulators, alongside the Federal Reserve and the Federal Deposit Insurance Corporation. In several areas, the comptroller was the first among equals. The comptroller approved every national bank charter. Later, the comptroller's examiners inspected those banks' books for compliance with federal law and the comptroller's rules. The understaffed comptroller's office was obscure, potentially powerful, and susceptible to a strong administrator's shaping directions.

In Kennedy's savvy hands, Saxon's appointment as comptroller offered a lonely outpost in his plan to speed up banking without having to work with Congress or seek to overcome standpat bankers and intransigent lawmakers like Congressman Patman. To be sure, the Senate had to consent to Saxon's appointment, which was for the standard five-year term. But the comptroller's office was financially independent. To pay employees and maintain the office, the comptroller levied semiannual assessments on member banks. Those same member banks also paid examination fees to the comptroller. Saxon was financially independent of Congress. Meddlesome congressmen, such as Wright Patman, lacked a direct path to control Saxon or another comptroller who headed off in new directions. Like any federal regulator, moreover, federal law and court holdings largely awarded deference to the administrator's determinations. In other words, the comptroller's office contained the potential for legal innovations. Up to Saxon's appointment, however, his predecessors had chosen not to expand their boundaries, much like the bankers they regulated. Saxon, once installed in office, was supposed to foster changes in bank rules that sped economic growth. Presidential authority and Saxon's administrative discretion would substitute for bankers' inaction and congressional obstruction. Kennedy no doubt hoped that Saxon would somehow prevail in the fearsome politics sure to follow his appointment.

Several years later, according to a *Time* magazine reporter, Saxon remembered simply that Kennedy had urged him to "start stirring things up."[5]

On September 21, 1961, Kennedy submitted Saxon's name and background materials to the Senate for confirmation. Saxon's career, which started in the Depression, had followed a series of upward steps. Beginning in 1937, Saxon worked in the U.S. Treasury Department, where by 1952, he served as assistant to the secretary. Between 1952 and 1956, Saxon was assistant general counsel to the American Bankers Association (ABA), with headquarters located in Washington, D.C. The ABA was a trade association that represented bankers before Congress and regulatory agencies. Saxon's assignments included tax and other legislative issues. Starting in 1956, Saxon took up the post of counsel to the First National Bank of Chicago, the city's largest bank. Up to 1961, Kennedy had not known Saxon. But Saxon enjoyed the support of C. Douglas Dillon, Kennedy's secretary of the treasury, and his undersecretary, Robert V. Roosa.[6] In 1961, as Saxon headed for his office in the Treasury Department building across from the White House, he had accumulated more than two decades' experience in the complementary realms of litigation, lobbying, bank operations, and federal and state bank politics.

Saxon Goes to Work

James Saxon had exchanged a well-paid, prestigious, and influential post at Chicago's First National Bank for the limited authority and visibility that inhered in a lowly and largely unknown federal office. In late 1961, about 1,200 employees worked in the comptroller's office, including 1,000 bank examiners in the field and some 196 employees located in Treasury Department offices. With such a small staff, including only five deputies, any comptroller's ability to learn about bank conditions, assess merger and branch applications, revise bank rules, and enforce administrative orders was necessarily limited. The former comptroller had approved several large mergers and, with the ensuing tumult, had to leave the office early.[7] Saxon, nevertheless, made merger applications his first order of business.

Saxon held his first merger hearing on December 4, several days after taking office. That hearing spotlighted Saxon's determination to reorganize the banking landscape in major ways. The case before him was whether First National City Bank of New York (where Walter Wriston won promotion to president in 1967) and the National Bank of Westchester, White Plains, New York, deserved the comptroller's approval to merge operations. Again, every merger between banks holding national charters required the comptroller's approval in advance. First National City was New York's second largest bank, behind Rockefeller's Chase Manhattan, and the nation's third largest. But in 1961, officials at the Federal Reserve as well as Attorney General Robert F. Kennedy opposed the merger. Those officials used words such as "undue concentration" and monopoly. Saxon, seeking to demonstrate his office's independence in public, sent objections to the merging banks' attorneys for reply at the hearing. Saxon was supposed to take account of views supplied by the attorney general, the Federal Reserve, and the Federal Deposit Insurance Corporation, but authority to approve the merger in the first instance rested squarely and exclusively in Saxon's hands.[8] Legally speaking, however, the attorney general could file a lawsuit to block this merger or any other. Saxon's responsibilities existed as part of a regulatory regime that allowed top officials to operate at cross-purposes.

Saxon denied the merger request. Antitrust ideals such as those put forward by the attorney general and Federal Reserve leaders, he contended, had played no part in his decision. The National Bank of Westchester already operated twenty-six branches. Larger banks brought improved banking services and lower costs, Saxon explained to members of the Federal Reserve Board on January 22, 1962. Yet Saxon wanted that growth to take place gradually rather than instantly through merger. The arrival of First National City and other large New York banks in the suburbs, Saxon warned, would unbalance the region's bank system. Precipitous was Saxon's word to describe these merger plans. In a moment, Saxon advertised the comptroller's office as the arbiter of the size, pace, and geography of bank mergers. Saxon, only recently installed in office, denied a merger sought by executives at the nation's second largest bank. Saxon had also disagreed in public with leaders of the powerful Federal Reserve Board of Governors and with the attorney general, the president's brother.[9] In brief, Saxon used the hearing and his decision against the merger to start on a course toward making his office the centerpiece of an American bank regulatory system that would emphasize economic growth spread around the United States.

Saxon, by any measure, favored bank growth and expansion. Between 1950 and 1961, former comptrollers had approved 468 mergers, consolidations, and purchases among national banks. During 1962–1963 alone, Saxon approved 201 mergers, the opening of 1,490 branch offices, and 295 new bank charters, including 68 in fast-growing states such as Florida, Colorado, and Texas. The award of new bank charters and branching rights undercut state regulations that had restricted branch banking. As well, the former comptroller, with fewer merger applications, required five months to make a decision. Saxon reduced the wait time to nine weeks.[10]

New branches and mergers fit with Saxon's conviction that American business firms were "under-banked." Since 1959, Chicago bankers had in fact used those very words in their effort to persuade the Illinois General Assembly to approve branch banking. Branch offices, if permitted to come into being, were supposed to draw deposit funds to the bank's headquarters and provide improved access to bank services for residents located in small towns and burgeoning suburbs. In February 1962, moreover, a *Wall Street Journal* writer used words such as "vexation" and "outrage" to characterize Saxon's views of Attorney General Kennedy's efforts to block several mergers. For public purposes, however, Saxon described their relationship as "fine."[11] In short order, Saxon had accelerated the pace of bank consolidation and branch growth; and he made journalists part of his public relations efforts, an adaptation no doubt cultivated during his years as counsel to the American Bankers Association.

Several of the mergers Saxon approved created the largest banks in their day. In September 1963, Saxon allowed a combination between San Francisco's Crocker-Anglo National Bank and the Citizens National Bank, with headquarters in Los Angeles. Officers of the new firm, the Crocker-Citizens National Bank, managed 202 branch offices and held assets totaling $3.2 billion. The merged operation, once the deal closed, would emerge as California's fourth largest bank and the nation's eleventh largest.[12]

By 1963, the arguments that Saxon and growth-minded bankers put forward in favor of these mergers assumed a codified form that consisted of idioms about the advantages of size. Saxon characterized business practices at one of the smaller merger candidates as "quaint." In contrast, officers at the merged banks would enjoy access to more capital, leading, so the argument ran, to improved service to the area's businesses. In an equally familiar refrain, Crocker president Emmet G. Solomon denied that size limited competition. Quite the opposite, Solomon asserted, as the combined firm would offer tough competition to the larger banks, especially Bank of America, and help meet the demand for credit among California's growing businesses. Similarly, Saxon justified another large merger on grounds that the combined bank would be in a position to approve loans up to $6 million to any one customer, nearly twice as much as before the combination. In his annual report for 1964, Saxon described national banks that were now equipped with the ability to stimulate economic growth.[13]

Americans admired economic growth. Growth, in fact, was one of those ideas, like markets, that commanded universal allegiance, at least when presented in the abstract. Yet, Saxon's aggressive rule changes and especially his quick merger approvals had already angered Attorney General Kennedy's antitrust attorneys. As well, the appearance of large banks like Crocker-Citizens, if the trend continued, threatened the livelihoods of smaller bankers, who lacked the capital, personnel, experience, and networks to deal with large corporate customers and mom-and-pop clothing store owners all at once. Those smaller bankers had already spoken more than once to their representatives in Congress about Saxon's high-handed ways. No one disliked Saxon's actions more than Rep. Wright Patman (D-TX).

Saxon and Representative Patman

In November 1928, Wright Patman won election to Congress. He was thirty-five years old. Patman represented a district in East Texas that included small businesses and small towns. Farming was a major activity, but more farmers were tenants than owners. Few had telephones and fewer had indoor running water. Like many in such areas during the 1920s and later, residents left East Texas in search of steadier incomes and a more comfortable way of life.[14]

Patman looked to the federal government to foster economic development, especially for the small producers and shop owners who populated his district and districts like his throughout the United States. Journalists characterized Patman as a populist. During the 1930s, Patman focused his energy on halting the rapid growth of chain stores. They harmed locally owned retailers, he contended. Patman characterized chain stores with terms such as "absentee ownership" that produced "absentee responsibility." If small businesses were destroyed, Patman told members of an outdoor audience on March 4, 1936, "the country will be destroyed." Patman was only one of many federal and state lawmakers with an interest in blocking chain store growth. Already, between 1931 and 1937, legislators in twenty-six states had approved bills against chain stores. In June 1936, President Franklin D. Roosevelt signed the Robinson-Patman Act, which prohibited manufacturers and wholesalers from selling their products to chain stores at lower prices than smaller retailers paid.[15] Patman's struggle against chain stores served as a run-up to his next major antitrust charge, this time against Saxon's program of approving bank branches and mergers.

In 1963, at age seventy, Patman achieved his lifetime ambition, that of elevation to the chair of the House Banking and Currency Committee. At last, he held a major post at a key congressional crossroads. Patman could initiate legislation, and he could stop it in its tracks. As part of his interest in bank size, Patman maintained a steady focus on bank regulators, whether Comptroller Saxon or the larger and more visible Federal Reserve Board. If Patman were to meet actress Elizabeth Taylor on an uninhabited island, powerful Texas congressman Samuel T. "Sam" Rayburn said of Patman, he would ask whether she knew how the Federal Reserve worked.[16] The chairmanship also brought reporters to Patman's office and to his hearings, where they prepared catchy leads and amusing anecdotes as he sounded off on events, people, policies, and regulatory agencies such as the Federal Reserve and the comptroller's office. As part of that habit of sounding off, Patman also displayed a crankiness that included personal attacks. Starting in 1963, Chairman Patman merged his dislike for big banks with his dislike for James Saxon.

In 1963, C. Herschel Schooley joined Patman in a mutual distaste for Saxon and his branch and merger policies. Schooley led the Independent Community Bankers Association (ICBA), a trade group that represented smaller bankers before state and federal governments. From his Washington, D.C., office located on Fifteenth Street, a few blocks from the White House, Schooley served as the independent bankers' political strategist and chief lobbyist. Schooley, with years of experience and solid connections among presidential staff and key members of Congress, such as Patman, enjoyed sufficient visibility to write directly to President Kennedy (and later to President Lyndon B. Johnson) about the harm Saxon had imposed on his small bank members. Schooley and his top officials were also important enough in national politics to expect a presidential audience to voice their concerns about Saxon's "divisive independence."[17] In the meantime, Patman held hearings that provided the national audience Schooley sought.

The hearings opened April 30 and ran for several days. Patman had not assembled a large group of witnesses to testify during the course of three days only to gain an understanding of Saxon's actions. Early in April, Patman had announced his settled conviction "that Comptroller Saxon has been trampling on the rights of state banks and state banking authorities." The hearings carried a weighty-sounding title, that of "Conflict of Federal and State Banking Laws." By common consent, however, lawmakers and bankers thought of those hearings with a simpler and more ominous title: "the Saxon hearings."[18]

Patman's hearings, however titled, created an opportunity for the officers and supervisors of smaller state banks to restate their case against Saxon's branching and merger policies. Patman invited S. E. Babington as the first witness. During 1963, Babington served a term as the ICBA's president. His full-time job was president of the Brookhaven Bank and Trust Company of Brookhaven, Mississippi. As part of his self-introduction, Babington reported that Brookhaven's population stood at eleven thousand and that he had served as a member of the American Bankers Association Agricultural Commission. In one swoop, Babington reminded committee members of his southern roots, his small-town place of business, and his service to the farm community. Babington also linked the ICBA's 6,200 members located in forty states to the "retention of free enterprise in banking." Prior to the start of his formal testimony, Babington had spotlighted respected symbols in American life that any small-town representative ignored at his political peril. Ultimately, Babington's argument boiled down to the simple but powerful notion that Saxon's rapid approval of mergers and branches had brought about "unhealthy competition" between state and federally chartered banks.[19]

Subsequent witnesses made equally reverential points about the virtues of a complex system of federal and state banking authorities, known to insiders as the dual banking system. Most basically, the dual banking system included both those banks chartered and regulated by the comptroller and other, smaller banks that the fifty state bank authorities chartered and regulated. (Several large banks operated under state charters.) Schooley's witnesses had not traveled to Washington, D.C., to provide a civics lesson. Instead, history and law proved favorite topics at the Saxon hearings, as Schooley's well-prepared witnesses cited bank legislation and judicial decisions dating to the nineteenth century to highlight the supremacy of state bank rules in the face of overweening federal regulators like Saxon. As one example, ICBA attorney Horace R. Hansen determined that Comptroller Saxon's "zeal" for large banks ran contrary to congressional policy. Left unchecked, Hansen charged, Saxon intended to remodel the American banking system along European lines, where a few large banks sponsored "hundreds or thousands of branches." Were Saxon permitted to create such an outrageous situation in the United States, who could doubt that bankers in distant cities would pass negative judgment on loan applications submitted by businessmen in Brookhaven and in every other small town. New York and Chicago bankers, ICBA members agreed, could not possibly understand the intricacies of the planting and harvesting seasons. As one example, Georgia leaf tobacco dealers launched marketing programs in July; but Virginia leaf tobacco dealers started their marketing efforts in September.[20] As small-town bankers well knew, farmers and businesspeople located in the nation's vast agricultural regions, with their diverse crops and climates, operated according to a different timetable than Chicago wholesalers or Detroit manufacturers. Here, by any reasonable standard, were reasons enough to delegitimize Saxon's merger and branching policies and accelerate his dismissal from the comptroller's office by firing or impeachment.

Schooley's witnesses such as Babington and Hansen were not small-town rubes; and, they were not engaged in a rearguard action against their approaching demise at the hands of large banks in a national economy. Neither had Schooley and Babington awakened recently to the fact that all or most ICBA members provided only a limited range of financial services to residents located in their town or in a nearby town. Schooley and Babington had to ask, what if Saxon managed to unhinge David Rockefeller and his Chase Manhattan executives to open branches and purchase banks nationwide? Schooley's goal, make no mistake, was to protect his members' limited fortunes, their esteemed place in small-town affairs, and their ability to make loan determinations for businessmen who were loyal customers, long-time friends, and influential figures in town, city, county, and state politics. When the ICBA attorney Hansen told Patman and his committee members that "commercial credit" offered by local banks served as the "lifeblood of our economy," in truth he described ICBA members' desire to retain their coveted space in the political economy of banking, a space that Saxon's rapid approval of large mergers and branch banking perhaps threatened.[21] Schooley and Babington, for all their efforts to sanctify free enterprise, could never have doubted that politics and public policy had produced the lifeblood that had brought them to their favored positions; and still more politics, they had to realize, was the only device capable of maintaining them in those positions. In the simplest terms, Patman and Schooley had to move Saxon away from their path. Saxon's decisions and his sometimes-aggressive disposition encouraged the appearance of staunch and vocal enemies in other quarters of the federal government.

Saxon and the Federal Reserve's William McChesney Martin

William McChesney Martin also wanted Saxon fired. Martin was chair of the Board of Governors of the Federal Reserve System. Disagreements between an energized comptroller such as Saxon and Fed chair Martin were probably inevitable. In these many clashes, however, Martin still held most of the cards. Saxon was "about as well known as an assistant postmaster general," a journalist reported in July 1963. By contrast, in 1938, Martin, at age thirty-one, was elected president of the New York Stock Exchange, prompting journalists to describe him as Wall Street's "boy wonder." Starting in 1951, as the Fed chair, Martin, like his predecessors, enjoyed private meetings with presidents and with influential members of Congress. Journalists reported Martin's every public observation. In 1965, Princeton University conferred an honorary Doctor of Laws degree on Martin, citing his "imperturbable wisdom" in guiding the Federal Reserve. During his first ten years as Fed chair, Martin disagreed frequently with Wright Patman, and he disagreed with Presidents Harry S. Truman and Dwight D. Eisenhower. Martin's position as an insider and confidant also fostered his ability to stand apart from presidents and legislators on economic policy issues, a position he characterized as the Fed's political "independence." In 1965, Martin was in the stronger position to describe Saxon as "a psychopathetic-case."[22]

The Martin-Saxon quarrel began with their joint service on a presidential committee. On March 28, 1962, Kennedy appointed Saxon, Martin, and other top federal officials to his newly formed Committee on Financial Institutions. Kennedy asked Walter W. Heller, head of his Council of Economic Advisers (CEA), to chair the committee. Kennedy's appointment letter made a customary reference to "our free enterprise system." In particular, however, Kennedy urged committee members to consider whether to develop legislation aimed at fostering development of bank branch offices. With a title like the Committee on Financial Institutions, moreover, Kennedy had rolled commercial banks, savings and loans, securities dealers, and even insurance firms into one. By that standard, Saxon's program of mergers and branching was in line with the president's wishes. But the Fed's Martin opposed Kennedy, and by extension Saxon, on those measures. In the course of committee meetings that continued to April 1963, Heller found "a bitterness [between Saxon and Martin] that has to be seen to be believed."[23]

The Martin and Saxon dispute, and their growing mutual distaste, spilled from Kennedy's Committee on Financial Institutions into arguments about additional areas of federal bank regulation. For example, Martin wanted the Securities and Exchange Commission (SEC) to regulate bank stock. In June 1963, however, Saxon urged members of a Senate subcommittee to assign that authority to one of the bank regulatory agencies, an approach that gave his comptroller's office a shot at taking on this new and important area. As early as March 1963, moreover, Saxon had sent a memorandum to officers of every national bank to advise against submitting to the SEC's regulation of bank stock.[24] Comptroller Saxon dared to challenge Chairman Martin's authority and prestige.

The Saxon-Martin argument widened into the arcane area of revenue bonds. In June 1963, Saxon awarded permission to national bank officers to underwrite state and local revenue bonds, as, for instance, the bonds issued by a turnpike authority. In 1933, authors of the Glass-Steagall Act had prohibited bank officers from entering this lucrative and risky field, with only a small exception for what were known as state "full faith and credit" bonds. State toll road bonds, however, did not rest on the state's faith and credit but on a stream of coins that motorists dropped in the toll box. An unexpected decline in the number of toll road users would lower revenues and leave the toll authority without sufficient funds to pay bondholders. As President Kennedy had hoped, Saxon's administrative action expanded bankers' authority to make loans. Saxon, often intemperate in his public language, asserted that investment bankers' control of revenue bonds constituted a "full-fledged monopoly."[25] Saxon, by authorizing commercial bankers to enter the revenue bond business, had also cleverly sidestepped Patman as well as the ICBA's Schooley and their nonstop drumbeat against the growth of large banks. And with equal deftness, Saxon had secured a head start on Martin's objections to bank underwriting of revenue bonds that was certain to follow.

Martin exercised the final word about revenue bonds. In September 1963, officers at Rockefeller's mighty Chase Manhattan Bank determined to underwrite a revenue bond issue. They would handle Washington State building bonds valued at $35,750,000. Yet, the Chase Manhattan held a New York State charter, and thus resided outside Saxon's reach and also outside his office's protection. Because Chase Manhattan was a member of the Federal Reserve System, Martin was in a position to rule against Chase officers who had approved the deal, and indirectly against Saxon. In September 1963, Martin determined that the bond sale could not proceed, even though Chase officials had purchased the bonds and their resale to investors was already under way. "This was an irresponsible act," Saxon announced, employing language that infrequently penetrated the doors of Chairman Martin's guarded and august office at Federal Reserve headquarters in Washington, D.C.[26]

Saxon and President Lyndon Johnson

On November 22, 1963, an assassin shot and killed President Kennedy in Dallas, Texas. A little more than two hours later, Vice President Lyndon B. Johnson took the presidential oath of office. Now Saxon had to rely on a new president for crucial support, starting with the ability to remain in office and continue the bank-expansion program started under Kennedy. But Saxon fared poorly in winning support among Johnson's closest officials. On February 28, 1964, Walter Heller, still the chair of the Council of Economic Advisers, described Saxon to Johnson as "dead wrong in riding roughshod" over Martin's Federal Reserve. Heller urged Johnson to meet with Saxon. At that proposed meeting, Johnson would tell Saxon to "work in harness" or leave. Heller and Johnson, however, could not simply fire Saxon. Federal law required the president to explain the comptroller's termination to the Senate, which Johnson did not want to do.[27] Besides, several top bankers holding national charters had warmed to Saxon's program of easing restrictions on expansion.

Johnson determined not to fire Saxon, allowing his spat with Martin to grow nastier. In March 1964, Saxon told members of the Senate Banking Committee that the Federal Reserve's regulation of the interest rates that banks paid savers amounted to price fixing. Again, presidential appointees did not speak in that fashion about the Federal Reserve. Perhaps in response, a member of Martin's Board of Governors asked in public about abolishing the comptroller's office.[28]

These disputes embarrassed Johnson's new administration, his top aides contended. Johnson, however, was willing to endure Saxon's inflammatory comments and the complaints lodged by opponents such as Heller, Martin, and Patman. To put it simply, Saxon ran the only office in the federal government in which top officials urged bankers to merge, branch, and enter new lines of business. Johnson would deflect angry critics like Patman and Martin, because Saxon offered something more valuable. Johnson needed Saxon as much as Kennedy had needed him—to foster economic growth through larger banks, especially when it came to pushing two Texas bank mergers.

Johnson, in office only a few weeks, asked John T. Jones, a well-connected Houston newspaper editor, to secure background information on the pending merger between Houston's National Bank of Commerce and the Texas National Bank of Houston, to create the Texas National Bank of Commerce. "New York banks have done more business in Houston," Jones reported to Johnson aide Jack J. Valenti on or around December 27, than "any city outside New York." Jones, likely anticipating Attorney General Kennedy's objection, added that each merger deserved consideration "on its merits," as opposed to the view of antitrust attorneys that size alone was sufficient reason to bring a lawsuit in an attempt to block it. "This is what . . . [the president] wanted," Valenti told Jones, and "I'll go over it with him when he gets in."[29] Early on, Johnson intended to push for creation of Texas banks that would rival New York and Chicago banks in their size and reach.

Protecting that merger against Kennedy's antitrust attorneys remained high on Johnson's agenda. Five days later, on January 2, 1964, Johnson telephoned George R. Brown, a key figure in Houston politics, a longtime Johnson friend and supporter, and among the owners of one of the merging banks. (The conversation was secretly recorded.) Johnson and Brown had traded favors for decades, and now Johnson sought to reassure Brown that the merger would go through. Johnson told Brown about his planned course of action. He would direct Pierre Salinger, President Kennedy's press secretary and still a member of the Johnson administration, to meet with Saxon. In turn, "we'll override the whole God-dammed outfit [Justice Department] and they'll do it to hold their own jobs." Whether Salinger and Saxon met remains unclear, but they had no need to do so. On January 13, Saxon approved the merger, a decision Johnson likely knew was forthcoming. That same day, however, Johnson was able to tell Brown in another recorded conversation, "we finally got that order out . . . on your bank thing." In this case Johnson's forceful rhetoric and multiple calls served mostly to impress upon Brown that the president still served as his benefactor. Johnson's fanciful talk also assumed Brown remained unaware of Saxon's expedited merger approval process. In truth, no one needed to persuade James Saxon to approve mergers and new branches that portended increased bank services and larger loans to local business executives. Johnson, to maintain his image as a lawmaker willing to push bureaucrats aside to help loyal constituents and promote bank growth, needed Saxon in the comptroller's office.[30] Johnson still needed him there nearly three years later.

In September 1966, Saxon approved another Houston-area bank merger. This new bank, more an acquisition than an assembly of equals, yoked the small Southern National Bank to the much larger First City National Bank of Houston. George Brown, always an important actor in Houston's politics and finance, sat on First City's board. On October 19, Justice Department officials filed a lawsuit to stop this merger, too. Their legal reasoning, as always, cited reduced competition and increased concentration. Saxon's office sent press releases with phrases such as "particularly unreasonable" and contending that were "dismayed." The combined bank "would be a fine thing for Houston," First City's president asserted.[31]

Unlike George Brown's earlier bank merger, Johnson could not pretend to intervene. Nor could the president of the United States disagree in the press with Justice Department attorneys about a high-visibility topic such as antitrust issues, where arguments were always strongly felt. Johnson avoided public comment, preferring to make his wishes know through a (recorded) telephone call to a top Justice Department official. On November 23, 1966, Johnson spoke by telephone with Ramsey Clark, the deputy U.S. attorney general. "There's no damn reason," Johnson asserted, "why we got to go from Houston to Dallas to borrow our money." Later in the conversation, Johnson added, "I think we're entitled to somebody who's big enough to meet our demands." Johnson described the author of antitrust ideas to Clark as "some theorist" who feared "somebody might get some size." "Well," Johnson urged, "size sometimes may be justified." Two years earlier, Saxon had defended the merger of National City and Texas National on grounds that the area's largest borrowers traveled to banks in New York and Chicago for loans. Banks in Houston should handle those loans, Johnson told Clark in their telephone conversation, virtually repeating Saxon's argument. Despite Johnson's bluster and the urgency of his advocacy, late in December Clark petitioned the Supreme Court to stop merger planning.[32] The savvy Johnson, at the peak of his presidential authority, failed to pressure senior Justice Department officials to drop a lawsuit against a Texas bank merger.

The Antitrust Tradition and Saxon's Last Days in Office

Proponents of the antitrust tradition led by Attorney General Kennedy and his successors also prevailed in other important cases. In June 1963, for example, Supreme Court Justice William J. Brennan cited antitrust violations in ruling against the merger of two large Philadelphia banks. That block-buster ruling overshadowed Saxon's contention that American businesses needed larger banks capable of writing bigger loans. Brennan's ruling, a writer in the *Duke Law Journal* contended soon after, would force bankers and regulators to "take notice . . . when considering mergers of similar pro-portions."[33]

Justice Department attorneys were also winning cases in the lower courts. The union of New York City's Hanover Bank and the Manufacturers Trust Company violated antitrust laws, a U.S. district court judge ruled in March 1965. Since 1961, the bank, with assets of $6.9 billion, had operated as one, the Manufacturers Hanover Trust Company. New Yorkers knew the com-bined bank by its nickname "Manny Hanny." Return the bank to its pre-merger status, the Justice Department's lead antitrust attorney recommended several days after the judge's favorable ruling. Manny Hanny's size, complexity, and more than three years' operation as a single firm mattered less to antitrust attorneys than the danger the combined firm seemingly posed to bank com-petition in the New York region. Because the two banks operated under state rather than federal charters, in September 1961, Federal Reserve officials and state bank regulators had approved the merger.[34] The merger's authorship at the hands of Saxon or Martin was not at issue. Proponents of the antitrust tradition led by Attorney General Kennedy had prevailed.

By February 1966, the high stakes and nonstop lobbying in these merger cases forced members of Congress to take a position. Leaders of the American Bankers Association, including, of course, merging bankers, supported a bill that stripped the attorney general of his authority to block mergers. Patman and his small-town bankers perceived another effort to undermine their busi-ness and their political and social clout. Congress gave something to everyone but did so in a way that heightened anger and distrust. In the future, Justice Department attorneys would have to file antitrust cases within thirty days after Saxon (or the Federal Reserve) had approved a merger. By congressional mandate, Saxon could not authorize a merger during that thirty-day period. Members of Congress had placed another hammer in the antitrust toolbox.[35]

But crafty lawmakers permitted all mergers started prior to June 17, 1963, to go forward. That exemption included the much fought over merger that led to the creation of Manufacturers Hanover. In the absence of congressional action, executives of a five-year-old bank, with countless business dealings as one unit, would have been required to return operations to their earlier form. A business writer asked whether the egg could be "unscrambled." No wonder senior Manny Hanny officials had mounted an intense lobbying campaign, even enlisting former President Eisenhower to telephone President Johnson with a request to help protect their merged bank. With tempers running high, Johnson's aides prevailed on congressional leaders to delay legislation, which kept Johnson from appearing too close to it. On February 21, Johnson signed an amendment to the Bank Merger Act of 1960 in private.[36]

Members of Congress had carved an awkward exclusion from antitrust rules. Despite that exclusion, competition emerged as the predominant standard by which Justice Department attorneys were required to measure future merger proposals. With that act, Johnson lost his ability to ward off antitrust enforcement on behalf of George Brown's bank merger. There's "not anything I could do" to protect the merger, Johnson lamented by telephone on September 21, 1966, to Brown, "including stripping down naked." Johnson's and Saxon's freewheeling days as merger advocates had run their legal and legislative course.[37]

By early 1966, Saxon could no longer quickly and reliably deliver the enlarged banks Kennedy and Johnson liked so much. Saxon had also encouraged powerful enemies. For several years, Wright Patman, Herschel Schooley, and Federal Reserve chair Martin urged Saxon's ouster, as had Attorney General Robert Kennedy. President Kennedy had not accepted their arguments. Johnson heard identical complaints and determined not to act on them. On February 7, 1965, Attorney General Nicholas Katzenbach, still fuming about Saxon's quick mergers and the decision by members of Congress to grandfather several of them into place, asked Johnson to remove Saxon "effective today."[38] Johnson, in the past, had turned aside negative remarks about Saxon. Instead, Johnson made secret telephone calls to Justice Department officials aimed at blocking antitrust litigation. Now Congress diminished Saxon's merger authority, leaving his many critics in a stronger position.

One of Saxon's supporters outlined a path toward dismissal. On April 21, 1965, First National City Bank president George S. Moore wrote to Jack Valenti, the Johnson aide who had worked on the Houston bank merger case for Johnson. Moore told Valenti what everyone recognized. Saxon had begun the process of overhauling bank rules. As part of that overhaul, Saxon's award of new charters and his rapid approval of branches and mergers had thrown state-chartered bankers into a more competitive environment, which they resisted. Saxon lacked a diplomatic touch in his dealings with U.S. attorneys and with bank regulators such as the Fed's Martin. Equally, Saxon possessed a "crusader" outlook, which made him unrelenting in his determination to push through a refashioning of the rules that governed commercial bankers. As if to punctuate Moore's observations, in February 1965 a *Los Angeles Times* reporter headlined a "banking donnybrook" in which Saxon had become involved with the chair of the Federal Deposit Insurance Corporation.[39]

Moore's key observations came next. Saxon's replacement, Moore advised, should extend his "progressive policies" and at the same time improve relationships with other bank regulators. Saxon judged his effort to reshape banking essentially complete, Moore added, and he was already looking for another high-level job. Moore did not need to remind Valenti that Saxon's eagerness to depart would allow Johnson to avoid an awkward firing. Valenti judged the letter "full of good meat," which he "chewed on" prior to sharing key points in a memo to Johnson. The importance of Moore's letter resided only in the fact that a top banker who had followed up on Saxon's invitations to enter new businesses did not promote his reappointment with Johnson.[40] Moore's highest priority resided in the pursuit of bank and regulatory innovations. Saxon's messy squabbles with Johnson's advisers and with influential figures like Federal Reserve chair Martin and Representative Patman threatened those plans.

By late April 1966, presidential aides had cleared a path for Saxon's departure. Johnson would not reappoint Saxon, but they were to exchange complementary letters. Saxon's departure would go largely unnoticed, and he would be at liberty to secure a top-level executive position at a higher salary.

With his fate determined, in April 1966 Saxon used an interview with a *Time* writer to settle scores. Saxon was practicing golf putts on his office rug when the writer arrived. Saxon, dressed as usual in a dark suit and sporting cuff links and a three-pointed breast pocket handkerchief, affected the image of the relaxed and disinterested golfer/executive. James Saxon was never relaxed; and he was always in control, or sought to be. He had introduced competition into banking, which disturbed "small monopoly people," an unveiled reference to Schooley, Babington, and their well-organized colleagues. "If I'd consulted with everybody, we'd still be in the doldrums," Saxon added. With that shot, Saxon questioned Fed chairman Martin's management of regulated banks and his oversight of the American economy. In contrast with Martin's apparent lethargy, Saxon had approved more than six thousand regulatory changes, with many aimed at accelerating bank growth.[41] Talk about the doldrums also permitted Saxon to maintain faith with President Kennedy, who had brought him to Washington to help get the economy moving. On November 15, Saxon completed the final day of his five-year term. Saxon's actual and promised rule changes, were they ever carried out in full, portended the elimination of long-standing bank regulations and a consequent upending of business practices at large banks like Chicago's First National and at Babington's small bank in Brookhaven, Mississippi. Instead, Saxon returned to anonymity, first as a senior officer at the largest bank in Indiana and soon after as an attorney in private practice.

The Challenges of Defending Saxon's Regulations

Johnson appointed William B. Camp to replace Saxon. Camp had worked in the comptroller's office since 1937, where he rose through the ranks. In 1963, Saxon made Camp the second in command, with the title of first deputy comptroller. Camp was almost certainly loyal to Saxon, and he shared Saxon's views regarding mergers, branches, and allowing banks to enter new lines of business. Camp was a finalist for the comptroller's job on a presidential list that included a Federal Reserve board governor and several state bank regulators.[42] Johnson knew in advance the outlook he wanted in Saxon's replacement.

In Camp, Johnson found a hardworking administrator who would carry Saxon's merger and branching policies forward. Johnson's administrative style included deep immersion in policy development and direct orders to subordinates, including independent federal officers such as the comptroller. A few days before announcing Camp's appointment, Johnson hosted him at his ranch near Austin, Texas. Although no record exists of their conversations, Johnson probably stressed the importance of extending Saxon's innovative bank policies and the equal importance of eliminating friction with members of Congress such as Patman and with bank regulators such as Fed chair Martin. Camp, in a follow-up note, described his ranch visit as "one of the highlights of my life," suggesting the honor he found in their direct conversation and the degree to which Johnson had impressed ideas on him about how to manage the comptroller's responsibilities.[43]

The Johnson treatment secured results. In September 1967, Camp told bankers gathered for their annual convention in New York City about the importance of identifying constructive devices to permit them to enter new business arenas. Here in unrevised form was Saxon's call to permit those bankers to participate in financial sectors such as revenue bonds and insurance sales. Unlike Saxon, however, Camp affirmed the importance of the dual banking system of state and federal regulators and added that it was time to cease disputes. The assembled bankers cheered and applauded Camp's speech, reported a writer for the *American Banker*, adding that bankers everywhere judged Camp convivial and cooperative. "I sleep better," the president of the First National Bank of Leesburg, Florida, wrote Camp in May 1967, with you in the comptroller's office.[44] Few had cheered for Saxon and fewer would have described him in such warm terms. In Camp, Johnson found the ideal person to carry forward ideas that still lacked an organized constituency.

In hard-edged regulatory politics, Camp's congenial ways brought only modest changes to bank organization. Camp, to be certain, maintained Saxon's emphasis on granting mergers. During 1968, he approved another eighty-one that finished successfully. The attorney general sued to stop four mergers; and his lawsuits encouraged executives guiding two additional mergers to quit their plans. In those two cases, Camp's attorneys repeated favored phrases about how the merged banks would foster economic growth, and the attorney general cited the mergers as likely to produce adverse competitive effects. With a ratio of eighty-one approved mergers to six denied or abandoned, Camp, by appearances, had maintained the Saxon tradition of granting mergers and guiding them to legal success. As a matter of fact, the denied and abandoned mergers would have created banks that ranked among the largest in their area. For instance, Camp had approved a union between two modest-sized Nevada banks intended to bring about "economic unification of the State now only united politically."[45] A succession of attorneys general starting with Kennedy had coalesced with Patman's small-town bankers. Together they mounted the political heights and used them to repel those who would permit distant and larger bankers to concentrate resources, expand loan sizes, and dominate the region's financial business. But again, most of the mergers had gone through.

Camp experienced far worse luck in defending Saxon's decision to permit bankers to enter new lines of business. In 1963, Saxon had authorized bank executives to sell insurance. Only officials at Atlanta's Citizens & Southern National Bank (C&S) took up the legally and politically risky challenge. C&S employees sold personal liability policies in conjunction with auto loans and property damage insurance. In 1966, bank officers ended sales, citing their inability to figure out a way to do so profitably.[46]

In December 1965, defense-minded attorneys representing national and Georgia insurance agents' associations brought a lawsuit to stop C&S's insurance sales. The fact that an insurance firm underwrote the policies and the equal fact that C&S officers had exited the business did not present reasons to drop the lawsuit. Like Babington, Schooley, and Patman, those insurance agents had a boundary to defend against future predators. In April 1967, a federal district court judge ruled against Citizens & Southern, and management appealed the decision. The question for them was not whether insurance was profitable, but whether C&S would be permitted to emerge as a full-service bank, a term better known among top bank executives than business journalists. True to the Saxon tradition, Comptroller Camp's attorneys joined Citizens & Southern's in bringing the appeal, which they abandoned in 1969 following a loss at the appellate level.[47]

Efforts to reverse Saxon's disruptive rulings did not end with insurance executives and their lawsuit against Citizens & Southern. In January 1964, Saxon had authorized bankers to underwrite a larger variety of state and local revenue bonds. Quick off the mark, leaders at the always-aggressive First National City Bank of New York and at the recently merged Continental Illinois National Bank and Trust Company entered the revenue bond business. But much like those nervous Georgia insurance agents, investment bankers at widely recognized houses such as Merrill Lynch had boundaries to maintain and revenues to protect against suddenly awakening commercial bankers. In 1965, investment bankers had placed more than $11 billion in bonds, including $3.7 billion in revenue bonds for cities, states, universities, and special purpose districts such as the massive Port Authority of New York and New Jersey. In January 1966, attorneys for ninety-seven investment banking firms, including Merrill Lynch, filed a lawsuit against Comptroller Saxon. Their legal footing rested on the Glass-Steagall Act, which, since 1933, had forbidden commercial banks from handling most securities dealings. In December 1966, when the judge ruled in the investment bankers' favor, he characterized Congress's decision to exclude Saxon and Camp's national banks from underwriting revenue bonds as definitive and unalterable.[48]

Banking's Partly Altered Landscape

In August 1967, a business writer asked whether Saxon and Camp's rulings had succeeded in their quest to open new fields.[49] Measured only in terms of concrete increases in commercial bankers' authority to create gigantic banks, sell insurance, and underwrite bond offerings, Camp and Saxon came up short. Much of that shortfall resided outside the comptroller's ability to leverage a small budget and few legal precedents into solid accomplishments on behalf of a small number of bankers eager to be unleashed.

Presidents had fared no better. Between 1961 and 1967, not even the massive authority accumulated in the office of the president of the United States proved adequate to turn aside the antitrust tradition. Given the president's weakness in this area, members of Congress, judges, and the U.S. attorney general prevailed to block several mergers, chill other merger plans, and maintain impermeable walls between bankers, insurance agents, and investment bankers.[50] In an environment so inhospitable to expanded bank size and scope, Kennedy and Johnson dared not expend presidential capital with grand announcements to Congress and the legislative slogging likely to end in defeat. Given Patman's and Schooley's undiminished hostility to large mergers and larger banks, one might be more surprised that Kennedy and Johnson permitted Saxon and Camp to serve their terms in full. In truth, Kennedy and Johnson were among only a few who advocated consistently for heftier banks offering more services—and Saxon and later Camp were their chosen instruments.

Still, where it was possible to do so, Saxon and Camp had carried out the wishes of their presidential sponsors. To begin, as part of Saxon's program of accelerated merger approvals, bank officers molded California's Crocker-Citizens and other merged firms into several of the nation's largest banks. In February 1966, members of Congress grandfathered several of those larger mergers such as Manufacturers Hanover. Whether those larger banks helped step up the pace of regional economic growth is not clear. More to the immediate point, Saxon and Camp's rule changes fit their contention that under different regulatory arrangements, stodgy bankers might emerge as aggressive entrepreneurs.[51]

Camp and Saxon also left future comptrollers with a stronger office than the hamstrung agency they inherited in 1961. In August 1962, several months into Saxon's term, the senior figures in the comptroller's Washington, D.C., office consisted of Saxon, an economist, a senior attorney, and four deputy comptrollers, including Camp. By 1969, the comptroller's office still included those four deputies and the senior attorney. Now, however, Camp and his successors supervised specialists in bank mergers, branching, and relationships with members of Congress. Comptrollers who followed Saxon and Camp suffered fewer indignities at the hands of hostile congressmen and overbearing Federal Reserve officers. Members of an enlarged legal staff defended lawsuits and scouted out creative avenues for bankers to expand their services.[52] In their brief time in office, Saxon and Camp were among that small group of federal officials, including Thomas H. MacDonald at the U.S. Bureau of Public Roads (1919–1953), who converted small, out-of-the-way offices into centers of information and federal authority capable of promoting construction of the Interstate Highway System. During the next decades, the comptroller's office emerged as a legal and political powerhouse and as an early stop for bankers and lawmakers seeking to build larger banks offering more services such as insurance and revenue bonds.[53]

Saxon and Camp also launched a change in the political and legal landscapes that surrounded commercial banking. Patman and Schooley had promptly recognized the danger that Saxon and Camp's actions posed for small bankers. Their early responses included the Saxon hearings and demands for Saxon's removal. But investment bankers, insurance agents, and heads of department stores that offered easy credit needed a few more years to catch on to the emerging threats. Their delay was generational in nature. During the late 1950s, members of a younger cohort of executives and attorneys—those with no adult memory of the money business before Glass-Steagall—had entered prospering firms in such apparently settled fields as investment banking and insurance. Those executives, seated in comfortable offices located downtown and in new suburbs, could not easily discern the invisible walls that federal and state officials had built around independent insurance agencies and investment banks. As long as those walls maintained would-be competitors like commercial bankers at a safe distance, talk about America as a market economy was always in order.

Starting in the mid-1960s, Saxon and Camp's actions alerted those newer financial executives to the presence of frightening political facts. Regulators as well as members of Congress, it now appeared, were capable of allowing and encouraging mergers that threatened careers, prestige, and a direct line to solid profitability. Mergers composed only one part of the changes that were at hand. Chicago's Continental Illinois Bank was enormous; and, its executives promoted credit cards. Executives at Rockefeller's massive Chase Manhattan had tried their hand with revenue bonds. Even more, officials at Atlanta's smaller Citizens & Southern had crossed the frontier to enter the insurance business. As these startling developments took place, members of this new generation of insurance executives and investment bankers realized how rapidly their expanding revenues and promising careers might come to naught were these predations allowed to continue.[54]

Starting in the wake of Saxon and Camp's rule changes, grinding politics in the form of endless litigation and lobbying emerged as a standard feature of bank politics. To be willing to go to court and Congress on a regular basis also required unstinting efforts to organize likely allies for the next foray against opponents and for the one after that. Full-time politics rather than markets, as any savvy executive like First National City Bank's Walter Wriston recognized, served as a mainstay of his firm's rapid growth. Among American business leaders, market talk supplied the language to wage those political and legal struggles. Presidents were equally alert to market talk's political value.

In 1970, President Richard M. Nixon restarted the search for legal and administrative changes to permit banks to grow larger and offer additional services. A decade later, President Ronald W. Reagan asked his treasury secretary Donald T. Regan to continue that hunt for devices to encourage creation of big banks and prosperity's certain return. Bank politics after 1970 was, however, only in part a direct extension of the changes Kennedy and Saxon had sought to bring about. During the 1970s and 1980s, presidents and their advisers brought new words and concepts like "regulatory reform" and "supermarket banks" to their efforts to create multipurpose financial institutions that spanned the nation. Presidents in the 1970s and later were also convinced that larger banks would help ward off the inflation and unemployment that afflicted corporate balance sheets and household budgets. By that point, the idea that larger, multipurpose banks bore a direct link to accelerated economic performance had achieved a lofty place in presidential imaginations and a permanent place in presidential politics. In the 1980s, few remembered James Saxon and William Camp and the decade when deregulation before deregulation took place.

CHAPTER 2

Supermarket Banks: Richard Nixon and Donald Regan

During the evening of Wednesday, May 27, 1970, President Richard M. Nixon hosted a formal dinner at the White House. At 6:30 p.m., the president and his guests convened in the Blue Room for cocktails. Bank of America's president attended the dinner, as did senior officers at the nation's largest banking, brokerage, and investment companies. Among the other financial executives present, several held top posts with insurance firms and with mutual and pension funds. Fourteen leaders of large industrial corporations joined the group. Arthur M. Burns, the Federal Reserve's new chair, mingled with the distinguished visitors. Following cocktails, everyone moved to the State Dining Room for dinner.[1]

Organizers had arranged the elegant and sumptuous dinner in haste. No one arrived in a celebratory mood. A *New York Times* reporter characterized the group's mood as a mix of "nervous bantering" and "grim" faces. Earlier in the month, Ohio National Guardsmen shot and killed four students on the Kent State University campus. Students had gathered to protest the Vietnam War and the president's decision to invade Cambodia. Inflation added to the problems troubling the president's guests. By 1970, the inflation rate had jumped to 6 percent, a big leap from 2.79 percent in May 1967. Rising costs had also invaded the corporate bond market. In May 1970, American Telephone and Telegraph (AT&T) bonds paid 9.19 percent, the highest in history for a major corporation. But AT&T was still in business. Officers of the Penn Central Railroad—the self-styled standard railroad of the world—had exhausted cash to pay employees and suppliers. In July, following Penn Central's bankruptcy filing, its president Stuart T. Saunders blamed the railroad's problems on inflation, money shortages, and high interest rates.[2]

Banks and savings and loan associations (S&Ls) were also in trouble. Between March 1969 and June 1970, as one example, depositors withdrew $278.6 million from New York City's Bowery Savings Bank. New Yorkers moving to the suburbs took their money with them. That type of disinvestment represented only part of the problem S&L executives soon faced on a daily basis. Beginning in 1972, interest-hungry savers throughout the United States removed cash from S&Ls and redeposited their funds in newly created money market funds, which paid higher rates of interest. As depositors withdrew savings, S&L executives pushed home mortgage interest rates skyward. By December 1969, even the large and still flush Great Western Savings & Loan in Los Angeles demanded 9.5 percent for a new mortgage. High mortgage rates and rising home prices meant that fewer prospective buyers qualified for loans. Even for lucky households with down payments and good credit, diminished funds crimped the number of loans that could be approved.[3] Falling home sales had already begun to ricochet into the construction industry, raising the specter of layoffs and bankruptcies in an economically important and politically visible industry.

Senior corporate officials and President Nixon had not gathered in haste for a midweek dinner at the White House to discuss inflation, home mortgage costs, and Penn Central's impending bankruptcy. Well-versed business leaders knew those dreary facts in detail. Instead, a sharp downturn in the stock market brought inflation, rising interest rates, money shortages, and an unpopular war into precise and scary focus. On December 3, 1968, the widely followed Dow Jones Industrial Average (the Dow) closed at 985, a record high. By April 30, 1970, however, investors had pushed the Dow average down to 736, a decline of 25 percent. In May, the stock market turned in an especially dismal performance. On May 4, the Dow fell 19 points, a loss that nearly equaled the 21-point falloff that had taken place on December 22, 1963, the day President Kennedy was assassinated. On May 25, the Dow tumbled again, this time by nearly 22 points. Stock market losses threatened insurance companies, stockbrokers, pension funds, and investment bankers. Falling stock prices put in doubt the savings of thirty-one million Americans who had purchased shares directly. Ordinary investors were in a squeeze, just like Bowery Savings' executives and prospective homebuyers. As prices tumbled, Bernard J. "Bunny" Lasker, the chairman of the New York Stock Exchange's Board of Governors, prevailed on President Nixon, his friend, to host the dinner.[4]

White House staff served dessert at 9:30 p.m., as scheduled. The time for plain talk about the war and the economy was at hand. Business leaders at the White House that evening sought assurances that the government would conclude the war, reduce inflationary pressures, and boost the economy's slowing pace. The costly and seemingly endless Vietnam conflict threatened still higher inflation and unemployment, already at 5 percent. In one year, employers had terminated and temporarily laid off 1,085,000 Americans.[5]

With the dessert dishes cleared, the president rose to speak. A large map of Southeast Asia served as his backdrop. The Cambodian invasion was on schedule, Nixon told guests, and would inflict great damage on the enemy. The economy was also on schedule to resume growth, Nixon observed, probably after July 1. Wage and price controls, Nixon added, would be voluntary in nature, if he even imposed them. In other words, Nixon promised to bring the economy under control in a slow and careful manner, without allowing it to lurch into recession or a full-blown depression. Stock prices rose as soon as news of the dinner became public. And stock prices continued to rise.[6] Those increases were temporary, however, much as the president's comments about the economy avoiding further downturns proved evanescent in nature.

Sixty-three business leaders attended that White House dinner. During the next decade and more, only a few among that extraordinary gathering possessed the clout, visibility, and longevity to put their ideas about banking and the economy into legislative and regulatory form. President Nixon was certainly a member of that group. Since World War II, Americans held the president responsible for the nation's economic functioning. In 1970, the levers of political and economic authority rested squarely in Nixon's hands. (Nixon was inaugurated January 20, 1969, and resigned effective August 9, 1974, eighteen months into his second term). Nixon did not seek only to create short-term economic cures (like White House dinners) that would jolt stock prices or get him past the next election. During his five and a half years in office, Nixon brought attention to ideas about bank mergers and expanded financial services that reverberated into the 1980s and 1990s. Nixon set in motion the idea of supermarket banks.

Nixon, the Hunt Commission, and Supermarket Banks

Nixon was a policy politician, in the mold of Kennedy and Johnson. He harbored ideas about how the economy worked and how reductions in government bank regulations might improve the nation's economic performance and put Americans back to work. In 1970, Nixon's ideas about how to change bank rules remained unsettled. He was clearly open to the merger policies and other innovative practices that Kennedy, Johnson, Saxon, and Camp had sought to promote. But Nixon also inherited the hardened politics of the 1960s. During the 1970s, as the stock market fluctuated and interest rates and unemployment climbed, investment bankers and insurance agents remained determined to stop any threat to the lucrative business areas that Congress and earlier regulators had set aside for them.

To complicate Nixon's task, S&L executives joined those anxious insurance agents and investment bankers in a righteous stand against commercial bankers. The nation's many S&Ls, such as California's Great Western, served as the financial backbone of the American housing industry. Homebuilders relied on S&Ls to foster home sales; and ordinary Americans relied on those same S&Ls to finance their new houses, including bedrooms for each of their children and a backyard with a swing for them to play. S&L leaders, with money flowing out of the till daily, advanced an audacious solution to their financial dilemma. Since the 1930s, S&Ls accepted deposits and wrote mortgages. Now, however, many S&L executives sought to escape the trap of rising interest rates and fixed mortgage returns by securing the government's permission to convert their firms to full-fledged commercial banks. Once through the political wringer, frightened S&L leaders would emerge as cocksure commercial bankers. Bankers were unlikely to accept the award of valuable franchises to stumbling S&L executives. Turf battles among business executives composed a standard feature of the American political economy.

Nixon had dealt with similar arguments his entire career. But with bad economic news arriving daily and with the election of 1972 looming closer, Nixon determined on a course that Kennedy and Johnson had refused to take. Nixon created a commission to investigate the organization of financial services. Commissions including this one were large, visible, and composed of senior corporate executives. Journalists paid attention to commission reports, especially in an area as important to members of Congress as the services and prices that bankers and S&Ls offered savers, home buyers, and loan applicants. Nixon did not appoint federal lawmakers to the commission, perhaps to keep Rep. Wright Patman off. But Patman was certain to have determined opinions about any commission recommendations that included tinkering with the rights of small banks and S&Ls. By way of contrast, Kennedy had appointed a committee on financial institutions, the one where the Federal Reserve chair Martin and Comptroller Saxon exchanged insults, but cabinet-level committees lacked a political presence and rarely garnered journalists' attention. Kennedy and Johnson had permitted Saxon and Camp to take the lead—and the heat from Patman and others—in fostering the growth of large banks. Nixon's course was a fraught one.

Nixon proceeded cautiously. Members of his Council of Economic Advisers (CEA) advertised the proposed commission on three pages in their 1970 *Economic Report of the President*. That proposed commission, Nixon's economists advertised, would study ways to permit increased branching. Removal of the cap on interest rates that S&Ls and banks paid savers loomed as another goal. Above all, CEA economists advocated the award of greater "flexibility" to bank and S&L leaders.[7] In the context of early 1970s bank politics, flexibility meant that bankers and S&L leaders would be permitted to enter new lines of business. Seeding the commission idea in the CEA's report provided cover for Nixon. In the event of a sharply negative congressional reaction, Nixon could always blame the out-of-touch PhDs who staffed the council.

On June 16, Nixon announced creation of his commission. Reed O. Hunt, the former chief executive of San Francisco's Crown Zellerbach Corporation, would serve as chair. Journalists described the group as the Hunt Commission, a name that stuck. Nixon's appointment of a presidential commission put his signature publicly on the idea of altering bank rules. The official title, the President's Commission on Financial Structure and Regulation, highlighted Nixon's concern that regulation had created overly specialized financial service firms and financial service industries walled off from one another.

Nixon wanted commission members to find ways to bring down those walls. Among its nineteen members, three were top-level commercial bankers and another three were senior executives with savings' societies, including Morris D. Crawford, Jr., Bowery Savings' board chairman. To balance Bowery's representation of savings banks, which were prominent on the East Coast, Nixon appointed J. Howard Edgerton, the chairman of California Federal Savings and Loan Association, to the Hunt Commission. In 1970, California Federal was among the state's largest S&Ls. The Prudential Insurance Company's chairman and CEO joined the committee, as did the president of CIT, a financial services firm. Nixon also placed the president of American Express on the Hunt Commission.

Nixon appointed Alan Greenspan to the Hunt Commission. In the late 1940s, Greenspan, a Columbia University graduate student in economics, had learned ideas about business firms that operated with fewer government restrictions. Following graduate school, Greenspan was a member of a small group, led by Ayn Rand, whose members studied and advocated for the elimination of all government regulation. Greenspan and others who attended Rand's seminars and get-togethers described themselves as libertarians. In his time as a member of Rand's group, Greenspan looked toward the arrival of a wondrous day when private firms operated without government rules. In the early 1970s, however, self-styled libertarians lacked clout in a policy arena dominated by bankers, lawmakers, and regulators. Among most bankers and regulators, federal and state rules offered predictability and security in an increasingly unsteady economy. Commission members wanted to change a few regulations, but no one sought anything as radical as the abolition of all regulatory agencies and the many rules that governed bank operations. To add to the complexity of their dealings, Nixon expected commissioners to transcend differences in background and outlook to produce recommendations for federal action that staunched the outflow of S&L funds, fostered bank growth, and inaugurated a period of renewed economic growth.[8] The Hunt Commission represented a heightened presidential commitment to writing new rules that were supposed to reshape a major swath of the American financial economy.

Hunt, alert to Nixon's goals, organized the commission's deliberations with an eye toward reducing distinctions between bankers, S&L executives, and heads of other types of money businesses such as American Express and Prudential Insurance. Hunt did not create specialized committees. Rather, at each of the commission's fifteen meetings, members worked as a committee of the whole. Discussions that took place in a large group made it awkward for bankers or S&L officers to recommend policies that favored their industry and firms alone. Instead, Hunt reported, commissioners engaged in wide-ranging discussions about problems and policy recommendations that crossed industry lines.[9]

Hunt played a key part in fostering a harmony of views. One observer described Hunt as "a low-key, affable man." Hunt spoke in neutral terms. "A view was expressed" was Hunt's chosen phrase to deal with the wide-ranging ideas commissioners brought to each meeting. Meeting minutes recorded only that "a discussion followed" the introduction of ideas certain to provoke sharp debate, as, for instance, whether S&Ls should retain the right to pay a higher rate of interest than commercial banks to attract deposits. The idea underlying that higher rate of interest was that S&Ls served as the nation's mortgage lenders.[10]

Insiders knew the government's ability to determine interest rates paid savers by its official name, the Federal Reserve's Regulation Q. The curiously named Regulation Q was part of the 1933 Glass-Steagall Act. In 1966, President Johnson and Congress approved the Interest Rate Control Act, which authorized S&L executives to pay a higher rate of interest to savers than banks paid them. Nervous S&L officers had urged this action. Federal Reserve officers in turn approved a 0.25 percent differential. In earlier years, prosperous bankers had accepted Regulation Q's limits on their ability to change interest rates paid to savers. But now, the Hunt Commission provided an official opportunity for those bankers to make their case against Regulation Q's restrictions. The Hunt Commission's S&L members, such as Edgerton, were equally passionate in defending the regulation and the 0.25 percent higher rates they were now authorized to offer as vital protection to their firms and to American home construction.[11] Hunt could not meld these sharp differences, but his rhetorical style made it easier for commissioners to entertain divisive ideas in the abstract. On the surface, Hunt appeared almost without a point of view.

Hunt's evenhanded style allowed commissioners to avoid making politically difficult choices. Nixon had created the commission to advance ideas that would lead to large changes in the political economy of finance. Yet, in the course of their deliberations, Hunt and his commissioners slowly narrowed the topics to be discussed. On October 28, 1970, Hunt informed members that they needed to devise ways to make more money available at lower rates of interest. Hunt did not need to inform commissioners that additional funds would help meet the needs of homebuyers and businesses.[12] High interest rates, went the reasoning, had hastened Penn Central's bankruptcy. Hunt Commission members along with every businessman at Nixon's dinner favored cheaper loan rates.

But the committee tripped up on whether S&Ls should remain the principal place where Americans took out home loans. At one point in that late October meeting, several commissioners asked whether home ownership was a matter of "national interest," and even whether the federal government was obligated to make credit available to homebuyers.[13] To proceed further with that question was to head down a path toward the S&Ls' extinction and a heart-stopping interruption in suburban growth. In that one moment, Hunt and his commissioners determined not to explore in detail the boldest question of all, which was whether the nation needed a separate and distinct group of S&Ls and another group of separate and distinct commercial banks. As with every aspect of American finance, history and politics dominated the way commissioners framed questions, and even whether those questions could be asked.

Yet, even within those limits, the accommodating Hunt was capable of advancing recommendations certain to challenge commissioners, bankers, and S&L leaders. Hunt had determined beforehand that the system of banks making commercial loans and S&Ls writing mortgages should not continue. Instead, at that crucial meeting on October 28, Hunt urged changes in federal and state law so that banks and S&Ls would receive nearly identical treatment and turn out nearly identical financial products. According to Hunt, S&L executives such as Edgerton would offer checking accounts and make commercial loans, the very business that authors of the 1933 Glass-Steagall Act had reserved to commercial bankers. In turn, commercial banks would move full force into home mortgages. In the course of five years, Hunt recommended, the federal government would phase out the nettlesome Regulation Q. At the end of that period, S&Ls such as Edgerton's California Federal would lose its legal right to offer savers a higher interest rate.[14] No one would be set on a path toward going out of business.

In October 1970, commissioners, including Hunt, lacked an agreed-upon phrase to describe the process whereby banks and S&Ls were to become much the same. Rather, commissioners invoked phrases such as "free entry [and] right of exit" to describe a situation in which banks and S&Ls easily entered financial areas rather than remaining holed up in a specialized niche such as home mortgages. As another phrase to describe the type of firm they hoped would emerge from "freer markets," commissioners talked about "supermarkets." During the years between the 1920s and 1970, supermarkets offering a variety of foods had replaced bakers, butchers, and candy shops that were individually owned and operated. Whether described as a bank or an S&L, the supermarket Hunt Commission members had in mind would offer a similar array of financial products. Old-fashioned restrictions like charter provisions limiting S&Ls to mortgages would no longer apply.[15]

"Supermarket" as a word to describe this new type of money business was never foreordained. More likely than not, "supermarket" was one of those terms that was familiar and also popular among business leaders and big city and suburban shoppers. And, as well, Merrill Lynch executives led by

Donald T. Regan had begun to describe their many financial offerings as a "supermarket," which awarded the term a positive cachet. Following Nixon's lead, Hunt and his commissioners were striving to create a politically acceptable way to reorganize banking and solve economic problems. At one point, still searching for the right phrase to describe what they hoped to accomplish, commissioners talked about a "merging toward the center."[16]

In December 1971, members of the Hunt Commission recommended eighty-nine changes to federal law and regulation. Anyone who had observed bank politics during the previous decade could have predicted most of them. In its essence, commissioners wanted S&Ls and banks to become more alike in the types of loans they were allowed to make. As one example, commissioners would permit S&Ls to issue checks, sell mutual funds, underwrite insurance, and make personal loans. As another, S&Ls as well as banks would enjoy statewide branching rights, knocking down barriers many states had erected. The commissioners also proposed a two- to five-year phaseout of Regulation Q, the ceiling on the rate of interest that banks and S&Ls paid depositors. For everyone, banks and S&Ls alike, federal and state caps on interest charged loan customers would disappear. According to members of the Hunt Commission, specialization of banks and S&Ls into distinct niches had contributed to rising interest rates. Not ready to dissolve every boundary, Hunt's members elected to permit commercial bankers to retain the sole right to make business loans, their bread-and-butter work.[17] If Congress approved each of the commission's recommendations, banks would soon underwrite revenue bonds and sell insurance, putting into effect the proposals that Comptrollers Saxon and Camp had urged.

Hunt relied on favored American idioms to introduce these complex recommendations. Rather than dwell on difficult-to-grasp rules about branch banking or Regulation Q's cap on interest rates, Hunt framed the report around undeniable ideas such as "freedom for the financial system." Saxon and Patman in contrast had employed opaque terms such as "monopoly" and "antitrust" to argue for and against mergers and bank entry into fields such as insurance sales. Only a few years earlier, Wright Patman and his small-town bankers stood shoulder to shoulder to defend state anti-branching rules. Now, Hunt judged those rules and every other rule that limited competition "socially harmful." Competition, Hunt promised, would lead to improved financial services for everyone. With "unworkable regulatory restraints" removed at last, Hunt predicted the appearance of a stronger economic system, one where interest rates stabilized and inflationary pressures subsided. Bank publicists further embellished Hunt's promised growth with phrases such as "free market forces" and "let freedom ring."[18] Stripped of these rhetorical excesses, here in condensed and specific form was the now decade-old proposition of Presidents Kennedy and Johnson that a change in bank rules would produce a growing financial system and a growing economy.

Hunt was a deft political operator. He had wisely steered clear of a direct assault on the nation's antitrust tradition. Neither had Hunt produce ideas that were new and startling to the executives who directed large financial corporations. One business writer characterized the report as "cautious and sometimes platitudinous."[19] Hunt's achievement resided in the consensus he had achieved among powerful commission members to break down barriers on which their firms and industries had long relied. That consensus also gave Hunt a running start at the prospect of winning support in Congress and among financial executives for ideas certain to be judged anything but cautious and platitudinous.

Freedom in the abstract did not count for much among self-protective bankers and their S&L counterparts. Criticism of Hunt's report arrived hard and fast. Only a few weeks after the report became public, Hunt Commission member Edgerton broke ranks with his former colleagues to denounce the "blurring of distinctions between financial institutions and tending to discourage specialization" in home mortgage lending. S&Ls, including Edgerton's California Federal, worked almost exclusively in the home mortgage business. Edgerton and other S&L leaders celebrated the Hunt report's promised access to new markets formerly owned by commercial bankers and simultaneously protested furiously at the prospect that unbridled commercial bankers would enter the home mortgage field, which by law and tradition belonged to them. Nor could Edgerton and other S&L leaders imagine relinquishing that extra quarter point in interest that authors of Regulation Q and the 1966 Interest Rate Control Act permitted them to pay savers. The report had been available for only a few weeks when former Hunt Commission member Richard G. Gilbert, chair of Citizens Savings Association, told fellow executives that high inflation levels were not permanent. By this reasoning, diminished inflation made the case for business as usual. And in fact, S&L deposits had stabilized during this period, allowing executives like Gilbert to characterize the Hunt report's recommendations as the harbinger of "revolution not evolution."[20]

Federal Reserve officials, such as Arthur Burns, also found problems in Hunt's report. Hunt had recommended creation of a new federal agency that would be empowered to regulate the S&Ls alongside state-chartered banks. Such an agency would undercut the often-celebrated state-federal bank regulatory system Patman favored. At its most basic, however, Hunt's proposal, if enacted, stood to create a rival agency that might instantly diminish Chairman Burns's ability to administer one part of a national regulatory regime. Creation of a new agency also threated Burns's acknowledged position as the most influential bank regulator. Presidents took counsel with Federal Reserve chairs, and that was a position not to be surrendered without a fight. Only a few years earlier, Saxon had threatened the Fed's regulatory overlordship and felt Chairman Martin's stinging criticism. Creation of another regulator would only add to the fragmentation of federal bank supervision, Alfred Hayes, president of the Federal Reserve Bank of New York, contended. During the 1970s, Federal Reserve chairs as well as the twelve district bank presidents guarded their portion of the financial regulatory system as carefully as insurance agents, small-town bankers, and S&L executives guarded their prestige and autonomy in dealing with customers and clients.[21] Federal Reserve officials also posed a silent but visible barrier against anyone who dared threaten their top-tier standing. A well-publicized speech by Burns or Hayes about Hunt's threat to the Federal Reserve's much-vaunted singular independence was certain to unleash strong emotions and political action among bankers large and small. Hunt's proposals, only recently heralded as a beacon of freedom, were not off to a propitious start. As a policy politician, Nixon took them up nevertheless.

Richard Nixon, Bill Simon, Gerald Ford, and the Small Saver

In August 1973, safely reelected, Nixon submitted a modified version of Hunt's proposal to Congress. Nixon urged narrowly constructed changes to S&Ls' authority to permit them to write consumer and business loans. Nixon would also make S&Ls and banks nationwide eligible to offer interest-paying checking accounts. State legislators in Massachusetts and New Hampshire had already authorized savings banks in those states to offer negotiable order of withdrawal (NOW) accounts, another name for a checking account that paid interest. S&Ls, such as Edgerton's California Federal, would provide services similar to those that commercial banks offered. Regulation Q would disappear in five and a half years, just as Hunt had proposed. Nixon, however, left the complex system of multiple bank regulators untouched. Nixon also stripped out ideas about banks and S&Ls underwriting insurance, administering mutual funds, and setting up statewide branches. In 1973, Nixon had no intention of debating insurance agents, mutual fund administrators, Federal Reserve chair Burns or Wright Patman and his band of well-organized small-town bankers. Instead, Nixon identified the small saver "who received an unfairly low return on his savings" as the likely big winner once Congress enacted his proposals. Nixon's focus on the politically forgotten small saver at once cast him as a friend of the ordinary wage earner and allowed him to avoid politically freighted terms like "antitrust" and "supermarket banks." Now it was up to William E. "Bill" Simon, a top Nixon appointee and a former investment banker, to convert the politically safer promise to help small savers into legislative action.[22]

William Simon was the treasury department's second-ranking official. With prices for most products and consumer anger rising in concert, savvy lawmakers such as Nixon and Simon urged enactment of one part of the supermarket idea that Hunt Commission members had advocated. On August 3, 1973, Simon told reporters about Nixon's plan to provide "freedom for our financial markets." In Nixon's hands, the idea of banks and S&Ls as interchangeable businesses had now moved from the Hunt Commission's report to a presidential recommendation to Congress. In 1973, although most Americans lacked experience with the language of market barriers and market entry, Simon and Nixon pointed to an experiment in the reorganization of financial services that might perhaps diminish inflation and improve employment. But creation of free-flowing markets was never Simon and Nixon's primary goal. Simon and the president, unprepared to do away with the federal government's helping hand, urged Congress to create tax incentives for S&Ls and bankers to invest in housing. The less visible tax code would help maintain the flow of loans to homebuyers. Federal Reserve chair Burns, a keen political observer, had already warned a senior treasury official that Congress would pass no legislation that failed to support homebuyers.[23] But Simon's proposals were already bogged down in arguments among banks and S&L executives, the squabbles that Hunt had sought to go around.

By mid-September, Simon judged bleak the prospect of passing Nixon's bank legislation. As part of an effort to revive the bill's chances, Simon granted an interview to a writer for *Banking*, by any measure a business-friendly publication. Simon employed grand phrases such as "Congress is a big give-and-take institution," suggesting that he and members of Congress might yet work out a deal. Yet, for Simon, Regulation Q was not susceptible to a vague give-and-take. "Regulation Q is where we must begin," he announced. Edgerton and other S&L leaders also drew the line at Regulation Q. In an uncertain economy, no one was willing to serve as the test patient for the idea that supermarket banking would hasten the return of widespread prosperity. "Leave this part of the status quo alone," Simon reported S&L executives had told him, "this is our franchise."[24] With President Nixon facing impeachment, members of Congress were in no mood to take up anything as uncertain and unsettling as eliminating Regulation Q and changing other bank rules.

On August 9, 1974, Gerald R. Ford took the presidential oath of office. In 1975, Ford submitted bank legislation that followed Nixon's in substantial detail. Like Nixon, Ford promised a phaseout of Regulation Q. Bankers still detested Regulation Q, while S&L executives and homebuilders continued to hold it dear. Inflation remained high, and savers in turn continued to transfer funds from S&Ls to higher yielding money market accounts.[25] Simon now served as Ford's treasury secretary, which added to the political standoff. During the short window between Ford's swearing in and the start of the 1976 presidential campaign, Simon had no greater luck changing bank rules than his predecessors extending back to Kennedy and Saxon.

Since the early 1970s, everyone who bought groceries, paid their family's bills, or drove an automobile could plainly see the extraordinary increases in prices for most products and especially for gasoline, natural gas, and heating oil. Rising prices for household necessities made it difficult for Edgerton's S&L to raise inexpensive cash; and, just as important, those rising interest rates had pushed the cost of loans to meet payrolls, buy new equipment, and absorb ever-larger energy bills nearly out of reach for managers of the largest and smallest firms. Financial hard times reached deep into the ranks of suburban householders. Just as certainly, no one, including Presidents Nixon and Ford, possessed the clout to assemble a successful legislative package that maintained a flow of funds to housing without at the same time distressing bankers and S&L leaders. As before, bankers and S&L executives were well organized and alert to legislative and regulatory innovations. One participant characterized the S&Ls' lobbying efforts as "aggressive without being obnoxious."[26] In contrast, the small saver, in whose name every piece of financial legislation had to go forward, remained without a comparably well-organized voice in House corridors and in the Senate cloakroom.

But the 1975–1976 congressional deadlock about changing bank rules was anything but a simple high-stakes contest among business interests and small savers, far from it. In May 1975, as hearings on Ford's bank legislation opened, Senator Thomas J. McIntyre (D-NH), the subcommittee chair, lamented the absence of legislation to deal directly with housing rather than with what he described as the "ad hoc, special-interest, piecemealing approach of legislation pertaining to financial institutions." S&L executives and commercial bankers, McIntyre contended that day, were as hamstrung as the president and the Congress in their ability to bolster housing and at the same time protect risk-averse stakeholders in a segmented financial economy.[27] During Ford's short presidential term, bank and S&L officers put the protection of their franchise rights in first place. But the day's legislative deadlock did not conclude there. Ford and Simon added another dimension to arguments that never seemed to end.

Like Nixon and Hunt, Ford and Simon left behind a residue of ideas that guided the way Americans began to understand the rapid economic changes taking place on a near-daily basis. Up to the early 1970s, few Americans possessed an insight or an opinion regarding how and even whether Regulation Q and other federal bank rules influenced unemployment, inflation, interest rates, and the movement of money out of S&Ls and into money market funds. Many, perhaps, had no idea how to explain such large and often devastating changes. Up to that point, economists, key members of Congress, and other experts tended to such matters.

Soon after becoming president, however, Ford and his top administrators introduced and standardized a new vocabulary by which those newspaper readers and TV viewers could begin to make sense of unseen connections among federal rules such as Regulation Q, Ford's legislative proposals, and household budgets, home buying, and jobs. During 1975, for example, Ford gave major speeches attacking federal rules that, he contended, added to inflation and reduced the number of jobs. In those speeches, Ford converted the word "deregulation" from one spoken only by his economic advisers and a few university professors to an everyday term that appeared in national newspapers and in television news broadcasts. Nixon and Hunt had advanced identical arguments against federal regulation including bank regulation. Nixon and Hunt had not barnstormed the country with their anti-regulation message. In Ford's hands, the disturbing effects of federal rules on employment and household budgets emerged as a political truth that Americans could begin to imbibe.[28]

Ford's speeches awarded special prominence to another word appearing in print more often—"freedom." Indeed, freedom was as old and revered as the republic. Starting after publication of the Hunt report in late 1971, a few bankers and bank publicists had begun to invoke freedom as a legislative cudgel. In speeches and in congressional testimony, Ford and Simon contrasted federal bureaucrats who issued detailed rules, called red tape, with freedom's promise of fewer rules, more jobs, and faster economic growth. Ford also highlighted the idea of rate freedom, the freedom for business executives to set prices rather than follow the dictates of anonymous federal bureaucrats. With Regulation Q out of the way, Simon promised, price-sensitive bankers and S&L officers would replace distant and heavy-handed Federal Reserve officials in determining interest rates.[29] By this reasoning, price freedom and easy entry among bankers and S&L executives into one another's fields would soon reignite economic growth.

"Freedom" suggested a simple relationship between fewer bank rules and prosperity. Yet Ford, like each president since 1961, never intended to return banking to an imagined state of nature. Perhaps at some future date, Ford and Simon or their successors might prevail on Congress to make Regulation Q disappear and render banking and S&Ls nearly indistinguishable in the kinds of businesses they undertook. Even when that happy day arrived, rhetorical freedom also faced practical limits. What sensible lawmaker or banker, as one illustration, would dare to demand that the comptroller no longer inspect banks' books, that the Federal Deposit Insurance Corporation stop insuring bank deposits, or that Arthur Burns and his colleagues at the Federal Reserve abandon their authority to determine interest rates for the economy as a whole? "Freedom," as Simon and Ford must have recognized, was a politically contrived term to modify the way federal rules organized banks and S&Ls. Freedom's passionate and determined advocates never sought to abolish federal bank regulations and usher in a period of financial anarchy.

All in all, "regulatory reform" was Ford's preferred term for loosening bank rules, and for good reason. "Regulatory reform" was a more subtle term, a term they could control, as opposed to "freedom," which was an open-ended concept with the potential to blow the doors off the administrative state. "Regulatory reform" meant the abolition of the onerous Regulation Q and the desegmentation of financial services. S&Ls and banks would become almost interchangeable once lawmakers pushed open those politically constituted fields.[30] Here resided Hunt's supermarket banks, with their seemingly natural propensity to reduce inflation and restart economic growth. By January 1977, as Ford prepared to leave the White House, an asserted relationship among regulatory reform, the appearance of supermarket banks, and the return of solid economic growth had emerged as durable features of the institutional office of the president. Jimmy Carter made regulatory reform a key feature of his campaign and presidency.

Jimmy Carter and Regulatory Reform

Jimmy Carter campaigned for the presidency on the promise of deregulation and economic improvement. He was inaugurated on January 20, 1977. Once in office, Carter adopted regulatory reform as his preferred goal, and he made the heavily regulated airlines his top target. Airfares were visible, especially among business travelers who flew in still-glamorous jets to meetings and holidays in European capitals and in fast-growing U.S. cities such as Los Angeles and Phoenix. Carter and his top staffers believed that success in lowering airfares would win those travelers to regulatory reform for trucking, railroads, and banking.[31]

No such constituency was in sight for bank regulatory reform. Commercial bankers remained adamant that S&Ls must never be permitted to offer checking accounts or enter any other aspect of commercial banking. And in turn, S&L executives stood solidly in favor of Regulation Q. To drive their points home, late in March 1977, more than one hundred savings executives, including former Hunt Commission member Morris Crawford, visited members of Congress and every federal bank regulator's office. Those S&L executives brought longtime contacts, a unified message, and a history of sustained lobbying with them. As a result, observers judged the chances of legislating Hunt ideas such as supermarket banks as no more likely to take place than the fanciful idea appearing in Sunday newspaper reports that Americans in the future would conduct their financial business electronically. Economic decline hardened their position. During 1979–1980, S&L executives wrote 25 percent fewer mortgages than the year before. Regulation Q protected their remaining business, S&L leaders like Crawford argued. In 1980, a writer for *United States Banker* described "positions seemingly locked in cement."[32] It was not only S&L and other financial executives who refused to run risks.

Carter was also reluctant to take risks to change the financial system. In 1978 and early 1979, his advisers exchanged memos that included terms such as "competition," "improved productivity," the small saver," and, of course, "regulatory reform." Carter's advisers still spoke about the desirability of permitting branch banking, eliminating Regulation Q's interest rate caps, and dissolving multiple bank regulators. The comptroller's office issued bank charters. But an entirely different agency, the Federal Home Loan Bank Board, issued S&L charters.[33] Leaders in the Kennedy administration and every subsequent administration had toyed with the idea of regulatory consolidation. By their reasoning, one regulator would produce one banking industry. Carter, again like each of his predecessors, sought to put his hands on legislative and regulatory devices that connected faster growing banks with diminished inflation, rising employment levels, and the politically popular small saver. Whether one or all of his advisers' ideas would actually lead the way to reduced inflation and rising employment remained anyone's guess.

A lawsuit altered the political dynamic. Regulation Q's capped interest rates for small savers resided at the center of the dispute. In 1978, leaders of a consumer group sued bank regulators on grounds that Regulation Q discriminated against small savers. Starting in June 1978, banks and S&Ls paid between 9 and 10 percent on deposits larger than ten thousand dollars, but the small saver still earned a comparatively paltry 5.25 percent at banks and 5.5 percent at S&Ls. Wealthier bank customers moved surplus checking funds to high interest savings accounts. In April 1979, a three-judge federal appeals court in Washington, D.C., ruled those transfers illegal. S&Ls and banks, the judges held, composed "separate and distinct types of financial institutions." Customers' ability to transfer funds threatened to create "homogeneous . . . financial institutions offering virtually identical services . . . without benefit of Congressional consideration."[34] Since 1961, Saxon, Kennedy, and leaders in subsequent presidential administrations had sought to create just such a homogeneous financial system but lacked the authority to do so. In the short run, the court's decision threatened interest payments and bank services. The judges gave Congress until January 1, 1980, to modify bank law.

The certainty of legislative action to protect savers created an opening for Carter and congressional leaders to act. Few Americans recognized the multiple laws and rules that governed banks and S&Ls. In May 1979, a month after the lawsuit was filed, Carter sent a message to Congress that once again placed the long-suffering small saver at its center. It was "unconscionable," Carter asserted, "for the Federal government to prohibit small savers from receiving the return on their deposits that is available to large and sophisticated investors." With the 1980 election fast approaching, Carter sought to win quick congressional approval. He abandoned a legislative effort to secure branch banking "to avoid antagonizing community banks and states' rights advocates," a top aide later reminded him.[35]

On March 31, 1980, Carter signed the awkwardly named Depository Institutions Deregulation and Monetary Control Act (DIDMCA). Congressional authors had focused their attention on reviving the fortunes of flagging S&Ls. Starting immediately, S&L executives like California Federal's Howard Edgerton could write a limited number of commercial loans and offer credit cards to customers at his branch offices. Regulation Q's phaseout during the next six years was the price Congress demanded for granting S&Ls these opportunities to return to profitability. Members of Congress, however, determined not to permit commercial bankers to underwrite revenue bonds, sell insurance, or open branch offices.[36] Carter's moment to foster creation of those much-discussed supermarket banks had passed.

Popular observers failed to understand Carter's modest legislative accomplishment in light of his larger bank goals. On November 29, 1980, a *New York Times* editorial writer thought Carter had turned around "the century-old movement toward ever greater Government involvement in the private economy."[37] The reverse had actually taken place. Carter and each of his predecessors had sought to reorganize banks and S&Ls from top to bottom. During the 1970s, presidents and top economic aides never lost sight of the Hunt Commission's recommended "convergence toward the center" and the supermarket banks that would follow. President Ronald W. Reagan's senior officials brought with them an identical urge to remake financial services from top to bottom. They described their effort as "regulatory relief," which represented an escalation from earlier administrations' antigovernment rhetoric. Reagan charged his treasury secretary Donald T. Regan to bring that relief to the nation's financial institutions.

Donald T. Regan's Appointment as Secretary of the Treasury

In 1980, Donald Regan was chairman and chief executive officer of Merrill, Lynch, Pierce, Fenner & Smith. Merrill Lynch, as it was known popularly, was the nation's largest brokerage firm with twenty-four thousand employees located in four hundred offices in the United States and another two hundred

around the world. Merrill Lynch employees sold stocks and bonds to customers who purchased a few shares at a time and also to wealthy investors
who placed orders for hundreds or even thousands of shares. Members of
Merrill Lynch's large sales force helped convert 1.7 million customers to the
idea of earning higher returns in bonds and stocks rather than in old-
fashioned fixed interest banks and S&Ls. Regan advertised Merrill Lynch as
"bullish on America."[38]

Merrill Lynch sold more than stocks and bonds. Regan guided the firm
into mutual funds and real estate sales as well as insurance, credit cards, government securities, and money market accounts. Regan's Merrill Lynch routinely underwrote bond issues, exactly the business that Saxon had urged on
bankers. In 1977, Regan presided over creation of the innovative "cash management account" that allowed customers to write checks and use their Visa
cards based on balances in stock accounts. Columbus, Ohio's Bank One
issued the Visa card. Regan had succeeded in assembling a firm and a financial network that dealt in multiple products throughout the United States.
Two decades later, a scholar described Regan as a "whiz kid."[39]

Regan at Merrill Lynch had accomplished what presidents and comptrollers had talked about for nearly two decades. In April 1972, federal law still
forbade interstate banking and the Hunt Commission report advocating creation of supermarket banks had only recently appeared. That month, however, Regan told a journalist about the how the "old corner grocery store" had
given way to the supermarket and shopping center. Americans wanted to
purchase houses, mutual funds, and stocks, he told the writer, and "why
should . . . [they] have to go to many institutions in order to find experts who
can satisfy . . . [their] needs?" Regan's visibility had probably encouraged
Hunt Commission members to adopt the "supermarket" term. And Regan's
success in turn brought the same attacks that Saxon and Camp had endured.
During the late 1970s, Merrill's supermarket-like business strategy had already prompted commercial bankers and S&L leaders to launch a lobbying
campaign in Washington, D.C., with the aim of disrupting Merrill's movement into business lines long reserved to them.[40] Regan, one of the four financial leaders who had organized Nixon's May 1970 White House dinner, was
long accustomed to working in fluid environments where high finance, hostile
competitors, congressional arguments, and the president's goals for improved
economic growth came together on a daily basis.

Regan was smart, innovative, and an adept political operator. His ability to guide a traditional investment banking and brokerage firm into

disparate products like mutual funds and Visa cards started with a keen reading of the way federal and state officials had jerry-built the American regulatory system over decades. Regan and every other financial executive understood that commercial bankers, whether the largest firms in New York and Chicago or the smallest banks in rural Iowa, accepted checks and offered savings accounts. As a result, those bankers came within the limiting rules imposed by authors of the 1933 Glass-Steagall Act and the 1956 Bank Holding Company Act. During the 1960s, investment bankers and insurance agents had sued to maintain those rules. Bankers, courts held, could not sell insurance or underwrite revenue bonds. The Federal Deposit Insurance Corporation (FDIC), which insured customers' deposits, also forbade bankers to risk customers' deposits in areas as speculative as bond underwriting. In contrast, the householder who invested in a Merrill Lynch mutual fund or money market account lacked the FDIC's guaranty.

Merrill Lynch was never without regulation, however. Officials at the U.S. Securities and Exchange Commission scrutinized Merrill Lynch's annual report for conformance with accounting principles. As well, state law and regulation guided Merrill Lynch's insurance and real estate operations. Yet, no rule or collection of rules at the federal or state levels forbade Regan to assemble insurance, checking, and real estate under one corporate roof. In all, Regan had worked between inconsistent federal and state regulations to convert Merrill Lynch from a large brokerage into a firm that looked like the much-hyped supermarket bank. "The bank of the future exists," Citibank's Walter B. Wriston regularly told audiences during the late 1970s, "and it's called Merrill Lynch."[41]

Regan had thought carefully about what that future bank should look like and how to bring it into being. In 1977, he drafted a book, "The Changing Market Place," which was not published. Regan prepared the manuscript to explain the development of financial services during the 1970s. The old financial marketplace, he reported, was like a camel—"It is a horse that's been put together by a Committee." In contrast, Regan advised, we are constructing integrated financial arrangements where experts in fields as diverse as securities sales and investment banking are assembled in one place. "The supermarket," Regan predicted, "is coming to the financial industry." But, as he recognized, the large grocer selling multiple food products had made enemies along the way. Small-town butchers, he asserted, had resisted the supermarket's frozen and packaged foods.[42]

Starting in January 1981, Regan served as President Ronald W. Reagan's secretary of the treasury. Like Saxon, Camp, and Simon under former presidents, Regan was supposed to push aside obstructions to the much-discussed supermarket bank's arrival on the American financial scene. Under Regan's tutelage, American financial firms would begin to look like Merrill Lynch. The politics of rescuing S&Ls in a high-interest-rate economy pushed in the other direction.

The nation's S&Ls remained in financial trouble. The sources of that trouble were unchanged from earlier years. To start, federal law kept S&L managers penned up in the home mortgage business. S&L executives such as the Bowery Savings Bank's Crawford and California Federal's Edgerton had been emphasizing that limit on earnings for a decade. And at the same time, during 1981, S&L loan officers locked in mortgages that earned low rates, perhaps 9 percent—just as the interest rates they paid to secure loan funds jumped skyward, as high as 15 percent by one estimate. Still more, the S&Ls' traditional customers continued to move savings to higher yielding money market funds. Those "hot money" flows were large and consequential. In 1980, the Bowery lost $60.8 million, demonstrating that even the largest firms could not escape these harsh changes. In April 1982, a writer for *Nation's Business* described the S&Ls as "practically prostrate."[43]

On April 9, 1981, Paul A. Volcker, the Federal Reserve chair, updated Regan on the S&Ls' plight. During the next year, Volcker expected reserve funds at around five hundred S&Ls to fall below 2 percent, the legal minimum. Volcker recommended a program of merging several of those weak S&Ls and putting federal bank and S&L insurance money in others. Bankers and lawmakers sometimes described putting money into banks or savings and loans as an "infusion." No one doubted that Federal Savings and Loan Insurance Corporation (FSLIC) officials already possessed the authority to rescue sinking S&Ls. (The FSLIC insured accounts held at S&Ls, just as the Federal Deposit Insurance Corporation insured accounts held at commercial banks.) Under law, FSLIC officials had to show that adding cash to a sinking S&L was "essential to provide adequate banking services in the community." That requirement presented a high legal and political hurdle to jump. In August, moreover, Regan took the view that S&Ls had sufficient cash on hand to conduct business. No infusions were necessary.[44] The outcome of this debate was substantial. Underfunded S&Ls promised to further retard home building, encourage negative headlines, and antagonize members of Congress such as Rep. Fernand J. St. Germain (D-RI).

In 1981, St. Germain was the newly installed chair of the House Committee on Banking, Finance, and Urban Affairs. He had been a member of Congress since 1961. St. Germain worried about S&Ls' financial health and home building. With the S&Ls weighed down with low-interest mortgages, St. Germain asked a business writer early in 1981, "where does the mortgage money come from?" As every lawmaker and financial regulator recognized, housing, S&Ls, and home furnishing were key factors in allowing householders to achieve the celebrated American Dream. St. Germain urged a relief package for ailing S&Ls.[45]

Much like the way he had turned away Volcker's infusion idea, Regan rejected St. Germain's proposed relief package. Until interest rates subside, Regan wrote St. Germain on May 29, ailing S&Ls could turn for assistance to the Federal Savings and Loan Insurance Corporation. Regan and his deputy also liked the idea of permitting leaders of healthy S&Ls to purchase insolvent operations across state lines. Otherwise, as Regan explained to President Reagan on April 24, he wanted "greater flexibility" for S&L executives to write business loans and pay higher interest rates to savers. (Greater flexibility for S&Ls, including the right to make business loans, was one of those ideas the Hunt Commission had put forward.) Regan's stance led to "strained" relations with S&L leaders, an official later recalled.[46]

By fall, however, Regan had set aside such difficult-to-achieve goals. Rescuing S&Ls and the housing industry took precedence. In October, with some five hundred savings institutions located in the Northeast still deeply troubled by cash outflows, Regan reversed his earlier opposition to the Federal Savings and Loan Insurance Corporation providing infusions on easy and automatic terms. Staunching the losses and shoring up S&Ls' capital represented the first step. As early as February 1982, members of the S&Ls' 160-member political liaison committee had lined up congressional support for a bill to permit members to loan up to 54 percent of their assets for nonresidential real estate ventures and conventional business loans. With that addition, S&L executives further entered a risky zone formerly set aside for commercial bankers. To avoid jeopardizing the S&L rescue, Regan asked Congress to permit banks and S&Ls to underwrite municipal revenue bonds and mutual funds, both seemingly modest steps on the road to full-service banks. Regan would not insist that members of Congress approve other Hunt Commission recommendations such as authorizing bankers to sell insurance. "We just do not want to . . . [undermine] the Bill's prospects," a Regan assistant treasury secretary reported to him on October 2, 1981, "by raising more issues than the Congress can cope with."[47]

Not even the emerging rhetoric of the marketplace slowed this bill's march. In February 1982, Regan's top officials characterized parts of the developing S&L legislation as "bail-out proposals." The application of that detested term failed to stop Regan from going along with it. In April, Regan wrote to the president about his pro forma desire to find "lasting solutions" that would take the form of permitting banks to enter every type of financial business. Regan ally Jacob Garn (R-UT), chair of the Senate Committee on Banking, Housing, and Urban Affairs, also wanted to assemble legislation to "revamp outdated Federal restrictions" and permit S&L executives to write commercial loans and underwrite insurance. Garn's proposals amounted to a "sweetheart S&L bill that leaves the commercial banking industry at a greater disadvantage than before," a bank lobbyist complained to a journalist in August 1982.[48]

President Reagan intervened to keep the S&L rescue package alive. The Garn bill was "must legislation," President Reagan told congressional leaders in September. In October, small bankers, now reorganized as the Independent Bankers Association of America, launched a last-minute effort to prevent authorization for S&Ls to make business loans. They lost that effort. But Garn and Regan also failed to win a great deal. They moved up Regulation Q's elimination date to January 1984, approved money market accounts for bankers and S&Ls, and secured authorization for S&L executives to offer no-money-down mortgages. A *Fortune* writer described bank politics as a "fight for financial turf." In a field as politically riven as finance, members of Congress needed until October 1982 to pass the Garn–St. Germain Depository Institutions Act. At the bill signing ceremony, Reagan asked Congress to approve "more comprehensive legislation."[49]

Regulatory Relief's Limits

In July 1983, Donald Regan once again launched the drive toward regulatory relief for financial service firms. Compared with his earlier and grander goal of creating supermarket banks, Regan's focus was narrower in scope. He urged members of Congress to permit bankers and S&L executives to own securities dealers and insurance companies. Comptroller Saxon had first authorized banks to enter these businesses, but successful lawsuits promptly terminated those initiatives. Starting as early as 1981, vigilant and well-organized insurance executives relied on Senator Christopher J. "Chris" Dodd (D-CT) to protect their firms and their industries' borders against predatory bankers. Dodd brought the same passion to looking out for the insurance companies domiciled in Connecticut that Wright Patman had brought to his decades-long defense of small bankers.[50]

During March 1984, Garn held another round of hearings on bank entry into securities and other financial dealings. His many witnesses needed six days to complete their testimony, which consumed 1,801 print pages. Garn titled the hearings "Competitive Equity in the Financial Services Industry," a goal that few would disparage in principal. But Garn recognized that important actors had staked a claim against unleashing bankers. "The conventional wisdom is that there's no chance for passage of a bill," Garn told journalists and bankers shortly before the hearings opened, but he held them anyway.[51]

Garn's hearings presented an opportunity for everyone with an interest in protecting and changing bank legislation to replay favorite scripts. In March, Richard R. Jenrette was chairman of the Securities Industries Association and chairman of Donaldson, Lufkin and Jenrette, a large brokerage and investment-banking firm. During the past three years, Jenrette had appeared five times before Garn's committee. In 1979 and 1981, Jenrette reminded committee members, bankers had sought permission to enter new areas of business. "The banks are back," Jenrette told committee members in 1984, "still seeking [to underwrite] revenue bond[s]" and "still asking . . . [to sponsor] mutual fund[s]." The president of the National Association of Realtors talked about the financial concentration certain to take place should banks enter the competitive home sales field. And so it went. "We are dealing not with real issues of public policy," Regan, the last to testify, told Garn's committee members, "but with simple protection of competitive turf."[52]

Turf protection extended farther than Regan realized. In May, FDIC officials infused $4.5 billion to prop up Chicago's financially troubled Continental Illinois National Bank. St. Germain described the FDIC's action as a "bailout for the powerful." St. Germain and other members of his committee seized on Continental's problems to vote, 32–16, to confine bankers to their current lines of financial services. Placing limits on bankers' movement into fields like securities dealings and insurance sales had a bipartisan appeal. Regan, after four years as treasury secretary, had failed to bring about supermarket banks with an interstate reach.[53]

In February 1985, Regan left the treasury department to become the president's chief of staff. Journalists published articles about Regan's Marine Corps service in World War II and about his rapid ascent at Merrill Lynch. They described him with words like "garrulous, sometimes short tempered, [and] vigorous." Regan, maintaining a rhetorical allegiance with the president, described himself as a "free-market person" and as "a political novice."[54] Business executives like Regan needed to reconfirm their commitment to get-the-job-done corporate governance and their impatience with horse-trading politics. In his public statements, Regan maintained the fiction that business and politics existed in separate spheres, or ought to do so.

Like Saxon and each president starting with Kennedy, Regan spent four years on a sophisticated effort to remake the financial services sector of the American political economy. Despite his free enterprise rhetoric, Regan never intended to abolish the rules that governed financial affairs. When Regan sought legislation to permit banks to offer mutual funds, the idea was that the executives who managed those new units would report to the president of a holding company. As well, officials in charge of insurance and investment banking would also report to the holding company's chief executive. And since 1956, Federal Reserve officials wrote the rules that governed holding company practice; and Federal Reserve examiners checked holding company books for compliance with those rules. Neither these holding company top executives nor the senior officials reporting to them were supposed to start each day anew, as if decades-old practices and regulators' directives had no meaning.[55] The financial holding company Regan had in mind looked like Merrill Lynch, and it was a regulated outfit. State insurance officials and Securities and Exchange examiners visited on a regular schedule. But Regan's idea for what banks should look like included the greater flexibility he had experienced at Merrill Lynch. Leaders at Regan's Merrill Lynch had flexibility to move operations across state lines and open new lines of business such as credit cards linked to a checking account issued by a bank.

Don Regan, with his determination to link supermarket banks to national economic growth, was among Comptroller Saxon's most innovative and influential successors. Yet Regan, for all his business know-how and obvious political acumen, proved unable to crack open the hard barriers that kept commercial bankers from offering a full range of financial services. Insurance agents and insurance corporations, for instance, maintained political links that flowed from Rotary Club lunches and Little League sponsorships to staunch supporters in Congress such as Senator Dodd. The day's still grinding politics flowed against Regan's threatening innovations. During the early 1980s, the politics of maintaining the S&Ls with their vital connections to home building and furnishings exerted a stronger claim on congressional attention and allegiance.

Starting in the early 1960s, Comptroller Saxon invited bankers to open branch offices, sell insurance, and underwrite revenue bonds. Between the early 1960s and 1984, First National City's Walter B. Wriston showed regulators and bankers throughout the United States how to exploit Saxon's innovations. Wriston brought a special urgency to his message to bankers. Unless rules were relaxed, Wriston regularly told large audiences, Donald Regan's Merrill Lynch and upstart money market funds would soon replace commercial banks as the source of business growth. Like every president, comptroller, and treasury secretary since Kennedy and Saxon, Wriston linked a promised return to national prosperity with bank expansion into new financial services.

PART II

Bankers in Politics

CHAPTER 3

Rescuing Banks Through Growth: Walter Wriston and Citicorp

On March 31, 1980, Citibank's Walter B. Wriston spoke to an audience of bankers. Wriston had worked for the bank since 1946. Under his innovative guidance, Citibank (up to 1976, the First National City Bank of New York) emerged as the nation's largest bank, eclipsing Bank of America and David Rockefeller's Chase Manhattan Bank. In 1984, as Wriston prepared to retire, a *New York Times* writer described him as "the nation's most influential banker."[1]

Officers of the Association of Reserve City Bankers had asked Wriston to address them. It was an exclusive gathering. The association limited its membership to four hundred senior bank officers.[2] Consistent with their members' notable rank, officials of the association invited only top bankers and senior federal bank and treasury officials to their meetings. Wriston, who met with U.S. presidents, conducted business with major corporate executives, and negotiated with top federal bank regulators, fit right in with members of this group.

As reserve city bankers took their seats for Wriston's presentation, they occupied an ambiguous position in the nation's financial system. Undeniable wealth and access to political and business figures at the highest levels surrounded meetings of the Association of Reserve City Bankers. Federal Reserve chair Paul A. Volcker and Merrill Lynch CEO Donald T. Regan were also scheduled to address the group. The meeting took place at a first-class hotel in posh Boca Raton, Florida. Yet, those reserve city bankers, like many business and political leaders at that moment, recognized that the national economy and the bank business model they had inherited was in the middle of a time of change. Leaders of the association set the room for Wriston's important address. They dismissed spouses to off-site hotels, excluded reporters, banned personal recorders, and permitted casual attire. The emphasis among members of Wriston's audience was on frank talk about the future of their banks.

Wriston told a story of the relative decline of commercial banking no doubt already familiar to his audience. In 1946, commercial banks held 57 percent of the nation's financial assets. By 1979, he reminded them, commercial banks held only 38 percent. The financial services business was larger, but commercial banks' share of that business had diminished. Insurance companies, S&Ls, and Sears, Roebuck, as well as credit unions, department stores, and stockbrokers such as Merrill Lynch, had scooped up business that formerly resided squarely and safely in bankers' hands. Money market funds, able to pay higher rates of interest to savers, siphoned deposits that bankers relied on to make loans. "It is doubtful," Wriston told the assembled bankers, "if any of us could come up with anything a bank can do that somebody else is not also doing—and doing nationwide." Wriston once again identified Donald Regan's Merrill Lynch, with its nationwide ability to offer checking and brokerage services, as an ideal model for their banks. Unless bankers undertook fundamental changes, Wriston prophesized, within ten to twenty years commercial banks would no longer exist in the United States. Wriston chose shocking words such as "tombstone" and "graveyard" to describe their future.[3] Even Wriston's mighty Citibank would presumably be out of business, forced, like the others, to relinquish its charter. Here, for all to see and hear, was the nation's best-known banker telling an audience of affluent bank executives that their jobs and firms would soon be in jeopardy.

Wriston judged fellow bankers compliant in their decline. Those bankers had adopted a defensive stance, a "fortress mentality," as Wriston characterized it. Commercial bankers, perhaps including audience members, sought to protect their place in segmented financial arenas. In lunch-hour speeches to the Lions Club and other business groups, Wriston observed, bankers offered a "ringing defense of free enterprise." Once returned to their offices, those same bankers contacted regulators and lawmakers to demand protection from competitors. Wriston cited several examples of this fortress mentality, including efforts by members of thirty-two state bankers' associations to overturn a comptroller's ruling permitting national banks to offer interstate trust services. Following the talk, and as if to draw additional attention to Wriston's remarks, a Missouri banker in the audience asked why Wriston had sent a charge card to his wife and further urged Wriston to "stay out of my market."[4]

Wriston's talk was at its heart a call to political action among bankers. Wriston brought several distinctive features to that call. He innately disliked government regulation. Wriston also had the good fortune to work at Citibank, where bosses and mentors were early enthusiasts for Saxon's ideas about bankers dismantling government regulations to enter new business lines. Wriston had only to emulate his superiors, not buck them. Wriston's preoccupation with growth also connected directly with the tumultuous changes taking place in the U.S. economy. Since the early 1970s, those changes included rising inflation, sagging productivity, and lost purchasing power for middle-class Americans. In concert with other bankers or acting alone, Wriston and his skillful attorneys at the gigantic Citibank fostered changes in bank rules aimed at restoring and accelerating that economic growth. They did so, it seemed, in contrast to members of Congress, who in past decades had refused to pass the legislation that would presumably lead to additional bank growth and restore prosperity throughout the United States.

Walter Wriston did not expand Citibank in order to create methods for Americans to prosper. But his many growth-oriented projects at the bank, such as credit cards and branch banks, spoke to a widespread interest among business and political leaders in bringing more investment to underserved parts of the United States, including burgeoning suburbs in the Northeast and small towns in South Dakota. As a start, credit cards meant more spending, and branch banking promised improved access to money for underserved areas. If regulators would only make it easier for Wriston and other bankers to expand services, those bankers would in turn lead the way back to a prospering economy, or so the promise ran. Johnson, Nixon, Ford, Carter, and Reagan made an identical case against antitrust lawsuits and anti-branching rules and in favor of supermarket banks. Wriston's special skill was in representing that promised growth as the handiwork of a modest, can-do executive arrayed against federal officials whose clumsy and ill-fitting rules stymied national prosperity. Wriston promised the fruits of a public-private partnership at which Saxon and Kennedy had first hinted and that Reagan put at the center of his presidency.

Wriston's Early Years

Walter Wriston was born on August 3, 1919. He reached young adulthood during the New Deal, when Congress and President Roosevelt approved historic legislation regulating banks, trucking, airlines, and consumer prices. Wriston grew up in an anti-statist household. His father, who taught history at Wesleyan College (later University) and was later president of Brown University, detested Roosevelt's new regulatory agencies. Wriston attended Wesleyan, where several faculty members reinforced his views about the dangers of central regulation. For young Walter, a family trip to Nazi Germany in August 1939 confirmed still-forming ideas about the dangers of power unchecked.[5]

Wriston was never a top student. In college and later in life, he was self-disciplined and self-confident, even when his grasp of a topic was incomplete. During his Wesleyan days, Wriston held determined views about limiting government regulation and equally determined views about campus issues such as the perceived need to break down disciplinary barriers. As a sophomore, Wriston won the college's public speaking prize. As editor of the college newspaper, the *Argus*, Wriston had a vehicle to assert and spread his views.[6]

In the fall of 1941, following graduation from Wesleyan, Wriston enrolled in Tufts University's Fletcher School of Law and Diplomacy. In October 1942, Wriston married Barbara "Bobby" Brengle. Her outgoing nature offset Wriston's reserve. In 1942, with a master's degree in hand, Wriston joined the State Department as a junior Foreign Service officer. Now all of twenty-three years old, Wriston drafted cables for American diplomats, one time visiting the White House to secure President Roosevelt's signature. Although the United States was engaged in World War II, Wriston perceived his future as open and perhaps worldwide in scope. In 1943, Wriston entered the U.S. Army as a private.[7]

In 1946, Wriston accepted a position at National City Bank of New York (renamed the First National City Bank in 1955, following a merger with New York City–based First National Bank). His father knew the bank's president. Wriston, always confident in his abilities, drove a hard bargain. He secured a starting wage $200 above the bank's customary salary for new college graduates. That first year he earned $3,000. The bank's assets totaled $5.59 billion, with $2.93 billion invested in U.S. government obligations. Bank officers were equally conservative in making loans. Compared with David Rockefeller's Chase National Bank, Wriston's friends could still ask why he had launched his career at a "second-class outfit." With headquarters at 55 Wall Street, Wriston worked nevertheless in a strategic location, near major competitors as well as the massive Federal Reserve Bank of New York (New

York Fed). Managers assigned Wriston to the bank's less-than-glamorous comptroller's office and then to a series of obscure posts. Wriston's colleagues judged him intelligent, driven, and willing to devote long hours to the bank's business. Yet in those early years, Wriston did not mesh with the bank's culture, where the few who won promotions were well connected, graduates of more prestigious universities, and sporting low golf handicaps. Wriston played poker.[8]

Wriston's break came in the late 1940s, when he met Aristotle Onassis, a Greek shipowner and a bon vivant who married Jacqueline Kennedy in 1968. Onassis borrowed large sums to pay for his growing fleet. Wriston, for his part, helped develop innovative finance methods that boosted bank lending. Prior to World War II, all U.S. banks together held approximately $100 million in loans outstanding to shipbuilders. By 1956, Wriston's First National City ranked first among banks with loans of $400 million to Onassis and other shipbuilders. Because of his work with Onassis, Wriston emerged as a First National City's expert on ship loans. Still more, Wriston's success with ship loans brought him to the attention of the bank's top managers, who placed him among that small group of junior executives thought to be ready for promotion to the highest levels. In 1961, Wriston scored another coup with development of the negotiable certificate of deposit, known popularly as a CD. Wriston priced CDs at $100,000 or higher. In turn, corporate treasurers placed surplus funds in CDs. Those CDs could be traded, and they also earned interest, unlike money kept in checking accounts. The notorious Regulation Q did not apply to CDs. With the CD, First National City and many other banks secured additional funds to loan, helping to fuel part of the 1960s' economic growth spurt. Wriston sold the CDs nationally, nimbly stepping across state borders. Going around regulations with the CD fostered the bank's profits and liquidity, assisted national economic growth, boosted Wriston's career, and knocked another small hole in rules limiting banks to one city or state.[9]

Wriston extended his successful dealings outside the United States. In 1956, bank officials assigned him to head their European district. Later, working with his mentor and future First National City president George S. Moore, Wriston opened branches in far-flung places such as New Delhi, India, and Durban, South Africa. In 1967, Wriston directed 148 overseas branches that had booked $2.7 billion in loans, an increase each year since 1960 of 16 percent.[10]

By the early 1960s, Wriston occupied a place near the top of the bank's management team. He used that proximity to talk with senior executives about the bank's growth under fewer rules. Open access to new territories over-seas and across state lines was clearly one such idea, as was Wriston's desire to extend the bank's reach into prohibited financial activities. The fact that foreign governments sometimes approved his plans faster than the Federal Reserve only added to Wriston's contempt for American bank regulations and regulators.[11] During these years, bank president Moore mentored Wris-ton. Moore and Wriston shared a desire to loosen Federal Reserve rules and avoid Wright Patman's gaze.

Wriston's and Moore's ideas meshed. Moore was an early and avid sup-porter of Saxon's rule changes to permit bankers to enter new fields. During the mid-1960s, as examples, Moore underwrote $115 million in Common-wealth of Pennsylvania tax anticipation notes and purchased computers, airplanes, and railroad cars for lease to bank clients. In October 1963, the president of the Investment Bankers Association appeared before a con-gressional committee to protest Moore's invasion of the underwriting busi-ness. Moore's quick adoption of computers also put the lie to bankers' and regulators' assertion that bank computerization was a nearly autonomous activity that had sprung up without human guidance. Rather, bankers' use of computers, especially in lease finance arrangements, was and remained another development that Comptroller Saxon nurtured and that Moore, with Wriston at his side, implemented. At a future date, Moore told a jour-nalist in 1966, the bank's computer system would permit him to charge his hotel room in Sydney, Australia, and have funds withdrawn immediately from his account in New York.[12] Moore's expansion plans offered a daily lesson to Wriston on the advantages of ignoring investment bankers, work-ing with and against regulators, and arriving early with new financial products that could be marketed as a service to millions of Americans.

In June 1967, the bank's board appointed the forty-seven-year-old Wris-ton the next president. Moore moved up to the post of chairman. During the next seventeen years, Wriston focused his considerable talent and limit-less energy into transforming First National City from a commercial bank to a company offering a wide range of financial services to corporate execu-tives and ordinary depositors. Wriston's wife, Bobby, had died in June 1966. In her absence, Wriston's directions to employees and his negotiations with regulators took on a harder edge.[13] Wriston's appointment as president corresponded with a new development in the organization of bank holding companies.

Wriston's Holding Company and Supermarket Banks

In 1967, California banker Harry J. Volk discovered a path toward supermarket banking. Volk had identified a loophole in federal bank law that allowed him to convert his Union Bank of California to Union Bancorp, Inc., a holding company. Holding companies were a standard feature of American corporate organization; and several well-known firms including Sears, Roebuck operated as holding companies. Up to that point, however, bankers like Volk and Wriston had thought that federal law prohibited them from organizing a single bank as a holding company subsidiary. Now, under this arrangement, Volk's holding company owned his bank. Officers of that same holding company could also operate outside the constraints of federal bank law that Wriston and Saxon had so disliked. No law or regulation stopped the holding company from owning insurance firms, securities dealers, and other types of financial businesses. And in turn, insurance or securities firms that the holding company owned (not including the bank) could also cross state lines. In October 1968, Wriston followed Volk's lead, creating a holding company. Comptroller Camp approved the change promptly, citing a stronger bank and improvements to "related services" that were certain to follow.[14]

In 1970, members of Congress amended the Bank Holding Company Act to accommodate the ambitions of bankers like Volk and Wriston. Those changes served as the "big bang" for bankers seeking diversification. By late December 1970, bankers had already created more than 1,350 holding companies. But traditional banking and regulatory ideas continued to predominate. The holding company, in other words, did not abolish regulators' limits.[15] A decade later, Treasury Secretary Regan continued to advocate for the holding company as the best and only device for bankers to create firms that performed services similar to his Merrill Lynch. As Regan understood, neither Congress nor the Federal Reserve had authorized bank holding companies to undertake anything that bold.

Walter Wriston never waited for congressional or regulatory approval to launch a favored program. He went on a buying spree even before Congress passed the revised holding company act. In January 1969, Wriston announced plans to purchase Chubb, a major insurance corporation. The price was $376 million in stock.[16] Moore and Wriston had long envied the freedom of action available to insurance executives, who were not subjected to tough federal regulation.

Chubb was only the start. Early in 1969, Wriston held a staff meeting outside the bank. He directed employees to search the United States for compatible opportunities. As part of his headlong rush into new businesses, officers of a bank subsidiary, the First National City Overseas Investment Corporation, purchased a minority interest in Ramada Worldwide, the hotel chain. The Overseas Corporation could enter nonbank businesses more easily than a bank firm housed in the United States. As a related move, in August 1970, Wriston opened an international office in Los Angeles under the authority of the Edge Act (1919) and known among bankers as Edge Act offices. Wriston's Los Angeles staff handled foreign trade and other bank transactions outside New York State. In Wriston's hands, Edge Act offices created an avenue toward interstate banking. Wriston also purchased FNC Credit, a company he used to buy loans. With FNC purchasing those loans, Wriston avoided stringent Federal Reserve rules about the amount of financial cushion First National City had to keep on hand.[17]

Federal officials slowed Wriston's breathless pace. Early in 1969, Richard W. McLaren, President Nixon's new head of the Justice Department's antitrust division, threatened a lawsuit to stop the Chubb purchase. McLaren cited the widespread fear that Wriston would force the bank's loan customers to patronize Chubb. Wriston's lawyers judged his case weak, and he backed down. That same year, Federal Reserve officials turned down Wriston's application to purchase a life insurance company in Taiwan. Insurance was not "closely related to banking," Fed officials contended.[18] Antitrust advocates like Patman had repeated these arguments since the early 1960s.

These early losses to regulators failed to slow Wriston's expansion plans. For a short time, in fact, Wriston sent a proposal a day to Federal Reserve officials seeking permission to enter new businesses. At this stage, profitability was only one factor Wriston considered. He was testing Federal Reserve officers regarding the range of financial services open to him.[19] Saxon and Hunt had advocated all or most of Wriston's sharp-edged growth activity, but they never encountered a bank executive so eager to embrace them.

Several purchases illustrate Wriston's strategic approach. Insurance was first. Shut out of Chubb, in April 1971 Wriston joined with Connecticut Gen-

eral Life Insurance Company to offer life insurance to his savings' customers. Every saver whose account earned at least $2.50 in quarterly interest was
eligible to purchase up to $15,000 in term life insurance. Wriston deducted
the premium from the saver's interest earnings. Because the bank rather than
the holding company offered the insurance, Wriston did not need to seek
Federal Reserve approval. New York State insurance department officials authorized bank sale of insurance, which was perhaps a sign of modest cooperation among regulators in a rigidly segmented field. Insurance executives
proved less cooperative, filing a lawsuit to prevent Wriston's sale of insurance. In October 1971, judges in the New York Supreme Court's appellate
division ruled in Wriston's favor. With more than five hundred thousand
depositors located throughout the United States, Wriston had created a nationwide business that rendered state boundaries irrelevant.[20] Wriston's
entry into the insurance business came only a few years after two courts
had sided with insurance agents to block Saxon, Camp, and Atlanta's Citizens
& Southern Bank from selling insurance policies.

Wriston and his creative attorneys also forged a path into mutual funds.
As far back as 1962, Comptroller Saxon had authorized bank executives to
operate a mutual fund. Attorneys for the Investment Company Institute, the
trade association for the mutual fund industry, naturally brought a lawsuit to
prohibit bankers from underwriting mutual funds. Adhering to the Saxon
tradition, Comptroller Camp defended his decision at the original trial (and
won) and before an appeals court, which he lost. In 1971, however, the U.S.
Supreme Court ruled 6–2 that the Glass-Steagall Act prohibited bank ownership of a mutual fund. By one account, Justice Potter Stewart "pissed all over
it."[21] For all the fervor gathering among bankers like Wriston to create supermarket firms, federal judges still directed those bankers to adhere to traditional lines of business.

In June 1972, Wriston moved with greater legal care into mutual fund
operations. He created Advance Investors Corporation. Bank executives
would make investment decisions for this new fund, the same as before.
Rather than position Advance Investors inside the bank or as part of the
bank holding company, Wriston set it up as an independent firm with its
own board of directors and its own listing on the New York Stock Exchange.
In December, Wriston headed deeper into the investment business, creating
Citicorp Investment Management, Inc. With offices in San Francisco, Citicorp
employees offered investment advice to corporations and individuals. Once
again, Wriston had entered new business arenas, crossed state boundaries,

and avoided judicial scrutiny. Wriston also hoped his aggressive purchase of businesses would encourage normally cautious employees to take on some of the entrepreneurial spirit found among those firms' founders. "By God," Wriston told a bank official, "we need more of that here."[22]

In 1972, Wriston's First National City emerged as the largest commercial bank in New York City, overtaking Rockefeller's Chase Manhattan. To symbolize the bank's majesty, rank, creativity, and solidity, in July 1973, Wriston announced construction of a new office tower at the corner of Fifty-Third Street and Lexington Avenue. The building, constructed of glass and aluminum, rested on four 115-foot columns set toward the center rather than at the corners, creating the illusion that the edifice might sway dramatically. Including the support columns, First National City's headquarters soared more than sixty stories into New York City's skyline. In October 1977, bank executives dedicated their new headquarters, described by a *New York Times* writer as "a brilliant, dazzling achievement."[23] Wriston's new headquarters opened as Americans struggled with inflation, closed plants, and unemployment. The new building, however, was supposed to show employees, passersby, and corporate and political leaders everywhere that Wriston's model of fewer regulations and international growth was capable of producing large and visible results.

The sparkling headquarters, Wriston hoped, would also attract millions of small customers. Starting in the mid-1970s, Wriston reoriented the bank to capture a larger share of consumer business—replicating Regan's approach at Merrill Lynch. During 1977, for example, Wriston spent $50 million to install automated teller machines in each of his 276 New York City branch offices A more user-friendly name was part of the plan to attract consumers. In 1974, Wriston had changed the holding company's name to Citicorp; and in 1976, he converted the bank's name from First National City Bank, a mouthful, to the catchier Citibank.[24] In looser fashion, journalists referred to both firms as "Citi."

Credit cards were the next big thing in banking. The Visa card represented yet another effort to woo the consumer and strike a blow against regulators and their rules. Widespread Visa card use would help boost bank profits. A number of banks already offered them, including Citi. Midway through 1977, Wriston launched a massive step-up in card operations. Citibank officials mailed more than twenty million invitations to potential customers, asking them to accept their Visa card, and secured four million approvals. A Visa card customer located in Pennsylvania or in another state was taking a loan at a New York bank. Each purchase invisibly subverted cumbersome rules that hobbled interstate banking. But Wriston still paid more to borrow funds than state usury laws allowed him to charge credit card customers. What started as a potential profit center turned into a sinkhole of costs—a sinkhole from which Wriston as head of the nationally known Citibank dared not withdraw for fear of harming consumer confidence.[25]

A timely Supreme Court decision created an opportunity for Wriston to rescue and then expand his credit card business. In 1978, justices ruled that interest rates on loans of every type were to be determined by the bank's home state rather than by the borrowers'. The court's decision offered savvy bankers like Wriston a potential way around New York State's usury limits, if only they could locate in an accommodative state. Meanwhile, unknown to Wriston, in January 1980, members of South Dakota's legislature approved a bill to exempt regulated bank lending in the state from usury laws—bankers could charge any rate customers agreed to pay. Wriston, now alert to this opening, promptly started negotiations with local bankers and the governor about relocating his credit card business. Two months later, the legislature passed another piece of legislation that outlined the terms of Citibank's dealings in the state's banking scene. In June 1981, Wriston moved his credit card operations from Long Island to Sioux Falls. Now, Citibank offered credit cards in thirty-five states, charging 19.8 percent on balances not paid within thirty days. In one swoop, Wriston added new outposts to his interstate ambitions and sent a powerful message to uncooperative New York lawmakers. Wriston was among the first bankers to exploit the expansion potential in playing off one state legislature against another. Under Wriston as well, the credit card became a major profit center at the same time that the card's national distribution allowed him to extend the bank's presence beyond state borders.[26] Meanwhile, Wriston's emerging supermarket bank still faced regulators' stern review.

Wriston, Fast Growth, and Regulation

Wriston's go-go days were ending. The new bank tower had just opened, a writer for *Business Week* observed in November 1977, but the "glitter appears gone." Managing such a large enterprise was proving difficult. By late 1977, Citibank operated 208 branches in ninety-three nations; and executives with

Nationwide Financial Services, only one of the holding company's many businesses, directed operations in another 171 offices located in twenty-four states. With so many businesses and offices spread around the nation and globe, Wriston and his top executives often could not remember what each firm's employees actually did. As well, many of those new firms failed to deliver promised earnings, which meant that Citibank, or its holding company Citicorp, subsidized their operations. In 1971, a confident Wriston had promised 15 percent annual (compounded) growth in Citicorp's operating income. For the period January–September 1978, Citicorp returned a paltry 1.8 percent. Late in 1977, Citicorp's share price declined 38 percent from its high point that year. Still, Citicorp's president, William I. Spencer, predicted that "the personal finance business could well be worth $200 million on the bottom line in eight years."[27] Under Wriston, talking up share prices constituted another part of commercial banking.

Not everyone bought the hyped-up rhetoric. Federal Reserve officials, who had approved Wriston's entry into so many new lines of business, now began to worry about Citibank's capital levels. Federal and state bank regulators had always insisted that every banker retain funds on hand in case of emergencies. At a lunch meeting held June 7, 1977, at the Federal Reserve Bank of New York, the New York Fed's president, Paul A. Volcker, told Wriston directly, "Citibank continues to have one of the lowest capital ratios of the major New York City banks." Early in 1978, the author of a New York Fed report still described Citicorp, Wriston's holding company, as "somewhat overleveraged." In plain language, regulators worried that the holding company's $5.3 billion assets rested too heavily on short-term, borrowed money. By 1977, starting with Arthur Burns at the Board of Governors and Paul Volcker at the New York Fed (and in August 1979 as chair of the Board of Governors), top Fed officials sought both to replenish bank capital levels and to avoid unsettling news or a bankruptcy. Bad news at a bank like Citi, Fed officials agreed, was certain to undermine confidence in an economy already strained by plant closures, layoffs, inflation, and an inability to deliver regular and solid wage increases.[28]

Wriston had nurtured Citi's worldwide presence but was less mindful of its size and visibility as part of a national financial system. Instead, he complained more frequently about the Fed's focus on the bank's capital level. Wriston viewed bank examiners' reliance on fixed ratios to determine Citicorp's and Citibank's ability to withstand a severe run or sharp loan losses as old-fashioned, comparable to evaluating the auto against the horse-drawn buggy. By way of contrast, in March 1975, during a regularly scheduled lun-cheon, the Chase Manhattan's David Rockefeller told Federal Reserve Bank of New York's top officials that "closer contact between [the Chase's] senior officers and examiners" had proved "beneficial." Wriston, however, directed his top executives to author books and papers to demonstrate the irrelevance of high capital ratios. More important than those arbitrary ratios, Wriston liked to argue, was his top bankers' demonstrated intelligence and ability to manage funds. Presiding over an increasingly diverse and far-flung network of businesses, Wriston perceived himself to be a smart chief executive who was capable of managing increased risk—and in need of fewer directives re-garding capital ratios. He always had. Soon, both the comptroller of the cur-rency and top executives at Chase Manhattan took notice of Wriston's argument that large and diverse banks were perfectly safe even with lower capital levels.[29]

With Ronald Reagan's election in November 1980, the antiregulation views Wriston so enjoyed espousing ascended to a top rung in the nation's legislative and cultural agendas. And as part of that convergence, Reagan's senior officials no doubt admired Wriston's quest to build supermarket banks, his dismissive tone toward government officials, and his preemptory challenges to regulators' authority. The president-elect's advisers considered Wriston for appointment as secretary of the treasury, but that post went to Donald Regan. Perhaps as a consolation, Reagan appointed Wriston to the President's Economic Policy Advisory Board. Others on the advisory panel included Arthur Burns, who had retired from the Federal Reserve Board, and economist Alan Greenspan, who had served on Nixon's Hunt Commis-sion and then as chair of Ford's Council of Economic Advisers. With members of such a distinguished group, including Donald Regan, committed in theme and detail to the idea that the federal government should dismantle the legal and regulatory barriers that separated commercial banking and other fi-nancial services, Wriston, professionally and rhetorically, was located in a congenial environment. As part of the buzz that surrounded Wriston's talked-about nomination to head the Treasury Department, late in Decem-ber 1980 a *New York Times* writer described Wriston as "an apostle of unfettered capitalism."[30]

In the middle of this undiluted talk about capitalism's natural workings, even Wriston, it turns out, perceived value in federal bank regulators. In a letter to New York Federal Reserve Bank president Anthony Solomon, on July 17, 1981, Wriston asked him to implore top Fed officials such as Paul

Volcker "to advocate for our survival on the Washington scene" against non-bank competitors. In this way, Wriston wanted Volcker to create a fortress for commercial bankers as a whole. Federal Reserve officials, of course, did not make Wriston's inconsistent views public. Two years later, in 1983, Treasury Secretary Regan sought to nominate Wriston to replace Paul Volcker as chair of the Federal Reserve's Board of Governors.[31] In the long run, Wriston, as the Fed's chair, might have been able to hasten the development of supermarket banks featuring reduced capital requirements. In the short run, Wriston would have had to implement policies he plainly detested.

With few aware of his inconsistent rhetoric, Wriston was able to make the most of this newfound attention with a threat to sell Citibank. In July 1981, Wriston granted an interview to a *New York Times* reporter. Reworking themes he had pronounced in March 1980 at the Association of Reserve City Bankers in Boca Raton, Wriston mused about having his holding company sell Citibank and buy an insurance company and securities dealer. Without saying so, Wriston's refashioned firm would look more like Merrill Lynch, which offered a range of financial services, but without the Federal Reserve's smothering regulations. To heighten interest in this proposal, Wriston threatened to sell Citibank to a foreign bank.[32] In the early 1980s, with reports of unemployment appearing daily, TV and print journalists flooded American households, factories, and offices with scary news about European and Japanese firms taking control of automobile, machine tool, and other threatened industries. Wriston had no intention of selling Citibank with its credit cards, automated teller machines, and far-flung offices. Wriston was instead alerting a national audience including, President Reagan and Treasury Secretary Regan, of his often-stated argument that failure to ease bank rules threatened the return of the prosperity they so demonstrably sought. Citi mattered in the national economy, and Wriston intended to leverage that size to advance his supermarket bank agenda.

Wriston was soon off on another growth tack. His goal, Wriston told a *New York Times* reporter on July 31, 1981, was to "start a consumer bank in every state." Similar to his earlier undertakings, Wriston moved quickly to open those consumer banks. In 1982 Wriston's Citicorp, the holding company, purchased California-based Fidelity Savings & Loan, a failing thrift from the Federal Savings and Loan Insurance Corporation (FSLIC). According to a writer for *American Banker*, FSLIC officials had been "knocking on the doors of bank holding companies" in search of a buyer, suggesting a growing willingness among officers in yet another federal agency to blur the distinctions between banks and S&Ls. Later in the year, Congress approved the Garn–St. Germain Depository Institutions Act authorizing that type of sales. Yet, never before had a bank holding company purchased an out-of-state S&L. The comptroller, alerted two years earlier to Wriston's interest in buying down-and-out S&Ls, approved the purchase. Wriston, always critical of government and rules, never turned down a helpful regulator along the way. Wriston has "blow[n] the structure of banking in this country apart," lamented the Independent Bankers Association executive director.[33]

Wriston's Advantages

In August 1984, Wriston, age sixty-five, stepped down as Citicorp's chair. Business writers described him as "brilliant" and "visionary." Wriston had "staggeringly transformed" his bank, one writer gushed. Citibank was the nation's largest bank by any measure, having surpassed the slower-moving Bank of America. Wriston's carefully cultivated image of executive sure-footedness and small-town accessibility helped make him the nation's and perhaps the world's best-known banker, surpassing Donald Regan. Appearances on television programs such as *Face the Nation* added to Wriston's image as a serious and capable banker with ideas about government, business, and how to nurture economic growth. In a survey conducted by the editors of *Euromoney*, bank chairmen located in Asia, Europe, and the United States selected Wriston the 1984 Banker of the Year. A period of remarkable growth composed part of their positive evaluation. Since 1967, Wriston had boosted Citibank's assets 761 percent, increased net income 764 percent, and expanded total loans 937 percent, to reach a staggering $102.7 billion.[34] Wriston produced growth that every U.S. president sought; and perhaps, by some magic, Wriston would make that growth rub off on the larger economy.

Observers also admired Wriston's political accomplishments. Between 1967 and 1985, Wriston challenged haughty Federal Reserve officials about reserve requirements; and for a time, each and every day he filed to secure permission to enter insurance, mutual funds, and mortgage banking. Few Americans, including Wriston, sought to eliminate the many state and federal rules that guided banking. But in an era when a small number of Americans began to talk about untrammeled capitalism's supposed advantages, Wriston pushed past state and federal lawmakers to create national and international capital flows that matched the pace and multiple directions in which Merrill

Lynch moved money around. As part of the moment's rhetoric, Wriston and his many followers described changes at Citi as a response to markets.[35] But Citi's fabulous growth rested far more on Wriston's careful reading and reshaping of the bank's political economy.

As bankers heaped praise on Wriston for Citi's growth record, few took notice of the advantages at his disposal from the outset. Starting in the late 1950s, Wriston was Moore's protégé, his chosen successor. Beginning in 1967, Wriston presided over a worldwide bank with immense resources. Wriston and his team also possessed years of experience in following up on Comptroller Saxon's innovative ideas about dissolving the legal walls that separated banking, insurance, and other financial services.[36] Citicorp's institutional setting and Wriston's ideas about growth and regulation reinforced each other.

During the next seventeen years, Wriston was rare in his ability to finance so many new businesses. He commanded the resources to open new bank offices, subsidize the faltering credit card business, and even to pay the immense costs associated with relocating those operations from New York to Sioux Falls. Wriston also commanded the legal and financial resources to tangle with powerful Federal Reserve regulators about new businesses and reserve ratios. "As is usually the case with Citicorp," an official at the Federal Reserve Bank of New York wrote Paul Volcker on November 1, 1977, "it did not seek prior regulatory review or approval of its action."[37] Insurance agents, mutual fund managers, securities dealers, and small-town bankers had good reason to urge regulators and legislators to maintain the resource-laden and boundary-crossing Wriston at a distance.

Money alone had not allowed Wriston to best Rockefeller's substantial Chase Manhattan or Bank of America, the West Coast giant. Walter Wriston, for all his ambition, intelligence, and drive toward creation of a national bank supermarket, was most fundamentally a policy entrepreneur backed by the resources of the nation's largest bank. Wriston possessed the patience and talent to look through the maze of state and federal regulations and perceive paths toward a national financial supermarket. Wriston in the long run expected to build Citicorp into a large firm that earned immense profits. And yet, for Wriston, as perhaps for many similar-minded executives, the challenge resided in the exhausting, long-haul business of outwitting regulators and outdistancing competitors.[38]

Wriston understood his success in precisely this fashion. "Members of the Federal Reserve Board . . . consider Citicorp an institution which tends to push to their outer boundaries the laws . . . which the Board administers," Wriston frankly told Fed chair Volcker in a letter dated July 17, 1981. According to Wriston, however, Citi's executives had "appli[ed] novel but fully defensible interpretations to prevailing laws and regulations" to ward off the challenges brought by Merrill Lynch and other non-bank financial service firms. Wriston had brought that message to bank president Moore and others in the executive suite in the 1960s, and he brought that identical message to the Association of Reserve City bankers at their March 1980 meeting in Boca Raton.[39]

Between 1967 and 1984, Wriston's many innovations and his widespread acclaim helped set a standard for bankers who were both entrepreneurial in nature and also willing to engage for many years with attorneys, regulators, and legislators with no end in sight. Wriston sought above all to alter the political economy in which Citicorp operated, and he judged his efforts a success. "We've changed the environment," a boastful Wriston told a journalist in May 1983.[40]

Starting in the late 1960s, Hugh L. McColl, Jr., and his fellow executives at the North Carolina National Bank took note of Wriston's innovative ideas. Like Wriston, McColl's rapid advance at the bank rested on close mentorship and an equally close alignment with his superiors' goals. McColl worked in harness with regulators more often than the cantankerous Wriston. Yet, McColl operated from remote Charlotte, where he also lacked Wriston's advantages of widespread recognition, political and financial resources, and experience working with Federal Reserve leaders and with Comptroller Saxon and his successors. McColl was certainly as aggressive as Wriston, and, like Wriston, McColl understood that only regulators and lawmakers possessed the authority to make his bank national in size and scope. McColl was also far more given to bluster.

CHAPTER 4

A Marine in Banker's Clothing: Hugh McColl and North Carolina National Bank

In 1985, Hugh L. McColl, Jr., was North Carolina National Bank's president and chief executive officer. North Carolina National Bank was headquartered in Charlotte. During the 1980s, growth-oriented bank officers like McColl created legal pathways to limited interstate expansion. Walter Wriston's earlier success at Citicorp served as a standing example that bankers like McColl followed in detail. And, as Wriston demonstrated, the fastest way to build an interstate network was to buy banks and S&Ls located in other states. At some point in the future, McColl told a *New York Times* writer in July 1985, regional firms like his North Carolina National would compete with the largest banks located in New York, Chicago, and Los Angeles. McColl had already purchased banks in North Carolina and Florida. His next acquisition target was First Atlanta Corporation, which operated more than one hundred branches in Georgia. McColl also liked the prospect of bringing First Atlanta's aggressive executive team into his organization.[1]

First Atlanta's executives rejected McColl's offer. McColl's acerbic personality was the key impediment, a *Wall Street Journal* writer later reported. McColl had used "military jargon and Anglo-Saxon expletives," to which First Atlanta's president replied, "Hugh, you're not being very friendly." McColl, teeth clenched, replied "I *am* being friendly, damn it." McColl's negotiating style reminded the *Wall Street Journal* writer about "the way troops took Iwo Jima." Rather than submit to the hostile McColl, First Atlanta's executives sold out to Wachovia, at a lower price.[2]

For decades, McColl's reputation for caustic remarks preceded him into meetings with executives at takeover targets. McColl built part of that reputation. He rewarded employees with crystal grenades, which they displayed proudly on their desks to signify success in meeting McColl's goals. The grenades were more than a showman's trick. McColl had served a two-year stint in the Marine Corps, where he undoubtedly received training in the use of many weapons. McColl's contact with physical danger and adversity ended there. Without doubt, however, McColl admired the Corps' reputation for achieving its objectives.

McColl's celebration of the Marine Corps' use of grenades in dugout-by-dugout combat contained a business purpose. Regular invocation of marine determination signaled McColl's intention to create a nation-spanning and even worldwide organization, just like the Marine Corps. No obstacle, it appears, was too large. McColl, as a start, sought to build a financial services firm that matched up with Wriston's far-flung Citicorp. McColl wanted not only to dominate banking. Starting in the 1960s, regulators and bankers including Saxon, Hunt, Regan, and Wriston had fostered creation of a legal and political environment that encouraged predatory behavior among bank executives. McColl was now one of those predators. In this new setting, McColl had to protect his CEO post and his employees against equally aggressive bank presidents. In a dog-eat-dog banking environment, McColl told a business writer in 1986, he "want[ed] to be the dog that does the eating."[3] In 1959, McColl had accepted a modest position at a small bank in Charlotte. In 1998, that small bank was one of the largest in the United States, and McColl served as its chief executive officer.

McColl's success rested only in small measure on real and cinematic Marine Corps exploits. Most fundamentally, McColl built his bank through entrepreneurial daring, some bullying, and mentorship at the hands of expansion-minded bank executives. And unlike Walter Wriston, McColl avoided confrontations with Federal Reserve officials and lawmakers regarding rules that supposedly obstructed growth. Instead, McColl worked with lawmakers and regulators to mesh their goal of achieving solid economic growth and his goal of making the North Carolina National Bank into a nationwide financial services firm. McColl's first days in banking were inauspicious, hardly the material for a story about intrepid behavior and fabulous growth.

McColl's Early Experiences as a Banker

Hugh McColl, Jr., was born in 1935 in Bennettsville, South Carolina. In high school and college, McColl was a mediocre student, his fraternity's president, a fun seeker, and an excellent athlete and poker player. In 1957, McColl graduated from the University of North Carolina at Chapel Hill. "You could put all I learned about banking and finance in an ashtray," McColl later recalled.[4]

McColl's start in banking lacked glamour. In 1959, fresh out of the Marines, McColl did not have a job. McColl's father, a former banker and a successful businessman, telephoned a well-placed friend at American Commercial Bank in Charlotte, North Carolina. The senior McColl's telephone call secured his son's post as the last of six trainees. McColl's early assignments at the bank included the bookkeeping department, where employees carried out the mundane work of posting deposits. McColl detested those tasks. McColl married after starting work at American Commercial and the couple was soon expecting their first child.[5]

McColl brought few of the advantages that accompanied Wriston to his early positions at First National City Bank. McColl and Wriston were born to successful families dominated by their fathers. McColl, like Wriston, attended a highly rated university. Wriston and McColl married the daughters of prominent businessmen. Yet in 1959, American Commercial offered only modest prospects for growth, especially compared to the international operations and connections Wriston commanded at First National City. In 1959, moreover, Charlotte, a third-tier commercial and manufacturing city, remained far removed from the maps of ambitious financial executives such as Walter Wriston and Donald Regan, with their bold plans for financial innovations such as securities' dealings and growth centered in New York and other major cities. Rather, North Carolina residents, like many of their counterparts across the American South, were capital poor; Charlotte and cities and like it were among the places President Johnson likely had in mind when he encouraged Comptrollers Saxon and Camp to permit mergers and branch banking. As a consequence of these many limits, McColl, during his first decade and more as a bank executive, could not rely on savvy attorneys and on plentiful cash and credit to guide the purchase of multiple businesses such as insurance and mortgage banking, at least not all at once. McColl's success between the early 1960s and the late 1990s rested on his ability to link his bank's future growth to lawmakers' and regulators' passion to find cash to support economic development projects such as roads, factories, home furnishing stores, business expansion projects, suburban subdivisions, and rising employment levels.

In 1959, when McColl arrived as a trainee, Addison H. Reese was American Commercial Bank's president and CEO. Reese expected the smallish

American Commercial to grow bigger than Wachovia, the largest bank in the region. As a start, Reese constructed a new bank building in downtown Charlotte. American Commercial's headquarters rose eighteen stories, modest by New York standards, but three stories taller than Wachovia's planned building. In 1960, Reese guided a merger with the Security National Bank in Greensboro, North Carolina. Naturally, Security National's officers wanted their city to serve as the combined bank's headquarters. But the comptroller's rules mandated only one headquarters address. Because the Federal Reserve operated a regional office in Charlotte, directors chose that city for their headquarters. Directors also determined to operate under Security National's federal charter, which removed the new bank from supervision by the state's bank commission and state legislators, both well connected to Wachovia executives. The growth-oriented comptroller in far-off Washington, D.C., set the rules that guided Reese's operations. These maneuvers eventually benefited Reese and McColl's plans for rapid expansion. North Carolina law also permitted branch banking, eliminating in advance an impediment faced by ambitious bankers in other states.[6]

Selecting a name proved the final hurdle to launching the merged bank. Directors were prepared to open as the National Bank of North Carolina. The comptroller's office rejected that name within a week. Directors then selected North Carolina National Bank, a name suggestive of a statewide bank with national operations. On July 1, 1960, opening day, Reese directed a staff of one thousand employees located at headquarters and in forty branches spread across twenty cities. North Carolina National Bank's assets totaled $500 million, compared with Wachovia's $658 million. Still smaller than Wachovia, Reese's bank was the largest in the Southeast holding a comptroller's charter.[7] Soon, many referred to the new bank by its catchy acronym, NCNB. Regardless of the bank's name or size, employees, including trainees such as McColl, recognized Reese's emphasis on fast growth. Less certain was whether those employees perceived the importance of state banking law, Federal Reserve regulations, and the comptroller's office in framing the bank's location, organization, and Reese's ability to foster that growth.

McColl did not join Reese and other senior executives in making these important decisions. Trainee McColl was still learning how each of the bank's departments worked. Late in 1960, NCNB executives shifted McColl to the correspondent banking office. McColl's new boss directed him to travel the state with Jack Ruth, an experienced banker who took an interest in McColl's career. Ruth invited McColl to join his family for dinners; and he also invited McColl and his wife to join his family's church.[8] Exactly like Wriston, McColl now had a senior bank official to teach him how to develop new bank business and who worked to protect him from other NCNB executives on the make.

Jack Ruth was McColl's first NCNB mentor. Ruth introduced McColl to the region's many small-town bankers. Each Monday morning, Ruth and McColl departed Charlotte to meet with them. McColl learned that many banks remained so undercapitalized that the Federal Reserve would not accept their checks. Still other banks were not even Fed members. NCNB and other larger banks handled the checking business for those banks. Another group of small banks operated under state charters, which limited their loans for any one customer to no more than 15 percent of the bank's capital. In order to write larger loans for customers such as auto dealers, those small bankers relied on correspondent banks such as NCNB and Wachovia to pick up the loan's outstanding portion. The only alternative open to underfunded clients was to contact a New York bank. McColl soon learned a valuable device to retain that business. Because NCNB's rules did not require formal review of loans less than $100,000, McColl announced approvals on the spot. In another move, the young McColl offered to purchase the loans South Carolina bankers had made to a conniving auto dealer, provided they allowed the dealer to remain in business.[9]

McColl had the luck to work at a growing bank. President Reese had launched a drive to increase the bank's size and reach. In 1962 alone, he added two banks, bringing employment to more than 1,700 executives and staff. In 1963, Reese guided a merger with the Bank of Chapel Hill, establishing NCNB's presence in the fast-growing Research Triangle Park. That same year, Reese started to write loans for residential lots on the Duke Power Company's Lake Norman development. While other bankers stayed away from the risky project, Reese, with permission from the accommodating comptroller's office, even wrote those loans without first securing deeds of trust. By late 1963, Reese presided over fifty-eight branch offices located in eleven cities. NCNB's assets totaled $654 million, a whopping increase over the $500 million with which the combined bank had opened in mid-1960.[10]

As yet another item in McColl's good fortune, in 1962 Reese assigned him to the bank's newly created National Division. Long before the advent of interstate banking, Reese planned for National Division executives to expand the bank's business beyond North Carolina's border. As a start, McColl and others would take business from their correspondent banks. McColl concentrated on starting banks, from scratch, in South Carolina, including loaning start-up funds and then processing their loans. "We would cradle to grave it," McColl later reported.[11] Too small for Wright Patman and his minions to notice at the time, NCNB's National Division staff, with the comptroller's expansive backing, posed a threat to the prestige and the predictable business that those small-town bankers had long enjoyed.

Assignment to the National Division also put McColl in regular contact with NCNB's senior executives. One of those executives, Thomas I. Storrs, a Harvard PhD in economics and a former manager of the Federal Reserve's Charlotte branch, took a special interest in the brash former marine. Storrs believed that McColl possessed a "nose" for identifying good and poor loans. In turn, McColl perceived Storrs, likely the bank's next president, as the person who would help boost him into a top post. In February 1967, NCNB's board members elected Storrs vice chairman. McColl, now the senior vice president, was "Tom Storrs' man," a bank director later reported.[12]

Buying Banks and Other Financial Companies

Storrs and McColl arrived at the top rungs at a good moment. President Reese was always on the lookout for growth ideas. In July 1968, Reese filed paperwork with the North Carolina secretary of state to form the NCNB Corporation, a holding company. Under this arrangement, the holding company owned NCNB, the bank; and holding company executives were free to purchase insurance companies and other financially oriented businesses that NCNB could not purchase. Reese named Storrs the holding company's president. Reese and McColl were now emulating Wriston at First National City Bank, but on a more modest scale. Similar to Wriston, Storrs quickly bought an insurance company and a real estate management firm. In 1969, bank officers opened an office in the Bahamas, their first branch outside the United States. The unstaffed Bahamas office allowed NCNB to make loans to North Carolina manufacturers looking to finance their European operations. In 1972, Reese purchased C. Douglas Wilson & Co., South Carolina's largest mortgage banker, as well as the Trust Company of Florida, located in Orlando. Federal Reserve officials approved each nonbank purchase.[13] In the course of a few years, Reese, Storrs, and McColl had established footholds overseas, in South Carolina, and in fast-growing Florida.

NCNB began to look like a smaller version of the largest banks, such as Wriston's Citibank. Between September 1967 and April 1972, NCNB's assets increased from $1 billion to $2.9 billion, surpassing Wachovia's $2.7 billion. Not stopping, NCNB officials entered the credit card business, purchasing the North Carolina franchise to issue the BankAmericard. The credit card brought out-of-state customers to NCNB, customers otherwise forbidden to NCNB by state and federal banking rules. As part of boosting the holding company's reach, image, and stock value, Reese and other NCNB executives flew city to city in a DC-3 to meet with stock analysts. Starting in 1970, editors of the *Wall Street Journal* and the *New York Times* published reports about NCNB's acquisitions. Newspaper editors began to quote bank executives on such timely matters as bank industry earnings. In his presentation to bank analysts, moreover, Reese highlighted the "brains, education, and training" that NCNB employees brought to their tasks.[14] Like Wriston, Reese made growth and boasting about it into regular features of the bank president's office.

Reese, Storrs, and McColl also purchased commercial banks. By the early 1970s, McColl led the purchase teams. Acquisition efforts started at parties and convention get-togethers, where heads of small-town banks talked shop and heard McColl's well-honed pitch. Targets were older men, anxious about the upheavals coming to banking such as credit cards and complex holding companies. Those bankers wanted to sell out for cash. If McColl and NCNB failed to land one of these bankers, Wachovia or another large bank would do so. McColl purchased banks such as Marion Bank & Trust Company for $4 million and the $15 million Industrial Bank of Fayetteville. Between 1971 and 1973, McColl and his associates purchased another five banks. Despite their modest size, the addition of those banks added to NCNB's expansion into small-town North Carolina. McColl also took part in banking seminars, where he spread the word about how NCNB set up specialized funds to invest in small banks. With McColl's visibility rising alongside NCNB's, a banker's magazine even published his remarks.[15]

McColl's success in guiding those purchases to completion solidified his position at the top of NCNB's ranks. Reese retired at the end of 1973. NCNB's board members, as expected, appointed Storrs to the top post, the holding company's chief executive officer. In turn, board members selected McColl to serve as North Carolina National Bank's next president. In the course of thirteen years, the eager McColl ascended from the trainee ranks to the top post in a fast-growing bank. In May 1974, a *New York Times* writer described NCNB as larger than "any other bank holding company in an arc between Philadelphia and Texas."[16] A few years earlier, writers had regularly used that description to characterize Wachovia's once commanding position.

Visibility and size encouraged regulators to pay more attention to NC-NB's holdings. In 1970, Storrs assigned McColl to purchase a finance company for the NCNB Corporation, the bank's holding company. Storrs in turn used that firm to create TranSouth Financial Corporation, to underwrite house and mobile home mortgages. TranSouth was a finance company rather than a bank, and Federal Reserve rules did not require reports about its operational details. In May 1978, those same Federal Reserve officials directed Storrs to sell TranSouth. NCNB's and TranSouth's substantial presence in many cities reduced competition, Fed officers contended, repeating the argument made against Wriston's ownership of Advance Mortgage. Now, Storrs had until December 1980 to unload TranSouth, the same termination date applied to Wriston.[17]

The TranSouth case highlights a fundamental difference between the way Wriston and McColl dealt with regulators. In his usually high-handed and antagonistic fashion, Wriston brought a lawsuit against the Federal Reserve Board, which he lost. McColl and his senior associates kept tabs on Wriston's Citi operations in detail. McColl could have built on Wriston's headlines to assert a similar legal and public relations case against regulators with the temerity to interfere with one of the holding company's businesses. Here was a moment surely in which to invoke his beloved Marines charging uphill in a fight to protect managerial judgment. Instead, Storrs and McColl chose to negotiate with Federal Reserve officials. In July 1979, Storrs sold twenty-five TranSouth offices to a finance company. In return, Federal Reserve officials permitted Storrs and McColl to retain ownership of their remaining offices.[18]

Storrs retired in August 1983. He left behind a bank with assets totaling nearly $9 billion and more than 250 branches in North Carolina. NCNB's board members named McColl, age forty-seven, to the posts of president, chairman of the board, and CEO. McColl also inherited Reese and Storrs's growth emphasis. But in the process of making that growth take place, McColl never fully internalized Reese and Storrs's smooth demeanor. Like his predecessors, McColl conducted mostly friendly negotiations with regulators and lawmakers at the same time that he often cursed in negotiations with bankers. Wriston's mixed reputation followed him across state lines, to

Florida, Georgia, and Texas. In 1982, McColl started NCNB's out-of-state expansion in Florida. That same year, a *New York Times* writer characterized Florida as "banking's hottest market."[19]

Beyond North Carolina's Borders

"We are absolutely convinced that interstate banking is coming," NCNB's Storrs told a business reporter in June 1981, and "we need more geography." Florida, with its rapidly growing population and fast-increasing bank deposits, was a natural place for nearby North Carolina bankers to operate. At the same time, leaders of the Florida Bankers Association, newly alerted to the looming presence of out-of-state competitors, had already asked their attorneys to study methods to stop those invaders. Florida bankers' hopes rested on earlier state legislation that plainly and simply prohibited outsiders like McColl from doing business in the state. Wriston, in his 1980 talk to reserve city bank executives in Boca Raton, probably had Florida bankers in mind as another case study of a fortress mentality. (And Storrs, as president of the Association of Reserve City Bankers that year, was surely alert to avoiding that negative designation.) Besides, federal law prohibited interstate branching without prior approval by the receiving state. The expansion-limiting banking acts of 1933 and 1956 still held sway.

In December 1981, however, Federal Reserve officials had permitted Storrs to purchase the tiny First National Bank of Lake City, Florida. In approving the purchase, Fed officials cited NCNB's prior ownership of the Trust Company of Florida, which the farsighted Storrs had purchased in 1972.[20] Federal Reserve officials possessed the administrative authority to turn aside panicky, in-state bankers. In the early 1980s, Congress refused to enact similar proposals, despite Treasury Secretary Regan's importuning.

The quest for growth in Florida did not end with those early purchases. McColl, Wriston and other heads of the largest bank holding companies sought to devise legally and politically defensible strategies for their out-of-state expansion plans. One such strategy rested on the ability and willingness of state government officials to create interstate compacts, permitting bankers to open a main office with branches in a neighboring state. Again, federal legislation blocked interstate banking except through state compacts or explicit state permission.[21] At this stage, interstate banking was less an ideological imperative pushed by free-market advocates than a gloves-off fight among bankers in several states for the best spaces to secure Floridians' deposits and loan applications.

On the surface, interstate reciprocity contained an evenhanded, come one, come all message. In truth, bankers like McColl argued for their right to branch out of state at the same time that the North Carolina commissioner of banks appealed to the Federal Reserve to block aggressive bankers like Wriston from opening operations in their state. Despite the complexities and inconsistencies inherent in creating these compacts, several Florida officials, including Governor Robert "Bob" Graham, were already on board with the compact idea. Graham, sounding much like Comptroller Saxon and Presidents Johnson and Kennedy fifteen years earlier, perceived larger banks as better equipped to handle the needs of Florida's midsized business firms. Graham even advocated for a "Southern Common Market," analogous to the way European leaders were reducing trade barriers between their nations.[22]

In 1984, Florida legislators approved an interstate banking compact with Georgia. McColl enjoyed several advantages in the fight for legislators' attention. Early on, Governor Graham signaled his support for NCNB's Florida presence by attending a breakfast with top NCNB executives the day they closed on the purchase of the Lake City bank. Still, Graham had wanted to bring full-fledged interstate banking to Florida. If Graham prevailed, bankers from anywhere in the United States would be able to open branches in Florida. But NCNB's skillful Tom Storrs subtly encouraged Graham to adopt the regional approach. As important in assembling legislative support, Gordon W. Campbell, the new head of the Florida Bankers Association, rallied the state's divided bankers to the cause of a regional compact. Campbell had recently sold his Exchange Bancorporation of Tampa to McColl and now served as vice-chairman of NCNB National Bank of Florida. In press conferences and in meetings with bankers, Campbell sounded the alarm about the dangers of unlimited interstate banking, where "the credit decisions and credit allocations would be decided 1,000 miles away from Florida." Patman and his small-town bankers had regularly cited the threat posed by distant bankers to ward off interstate banking. No one, including Campbell, mentioned that Miami and Atlanta were located more than six hundred miles apart. Storrs's foresight, McColl's negotiating skill, and Governor Graham's determination to bring additional capital to Florida allowed NCNB's top executives to establish a sizable and politically formidable presence in Florida. In the language popular at the time, NCNB was now a superregional. And in April 1984, a writer for *American Banker* described McColl as the "tough new kid on the block in Florida."[23]

McColl had to act quickly to extend his Florida franchise into Georgia. Under terms of the Florida-Georgia interstate bank compact, McColl and heads of two other Florida banks enjoyed a one-year head start before outsiders such as Wriston's Citicorp could begin to purchase Georgia banks. In June 1985, moreover, a unanimous U.S. Supreme Court approved a similar compact between Massachusetts and Connecticut, turning aside the challenge brought by executives at Citicorp and Northeast Bancorp. Those states, by excluding Citi and Northeast, violated the Constitution's guarantee of equal protection of the law, the two banks' avid attorneys had asserted. The court's decision brought legal finality to the regional concept and to the head start awarded McColl and NCNB in the race to buy Georgia banks certain to ensue.[24]

The Supreme Court's decision also set off a merger craze. In 1984, then a record year, 68 of the 300 largest banks purchased 150 other banks, adding $22.2 billion to their assets. In 1987, however, 649 banks merged, adding a fantastic $123 billion in assets to the acquiring banks' balance sheets. The interstate bank compacts created a legal and political environment for which growth-oriented bankers such as Wriston and McColl had been looking. Bankers were not the only ones to jump into the booming merger and acquisition field. Between January and September 1988, dealmakers at Shearson Lehman Hutton, a brokerage firm and investment bank, presided over 140 corporate purchases valued at $57 billion.[25]

There was no denying the immense sums to be earned in putting deals together. With corporate leaders and corporate raiders leading those widely reported and wildly lucrative mergers and acquisitions, McColl and other bankers had every reason to pursue their share of the action. Self-protection was yet another reason to seek mergers. "We won't have to worry about the other guy acquiring us," McColl told a *New York Times* writer several years later, "they have to worry about us acquiring them." Self-preservation and a cut of the revenue came together in the merger and acquisition departments that bankers like McColl created.[26] During the 1960s, Patman had fought Saxon to stop bank mergers and branching that appeared to threaten the livelihoods of his small-town supporters. Two decades later, McColl and other big bank heads had crossed state lines, joined the merger movement, and taken on the coloration of amoral investment bankers at firms like Shearson.

Texas-Style Growth

In an era only a few years removed from the Justice Department's antitrust enforcement actions, bankers needed sturdier arguments for their aggressive buying than self-defense. Once again, McColl and other acquiring bankers returned to the promise of a deep deposit base for economic activity in the vast and still underserved South. As well, McColl promised brokerage and other financial services to small-city residents, much as Don Regan had accomplished at Merrill Lynch.[27] And as much as words such as "markets" and "deregulation" had permeated popular and business vocabularies, expansion-minded bankers like McColl recognized their dependence on regulators to maintain their fast-paced growth through mergers. McColl's Texas acquisitions required luck, tenacity, a startling collapse in oil prices, and his ability to fashion a deal with Bill Seidman, another federal regulator.

In 1985, Reagan appointed L. William "Bill" Seidman chair of the Federal Deposit Insurance Corporation. In 1933, Congress had created the FDIC to insure customers' deposits in commercial banks. Seidman possessed an ideal background for work at the FDIC during a troubled time. In 1943, he earned an undergraduate degree in economics at Dartmouth College. Following service in the navy during World War II, for which he was awarded a bronze star and eleven battle stars, Seidman completed a law degree at Harvard University and then earned an MBA at the University of Michigan. In 1949, he joined the family's Michigan-based accounting firm, which, by the late 1960s, was one of the ten largest in the United States. During the 1970s, President Ford appointed Seidman to top-level economic posts.[28] By 1985, when Seidman was heading the FDIC, Texas's overextended banks loomed among his greatest challenges.

During the early 1980s, the Texas's economy experienced fast-rising oil prices and skyrocketing property values. In a perverse turn, Texans profited from the high oil prices and inflation that wracked businesses and house-holders in most parts of the United States. Families moved from Michigan and other regions experiencing economic decline to Houston and Dallas in hope of finding a steady job.

Texas banks funded much of the prosperity, fulfilling President Johnson's hopes of two decades earlier. Confident Texas bankers liberally extended loans for homes, offices, and especially energy production. In 1972, changes in state law also allowed those bankers to merge with competitors and open branches throughout the state. In the late 1970s, the four largest banks in Texas grew faster than the largest banks in the United States, including the mighty Citicorp and Bank of America. Confident Texas bankers started to talk about buying New York banks.[29]

No banker was more active in funding the Texas energy economy and in expanding the scale of his bank's operations than Charles H. Pistor, Jr., the chair and CEO of the Republic National Bank of Dallas. "There's been this tremendous corporate in-migration to the Sun Belt and . . . a tremendous influx of [bank] competition," Pistor told a reporter, and "we intend to strengthen our competitive defenses and be more aggressive." On January 1, 1980, Republic National, with $10.8 billion in assets, was the largest bank in Texas and the twenty-first largest in the United States.[30]

Only a few years later, the great energy boom ended. Home and office prices followed oil's downward trajectory. Mortgages and loans went unpaid. Between April 1985 and April 1986, the assets of several of those booming Texas banks including Pistor's Republic National fell a whopping $4.7 billion. A top Republic National executive blamed the losses on the presence of too many banks and savings and loans. In 1986, the Texas legislature, following the lead of Pistor and other bankers, approved interstate banking on the grounds that Texas banks and businesses needed to attract out-of-state capital.[31]

Still, the promised recovery never materialized. During this period of unpaid loans and falling oil and property values, bank officers scrambled to save their jobs and their firms. In December 1986, Pistor's top executives arranged to purchase the InterFirst Corporation, another large and troubled Dallas bank. The combination would rescue Republic National, went the reasoning. In June 1987, the First RepublicBank Corporation opened with combined assets of $35 billion, instantly making the new bank the nation's twelfth largest. To launch the firm, Pistor fired 400 employees, the first round of some 2,700 persons scheduled for termination during the next two years. The guiding idea behind those dismissals was to reduce costs and subsequently boost the firm's stock price, a process advocates described as boosting shareholder value.[32]

The firings and brave talk about shareholder value failed to reverse First RepublicBank's dismal performance. In April 1988, bank officials announced a quarterly loss of $1.5 billion, the second largest in banking history. Ordinary depositors began to withdraw funds, totaling another $1.1 billion.[33]

In March 1988, the FDIC's Seidman determined to rescue First Republic's remaining assets and branch offices. Seidman guaranteed the bank's deposits, even those larger than his agency's $100,000 limit per account, and he "injected" $1 billion. Bankers used the term "injected," like "infused," to describe a regulator's decision to add funds, rather than a loan Pistor would have applied for. Meanwhile, top executives at Wells Fargo and other banks announced their interest in buying First Republic. Large Japanese banks would enter the bidding, some speculated. In late June, Citicorp officials installed a team of twenty employees in First Republic's office to examine the failing bank's books with an eye toward putting in a bid. No one mentioned McColl's NCNB.[34]

McColl had actually been working with Seidman for several months to purchase First Republic. A key member of McColl's management team had alerted him to the bank's impending failure. McColl hired a visible Washington, D.C., attorney to secure a meeting with Seidman early in April 1988. McColl left that first meeting convinced that Seidman "liked him."[35]

During the next months, McColl and Seidman enjoyed a friendly and tumultuous relationship. Seidman nicknamed McColl the "little general" and characterized him as "a former Marine" who led NCNB "with absolute determination." At that first meeting, McColl told Seidman that he was accustomed to meeting his objectives and that the First Republic purchase was among his most important. Seidman admired McColl's frank approach. McColl in turn judged Seidman "a man's man, a very straightforward person."[36]

McColl, by appearing first at Seidman's office, had advantaged his hand—despite angry conversations that often followed. McColl twice stormed out of Seidman's office. "The Allies invaded Europe in less time than you're taking to make up you mind about Texas," McColl told Seidman. By one account, an FDIC attorney told McColl by telephone that his staff needed another thirty days to make a decision. "Fuck you!" McColl replied. "You're just jacking us around." But McColl persisted. He secured a promise from H. Ross Perot, a prominent Texas businessman, to guarantee NCNB's bid. No one doubted Perot's ability to deliver a check if called upon, and his presence, according to Seidman, "show[ed] Texas connections, Texas support." In contrast, a writer for the *Wall Street Journal* reported that Citigroup's interest in buying First Republic raised the specter that Texas's largest bank would "become the province of Yankees."[37]

On July 29, FDIC board members rejected the Wells Fargo and other bids and voted to award the beleaguered First RepublicBank to McColl. The high drama and respect between Seidman and McColl perhaps played a small part in moving the deal forward. Maybe Seidman admired McColl's Marine Corps experience as a counterpart to his years in the navy. In that period, however, millions of American men had served in the U.S. armed forces. More likely, McColl's purchase simply worked for both sides. McColl agreed to invest $210 million in the new bank, which he acquired with all branches, but without the mountains of debt that the bank and the holding company had accumulated (and the litigation certain to follow). Bankers called it a bridge bank. McColl owned 20 percent and the FDIC held the remaining 80 percent. As part of the arrangement, Seidman's FDIC guaranteed payment of First RepublicBank's debts and waived repayment of the $1 billion injected months earlier. A top NCNB lawyer had also discovered that Mc-Coll could deduct whatever bad debt came with the First Republic purchase from NCNB's federal income taxes. "The tax benefits alone could offset our total investment [in the bank]," the attorney reportedly told McColl.[38]

McColl's investment in First Republic was not a simple adding up of profits and expenses. McColl risked control of NCNB. If the Texas economy languished, McColl's shareholders, his board of directors, and bank analysts would judge his Texas venture a failure and probably insist that he step aside. And yet, as McColl understood, were the Texas economy to recover, then, for a modest investment, he had secured a giant foothold in the state, including First RepublicBank's Dallas headquarters and some two hundred-branch offices. On the day McColl assumed control of First Republic, NCNB's assets increased to $54 billion, and it was instantly the eighth largest bank in the United States. "NCNB Strikes Gold in Texas," a writer for *Bankers Monthly* headlined a year later.[39] By the early 1990s, NCNB's massive size merited more journalistic attention than the increasingly common practice of interstate banking.

Seidman, a nearly anonymous political appointee, had negotiated with McColl from a different starting point. "We acted from necessity," Seidman later wrote. Seidman staunched First RepublicBank's mounting losses with that FDIC injection. In doing so, he protected the FDIC's Bank Insurance Fund, already experiencing heavy losses brought about by the increasing numbers of bank failures. By moving the First RepublicBank off the FDIC's books, Seidman protected his credibility with members of Congress, who would be asked to replenish those funds. As well, Seidman was mindful of

the FDIC's history in making large injections. In 1984, Seidman's predecessor had injected large sums into Chicago's failing Continental Illinois
National Bank, leading to the first use of the term "too big to fail." In 1988,
however, Seidman was able to describe the bridge bank's transfer to McColl
(and losses taken by First RepublicBank's shareholders) as another example
of too big to fail, "but in a more limited way." Later, when a member of Congress noticed NCNB's favorable tax treatment, Seidman described those
terms as "a matter for the IRS." Above all, Seidman had fixed on McColl's
NCNB to become a major actor in relaunching the Texas economy on an
upward trajectory. Seidman's goal of fast economic growth through large
banks was exactly the elixir that Ford and Reagan had long promoted. In
fact, authors of the 1982 Garn–St. Germain Act had expressly permitted federal regulators to arrange interstate sales of failing banks and S&Ls. Even
before Congress approved that bill, the nimble Wriston purchased a failing
S&L located in California. Still, Seidman had to perceive the value for the
economy and for his FDIC in making this deal. No wonder Seidman's colleagues in the Ford administration had described him as self-conscious
about "public reaction and the political consequences."[40] Seidman, the head
of a federal regulatory agency, was another policy entrepreneur.

A Nationwide Bank

In January 1992, McColl changed his firm's name from NCNB to Nations-
Bank. The new name reflected the bank's growing presence in the national
economy and McColl's ambition to assemble the largest bank in the United
States. NationsBank was already large, the third largest, in fact, with assets
of $119 billion and nearly sixty thousand employees. Southerners would have
a bank with the ability to "meet financial needs from Main Street to Wall
Street," McColl told reporters at the news conference that followed.[41] In the
1960s, Presidents Kennedy and Johnson and Comptrollers Saxon and Camp
had advanced an identical argument. The political moment was not right for
such dramatic bank growth at that time.

In 1989, McColl took a moment to reflect on the complex politics of bank
growth. In an article published in *American Banker*, McColl failed to curse
and he avoided his customary aggressive tone. Rather, he spoke to bank employees and top financial executives as a senior statesman of banking. "Laws
and regulations still hinder the ability of commercial banks to react quickly

to the marketplace," McColl lamented. And yet, McColl added, nonbank competitors such as Sears, investment bankers at Shearson Lehman Hutton, and money market managers did not suffer under those burdens. The cumulative effect of those rules for commercial banks was "much like the difference between turning a speedboat and turning an ocean liner." McColl, given a choice, now sought "to operate in a totally unfettered environment." Economies of scale would come about, McColl asserted, when banks operated across state lines from a single headquarters and when they offered additional services such as insurance. McColl, in fact, perceived no problem were insurance firms to own banks. By the late 1980s, McColl, the often foul-mouthed ex-marine, gave gentle voice to many of the themes Saxon and Wriston had promoted years earlier. But such supermarket-like bank combinations, most regulators and bankers agreed, were illegal. Supermarket bank advocates like McColl continued to search for that right political moment.[42]

In that same 1989 article, McColl also demonstrated an insight about government rules and rule makers. Regulators, McColl admitted, had "been instrumental" in bringing fresh interpretations to bank rules. At the same time, McColl reported, bankers, including top NCNB officials, had "pushed issues and found loopholes" to sway legislation that had earlier confined banks to the business of making loans in one state or even in one city. McColl enjoyed his greatest successes among Florida's legislators and with the FDIC's Seidman. By way of contrast, McColl complained, Congress had provided no help in clearing the way for supermarket banks.[43] The basic legislation governing bank organization and growth, the Glass-Steagall Act of 1933, remained on the books. Although McColl and Wriston had created early bank supermarkets, insurance companies and investment banks such as Shearson Lehman Hutton continued to operate in legally distinct fields, each subject to its own state and federal regulators.

Not even the sustained effort of every U.S. president since 1961 had managed to reduce the hostility that existed among insurance and securities executives and commercial bankers like McColl and Wriston. Nor had American presidents and many in Congress reduced the basic distrust between large and small commercial bankers. McColl and his counterparts at Shearson Lehman Hutton might talk about the inefficiencies that regulation imposed. At the same time, most small commercial bankers and many insurance executives were reluctant to enter anything as scary and unpredictable as a unified industry. History mattered, as insurance executives and bankers of the 1980s and 1990s repeated the fears and certitudes about nationwide banking and bank supermarkets taught to them by members of the retiring postwar generation. Those younger leaders might not have recognized the name Wright Patman, but they had imbibed his message about the dangers of relying on distant bankers for loans. Surely no insurance executive or investment bankers in the 1960s or in the early 1990s needed to be reminded that bankers like Wriston and McColl posed a danger to their independence, prestige, and livelihoods. Bank politics continued to grind.

Starting in 1993, however, commercial bankers, including Hugh McColl, coalesced with President Bill Clinton to push for nationwide banking and full-fledged bank supermarkets. Even alongside the unceasing drumbeat of bankers and lawmakers talking about competition, efficiency, deregulation, and shareholder value, members of that coalition almost failed to achieve their goals. In 1999, big bankers led by McColl and by Wriston's successors at Citi succeeded in persuading still reluctant members of Congress to permit supermarket banks to exist, but they only barely did so. President Clinton's search for big banks with sufficient funds to get the central city and the national economy moving proved decisive.

PART III

New Regimes for Bankers

CHAPTER 5

Full-Service Banks: Bill Clinton and Sandy Weill

On April 3, 1994, the University of Arkansas men's basketball team played a semifinal game against the University of Arizona, in the NCAA Final Four. Millions of Americans paid attention to the NCAA basketball finals, including President Bill Clinton, who attended the big matchup. For the president, this particular game presented an opportunity to root for Arkansas, his favorite team, nicknamed the Razorbacks after the feral hogs that populated the state. As part of the pregame buildup, the Arkansas coach claimed that one of his players was "pound for pound, the strongest kid in the universe." Journalists covering the game expected to witness equal evidence of the president's commitment and passion for his beloved Hogs, a local variant of Razorback. Clinton initially failed to provide staring reporters what they sought. In one account, Clinton appeared "uncharacteristically subdued during the first half," which ended in a tie. At one point during the second half, however, the Razorbacks went on a 12–0 roll, which led Clinton, the "first fan," to "bounce up and down in his seat and pump . . . his fist in the air." The Hogs won by a score of 91–82. "I was very worried," Clinton told waiting reporters. "It was a hard game."[1] Clinton's Razorbacks won the final game and the tournament, beating Duke University 76–72.

Journalists, anxious for an evocative quote or a glimpse of the president's gyrations, overlooked the many symbolic elements that surrounded his appearance at that game. For one, the Final Four tournament was played in Charlotte. Only thirty years earlier, Charlotte was another modest-sized southern city. In 1992, however, Hugh McColl's large and powerful Nations-Bank opened its sixty-story Corporate Center in the city's downtown, known to locals as Uptown. First Union Corporation, another superregional, was also headquartered in Charlotte. McColl's original competitor, First Wachovia Corporation, also maintained a major presence in the city. With this assembly of big banks, Charlotte emerged as the nation's third largest banking city behind New York and San Francisco. For another, McColl joined the president and other guests in his skybox. Three decades earlier, McColl toiled as a low-level trainee, driving town to town to build the bank's loan business. By the early 1990s, McColl had emerged as a key figure in American banking and in Charlotte philanthropies. As of September 30, 1993, McColl's Nations-Bank ranked fourth in assets, behind only Citicorp, San Francisco–based BankAmerica, and New York City's Chemical Banking Corporation. After Clinton's election in 1992, NationsBank officials had to deny inquiries as to whether McColl was under consideration for secretary of the treasury.[2]

An invitation to sit with the president was an important form of recognition, an honor many prized for a lifetime. Clinton's invitation to McColl was also a profoundly political act. Clinton needed McColl to help push legislation that would free up banks to make more loans and accelerate the pace of economic growth. During the late 1980s, nearly nine hundred S&Ls and large banks, including Dallas's First RepublicBank, went bankrupt. In turn, regulators at the Federal Deposit Insurance Corporation and the comptroller of the currency forced bank executives to tighten credit standards. Bankers approved fewer loans as a result. The economy was also in a slump, with the unemployment rate during the final three months of 1992 hovering between 7.3 and 7.4 percent. In December 1992, soon after his election, Clinton told a "summit" of business, labor, and political leaders meeting in Little Rock, Arkansas, that federal spending on roads and bridges amounted to "peanuts" compared to the stimulus that would come about with increased bank lending.[3]

Additional loans represented only Clinton and McColl's first steps in a promised rekindling of economic activity. Clinton wanted bankers to direct a portion of those increased loans to low-income areas, rural and urban. More cash, went the reasoning, would benefit local residents and accelerate the pace of rural growth and central city revitalization. And indeed, in 1991, when McColl purchased Atlanta's C&S/Sovran Corp, he had committed to invest $10 billion over ten years in low and modest income areas where NationsBank conducted business. On August 4, 1993, then, Clinton told audience members at a meeting of the National Urban League in Washington, D.C., that "my friend Hugh McColl [was] one of the most enlightened bankers in America." Early in 1994, moreover, the editors of *American Banker* chose McColl as their 1993 "Banker of the Year," adding to the idea that here was an executive committed to making his bank a partner in the quest for speeded up growth.[4] During the 1990s, McColl enjoyed the public acclaim and access to leading politicians that Walter Wriston and Donald Regan had taken for granted several years earlier. McColl's visibility, his willingness to engage members of Congress and hostile bankers, and his strong hand in guiding Charlotte's revival served as an ever-present reminder of what a business leader and a president acting together to foster nationwide and international economic growth might accomplish.

Interstate Banking

Clinton and McColl carried forward Kennedy and Saxon's original assertions that larger banks conducting business across the United States (and now to include central cities) would open a path toward accelerated economic growth. In similar fashion, Clinton as governor and as president supported reduced trade barriers. In 1993, he pushed members of Congress to ratify the North American Free Trade Agreement (NAFTA), a pact between Canada, Mexico, and the United States to reduce tariffs and foster business activity. Investments, farm products, and manufactures would soon roll across international borders by air, land, and sea, as if North America consisted of only one nation. This expanded trade, went the reasoning, would lead to lower prices, more shopping and buying, and increased employment. Whether the federal government developed international trade or encouraged community-level banking, a top aide wrote Clinton on July 14, 1993, "the message is the same—creating new jobs."[5]

Market talk added to the appeal of opening international borders for trade and state borders for the creation of branch offices and the movement of loans. In recent years, larger numbers of Americans had taken up the rhetorical obsession of citing markets as an explanation for nearly every event and as the antidote for nearly every human ailment. By that reasoning, market talk offered a patina of inevitability to the appearance of freer trade through NAFTA and larger banks, like NationsBank, conducting business throughout the nation.

McColl and Clinton certainly knew better than to put their faith in markets. Years of practical experience in dealing with feuding and litigious bankers, insurance executives, and securities dealers had taught McColl and Clinton that only politics could bring supermarket banks and their promised growth effects into existence. McColl's efforts in Florida and elsewhere just to create interstate banking compacts served as case studies of the muscle and perseverance required to make anything as important as nationwide banking a matter of federal law. If Clinton were to create the interstate banks that had eluded lawmakers and bankers since the 1960s, then he would need the help of resourceful and powerful supporters, much as Kennedy, Johnson, and Reagan had needed Saxon, Camp, and Regan.

McColl and Clinton's allies included Eugene A. "Gene" Ludwig, the new comptroller of the currency. In 1993, Ludwig came to the comptroller's post as an FOB, a journalist's term to denote a Friend of Bill. In 1968, Ludwig and Clinton met in England, where Clinton was a Rhodes scholar and Ludwig was a Keasbey Fellow. Following their year of study, Ludwig and Clinton earned law degrees at Yale University. After Yale, Ludwig became a partner at Covington & Burling, a major law firm located in Washington, D.C. By the 1980s, Ludwig's clients included NCNB and other large banks. In 1992, Ludwig joined Clinton's campaign part-time. During the transition, Ludwig chaired the president-elect's task force on financial services.[6]

Ludwig, as comptroller, maintained the office's decades-old tradition of promoting commercial banks' financial health. Ludwig worried about the slow erosion of bank deposits to nonbank competitors such as Merrill Lynch and growing numbers of mutual and money market funds. Heads of large banks like Wriston and McColl and every comptroller as far back as Saxon had shared Ludwig's goal of formulating policies that fostered commercial bank growth against these less-regulated competitors. In 1993, a leader of small-town bankers characterized Ludwig as an "advocate in regulators' clothing."[7]

Ludwig, as part of that advocacy, was equally enthusiastic about expanding bankers' authority to cross state lines and jump full force into insurance sales and underwriting. Making use of legislation passed in 1886, Ludwig allowed McColl to consolidate his Maryland and Washington, D.C., branches under one headquarters. As for banks selling and underwriting insurance, by September 1993, Ludwig had already determined that bank insurance sales benefited consumers and posed no problems for banks. The distinction between bank and nonbank products was "artificial," Ludwig told members of the Senate Banking Committee on October 5, 1993.[8] Judges had already backed up Ludwig's argument.

Bankers' authority to sell and underwrite insurance comprised a political and legal conversation that extended back to the 1960s. Judges brought about a partial closure. In June 1991, three judges sitting for Manhattan's

U.S. Court of Appeals determined that state-chartered banks could indeed sell insurance. As part of a lengthy history of testing legal limits, Citicorp operated a bank chartered in Delaware, and that bank owned an insurance subsidiary. Federal Reserve officials had ruled nonetheless that the subsidiary had no right to be in the insurance business. Now the court agreed with Citicorp. Once again aggressive Citi attorneys had carried the day for the right of every banker to arbitrage between state and federal law. As a practical outcome, banks were now undeniably in the insurance business.[9]

Justices of the U.S. Supreme Court also weighed in on banks and insurance sales. Since 1916, under federal law, national banks operating in towns with fewer than five thousand residents possessed the authority to sell insurance to local residents. In 1986, however, Ludwig's predecessor in the comptroller's office ruled that banks could use those local offices to sell insurance throughout the state. By the early 1990s, more than one hundred national banks were already in the statewide insurance business. Attorneys for the Independent Insurance Agents of America naturally brought a lawsuit to stop those sales. On what was actually a technical matter, in June 1993 the court was unanimous in supporting the comptroller.[10]

Those decisions altered banking's political landscape. Bankers such as McColl, with two victories tucked in their legal belts, were now much closer to achieving full-fledged insurance authority. To add to the burden now placed on insurers, Comptroller Ludwig ruled that federal bank law preempted Connecticut's ban on banks selling insurance.[11] Senator Christopher J. Dodd served as the last line of defense for those floundering insurance executives.

Senator Dodd represented Connecticut, the home of Travelers and other large insurance firms. Starting in 1980 with his election to the Senate, Dodd stood foursquare against permitting banks, securities dealers, or investment bankers to enter the insurance business. In 1984, insurance executives gathered outside the Senate to applaud Dodd for his efforts to mount a stouter defense of their industry against marauding bankers. In 1988, Dodd walked out of a Senate hearing to demonstrate his fidelity to the principle that his state's insurance companies were entitled to maintain legal barriers against threatened predations at the hands of securities firms. In 1991, Dodd sought and failed to write legislation to stop Delaware-chartered banks from selling insurance through their local offices, which state law permitted. Dodd likened the shield he offered Connecticut's insurance firms to efforts of Senate colleagues to protect key industries in their states, such as corn in Iowa. In

1992, Dodd's opposition to bank insurance sales helped kill President Bush's proposed legislation. Dodd was simply determined to block any effort to permit bankers to junk their interstate banking compacts and launch insurance sales in each and every state. Hardened bank and insurance executives and their legal staffs recognized that litigation, lobbying, and obstructing competitors constituted regular and reasonable parts of conducting business. Now, Dodd's opposition had run its legal and political course.[12]

By early 1994, those adverse court decisions forced Dodd to reconsider his opposition to interstate banking. On February 3, 1994, the flexible Dodd took to the Senate floor to announce his support for interstate banking. He lacked the "horsepower," Dodd told colleagues, to block interstate banking. As part of those floor comments, Dodd announced himself an enthusiastic supporter of interstate banking. Members of the House Banking Subcommittee on Financial Institutions voted 29–0 to support an interstate banking bill.[13]

Amid the excitement that followed Dodd's announcement and the House subcommittee vote, only a few bank and insurance industry observers explained the trade-offs that guided Dodd's sudden conversion. For one, the courts and Comptroller Ludwig had spoken; and, as a second factor, many insurance firms already sold policies inside bank branches. By resolving this lengthy impasse, bankers and insurance executives could now get on with the business of adding to sales volumes. Dodd, however, left the independent insurance agents, another group of supporters in his lengthy fight, unprotected. Agents, by one report, made nine calls for each sale and looked upon added bank competition as "disconcerting." A top official at the Council of Insurance Agents and Brokers, the agents' trade association, described Dodd's changed course as "a significant setback born of unfortunate political factors."[14]

Dodd's announcement proved revolutionary among members of Congress. During the 1980s, Dodd and his insurance allies had treated members of Congress to a no-holds-barred education on the importance of never linking insurance and banking. So successful was that campaign that one observer described a negative connection "in the Congressional psyche between branch banking and insurance" offerings. Bank and insurance company joint sales programs had loosened that linkage; and those court decisions and then Dodd's sudden reversal severed it. Starting in March 1994, with Dodd's insurance wall removed, hesitant members of Congress suddenly reversed course to adopt both interstate banking and a renewed emphasis on low-income lending.[15]

Senator Donald K. Riegle, Jr., and Interstate Banking

With most of the opposition to interstate banking suddenly evaporating, Clinton, Ludwig, and McColl still required leaders to shepherd legislation through Congress. Senator Donald W. Riegle, Jr., was another of Clinton and McColl's allies. In 1966, Riegle, a twenty-eight-year-old Republican, won election to the U.S. House of Representatives from Flint, Michigan. In 1976, Riegle, now a Democrat, was elected to the Senate, where he joined the Committee on Banking, Housing, and Urban Affairs. In 1989, Riegle emerged as the Banking Committee's chair.

To study Riegle's work as chair is to revisit arduous bank politics from the early 1980s through Clinton's election. Like many of his contemporaries, Riegle's views on key banking issues had evolved during his years in office. At first, he endorsed maintenance of the legal and regulatory walls that separated commercial banking from other financial services such as the sale of stocks and bonds. By the late 1980s, Riegle followed executives of the nation's larger banks, such as New York's Marine Midland, and nationwide securities dealers, including Prudential-Bache, as they swung in favor of interstate banking and creation of bank supermarkets. In 1987, Riegle, as part of his newfound commitment to full-serving banking, had even dared to question Dodd's insistence that bankers must never be permitted to engage in insurance sales.[16]

Riegle was no simple convert to ideas about substituting markets for banking's many rules. Riegle's constituents, he judged, could not afford to take a chance with such abstract and untested notions. Riegle represented a city, state, and region undergoing massive deindustrialization and population losses. As one tool to revive those cities and industries, he sought ways to strengthen the federal government's Community Reinvestment Act (CRA). Approved by Congress in 1977, CRA rules provided that bankers had to make loans in areas where they took deposits. The CRA's authors intended to force bank funds into underinvested central city and rural areas. In a handwritten memo to his office files in 1987, Riegle noted "growing dissatisfaction" among Michigan's urban leaders with aspects of the CRA. Riegle judged a review of CRA legislation by the Banking Committee a "worthwhile topic," and he promised to include community leaders' suggestions as part of that review.[17] By this reasoning, tougher CRA rules would force successful bankers to help fuel recovery of depressed areas in Michigan and elsewhere.

With his years of congressional service, Riegle had also learned how to swing a political whip at recalcitrant bankers and noncompliant Senate colleagues. In 1987, he supported a one-year moratorium on award by the comptroller and the Federal Reserve of additional authority to bank holding companies. That moratorium stopped cold the scramble among executives at insurance firms to get into banking and also blocked Citibank and NCNB executives from trying to sell insurance or underwrite mutual funds. Bankers and heads of insurance and securities firms needed to work out compromises among themselves, he announced publicly in October 1987, or Congress would do it for them. At the same time, Riegle asked Alan Greenspan, the new Federal Reserve chair, not to issue rules loosening regulatory constraints. That job properly rested in congressional hands, he announced, which was the only place Riegle and colleagues could influence the organization of financial services. But if Congress failed to act, Riegle warned colleagues, Greenspan would do so. In 1991, with Riegle chairing the Banking Committee, senators voted in favor of substantial loosening of federal banking restraints, only to see the legislation die in the House. In 1991, legislators had made the bill top-heavy with such difficult-to-achieve objectives as permission for bankers to sell insurance and underwrite new securities' issues, areas of business that federal law had relegated to investment bankers since 1933. In 1992, with a presidential election on the calendar, no one expected congressional action on thorny issues like the reorganization of financial services.[18]

In 1994, Riegle, McColl, and Comptroller Ludwig provided a formidable legislative and regulatory combination advocating for the right to open branches without regard to state borders. McColl spoke to influential business groups, where he regularly bragged about his urban lending programs and extolled the economic growth that changed bank regulations would bring about. Business journalists were always eager to interview McColl, and he used those sit-downs to drive home the identical message. McColl, as "Clinton's banker," also enjoyed access to the Oval Office, where he talked with an avid president about community reinvestment and interstate banking. McColl wanted CRA rules applied to insurance companies and other financial corporations. That idea, unlikely to win enactment, would increase inner-city lending and also force identical costs on his competitors. In the meantime, a NationsBank lobbyist spoke with more than 150 members of Congress to explain how the proposed legislation would work in practice.[19]

Ludwig added to pressure on members of Congress to approve interstate banking. He hung a portrait of former comptroller James Saxon in his office. In the early 1960s, Saxon launched the first assault on bank rules, approving large mergers as well as bank entry into insurance sales. Ludwig described Saxon to a writer for *American Banker* as "the father of modern banking." Saxon "saw the future," Ludwig added, "and he acted on it." In a similar way, Ludwig, sounding much like Saxon (and Wriston), issued public warnings about commercial banking's decline relative to less-regulated firms such as Sears and Merrill Lynch that issued credit and sold financial products. In other words, Ludwig, like Saxon, would promulgate insurance and interstate bank rules if members of Congress failed to do so. In February 1994, months before Congress voted, Ludwig issued consumer rules to govern bank insurance sales. He intended to preempt congressional restrictions.[20] Financial journalists added to Ludwig's visibility and stature with reports of his FOB status and his frequent visits with Clinton at the White House.

Leaders of the American Bankers Association (ABA) provided the final piece of legislative groundwork. Because the ABA represented every banker, its office took on the most neutral colors. McColl and his counterparts were bent on achieving interstate banking. Small-town bankers remained equally opposed to such a vast change. Up to 1994, those small-town bankers found comfort in Dodd's stolid opposition to bank sales of insurance, which also blocked interstate banking legislation. Once Dodd gave way on bank sales of insurance, ABA leaders worked with some one hundred bankers to assemble a final bill on which most could agree. Those negotiators provided scant assistance to small-town bankers. Their fate, every small-town banker understood, rested on preservation of state banking laws. Riegle's bill authorized states to opt out of interstate banking, an unlikely occurrence for most and an approach that provided no shelter for small bankers located in states that would never choose to exempt their banks. Small-town bankers were "stunned" by the speed with which Congress took steps to reorganize their corner of the financial business.[21]

On September 13, 1994, as senators prepared to vote, many sought to demonstrate their facility with the new language of national markets. "The time has come to lift the ban on interstate banking," Senator Duncan "Lauch"

Faircloth (R-NC) announced, "and to recognize the reality of . . . market forces." According to Faircloth, small bankers in his state feared government regulation more than they feared NationsBank and First Union. "We cannot fear the markets," Faircloth added, handing those cringing bankers an exhortation rather than a legally protected market segment on which to pin evaporating hopes. Senator Thomas A. Daschle (D-SD) liked the idea that bankers operating nationwide would be in a stronger position to adapt to ups and downs in regional economies. That argument gained currency with Riegle and others who kept abreast of the hard downtown Texas banks experienced during the late 1980s. Still other Senate members returned to McColl's concern with the high cost of maintaining headquarters in each state.[22] Market talk, it seems, got lawmakers and everyone else off the hook for their action. It was as if words such as "markets" would anesthetize lawmakers, bank employees, and customers against wrenching changes sure to come.

In reality, lawmakers were about to devolve authority to bankers like McColl to vacate their state-by-state headquarters and reorganize as nationwide holding companies. In a year, McColl and others would be able to purchase banks located in any state. Starting June 1, 1997, those bankers were entitled to direct national operations out of one corporate center. To quiet fears about heads of large banks stealing business from their smaller competitors, congressional leaders prohibited a bank from controlling more than 30 percent of the deposits in a state, or more than 10 percent nationally. Well-organized small-town bankers still wielded considerable clout when it came to protecting their very existence.[23] Decades before, Saxon had launched the prosaic business of authorizing bankers to enter new businesses and expand operations. In the exuberant days of the mid-1990s, however, Congress approved that new authority under more exciting names such as "regulatory reform."

On September 29, 1994, Clinton signed the Riegle-Neal Interstate Banking and Branching Efficiency Act. In his remarks at the signing ceremony, Clinton invoked popular themes in political economy such as "making government less regulatory and less overreaching."[24] Interstate banking represented only another step in Clinton's efforts to boost trade throughout the Americas and eventually throughout the world. The alternative, Clinton told the gathered dignitaries, was to play at a "zero-sum game," where economic growth in one place meant decline in another place.

Since the early 1960s, bank politics consisted essentially of just such a zero-sum struggle. In 1994, for a moment, Riegle, Ludwig, and McColl held the legislative upper hand, which they used to push through interstate bank legislation. Yet, Clinton's much-hyped plans to boost rural and central city loan making had nearly foundered because of its links to the Community Reinvestment Act. At one point, Senator William Philip "Phil" Gramm (R-TX) threatened to hold up interstate bank legislation to seek modest changes in the CRA, which he detested in total. McColl had worked behind the scenes for months to avoid just such a legislative catastrophe. Clinton in return singled out McColl for special praise at the signing ceremony, once again highlighting his conviction that a union of government and banks would boost economic growth. If McColl could be "rhapsodic" about interstate banking at 2:00 a.m., Clinton joked, then Clinton should support it.[25] But to achieve supermarket banking, Clinton and McColl still needed each other for future legislative maneuvers. They also needed Comptroller Ludwig and Robert E. Rubin. Ludwig and Rubin, with their offices in the Treasury Department across the street from the White House, stood as a formidable pair.

Robert Rubin, Eugene Ludwig, and the Run-Up to Gramm-Leach-Bliley

Robert E. "Bob" Rubin had no intention of waiting for lawyers and lawmakers to struggle toward agreement about whether banks sold insurance and dealt in bonds and stocks. Starting in the Clinton administration's first days, Rubin, born in 1938, served as director of the newly established National Economic Council and as assistant to the president for economic policy. Clinton and Rubin met several times a week. Rubin brought decades of experience to his new assignment. In 1964, he earned a law degree at Yale University. During the next two years, he worked for a large law firm located in New York City. In 1966, Rubin joined Goldman Sachs as a trader. By the early 1990s, Goldman Sachs was among the nation's most prestigious and powerful investment banking firms, and Rubin was a senior partner and co-chair. Colleagues and journalists described Rubin as "pro-business," "pragmatic," and as "one of the shrewdest executives on Wall Street." Clinton charged Rubin to find devices to accelerate economic growth.[26] In January 1995, members of the U.S. Senate confirmed Rubin as the next secretary of the treasury.

Rubin brought an active voice and decided economic ideas to the White House and then to the Treasury Department. Like many business, academic, and political leaders between the 1970s and early 1990s, Rubin had watched stagflation destroy firms and jobs in New York City and throughout large swaths of the United States. Academic and journalistic observers regularly reported the successes of Japanese and European firms as they outsold American competitors in the U.S. market. More generally, educated Americans described these vast changes with phrases such as "a lack of U.S. competitiveness." To make businesses and workers more competitive, Rubin sought to reduce government regulation and to boost investment in job training and infrastructure. As a young and prospering banker, Rubin had watched just such a program of business-first investment at first hand. During New York City's fiscal crisis of the 1970s, political leaders dismantled portions of the city's social services network and initiated programs to create friendly terrain for start-up firms and to retain older corporations inside city limits. As a device to draw the attention of lawmakers and ordinary Americans to his competitiveness concerns, Rubin used scary phrases such as "underperform . . . the rest of the industrialized world."[27]

Examples of such underperformance had constituted a routine part of the American experience for decades. Starting in the 1950s and extending up to the mid-1990s, firms that formerly turned out steel, coal, shoes, railroad equipment, clothing, machine tools, and televisions had reduced production, entered bankruptcy, and moved operations outside the United States. Executives of bankrupt and relocated firms left behind countless employees who suffered pay cuts in new jobs as restaurant service workers or who never again found steady work. By the 1980s, motorists passing through cities like Pittsburgh, Youngstown, Cleveland, Detroit, Chicago, and St. Louis could not help but notice the abandoned factories and homes and the absence of freight cars on formerly busy railroad sidings. The political and economic sun had been setting on coal and steel for a long time. Their fast disappearance served as unsettling background for news reports highlighting a diminished number of jobs. Meanwhile, formerly key parts of the American economy stood still, cold and rusting.[28]

Banking was different. Commercial banking remained a healthy and lucrative business, with prosperous and influential supporters among regulators and lawmakers, including Rubin. Starting in the 1960s, bankers like Wriston and comptrollers such as Saxon complained about stifling federal regulations that prevented commercial bankers from keeping pace with upstart rivals such as money market funds and investment banks like Merrill Lynch and Goldman Sachs. Wriston continued to ring the alarm in books, interviews, and public appearances for a decade and more after his retirement in 1984.

Commercial banking was in fact caught up in the middle of a period of vast change that replicated several of the upheavals taking place in other industries. After World War II, new firms and new ways of allocating credit stripped away part of bankers' traditional business. Department stores offered credit cards, for instance. Starting in the 1970s, Americans moved billions of dollars from banks to money market funds that paid higher rates of interest. Cash management accounts offered by Merrill Lynch and others offered customers the ability to write checks, once a commercial bank monopoly. Ford, General Motors, and appliance dealers made customer loans, cutting sharply into another part of bankers' traditional business. In 1980 and again in 1982, members of Congress and Presidents Carter and Reagan approved legislation that allowed hard-pressed savings and loan managers to encroach further on bankers' traditional realms, such as checking and business loans. In sum, during the postwar years, the game's rules were such that nonbanks snatched a whopping share of bankers' traditional business. To maintain profit levels, customarily cautious bankers made loans to less credit-worthy customers and got into riskier ventures such as securitizing mortgages. Between 1961 and the mid-1990s, Saxon, Wriston, McColl, and Ludwig attracted audiences among bankers, congressional leaders, and presidents by describing in concrete terms the industry's comparative decline and the riskier dealings that bankers had started to place on their books. In 1994, one legal scholar described the banks' situation as that of a "legally protected niche [that] can turn into a death trap."[29]

Up to 1993, Rubin never talked about death traps and he never lamented bankers' situation. As a trader and a Goldman Sachs executive, Rubin had sought to profit by getting a jump on industrial change. But, as treasury secretary, the president expected Rubin to propose measures aimed at putting the economy and especially the financial sector on a path toward sustained growth. With nationwide banking now officially in the offing, Rubin sought to eliminate the Glass-Steagall Act. That 1933 legislation remained on the books and prevented banks, securities dealers, and insurance executives from fully and unreservedly entering each other's business. At its most fundamental level, Rubin, Ludwig, and Clinton viewed Glass-Steagall's abolition as another device to boost bank growth and U.S. economic expansion.[30] In their hands, Glass-Steagall's termination was never an ideologically driven campaign to restore markets in the abstract.

Members of the Republican Party faced a different set of circumstances. In 1994, Republicans won majorities in the U.S. Senate and House. Led by

Congressman (and future Speaker of the House) Newton L. "Newt" Gingrich, Republicans campaigned on the promise to reduce government's influence in areas such as telecommunications and banking. With those predilections as routine campaign themes, seasoned observers predicted near-certain elimination of Glass-Steagall's remaining rules. Gingrich and his allies quickly discovered that only government created and rearranged the markets they had talked about with such fervor.

Republican leaders failed to keep their promise to ease bank controls. Early in May 1995, members of the House Banking Committee approved a bill to allow banks, insurance companies, and securities dealers (including investment banks) to merge. Quite a few Republicans liked the idea of including insurance as part of their effort to eliminate all barriers to the creation of fully integrated financial service firms. Several Democrats signed on with that effort. They wanted to protect the Community Reinvestment Act and figured that the insurance provision would raise the anger level among insurance agents enough to sink the entire bill. In the language of the day, Democratic members backed a poison pill. As those Democrats hoped and predicted, during the weekend of May 13–14, some seven hundred outraged insurance agents went to Washington, D.C., and to members' home offices to protest this attack on their future sales prospects and their place as members of Kiwanis and other solid symbols of respectability. Crusading insurance agents, alert to the day's political language, represented themselves as favorable to financial modernization and opposed to "domestic protectionism." But when it came to protecting their right to sell insurance, it was a "life or death" matter, they told representatives.[31]

The insurance agents prevailed. In early June, Speaker Gingrich joined with committee chairs James A. "Jim" Leach of Iowa and Thomas J. "Tom" Bliley, Jr., of Virginia to support legislation to bar the comptroller from authorizing bankers to sell insurance. In October, leading bankers like McColl, who had been insisting on their right to sell insurance, reversed course and withdrew support for the stripped-down Glass-Steagall repeal bill. In mid-November 1995, keen observers of bank politics recognized that the House bill and Rubin's first run at supermarket banking were dead.[32]

It was Comptroller Ludwig's turn. His chances of bringing banks, insurance companies, and securities dealers into one firm rested on different media and legal environments from those Rubin occupied. Rubin, the president's spokesman on financial matters, was always in the media spotlight. Rubin brought the added advantages of good looks, a calm demeanor, and stunning business success to his many interviews and congressional appearances. Rubin relied on his persuasive powers and on the threat of a presidential veto.

Ludwig relied on the authority of his office. That authority was a curious one. Ludwig and the comptroller's office were no more visible to ordinary Americans than in Saxon's era. Reporters for national publications such as the *Wall Street Journal* and the *New York Times* and TV networks such as CNBC and ABC failed to station reporters and camera crews outside Ludwig's office. Ludwig, as comptroller, lacked the image of authority and audacity that were prerequisite to emergence as a TV personality. Yet, the financial and business press covered Ludwig's fewer pronouncements in scrupulous detail. Copies of *American Banker* (daily) and *National Underwriter* (weekly) regularly landed on bankers' and insurance executives' desks. Reports in those publications about crucial topics such as bank sales of insurance formed the basis for lunchtime fulminations and political action campaigns that could slow and then stop unfavorable legislation. Once insurance executives mobilized to oppose a bill, Rubin and congressional leaders such as Leach, Bliley, and Gingrich negotiated with them. Rubin exhorted everyone to legislative action; but Ludwig, his office newly clothed in a 1995 Supreme Court decision authorizing bankers to sell insurance, could issue a rule and send examiners into bank offices to check on its implementation. "Ludwig is in the catbird seat," an industry observer told a *Financial World* writer in April 1995.[33]

Ludwig launched his supermarket bank efforts without waiting for Rubin's to fail. In January 1995, Ludwig threatened to rewrite a comptroller's rule to permit bank subsidiaries to undertake businesses such as real estate, data processing, travel agencies, and, of course, life insurance. The rule was known to bankers and other insiders as rule 5. Ludwig's announcement, couched in the complex language of bank regulation, necessarily resided outside the reach of ordinary Americans. But, as a *Barron's* writer explained to his business readership, Ludwig's plans would virtually abolish the separation of banking and other business activities in place since 1933. During the next months, affected business executives and business writers speculated about whether Ludwig would go forward with this bold proposal, and where, if at all, he would draw a line that bankers could not cross. Would Ludwig "blindside Congress"? asked one writer in April 1995. The one certainty, Ludwig's predecessor observed, would be lawsuits brought by competitors such as insurance companies and travel agents. At this point, speculation about Ludwig's intentions stood as a warning to Congress and to resistant insurance executives that the time to make a deal had arrived. In July 1995, turning to the language of an upcoming boxing match, a writer for *American Banker* headlined Ludwig as the "bankers' champion."[34]

In November 1995, after negotiations in the House of Representatives to change bank legislation collapsed, Ludwig followed through on his announced threat. Ludwig's staff, as promised, had revisited rule 5. Starting in 1997, banks would be able to enter those new business lines. A plain-vanilla bank could launch or purchase an insurance firm and organize it as a bank subsidiary. Authors of earlier rule changes had required bankers to set up subsidiaries in holding companies, a costly and complex maneuver for small operators. The Federal Reserve regulated bank holding companies, but Ludwig and the comptroller's office alone would regulate these innovative banks. In turn, the president, who appointed the comptroller, would exercise nearly direct control over bank subsidiaries—and, presumably, the president, through his choice of comptroller, would expand bank services and speed up economic growth. Kennedy, Johnson, and Saxon promoted a similar idea three decades earlier. To justify this sweeping change, Ludwig returned to a favored theme, "the survival of commercial banking."[35]

Safety was another factor Ludwig cited in favor of his proposed changes. Nationwide commercial banks engaged in multiple activities would be better equipped to withstand downturns, he contended. Wriston had advanced an identical argument starting in the 1970s. In November 1996, Ludwig issued rule 5's final revisions, which included authority for bankers to enter lower-risk businesses without first seeking his office's approval. Bank subsidiaries had only to engage in the "business of banking." Left standing, Ludwig's revised rule substantially abolished the Glass-Steagall Act. On learning about these changes in draft form, leaders of the American Council of Life Insurance, an industry trade association, promised an "all out fight against Ludwig's power grab."[36]

Members of a Senate banking subcommittee held a special hearing to manifest their fury with Ludwig's behavior toward insurance companies and agents. On May 1, 1997, the committee met for one day to take up Ludwig's apparent challenges to the authority of state insurance commissioners to determine who sold insurance. Banks had the right to sell insurance, the market-oriented Senator Faircloth conceded, but Congress had "a right . . . [to] maintain a level playing field." Insurance agents invoked identical language. In a similar vein, Senator Alfonse M. D'Amato (R-NY) denounced

Ludwig for entertaining one bank's proposal to get into real estate development. Still more, D'Amato continued, Ludwig's actions diminished the authority of state insurance regulators. Meanwhile, D'Amato had introduced a bill to allow banks to merge with any type firm, even automobile manufacturers such as Ford or General Motors, which already owned automobile finance companies. But during that day in May at least, one senator who favored creation of unhindered markets and another who was prepared to restructure banking in its entirety might still refashion themselves as true friends of under-siege insurance executives and agents. Between 1994 and 1997, those long-suffering insurance agents and executives (with help from Speaker Gingrich) had stymied the concerted efforts of many in Congress, Treasury Secretary Rubin, and Comptroller Ludwig to create bank supermarkets. As late as December 1996, according to a writer for *Euromoney*, American bankers still went "through contortions" to enter new lines of business such as securities sales and underwriting.[37] Starting in 1998, Ludwig's complicated rule 5 changes merged into the legislative wrangling that surrounded Sandy Weill's newly created Citigroup and Glass-Steagall's subsequent abolition.

Sandy Weill and Citigroup

In 1998, Sanford I. "Sandy" Weill was chairman of the Travelers Group. The company's symbol was an umbrella, suggesting that the firm's many products, such as insurance and mutual funds, shielded middle-income Americans from financial storms. Weill projected the dual image of a prosperous executive and a no-nonsense boss. With his characteristic big smile and rotund appearance, Weill enjoyed upscale restaurants such as New York's Four Seasons. He also liked spirited refreshments, often in the company of large groups, and he smoked cigars until 1992. During the workday, Weill sometimes walked the company's floors, where he cursed, cajoled, and directed employees. People who liked Weill described him as "smart, loyal, and bold." A *Wall Street Journal* writer characterized Weill's decision-making as "going with his instinct, a style that has worked remarkably well." Others who disliked Weill chose words such as "ruthless, rumpled, and abrasive" to describe him. Weill also surrounded himself with a loyal and seasoned cadre of top executives, including James "Jamie" Dimon and Charles O. "Chuck" Prince. Dimon, Prince, and others managed daily operations and advised on acquisition targets.[38]

During several decades as a corporate executive, Weill's strategic vision rested on two simple ideas. First, he purchased sagging corporations and reduced costs by terminating part of the workforce. In the process, Weill created profitable firms that (often) enjoyed rising stock prices. Regular news reports of Weill's dinner choices, philanthropies, and successful corporate purchases added to his reputation as an executive who knew how to assemble deals that added to his stock's price. Small shareholders took their investment cues from Weill's deals; they "invested with Sandy."[39] Second, Weill's corporate purchases were anything but random. Weill built his Travelers Group empire by assembling diverse parts of the fragmented financial services industry into a full-service provider, including charge cards, insurance, securities, and the like. Those firms were supposed to add to each other's business by cross-selling, as, for instance, by pitching the same customer on an insurance policy and a mutual fund. Weill aimed to make his firms the largest and the most visible in their field, replicating Donald Regan's success with a similar approach at Merrill Lynch.

Weill sought to make one more large acquisition. Early in 1998, he boldly offered to merge his Travelers Group with the gigantic Citicorp, the firm Walter Wriston had done so much to build into a worldwide behemoth as well as a legal and political force in battling regulatory constraints. That federal law prohibited an insurance company like the Travelers Group from owning a commercial bank such as Citicorp was only one of several hurdles standing in Weill's path. But Weill, unlike still-constrained bankers such as McColl, was accustomed to exercising a flexible hand in his multiple undertakings.

Weill's approach to Citicorp's leader, John S. Reed (Wriston's chosen successor), was conventional and audacious, all at once. The Business Council, a group of top corporate executives, was scheduled to meet in Washington, D.C.'s Park Hyatt Hotel on February 25, 1998. Weill was, of course, a Business Council member, as was Reed. Several weeks prior to the meeting, Weill telephoned Reed to schedule a conversation in his hotel room at 9:45 p.m., after the Business Council meeting concluded. Weill regularly conferred with top executives in restaurants and other public places, but the meeting with Reed had to remain secret. After offering the customary glass of wine, Weill asked Reed, "Will you merge?" Weill stressed the combined company's ability to cross-sell insurance, annuities, and credit cards. Citi would be in a position at last to launch investment-bank activities such as underwriting stock and bond issues, completing Wriston's quest to create a supermarket bank. For legal purposes, Travelers Group would buy Citicorp, and then apply to become a bank holding company. On April 6, at a news conference to announce the combined Citi-Travelers, Reed emphasized the "one-stop shopping" that the merged company would soon provide.[40]

The Travelers-Citi combination was no ordinary bank merger. It contained novelties of size, management, and political economy. First, with assets valued at $698 billion, the combined firm would emerge as the world's largest financial services corporation. As another measure of this new company's potential size and reach, it served more than 100 million customers in some one hundred countries. Second, a large insurance company was to buy a large bank, perhaps leading to the conclusion of four decades of regulatory, legal, and political disputes. Still, at that point, no one could predict how Greenspan's Federal Reserve would rule or whether Congress would legislate favorably. At that same April news conference, Reed expressed hope that "over time the legislation will change." To get that needed legislation rolling, Weill had earlier telephoned Alan Greenspan, Robert Rubin, and President Clinton. In an effort to present the merger as an accomplished fact, Weill and Reed announced that the new firm would use the Travelers' umbrella as its logo but take the name Citigroup, discarding Citicorp.[41]

Weill and Reed brought tremendous clout to any business proposal. Still, the environment for permitting banks and insurance companies to merge remained muddy. As recently as November 1997, feuding bankers, insurance and securities executives, and congressional leaders had failed yet again to reach accord about intractable matters like state insurance regulation. An editorial writer for an insurance industry publication described one proposal as a "knife in the back." Insurance agents in particular remained agitated at the prospect that Ludwig would permit banks to enter insurance sales everywhere and at once. Those agents invoked time-tested phrases such as "anticompetitive and protectionist." Ludwig was the banks' best friend, agents asserted as often as possible. Bankers were nearly as uncomfortable. Quite a few worried about any congressional action that would permit voracious and cash-rich insurance executives to purchase undervalued banks. To worsen legislative prospects, Federal Reserve chair Greenspan, Comptroller Ludwig, and Treasury Secretary Rubin were still engaged in a public debate about how to regulate those massive bank holding companies. "Getting any legislation through Congress may still be impossible," a writer for the *Investment Dealers' Digest* had observed in May 1997.[42]

In September 1998, Greenspan's Federal Reserve approved the Weill-Reed merger. The co-executives had between two and five years to secure congressional and presidential approval to blend insurance and banking. Prospects for that approval had dimmed a month earlier, however, when Clinton threated to veto any legislation that shifted regulatory authority to the Federal Reserve and away from the comptroller's office. Clinton was not protecting Ludwig, his longtime friend, who had in fact completed a five-year term and left the comptroller's office in April 1998. Rather, Clinton, who appointed the comptroller, sought to advance the president's ability to influence bank policy with a view toward promoting faster economic growth nationwide and in central cities. Pending bank legislation, Rubin wrote to the president's chief of staff and to a top economic adviser on September 22, will "greatly diminish the role of the elected Administration in financial services policymaking and adversely affect the Community Reinvestment Act." Weill and Reed were scheduled to meet with key officials at the White House the next day. "We told the bank CEOs that our veto is still in place," a presidential adviser later reported. For Clinton and his top advisers, guaranteeing the president's ability to foster bank and financial industry development and central city economic growth took precedence over the largest bank merger in history.[43]

Not even the president's veto threats could stop this bill's momentum. In May, House members passed the long-awaited legislation by one vote. In September, the more enthusiastic members of the Senate Banking Committee approved a roughly similar bill, 16–2. Senator D'Amato of New York, the committee's chair, had cobbled divergent interests into a bill that few loved, that leaders of larger banks opposed, but that many reported they would be able to "live with." In October, bank and insurance industry leaders even reached an agreement to prevent the imperious comptroller from preempting state insurance regulations. Supermarket banking, the object of decades of presidential urging, endless congressional talk, regulatory innovations, and lawsuits stood at the verge of becoming national law. Fear among members of Congress and insurance agents that Greenspan and other regulators would promote more onerous regulatory changes added to the bill's momentum. In the near term, moreover, Weill and Reed needed this legislation for their "mega-merger" to go forward. Billions of dollars and reputations for smart deal making, developed over decades, were at stake.[44]

Senator Gramm was positioned to halt that momentum. Gramm had no problem supporting the Citi-Travelers merger; nor did he object to insurance firms and bankers mingling operations. But he disliked two other parts of the bill. First, Gramm opposed an obscure section of the legislation having to do with the sale of thrift institutions to nonbank firms. Large and small bankers alike feared that insurance companies like State Farm would purchase a thrift charter and use it to offer bank services. That horrifying prospect had made it easier for Senator Robert F. Bennett of Utah to foster a compromise between the usually opposing American Bankers Association and the small-town bank managers and owners who made their political weight known through the Independent Bankers.[45] Gramm was willing to cross swords with unified bankers and Senate colleagues on matters important to him alone.

Gramm carried a special animus toward the Community Reinvestment Act (CRA), which Congress had enacted in 1977. By the late 1990s, many bankers including leaders of the American Bankers Association grudgingly accepted the CRA as another cost of conducting business. And the CRA remained vitally important to Clinton's economic plans, to many central city members of Congress, and to merging bankers such as McColl, Reid, and Weill. Up to 1994, Donald Riegle, the now-retired senator from Michigan, had stressed the importance of CRA provisions so that banks would continue to make loans in his deindustrializing state. As such, authors of the Senate bill provided that banks would have to earn a "satisfactory" CRA rating before entering the insurance and securities fields. In 1994, Gramm had disapproved the CRA's extension. In 1998, Gramm, now the next person in line behind committee chair D'Amato, described the CRA's stipulations as forms of "extortion," "piracy," and even "slavery." On October 9, Gramm, perceiving those dire threats to American liberties, stopped the pending legislation almost by himself. "We are changing the rules of the game," Gramm told Bank Committee members only the month before.[46]

In November, Senator D'Amato lost his reelection bid. Gramm would take D'Amato's place as chair of the Finance Committee. Gramm's Senate colleagues judged him abrasive and more partisan than usual. Gramm was ornery, self-confident, and ambitious—in 1996, he sought the Republican nomination for president. Gramm's abstract ideas made bankers uncomfortable. In his public presentations, Gramm was an unflinching admirer of the notion that business executives, responsive to market pressures rather than government rules, should make loan decisions and organize financial services. Gramm's PhD in economics added to his rhetorical certainty about the value of unhindered markets. Bankers such as McColl and Weill always genuflected before the altar of markets free of government. Still, in November 1998, the prospect of Gramm's elevation to the post of Banking Committee chair "sent . . . shivers through" financial service executives.[47] Gramm's market fundamentalism appeared too much of a good thing.

Bank Supermarkets on Clinton's Terms

Between 1961 and 1998, every issue surrounding creation of bank supermarkets had been litigated, lobbied, studied, and talked about. Several generations of lawmakers and bankers had devoted large portions of their careers to efforts to modify the rules under which banks organized and operated. Few had achieved much headway. Walter Wriston, the head of the mightiest bank of all, failed to change federal law. Instead, he pursued a strategy of aggressive regulatory filings. As of 1994, Clinton and McColl helped make nationwide banking a legislative fact. But neither Donald Regan nor Robert Rubin had been able to usher supermarket banking into existence. Instead, right up to 1998, bankers, insurance agents, and regulators still scrambled for the right legislative wording to speed up economic growth, to preserve an advantage in their national and international dealings, or to send competitors into a tailspin. Nor had the recent creation of the gigantic Citigroup, headed by the influential Weill and Reed, proved sufficient reason for lawmakers, bankers, and insurance executives to set differences aside. In 1998, the weight of recent bank history, four decades' worth, determined the language and the range of actions that were "thinkable" in Congress and in the Oval Office.

Again, the question before Congress and the president was not whether to create an unspecified free market or to maintain bank regulations. Legislators rarely worked inside such binary options. Banks had always been subject to regulation, and they would remain regulated in the future. Instead, as Rubin told members of the Senate Banking Committee on June 17, 1998, they and other lawmakers were about the business of negotiating "the constitution for the financial system for the next century." Federal officials, in other words, would continue to determine rules for the next banking regime.[48] Three questions remained unresolved—first, how would bankers organize their holding companies and subsidiaries? Second, who would regulate them? And third, whether bankers should have to observe CRA rules? President Clinton insisted that the CRA would continue as part of banks' regulatory regime as much as Senator Gramm insisted that they would not.

The much-acclaimed Fed chair Alan Greenspan remained a key voice in these negotiations. Greenspan favored awarding bankers the authority to enter new and challenging fields such as investment banking. In testimony to members of a House commerce subcommittee on April 28, 1999, however, Greenspan urged the continued use of holding companies to keep banks and their subsidiaries operating at a safe distance from one another. Federally insured banks such as Citicorp and freewheeling securities dealers such as Salomon Smith Barney, for example, would exist in the same firm, in this case Citigroup. But, in Greenspan's version, Citi and Salomon leaders would report to the head of the bank holding company rather than to Citibank's executives. Salomon executives, in Greenspan's version, would not have direct access to Citi's customer deposits and its carefully regulated capital to finance their less certain operations. Nor would executives at the bank's subsidiaries enjoy access to operating cash at the lower rate that insured banks enjoyed, which in an extreme case might place the bank itself at risk. Greenspan's future bank, centered in the holding company, looked like the supermarket bank that he and others on Nixon's Hunt Commission had talked about in the early 1970s.[49]

Greenspan was equally certain that only the Federal Reserve could supervise these massive holding companies in their entirety, which had been the case since 1956. His successes starting in 1987 in working with bankers and presidential advisers to deal with stock market and financial crises in Russia, Asia, and at a failing hedge fund (Long-Term Capital Management) added to his credibility on any financial topic. Soaring stock prices and adulatory reports of his deft financial touch added to Greenspan's credibility among ordinary Americans and enthralled members of Congress.[50]

President Clinton and his new comptroller still held out for the idea that securities dealers, investment banks, and other bank-owned firms would report to bank executives rather than to the holding company's top executive. This matter was not some arcane law school debate. If Clinton prevailed, the head of Weill and Reed's Citibank would be entitled to authorize subordinates at their investment bank (Salomon) or at another part of the firm to engage in highly speculative dealings, some of which were clearly off-limits to the bank, such as real estate development. Perhaps Citibank executives would also loan or give operating funds to Salomon, with those funds obtained at the lower rate available to insured banks. For years, Ludwig and Rubin had championed this arrangement as a device to accelerate the pace of national economic growth. As well, Clinton's top officials insisted, to permit

banks to organize as holding companies placed parts of those banks' capital outside the reach of the Community Reinvestment Act. All in all, Clinton
and Ludwig sought to add to the president's arsenal of economic weapons
in central cities and throughout the United States. After all, they had also
concluded, Americans held the president responsible for the economy's performance. By that standard, the president, any president, needed to control
several of the economy's levers. Just to make certain everyone had heard and
understood his concerns, Clinton's veto threat remained standing.[51]

Outside observers characterized the Clinton-Greenspan debate as a turf
battle, which it was in part. The more fundamental question was who within
these massive banks, such as Citigroup and Bank of America, would make
major investment decisions, and whether those decisions in turn could be
leveraged with a eye toward boosting the pace of national economic growth.
To insist that banks organize only inside holding companies, Rubin had advised members of the Senate Banking Committee in June 1998, was to "limit
the ability of market participants to make their own judgments about how
best to lower costs [and] improve services."[52] The preamble to Rubin's
imagined financial constitution cited market ideals. As a top member of the
Clinton administration, however, Rubin also labored mightily to maximize
the president's ability to influence the market's pace and direction.

In mid-October 1999, Senate and House conferees met, creating an opportunity for Gramm and presidential aides to negotiate their deep differences. Within a few days, they worked out a compromise on how bankers
would deal with their nonbank subsidiaries, such as their investment banks.
Gramm, the strident market advocate, had originally wanted to keep those
operating subsidiaries outside the banks. Now, he reversed position to join
presidential advisers and bankers like Weill and Reed to permit banks to
place investment bank affiliates inside a subsidiary directly in line with
the bank, or even inside the bank. The comptroller, a presidential appointee, would regulate those operations, exactly as Clinton insisted. But as a
countermeasure, Treasury and Fed officials could veto each other's decisions,
an arrangement that awarded the upper hand to more cautious Fed officers.
As part of the deal, Gramm and Lawrence H. Summers, the new treasury
secretary replacing Rubin, added provisions to stop growth-minded bankers
from investing insured funds in their securities and other firms.[53]

Gramm, in private negotiations, was amenable to additional changes. Although Gramm represented himself as a cowboy capitalist, he actually demonstrated a keen appreciation for bankers' excesses. Gramm insisted that

Greenspan's Federal Reserve continue to act as the overall holding company supervisor. Gramm trusted Greenspan and senior Federal Reserve officials more than he trusted Clinton and his White House team. In negotiations that ran to the early hours of the morning, Gramm permitted regulators to check on bankers' compliance with the Community Reinvestment Act. As one key example, expansion-minded bankers would have to produce Federal Reserve documentation to show their compliance with CRA provisions before purchasing a securities dealer or an insurance company. Altogether, regulators located at the Fed, the comptroller, and other federal and state agencies remained ubiquitous and sometimes uncoordinated features of American banking. Authors of the Gramm-Leach-Bliley Financial Services Modernization Act of 1999 needed 79 pages to explain the pending legislation to congressional colleagues and more than 140 pages to lay out the law's complex details.[54]

Lawmakers never intended to make regulations disappear. Financial modernization, as the legislation was labeled, was not about emancipating bankers from rules. At its most basic, leading bankers such as Weill and McColl had joined congressional and White House officials to permit executives like themselves to build still more complex and larger companies. Once in place, those firms' clearly talented leaders would produce valuable products, create sought-after synergies, and launch another round of economic growth both for central cities and throughout the United States. President Clinton, in his signing statement on November 12, spotlighted the road from Gramm-Leach-Bliley to "greater innovation and competition."[55] Such, anyway, ran Clinton's hopeful reasoning, which was commonplace among lawmakers and bankers.

Without doubt, however, Congress and Clinton had restored the commercial bank and commercial bankers to a center place in American financial affairs. "Ten years ago," chief bank lobbyist Edward L. "Ed" Yingling told an interviewer in December 1999, it was not clear "who . . . [was] going to be the big dog in this fight." With Gramm-Leach-Bliley, Yingling boasted, "we basically won it all." Starting in 2000, well-capitalized bankers held the upper hand in buying insurance and securities firms. Congress and the president freed commercial bankers to internalize the activities of financial service firms (like Salomon Smith Barney) that had taken away a big chunk of business in the past half century. During the 1980s and 1990s, interstate banking legislation and key regulatory and court rulings had already cleared the way for bankers to enter formerly closed business fields. Ludwig, Gramm,

Greenspan, and Clinton authorized bankers in the future to move into new types of businesses without first having to seek regulators' approval.[56] Legislators, following Ludwig and Rubin's lead, called this new, flexible type firm a "financial holding company," to distinguish it from the old-fashioned bank holding company.

Markets or economics never preordained the appearance of these financial holding companies on the American scene. President Kennedy and Comptroller Saxon and their successors embarked on a political project aimed at creating a legal space for the development of supermarket banks. Bankers like Wriston, McColl, and Weill joined in their undertaking. Their entire project, with its litigation, debate, and legislative obstructions, required four decades to accomplish. Along the way, presidents and bankers also repositioned the commercial bank to reemerge as a key actor in accelerating the nation's economy. No longer would contemporary bankers and up-to-date regulators have to follow the dust-laden rules created by the decidedly old-fashioned Glass-Steagall Act of 1933. In symbolic fashion, moreover, the bank rules of the last century ended just as the new one began.

Starting in 2000, ordinary Americans heard less about remote topics such as holding companies and bankers who sold insurance and dealt in securities. Those topics largely disappeared from news reports. Instead, in the popular telling, markets, liberated at last from government, would hasten the pace of economic growth. Lawmakers and popular writers even recast the executives who had labored and lobbied to assemble those new banks—Weill, McColl, and the others—as savvy students of the market's sovereign determinations.

At this moment of nonstop market talk, few had reason to doubt that the great banks assembled so recently would continue to pull the nation's economic cart upward. In December 1999, only a few weeks after Clinton signed the Gramm-Leach-Bliley Act, one business writer suggested that economic growth would take place without human intervention. "Technological advance," he announced, "has installed a new set of automatic stabilizers for squeezing inflation out of the system."[57] In truth, regulators and lawmakers had assembled the new bank regime, and they remained important in its every facet.

During 2008 and 2009, the bank-led economy tumbled inward at a frightening pace. Great financial corporations shut their doors and millions of Americans lost their jobs and homes. The American economy had entered a period of "free fall," a distinguished economist later reported.[58] Federal officials such as Treasury Secretary Henry M. Paulson, who had spent his business career as a market celebrant, now injected billions into wobbling banks and insurance firms. At that point, Americans briefly rediscovered their preference for hard links between regulation and bank behavior. No sooner had the economy begun to recover than many of those same lawmakers and journalists returned to a celebration of the canny executives who presided over vast commercial banks. Sounding like their counterparts in the last decades of the twentieth century, those critics asserted that government limited bankers' creativity and the nation's financial growth. Market talk, it seems, pervaded the new century's first decade.

CHAPTER 6

God's Work in Finance: Ken Lewis, Charles Prince, Richard Fuld, and Henry Paulson

On May 3, 2000, Bank of America's Kenneth D. "Ken" Lewis spoke to members of the Greater Miami Chamber of Commerce. Lewis, long a visible member of Hugh McColl's senior executive team, had made countless speeches to business groups. Yet, the timing of this address was special in two respects. First, in April 1998, a few days after Sandy Weill and John Reed announced creation of Citigroup, McColl's NationsBank purchased San Francisco's mammoth BankAmerica. McColl moved the merged bank's headquarters to Charlotte and renamed the combined entity Bank of America. And second, late in 1999, Congress and President Clinton had approved the Gramm-Leach-Bliley Act. And now Lewis was Bank of America's president and chief operating officer. McColl, the former marine and the key person guiding the bank's growth, was scheduled to remain as CEO only a short time longer.

Members of Lewis's business audience would naturally want to know how the top officer at one of the nation's largest banks planned to integrate insurance, investment banking, securities sales, and plain-vanilla banking, such as taking deposits and approving loans. Lewis's speech and conversations before and after provided an opportunity for local bankers and business executives to evaluate the new top executive's leadership. Chamber members sought an insider's look at how Lewis's plans for the bank's development intersected with their firms' prospects and with their ambitions for regional and national economic vitality at the century's start.

Lewis offered no such big picture of the bank and the national economy. Instead, he turned audience members' attention to the bank's financial strength and to his employee's ability to service millions of customers, as they had before. Bank of America earned an $8.2 billion profit in 1999, he reported. That week, moreover, bank employees started to install new signs and a jazzy logo in their far-flung offices. The bank would continue to offer "convenience and service . . . 24 hours a day." As well, Lewis reminded audience members, Bank of America's 156,000 employees still took deposits, cleared checks, serviced online accounts, and wrote loans for schools, bridges, and factories. In the language of American business officials at the century's start, Lewis's "takeaway" points included rapid growth, whopping profits, nationwide operations, and a large staff with the know-how to deal with current business. "In our banking centers and offices," Lewis promised Miami Chamber members, "there will be no disruption of business as you know it." Charlotte's modest North Carolina National Bank, where McColl worked in the early 1960s, was now a nationally recognized brand, and executives had to make the parts mesh. "Where McColl was a builder," a writer for *American Banker* observed in December 2002, Lewis was a "manager . . . and tuner."[1] No one in the audience at that splendid lunch could have doubted Lewis's immersion in McColl's ideas about the importance of servicing clients' needs, avoiding a takeover, and outdistancing the other supermarket banks, such as Citigroup and Wells Fargo.

In the early 2000s, officers at Bank of America's largest competitors placed a similar emphasis on the appointment of new executives, impressive balance sheets, and solidification of customer relationships. After four decades during which bankers and regulators promoted mergers, national branching, and development of supermarket banks, top executives such as Richard M. "Dick" Kovacevich at Wells Fargo & Company marked the decade's first years as a moment of stability. Bankers' efforts to secure access to insurance and securities dealings, led by McColl and Wriston, resided in the past. The days of litigation, endless politicking, and experimentation, it seemed, were over.

Venerated institutions, trusted leaders, and traditional ways of managing banks and the economy remained in the ascendance. Early in the decade, the collapse of the dot-com boom and the September 11 attacks on the World Trade Center fostered a recession. But Alan Greenspan remained as chair of the Federal Reserve's Board of Governors, a post he had held since 1987. As in the past, Greenspan's Federal Reserve lowered interest rates to support prosperity's quick return. Greenspan's hand on interest rates and his demonstrated support over decades for the development of larger, more freewheeling banks suggested that the return of solid growth could not be far off.

The divided regulatory scheme that Congress brought forward into the twenty-first century added another predictable element. Regulation at the hands of the Fed's Greenspan, the FDIC, and the comptroller of the currency represented a system bankers had known for decades. During these years, Comptroller John D. Hawke, Jr., stood at the side of bankers to defend their hard-fought gains. Hawke, a Clinton appointee and an attorney with decades of practical experience in the realm of bank regulation, went to court to pre-empt state insurance commissioners and agitated insurance agents who still sought to limit bankers' access to the insurance business.[2] All in all, the legal landscape, confusing to outsiders, extended familiar bank regulation methods. And protective federal officials continued to hover nearby.

As yet another measure of continuity, senior executives at the other large banks also had lengthy and deep connections to Walter Wriston's and Sandy Weill's ideas and practices. Charles O. "Chuck" Prince, heir to the Citigroup empire, had worked with Weill since 1986. "Their friendship is a powerful one," a *New York Times* reporter noted in July 2003. Similarly, Wells Fargo's Kovacevich had once served as an executive at Citicorp, where he had an opportunity to observe Wriston's methods at close range. In 1998, Kovacevich, then the president and CEO at Norwest Bank, purchased Wells Fargo & Company. "Is this guy the best banker in America," asked a starstruck business writer. Kovacevich moved Norwest's operations from Minneapolis to San Francisco, Wells Fargo's home base. By 2001, Kovacevich's Wells Fargo, with assets totaling $272 billion, had emerged as the nation's fourth largest bank.[3] Wells Fargo was the West Coast banking powerhouse. And Wells Fargo, like Citigroup and Bank of America, was a nationally recognized brand.

James "Jamie" Dimon represented another highly regarded figure in the constellation of powerful bankers with years of experience. Dimon, who held a Harvard University MBA, had worked side by side with Weill to build Travelers Group. Late in 1998, soon after the Citigroup merger closed, Weill fired Dimon. In 2000, however, Dimon accepted appointment as CEO of Chicago's Bank One. In 2004, executives at New York's JPMorgan Chase purchased Bank One for $58 billion and appointed Dimon to the CEO's post. JPMorgan Chase & Co. was itself a 2000 merger product that included David Rockefeller's fabled Chase Manhattan. The enlarged JPMorgan Chase & Co. now ranked second in assets. Enthusiastic observers described Dimon with terms such as "straight-talking," "demanding," and with "a temper that can flare." Dimon also brought an aggressive side to his dealings. "I hate [our competitors]," Dimon told a gathering of Bank One employees in 2002, "I want them to bleed!" In these pronouncements and in the adulatory accounts that accompanied them, Dimon emerged as an executive focused on reducing expenses and fostering additional cross-selling by better aligning the bank's multiple divisions, such as home mortgages, credit cards, and investment banking.[4] Dimon, like Kovacevich, Prince, and Lewis, had absorbed McColl, Weill, and Wriston's ideas and methods about building and maintaining supermarket banks that conducted business around the world.

Elements of the older order in banking extended in myriad ways into the post Gramm-Leach-Bliley regime. As one example, Dimon and the others inherited massive and prosperous banks. During 2004, Citigroup, Bank of America, JPMorgan Chase, and Wells Fargo reported earnings of $27.6 billion. They owned assets valued at more than $4 trillion and employed 785,000. Citigroup, the largest by far, employed 300,000 stationed around the world. Citigroup was "a $900 billion financial aircraft carrier," a business writer observed in 2001.[5] To be president of any those banks, moreover, was to occupy one of the most visible and admired posts in corporate America.

As before, Dimon, Lewis, and the others were among the brightest and most discussed stars in the American business galaxy, taking the place of Wriston and Regan before them. Reporters wrote about their larger-than-life presence, their relentless focus on financial performance, and their blunt approach to subordinates and even to members of Congress. Still, compared with earlier bank leaders, an observer reported in June 2003, members of a new generation of bank executives, such as Lewis and Dimon, were "more realistic, more hands-on, and more risk-averse."[6]

Mentors such as Weill and McColl had also handed down a few easily grasped ideas to guide members of the next generation of senior officials. Cross-selling products such as mortgages and credit cards was one such idea; and nationwide operations that included small depositors, major corporations, and investment banking was another. In word and deed, moreover, Weill and McColl and other leaders in that earlier generation had instructed senior executives that both their banks' and the nation's economic growth must never be allowed to stand still. Once convinced "that we have arrived," the frank-speaking McColl told an interviewer in 1993, "somebody will take you out."[7] Lewis and Prince in turn were among their mentors' keenest disciples—unwavering loyalty to bosses and unflinching commitment to the growth ethic they espoused were among factors that helped move Prince, Dimon, and Lewis to top posts. Since the 1960s, investors, analysts, and American presidents had preached a similar gospel that centered regulated commercial bankers as key actors in fulfilling national goals of low inflation, high employment, and fast economic growth. Bill Clinton made Hugh McColl "his banker" based upon their shared growth goals.

By word and deed, successive teams of bankers like Hugh McColl and Ken Lewis and regulators such as Eugene Ludwig had built supermarket financial service firms. Up to 2003, for all appearances, American banking resided safely in the hands of disciplined chief executives and seasoned regulators. During 2007–2008, however, the nation's investment banks such as Merrill Lynch and supermarket commercial banks including the massive Citigroup and Bank of America entered a period of financial crisis. And, as it turned out, self-congratulatory bankers and lawmakers were not really practiced in setting upright the out-of-control markets they had made in detail since the 1960s. As one of the great ironies of the American political economy, the vast networks created to disperse financial risk actually concentrated it in fewer hands. Millions of Americans in turn lost their homes and jobs and a place in their communities. In 2003, when Bank of America's Ken Lewis launched another acquisition phase, he thought he was adding to the bank's profitability, extending a protective set of relationships, and reducing his risk exposure.

Another Buyout Craze and Its Benefits

Late in October, Lewis purchased FleetBoston Financial Corporation, New England's largest bank. Lewis paid $48 billion, a 40 percent premium over FleetBoston's share price the day before the deal's announcement. Citigroup and Wells Fargo officials had expressed interest in buying FleetBoston, a fact that no doubt pushed the competitive Lewis to pay such a whopping price. To head off merger opponents (as well as the Boston area's powerful congressman Barney Frank), Lewis promised to lend or invest $750 billion over ten years in modest income housing, including $100 billion in Fleet's home market. Like Weill before him, Lewis acted to preempt opponents who would cite the Community Reinvestment Act as a reason for Federal Reserve officials to deny the merger. When the deal closed, Lewis's Bank of America served 33 million retail customers and another 2.5 million business clients through 5,700 branches located in twenty-nine states. In 1988, McColl had purchased the failing First RepublicBank Corporation, an act that established his NationsBank as a key actor in Texas and national finance. In 2003, Bank of America under Lewis emerged in one swoop as the dominant consumer bank for a large part of wealthy New England. "If you live in New England and winter in Florida," Lewis announced after the merger, "your bank goes with you."[8] McColl could just as well have made similar announcements anytime between 1970 and 1998.

Lewis was one of many bankers who regularly sought to add to their firm's size through large and complex mergers. Between 1990 and 2003, bank executives assembled more than five thousand mergers that included some $4.9 trillion in assets. Those mergers concentrated wealth in fewer banks. By 2003, the four largest banks, including Citigroup and Bank of America, held 25 percent of the nation's bank deposits. In Dallas alone, by June 2004 only two banks, JPMorgan Chase and Bank of America, held 52.6 percent of deposits. Lyndon Johnson's plan to make larger loans available to Texas business executives without requiring them to apply at the big New York or Chicago banks had materialized, but not always in the form of Texas-owned banks directed by local officers. Regardless of ownership or location, Federal Reserve officials invented a new term for these giant banks, describing them as "large complex banking organizations." In contrast, 4,390 banks owned 3 percent of domestic deposits in 2003.[9]

Scale created advantages. With their national presence and vast holdings, Lewis and the others who presided over these supermarket banks heightened their brand's visibility and brought in additional customers for cross-selling products like insurance, stocks, mutual funds, and credit cards. When Lewis and other CEOs purchased a bank, they also added low-cost savings and checking funds to their deposit base.

Size also conferred less visible benefits. Large banks were more difficult for competitors to buy. Big banks protected top executives' jobs against predators, whether McColl in one generation or Lewis in the next. Again, McColl and Weill had driven these points home to their executives for decades. Lewis and the other largest bankers simply carried them into the next decade at a higher level of size and concentration. A global scale of operations protected top executives' jobs in the same way that scale seemingly produced fundamentally stable banking organizations. "The perception" among bankers, a financial writer reported in June 2003, "is that in rough seas an oil tanker is safer than a fishing boat."[10] Federal Reserve officials, describing Wriston's similar behavior decades before, had made nearly identical observations about how size anchored CEOs in the executive suite.

Vast assets and worldwide operations also permitted bankers to go head to head with less-regulated financial service firms and come out ahead. During 2003–2004, for instance, executives at Wachovia Corporation, a large Charlotte bank with which McColl had competed for regional supremacy, took the lead from GMAC Commercial Mortgage Corporation in acquiring the right to service business mortgages. Basically, local banks originated mortgages on commercial buildings. In this instance, those originators sold twenty-seven loan packages (each stuffed with individual mortgages) to Wachovia for $25.6 billion. In turn, Wachovia officials assembled a large staff to handle the incoming payments. Wells Fargo and Bank of America had also emerged as major actors in the commercial loan-servicing field, finishing the year among the top five.[11] An obvious hype surrounded these rankings. Nevertheless, those fleeting reports highlighted Prince and Lewis's ability to marshal personnel and resources in a search for domestic and worldwide business that only the largest banks could handle. At one time, bankers at GMAC and Lehman Brothers (a large New York investment bank), not subject to the comptroller's stringent regulations, took that business for granted. Saxon, McColl, and Wriston had worked for decades to bring large commercial banks into existence and secure their place in line for national and worldwide servicing contracts.

Size bestowed yet another edge in the race for growth with stability. In 1984, FDIC officials had rescued the failing Continental Illinois National Bank's uninsured creditors and largest (and uninsured) depositors.[12] That rescue created an implicit guarantee far into the future. Federal officials would never permit a big bank to fail, all seemed to agree, although no one could point to a written policy that made such a guarantee a matter of public policy and public record. Observers and officials described that implicit guarantee with the term "too big to fail" (TBTF), which (in later years) extended to the bank's nonbank subsidiaries, such as its insurance firm, securities dealings, and mutual funds. By the 1990s, McColl and then Lewis and other large bankers, holding that vague TBTF guarantee in their pockets, paid lower rates of interest on borrowed money. More than smaller bank leaders, Lewis, as well as his largest competitors, possessed the ability to finance subsidiaries, write loans at lower rates, and earn higher profits on a wider spread. Decades earlier, Citicorp's Wriston had demonstrated the advantages of size and sharp lawyering. Starting in 2000, Lewis and Prince, blessed with a large asset base and a strong legal position, added to the financial and institutional inheritance that founders had left behind. Federal rules helped make credit cards another safe growth opportunity.

How Did Ken Lewis Transform Debt into a Dividend-Paying Security?

On June 30, 2005, Lewis announced an agreement to purchase MBNA, a major credit card firm located in Wilmington, Delaware. Lewis paid $35 billion, a 30 percent premium over the firm's stock market valuation. Days earlier, executives at Wachovia Corporation had rejected a deal to purchase MBNA. They cited MBNA's sky-high asking price. In October 2003, Lewis had paid a hefty premium to purchase FleetBoston. By mid-2005 that merger had helped boost Bank of America's stock by 7.8 percent compared to 2.5 percent for other banks, confounding critics. "Sure it [others' criticism] gives you a bit of a chip on the shoulder," Lewis announced that day, "but it also makes you want to prove you can do it to them one more time."[13] Lewis did not curse in public, but he brought McColl's competitive, thumb-in-the-eye style to his undertakings.

Lewis and his top officials still had to judge that buying MBNA made financial, strategic, and regulatory sense. Thanks to McColl, Bank of America was already a large credit card issuer. With MBNA's addition, Lewis's Bank of America managed $143 billion in outstanding credit card debt for 132 million customers in the United States, Canada, and Europe. MBNA in fact handled Wachovia's credit card business, but with the expiration of that contract, Lewis would own those accounts. Like McColl, Lewis had bested Wachovia executives once again. The timing looked right as well. Dimon at JPMorgan was still occupied with the details of the Bank One merger; and Federal Reserve officials had warned Citigroup's Prince against large acquisitions until his executives tightened their internal control system. Shifting from his pugnacious style to standard business talk, Lewis highlighted "size and scale" and, another favored term, "distribution and marketing efficiencies" to explain the MBNA purchase.[14]

Lewis's MBNA purchase fit with a larger strategy that was less visible to observers focused on quarterly profits and daily stock price gyrations. Credit card companies like MBNA and Bank of America did not simply extend credit and collect customers' payments, including interest charges. That model was increasingly out of fashion. Instead, bankers channeled cardholders' payments into asset-backed securities, which they sold to investors who liked the promise of a steady, safe, predictable income stream. Bankers and other financial industry leaders described this process of converting cardholders' debt to bonds as securitization.

Securitization offered special advantages to bankers like Lewis. When bankers approved conventional loans, they had to worry daily about Federal Reserve and other rules that required them to maintain cash reserves on hand in case customers failed to make payments. Money held in reserve was and remained money for which bankers paid interest and yet could not earn a return. Walter Wriston had complained regularly about the seemingly high reserve levels his Citicorp had to maintain against outstanding loans. Securitization solved the reserve problem. Securitization permitted bankers like Lewis to "offload credit [card] risk to some third party," a business writer explained in 2002. In the process of securitizing credit card debt, that same writer explained, bankers "transformed a traditional loan into . . . [a] type of security."[15] With credit card debt now safely removed from their books, bankers no longer had to hold cash reserves in the event cardholders failed to make monthly payments. Massive nonpayment caused by a recession would become a problem for securities' owners, not the bank. Securitization, understood in this way, offered a safe and profitable work-around to the government's reserve rules. And securitization, by eliminating the requirement to hold bad debt reserves, also freed bankers to make additional credit card and other loans, creating a virtuous cycle of fresh debt and economic growth. Securitization offered a larger financial and political payoff. In earlier years, bankers like McColl and Wriston had clamored for the right to grab a much larger part of the business from dominant investment banks like Merrill Lynch and Lehman Brothers. Securitization allowed commercial bankers to emerge as investment bankers, fulfilling ambitions decades in the making.

Rules for Commercial Bankers as Investment Bankers

Ken Lewis's newfound success in securitizing debt and outdistancing formidable investment bankers at Merrill Lynch rested on changes in federal bank rules and bank legislation long in the making. Beginning in 1970 and extending through the early 2000s, regulators and lawmakers began a process of writing rules and legislation that helped widen, deepen, and legitimate the securitization field. In February 1970, leaders at two government-owned corporations made their first mortgage purchases and quickly used them as backing for new securities. The business grew rapidly but still needed additional federal assistance. In 1984, members of Congress and President Reagan preempted state legislation that had blocked banks from purchasing asset-backed securities. At that point, bankers had created $10 billion worth of these new kinds of securities. In 1985, the comptroller determined that bankers could cut up loan pools and sell them. In later years, angry securities dealers lost their lawsuit and their Supreme Court appeal. Securitization was "the hot new game in creative financing," an investment banker reported in mid-1985. As part of the S&L cleanup that extended into the early 1990s, officials at the federal government's Resolution Trust Corporation securitized more than $40 billion in good and bad loans.[16] In each of these undertakings, government action helped clear the regulatory and logistical paths toward larger and more frequent securitized offerings.

By the late 1990s, these government-led experiments had accelerated the arrival of a growing securitization field. Between January and June 1999, executives at Citigroup assembled seventy-seven issues of securitized debt totaling $21.14 billion. To achieve those remarkable figures, the highest in the industry, Citi officials prepared and sold more than twelve issues each month. Most Americans had not heard of these exotic financial instruments. Yet, members of the financial press were already filing stories about the fast growth of securitized issues and about American and European bankers' desire to accelerate that growth's pace.[17]

McColl and others had led their firms into securitization issues during this period of experimentation. By the late 1990s, building on their successes, top bankers like Prince, Weill, and Lewis redirected operations and funds to make securitizations a major part of bank operations. During the crucial period of 1999–2002, federal officials supplied three additional legal, legislative, and regulatory supports that were prerequisite to making securitized products easy to produce and safe from legal and political attacks.

First, most of the remarkable and lucrative growth in securitized issues took place inside banks' operating subsidiaries. Here is where the first piece of federal assistance made it easier for bankers to develop securitized issues. Late in 1999, as part of negotiations leading up to Gramm-Leach-Bliley, Clinton's top financial appointees—Rubin, Comptroller Hawke, and again Summers—stood firmly on the side of permitting bankers to move deals rapidly and perhaps innovatively among their many subsidiaries. Simple sounding,

Clinton's officials acted to put the comptroller, the president's appointee, in the key position to regulate banks' subsidiaries and perhaps write additional rules to keep the securitization gas pedal pressed on economic growth. The version of bankers' autonomy that Comptrollers Ludwig and Hawke had promulgated was not a matter of abandoning rules in favor of unregulated markets. On the contrary, Ludwig and Hawke had prepared a calculated and calibrated policy aimed at structuring bankers' expanded dealings in a way that fostered the production of a larger number of innovative products like asset-backed securities and a faster-paced economic growth.[18]

Less visible but equally important in protecting bank-issued securitizations, Comptroller Hawke also joined a lawsuit to prevent state bank officials from regulating bank subsidiaries. That lawsuit helped bring about a second government-inspired development that added certainty to bankers' securitization plans. Wells Fargo's Kovacevich played a key role in this unfolding drama. Wells Fargo owned Wells Fargo Home Mortgage, Inc., which held a California charter to originate home mortgages. In 2002, the state's commissioner of corporations asserted his authority to audit the home lending company's books. In particular, the commissioner sought to force the home mortgage firm to refund higher-than-permitted daily interest charges. Wells Fargo's attorneys predicated a defense on their mortgage company's status as a national bank subsidiary, subject only to the comptroller's authority. Comptroller Hawke's attorneys filed a brief to support Wells Fargo, contending that the comptroller was entitled to authorize every activity "incidental" to banking. Following state administrative hearings, however, the California commissioner stripped Wells Fargo Home Mortgage of its licenses. In May 2003, the United States District Court for the Eastern District of California determined that the comptroller possessed the right to preempt state law on behalf of a national bank's operating subsidiaries. In legal language, the judge prohibited the California corporation commissioner from exercising visitorial power. Starting in mid-2003, bankers like Kovacevich no longer had to deal with up to fifty state regulators and their conflicting rules aimed at protecting consumers.[19] The net result for Kovacevich and for every other Financial Holding Company executive was to facilitate the production of uniform, marketable, nationwide securitizations starting with mortgages in a protected bank subsidiary.

Federal Reserve chair Greenspan brought a third dimension to the legal foundations on which bankers' vastly enhanced securitization efforts rested. Greenspan never took a hand in assisting bankers to put the final trimmings on a securitization issue. Instead, during the late 1990s, before Congress enacted Gramm-Leach-Bliley, Greenspan had worried about losing the securitization field to less-regulated European bankers. Greenspan also liked the idea that securitization issues helped move debt off of banks' balance sheets. Securitization, according to Greenspan, was valuable for banks and beneficial to the nation's economic growth as a whole. In particular, Greenspan's approval of securitization issues meant that bankers like Weill, Prince, Kovacevich, and Dimon would not have to worry about adverse rules suddenly emanating from the Federal Reserve. By March 2000, in fact, Federal Reserve officials had approved the applications of 117 banks to reorganize as financial holding companies.[20] With that designation, Fed officials put the final touches on a process Comptroller Ludwig had initiated in 1995. Starting immediately, officers at each bank, including Lewis at Bank of America and Weill and Prince at Citigroup, held the authority to conduct their securities operations through their banks' direct subsidiaries—quickly, subject only to the comptroller's general oversight, and, in many cases, off the banks' balance sheets. Since the 1960s, judges and regulators like Saxon, Ludwig, Greenspan, and Hawke had played a large role in permitting staid bankers to emerge as celebrated executives of supermarket banks.

One more judgment, about risk, surrounded the momentous decision to legitimate bankers' securitization programs. Risk was inherent in any bank product, as every banker and regulator had always known. Greenspan, Gramm, and Summers had nonetheless concluded that bankers' conversion of debt to asset-backed securities would also move risk off of banks' balance sheets—and into the hands of traders and investors who sought it out. In 1998, the authors of a report prepared for senior treasury officials put the matter of balancing risk with the potential for accelerated growth in simple terms. In the "mercurial financial world now emerging," they contended, regulators needed to "focus less on preventing mishaps and more on ensuring that an accident at any one intersection will not paralyze traffic everywhere else." In other words, lawmakers and regulators had to expect occasional accidents, such as Long-Term Capital Management's implosion in 1998. But surely, Summers, Hawke, and others who worked on the matter for President Clinton agreed, few would opt to shut down all traffic to prevent infrequent smashups. Starting in 2001, with policy issues resolved and with Rubin's version of the nation's financial architecture solidly in place, bankers could get about the business of converting debt into securities in a way that was safe, profitable, and massive in scale.[21] And, with the computer boom ending and a recession already bringing layoffs and losses, complex financial products such as securitization issues looked like one of the next big things to which to hitch national economic growth.

Former senator Phil Gramm added a final invocation about securitization issues that made them appear almost risk free. In 2004, with the securitization boom solidly under way, Gramm (then an investment firm vice president) told securities traders in Chicago that they were doing "God's work."[22] In 1999, Gramm had exhibited considerable nuance in meetings with congressional colleagues leading up to Gramm-Leach-Bliley's approval. In 2004, however, his public lauding of unhampered markets and the men and women who made them work was among his characteristically inflated public utterances. In this way, Gramm added one more reason for ordinary Americans to think that markets produced results in a way that any earthly or heavenly God would have directed. In more prosaic fashion, a pickup in housing sales also encouraged the securitization of subprime mortgages.

Subprime Mortgages

Starting in the early 2000s, Citigroup's Chuck Prince and heads of other big banks looked to augment their securitization business by writing and packaging a larger number of mortgages for low-income householders. Bankers designated those mortgages "subprime." In earlier years, firms with names such as the Money Store originated (wrote) these subprime mortgages. Bankers, for their part, supplied credit lines to the Money Store and other subprime originators. By the late 1990s, however, bankers across the country began to look at subprime as a new profit center. In 1998, executives at First Union purchased the Money Store for $2.1 billion in stock. Chase Manhattan executives had equally large plans. Bankers possessed far larger resources than firms like the Money Store; and bankers were also in a better position to siphon up large numbers of mortgages and then package them for resale.[23] Like the way massive big-city banks were often able to siphon business from their small-town colleagues, big bankers like Weill were in a position to overrun undercapitalized firms such as the Money Store.

Subprime loans also presented a new set of challenges to the banking community. Bankers had decades of experience writing business loans and handling checking and savings accounts for higher-income households.

Bankers described wealthier account holders as customers and clients. Those same bankers lacked a word or phrase to describe subprime borrowers.

Subprime borrowers brought new, unfamiliar, and even uncomfortable characteristics to the mortgage application process. They resided in low-income neighborhoods composed of recent immigrants and persons of color. Spanish was often their first language, especially in parts of Florida, Texas, Arizona, and California, but subprime neighborhoods existed in every urbanized area. The American city was white on the outside and brown and black in the center, and a large number of subprime borrowers resided in the brown and black parts. Chuck Prince and his well-paid executives knew those neighborhoods as names on interstate highway exits and as stops on commuter lines. If subprime borrowers worked at banks, they flashed a badge in front of a security guard and entered through side doors and loading docks, more likely at night. Even as daytime employees, subprime borrowers—as low-level clerks or with first names sewn on building maintenance uniforms—remained invisible to handsomely attired office staff and top-floor executives. In April 2003, a U.S.-based writer for London's *Financial Times* characterized subprime borrowers as "untouchables."[24]

Race and space were not the only factors that set subprime borrowers apart from bankers. Subprime customers had poor credit scores and often lacked access to savings and checking accounts; subprime borrowers were, as the polite, official phrase went, unbanked. Lenders, to be sure, assumed extra risk in making a subprime loan for a property located in a central city neighborhood. Those same subprime borrowers, however, lacked knowledge about how to shop around for a better price, which left them vulnerable to predatory sales personnel. Subprime borrowers could not muster negotiating power. They accepted lenders' offers or went without. Unlucky subprime borrowers became victims. In 1998, as bankers shifted their attention to subprime loans, Comptroller Hawke warned them not to adopt the "predatory" sales practices that had tarnished reputations among first generation subprime lenders like the Money Store. Despite the comptroller's stern warning, homebuyers unable to document a job proved especially attractive targets for a subprime mortgage that could be securitized.[25]

President Bush added his support for homeownership among the nation's lower-income citizens. On June 17, 2002, Bush spoke at the St. Paul African Methodist Episcopal Church in Atlanta. "Too many minorities do not own a home," Bush told audience members, and in this decade "we must increase minority home owners by at least 5.5 million"[26] Bush, to be certain, never endorsed subprime mortgages or predatory loan making. Nor is there evidence that African Americans or anyone else purchased a home based on the president's urging.

Without doubt, however, bankers paid close attention to Bush's admonitions and policy prescriptions. On October 15, Bush hosted a White House conference on minority homeownership, where he urged real estate and financial executives to accept "America's homeownership challenge." That challenge included creation of new types of mortgages suited to persons without first-tier credit ratings and lacking conventional down payments. Homeownership, according to Bush, benefited buyers and the economy. On December 16, 2003, Bush signed the American Dream Downpayment Act, in which congressional authors focused on assisting the first-time homebuyer. Like his predecessors, Bush served as "consumer in chief," the nation's cheerleader for the idea and supporting legislation that patriotic Americans best assisted their nation through increased spending and borrowing.[27] Every president since the 1930s had taken up the idea that increased spending helped the economy. In this instance, Bush neatly blended calls for homeownership and bank production of new financial products, with both aimed at fostering a more inclusive form of speeded-up economic growth.

Even before Bush signed this legislation, heads of the nation's largest banks had experience in assembling and selling subprime mortgages. "We believe that low income borrowers are going to be our leading customers in the next millennium," explained a bank executive in November 1998. Bankers described the process of originating and securitizing mortgages as "residential production," borrowing a phrase from the more concrete business of buying vast tracts of land and building hundreds or even thousands of homes. By whatever term, residential production was growing rapidly, jumping from $288 billion during July–September 2000 to $513 billion during that same period in 2001.[28] Leading bankers wanted to increase their share of this lucrative action.

No two bankers possessed more experience in assembling subprime mortgages than Sandy Weill and Chuck Prince, Weill's long-term employee and ultimately his successor. The Travelers-Citi merger that created Citigroup included Weill's Commercial Credit Corporation, a Baltimore firm that had long made loans to low-income Americans. By late 1998, Commercial

Credit was already the nation's tenth largest subprime originator. But Weill intended to dominate every sector in which he was active. In April 1999, he purchased Source One Mortgage, housed in Farmington, Michigan. In 1998, Source One operated 160 sales offices staffed by three hundred brokers and two hundred correspondents. During 1998, they originated $10.8 billion in subprime mortgages. Volume was important in taking the lead in securitizing mortgages. The Source One purchase "will boost Citi's residential production," observed a writer for *Origination News*.[29]

Those acquisitions failed to satisfy Weill's appetite for subprime growth. In 1999, he paid $31 billion to buy Texas-based Associates First Capital and merge it with his Commercial Credit. He renamed the combined firm Citi-Financial, with headquarters in Baltimore, where employees managed 1,800 offices in forty-five states. The Associates purchase added 700,000 accounts in Western Europe and thousands more in the United States and Japan. Citi-Financial staff continued to write loans and subprime mortgages for those same lower-income buyers. Citigroup was "poised to dominate subprime," announced a business writer in September 2000.[30] Whether it was Wriston's expansion plans in the 1970s or Weill and Prince's big merger in 1998, Citi's subprime surge rested on an immense asset base, the presence of disciplined and experienced managers, a supportive regulatory regime, and a far-flung network that met or exceeded competitors' production. Weill and Prince's subprime network posed a challenge to any banker. But Kovacevich at Wells Fargo still challenged for a bigger cut of the fast-growing subprime business.

In 2002, Kovacevich's Wells Fargo was already large in assets and global in reach. Still, Kovacevich had his work cut out for him to keep pace with Weill and Prince's mortgage development and processing machinery. Like Weill, Kovacevich had to identify mortgage customers. Top bankers did not make cold calls to residents located in distant and unfamiliar neighborhoods. Instead, they followed Weill's path, purchasing companies that specialized in subprime originations and securitizations. At the next stage, Kovacevich built networks staffed by savvy sales personnel who initiated mortgages and traders who moved securitized mortgages off the books. Bankers often described those networks as "strategic relationships."[31]

Kovacevich enjoyed a head start in building those relationships. In December 2001, his Wells Fargo Home Mortgage already ranked number one in mortgage originations. Kovacevich's market share was 9.47 percent, outpacing Chase Manhattan's 8.89 percent. At that point, however, Kovacevich sold few subprime mortgages. In January 2002, Kovacevich purchased GE Capital Mortgage Services, assuring a large and steady stream of revenue for handling monthly mortgage payments. Kovacevich, as the servicer, did not own the mortgage-backed securities or the mortgages dedicated to their payment. Kovacevich, however, wrote so many standard mortgages that officials at Freddie Mac, a private firm that held a federal charter to foster home owner-ship, guaranteed to buy those mortgages or provide credit guarantees for them. Freddie Mac's officers could not take the chance that Kovacevich might shop around.[32]

Kovacevich's senior executives accelerated their lending among Hispan-ics, African Americans, and Native Americans. The totals still were not large—they counted in the millions of dollars at a corporation that tallied its mortgages in the billions. Yet, in November 2002, a Wells Fargo regional president described the loans as part of the corporation's mission. "The power of home ownership is the secret to building wealth," the regional president added, following up on one of Bush's assertions in his Atlanta speech and at the White House conference earlier in the year. During the last quarter of 2002, Kovacevich's subprime originations surged 286 percent over the com-parable period in 2001. Subprime loan numbers, a writer for *National Mort-gage News* reported, were "going through the roof."[33]

Part of that increased subprime volume perhaps rested on Kovacevich's regular exhortations to employees to cross-sell products such as credit cards and insurance. In earlier years, Sandy Weill assembled Travelers and Citigroup around the idea of cross-selling financial products. But subprime customers were not often on the lookout for insurance or other bank prod-ucts such as new car loans and home equity lines of credit; and many or most would not have qualified for any of those items. To motivate employees to sell additional financial products, including subprime mortgages, Ko-vacevich and his top executives staged performances where they sang and danced. They made "fools of themselves—to the delight of the tellers and loan officers in the audience," a writer for *American Banker* reported in December 2003. The so-called "method to the madness" was to "recognize employees, make them feel special—and they'd go home fanatics." Those shows composed a key part of Kovacevich's emphasis on building strong relationships among employees. In spring 2004, Wells Fargo remained the nation's largest mortgage lender; and Kovacevich's subprime unit had climbed into the top ten.[34] Falling house prices and a resulting downturn in the value of mortgage-backed securities quickly brought these boom days to a close.

Bank Runs and the Financial Crisis

The financial decline started in low-income neighborhoods, miles from Kovacevich's and Prince's elegant headquarters in San Francisco and New York City. On clear days, executives and staff located on higher floors could see those areas in the distance. In 2005 and 2006, many of the home-owners in those modest neighborhoods, including postal workers and teachers, discovered they could not pay the stepped up interest rates (as high as 11 to 15 percent) built into their adjustable rate mortgages. Soon after, home prices fell among members of groups suffering the first wave of eco-nomic dislocations such as black and Hispanic householders, persons under thirty-five years of age, and among low-wage employees. A large number of those householders stopped making payments; bankers in turn put their homes in foreclosure. Late in 2006, more than 13 percent of subprime mort-gage holders were delinquent on their payments. The default rate in neigh-borhoods featuring a large number of subprime mortgages was three times that of areas in the same city where homeowners had been able to secure standard mortgages.[35]

The crisis that lower-income Americans were experiencing in mid-decade soon made its way around the country. Between 2005 and 2010, home prices fell in every region, a situation that had not taken place since the Depression era. Home prices and the value of securitized investments moved rapidly downward as one. And yet, the system of originating mortgages and selling them off in the form of mortgage-backed securities at firms like Prince's CitiFinancial depended both on further increases in home prices and on confidence that those homebuyers would send in their monthly payments. Americans who took out those mortgages as well as the more knowledgeable investors (including top bankers) who purchased mortgage-backed securi-ties had actually bought "a modern form of snake oil," two economists determined in 2009.[36]

Prince's Citigroup was among the first of the large banks to experience the changed valuations attached to subprime. By mid-2007, his $2.3 trillion firm was in deep financial and regulatory trouble. "No one wanted anything to do with securitization," two business writers later reported. Citi's deterio-rating financial situation forced Prince and his top officials to take emer-gency measures. As a start, they brought $49 billion (eventually $58 billion) worth of investments back onto Citi's balance sheet.[37]

The return of those investments to Citi's balance sheet highlighted one of the mistaken assumptions that had bolstered mortgage securitization in the first place. For years, bankers and regulators had extolled the value of complex financial instruments to rid their balance sheet of risky loans and the reserves they were required in the event of default. By reducing the need to hold reserve funds, bankers made more money available to write loans, create another round of securitizations, and boost earnings. By this reasoning, securitization would also disperse risk away from banks and into the hands of those who chose to own it. As a matter of fact, however, Prince's Citigroup and other banks ended up holding part of those debts on their books. In the stylized language prevalent in 2008 and 2009, Prince retained many of the financial hot potatoes rather than selling them to the next greater fool. By December, the return of those billions to the bal-ance sheet reduced Citi's capital reserves. To add to the troubling news, Citi officials wrote off additional asset-backed securities, producing a fourth quarter loss of $9.83 billion and the termination of another 4,000 employees on top of the 17,000-person reduction announced earlier in the year. On Sunday, November 4, Prince resigned from Citigroup. Prince had "decided to jump before he was pushed," a business writer observed the next day.[38] Prince's sudden resignation and Citigroup's losses contributed to the fast-spreading conviction among bankers and many other Americans that Main Street businesses as well as the nation's great financial corporations were in trouble.

Bad news kept coming. In March 2008, Federal Reserve and treasury officials urged JPMorgan Chase's Jamie Dimon to purchase Bear Stearns, a large and now faltering investment-banking house whose leaders had plunged deeply into mortgage-backed securities. To finance these dealings, Bear's ex-ecutives borrowed short term, sometimes overnight, at a leverage ratio of ap-proximately $29 in loans to $1 in the firm's capital. Each day, Bear's leaders borrowed another $29 to repay yesterday's loans for a total of about $50 billion always turning over. By 2007, according to one estimate, short-term lending among investment and commercial banks overall was worth about $10 tril-lion. This massive system of short-term borrowing posed no apparent prob-lem, as long as the value of securities containing subprime mortgages used for

collateral held up. Bear's lucrative business model was actually normal practice among investment bankers. By March, however, Bear Stearns creditors
demanded instant repayment on those overnight loans, setting up a run on
the bank. Bear's president described "continued liquidity demands that would
outstrip our resources." Dimon and Bear Stearns's officers assembled the
buyout over a weekend in order to head off a greater panic when Asian markets opened Monday.[39] Dimon also emerged as the banker federal officials
turned to in a pinch. In a similar way, the FDIC's Bill Seidman had worked
with Hugh McColl to unload a troubled Texas bank in 1988.

Bear's demise was part of a much larger downturn just then coming into
partial view. In August 2007, months before the Bear Stearns crisis, leaders
of the French bank BNP Paribas suspended withdrawals from several of
their money market funds. Heads of other money market funds, fearing the
onset of large withdrawals, shifted to short-term investments, putting pressure on firms to whom they loaned funds. The first stages of a run emerged
at investment banks that worked with a business model like Bear's that
stressed overnight loans at leverage ratios of $29 to $1 and higher. The bank
run then moved outward from there, likely into additional money market
funds, to dealers in corporate short-term debt, and to Bank of America,
Merrill Lynch, and Citigroup's subprime and overnight operations—and, of
course, to Bear Stearns. All of a sudden, traders who conducted business
with regulated bankers like Prince and less regulated bankers like those at
Bear Stearns feared ending up as the last fool to hold the hot potato, which
in this case consisted of overnight loans backed by subprime mortgages.
Meanwhile, interest rates for those overnight loans increased rapidly, a sure
sign that bankers were losing trust in the firms and people with whom they
had long conducted business.[40] Despite the presence of well-trained economists and other experts, bankers still relied on an old-fashioned sense of
trust about the people they worked with before making small trades or big
deals.

During the past year, however, Henry M. "Hank" Paulson, the treasury
secretary, and Ben Bernanke, the Federal Reserve chair, had declared the financial crisis contained. Their observations, as it turned out, were wildly
inaccurate, but understandably so. In an old-fashioned bank run, observers
watched as worried customers lined up to demand their savings; but this run,
as one economist reported, "was invisible to almost everyone because it was
a run by banks and firms on other banks." By this reasoning, Paulson and
Bernanke had not misspoken nor were they seeking only to talk down the

crisis.[41] Bernanke and especially Paulson, as qualified as any observers about the way large financial firms borrowed short term to finance securitizations, could not yet identify the degree to which the nation's financial system was both opaque and deeply interconnected. The failure of Bernanke and others to identify and halt the crisis was and remains understandable. But their failure undermined confidence in government nevertheless.

Financial Crisis: The Conventional Way, August and September 2008

Paulson and Bernanke's comments also reminded ordinary Americans that lawmakers and regulators were prepared to bolster banks and seek to prevent a sharp economic downturn—as they had done many times in the past. During August and September, problems with the fast-declining value of securitized mortgages reached Fannie Mae and Freddie Mac, the privately owned firms originally created by federal officials to bolster home sales. In the first months of 2008, Fannie and Freddie officials purchased 80 percent of the mortgages written in the United States. Like their counterparts at Bear Stearns and Citigroup, Fannie and Freddie's executives borrowed short-term to finance their securitizations, often at ratios as high as $75 in borrowed money to $1 in their funds. In doing so, Fannie and Freddie's operations made it possible for Americans to buy houses and fit them out with new furniture and appliances at Sears, Lowe's, and Home Depot. Altogether, Fannie and Freddie's executives played a crucial role in the U.S. economy. By early September, however, Fannie and Freddie had little cash on hand; they had purchased or guaranteed $5.3 trillion in mortgages; and gloomy economic news arrived daily. On September 7, Paulson secured President Bush's permission to place Fannie Mae and Freddie Mac into conservatorship, a fancy word for government management.[42]

Merrill Lynch was next. Merrill was probably the nation's best-known financial services company. In the 1970s, under Donald Regan, Merrill was a supermarket bank before the term was coined. Between 2007 and September 2008, however, Merrill executives reported losses totaling $52 billion. On October, 2007, Merrill's CEO, E. Stanley O'Neal resigned, beating the sudden departure of Citigroup's Prince from the executive suite by a few days.[43]

By mid-September, Bernanke and other federal officials were on the lookout for a deep-pocketed executive to buy Merrill. Bernanke needed to stop the contagion; and Bank of America's Lewis expressed interest in making the purchase. "We'll work with you on capital relief and anything you might need," Bernanke told Lewis by telephone. On September 14, Lewis bought Merrill for $50 billion in stock. Lewis and his team, in their haste, failed to check Merrill's books in detail, and they paid a sizable price for a firm in such precarious straights. On September 15, then, Merrill Lynch at last in hand, Lewis issued a press release that included terms such as "global reach" and "synergy." Lewis "had long craved" Merrill Lynch, Paulson later reported. Lewis, like his mentor McColl, had run large risks (and often relied on government) to make Bank of America one of the nation's largest bank supermarkets. But in this case, the Merrill purchase made Bank of America's deteriorating balance sheet part of a large number of catastrophic developments.[44]

During the weekend of September 12–14, reports about the impending collapse of Lehman Brothers Holdings obscured news about Merrill Lynch, Bank of America, Fannie Mae, and Freddie Mac. Lehman was a large and storied investment bank that was now overexposed to securitized investments that had fallen sharply in value. Richard S. "Dick" Fuld, Jr., Lehman's CEO, and his top officials had been "aggressive even by pre-crisis Wall Street standards," Bernanke later contended. Fuld's nickname was the Gorilla. With Fuld and his lieutenants demanding reports from subordinates that showed improvements every quarter, Lehman's traders sold their securitized debt (credit card and mortgages, for instance) to knowledgeable as well as uninformed investors in the United States and around the world. Again like Bear Stearns, Lehman's transactions depended on funds that banks and securities dealers loaned on an overnight basis. Minute-by-minute news reports of Lehman's problems added to the growing conviction among bankers that the safest course was to pull their cash and lines of credit. The run on Lehman and the firm's impending collapse threatened countless firms and customers who conducted business with one or several of Lehman's clients. Because it was such a confused situation, it was not until later that many financial executives discovered the extent of their connections to Lehman or its subsidiaries. The interconnections were vast, all agreed, but no one could estimate their extent with any precision.[45]

Timothy F. "Tim" Geithner, president of the New York Federal Reserve, took charge of the next stage. To head off Lehman's bankruptcy, Geithner directed top officials of the largest commercial and investment banks to gather at his Lower Manhattan headquarters on Friday, September 12, at

6:00 p.m. Geithner's list included Jamie Dimon, as well as top officials at Citigroup, Goldman Sachs, Morgan Stanley, and BNP Paribas, a major French bank whose problems were first visible more than a year earlier. Those bankers had gathered at the New York Fed, Treasury Secretary Paulson later related, "to save a rival—and their own skins." Paulson along with Christopher C. Cox, chair of the U.S. Securities and Exchange Commission (SEC), joined the meeting, which extended into Sunday. One business writer described the stakes as "sav[ing] Western capitalism from financial catastrophe."[46]

Geithner exhorted bankers to act on the spot. Failure to protect Lehman and, by extension, the many firms that traded securities and made loans to Lehman put the nation's financial system at risk, he contended. Paulson went straight to threats. "This is about our capital markets, our country. We will remember anyone who is not seen as helpful." Most basically, Paulson wanted bankers to pool funds and rescue Lehman, much in the fashion that Greenspan had arranged in 1998 to prevent Long-Term Capital Management's derivatives' excesses from seeping out to banks and the larger economy. Paulson made clear that no federal money was available to rescue Lehman. He did not want the assembled bankers to "think that Good Old Hank would come to the rescue."[47]

Paulson's exhortations and bankers' fear went only so far. Bankers wanted federal guarantees, like those awarded Dimon to purchase Bear Stearns. Paulson refused to offer those guarantees, leaving assembled bankers to face an unknowable level of risk when, at some near date, Lehman's customers would demand payment. Paulson told Bush by telephone that Sunday around 3:30 p.m., "There was just no way to save Lehman." The next day, September 15, Lehman's attorneys filed for bankruptcy, instantly putting 25,000 employees out of work.[48]

The panic Paulson, Bernanke, and Geithner had feared and attempted to avoid was at hand. Two iconic financial names, Lehman and Merrill Lynch, had disappeared in the course of a few days. As news of the failed meeting and Lehman's bankruptcy circulated around the world, the Dow Jones Industrial Average fell 504.48 points, the steepest drop since the September 11 attacks on the World Trade Center. Americans who only watched TV news and read the daily newspaper, as well as bankers and lawmakers, treated the Dow's closing number as an index of the nation's economic well-being. More immediately, those same ordinary Americans were making panic-driven withdrawals from their money market funds. Bankers, including those with plenty of cash in the till, were equally panicked. In turn, they cut off credit to prominent longtime clients. The rush among financial executives at the largest and smallest firms to unwind positions only added to a decline in cash and asset values at closely linked firms, a process several economists colorfully characterized as a "negative vortex."[49]

The imminent bankruptcy of the insurance company American International Group (AIG) added to the terrible news arriving at Paulson's office on a near-hourly basis. AIG insured most of the asset-based securities sold around the world, including many that bankers had retained on their balance sheets. The ability of large and small firms to remain in business and the survival of the financial system as a whole rested on AIG's ability to put up collateral when the asset-based securities they insured fell in value. Paulson found "AIG's incompetence . . . stunning." "This is an economic 9/11," Paulson told staff members gathered in his office. All of a sudden, Paulson reversed direction and stopped talking about private market solutions. On September 16, Bernanke's Federal Reserve Board approved an $85 billion loan to AIG and took a 79.9 percent stake in the company. An administration on record in favor of disentangling government and business now controlled the nation's largest insurance company. The crisis took precedence. Financial problems that began to accumulate a year earlier, Bernanke reported in retrospect, had now mutated "into the worst financial panic in our nation's history."[50] Americans had entered a period of economic dislocation and sharpened politics.

The Troubled Asset Relief Program and a Sharpened Politics of Resentment

To reduce the panic, financial losses, unemployment, and the nasty politics surely ahead, Geithner, Bernanke, and Paulson sought new ideas. Between March and September, they had dealt with problems at Bear Stearns, Lehman, and AIG, to name only a few. No one set of ideas or institutions or ideas had guided their judgments about how or whether to keep firms alive. "Our constant zigzags looked ridiculous," Geithner observed a few years later. Several Federal Reserve district bank presidents described the AIG rescue as "an inconsistent lurch." During late September, moreover, the nation's financial situation continued to worsen. "The markets are frozen," Dimon told Paulson in a telephone call on September 17.[51]

At this uncertain moment, many lawmakers placed their diminished faith in Paulson and other regulators' ability to stop the downturn. Word that Paulson and Bernanke were scheduled to present a recovery plan to congressional leaders during the evening of September 18, encouraged investors to bid up the Dow Jones average by 108 points. Paulson wanted Congress to create a $700 billion fund to rescue failing banks, either by purchasing their depreciated assets such as those asset-based securities or by injecting funds directly, like the AIG rescue. Paulson and his top aides judged $700 billion a sufficient sum, and less than a trillion, which sounded too high to bring to Congress. His plan also invested substantial authority in the treasury secretary to carry it out, leading *Newsweek* editors to dub him "King Henry."[52]

The plan was simple and, like every important change in bank operations, contrived with politicians in mind.[53] Injecting cash into troubled banks that were interlocked with one another and with the larger economy was a standard practice among bankers and FDIC officials. William Seidman, President Reagan's FDIC chair, had injected cash into troubled banks. And, despite complaints about King Henry, placing administrative responsibility in one person's hands was a regular practice in government and business. To make $700 billion available to assist failed bankers who had brought on the crisis was the political fact that stood out.

Paulson's plan came up short among disgruntled and frightened members of Congress. On September 29, they voted 228–205 to reject his proposal. A few days later, recalcitrant House members reversed course. News of sharp stock market declines and more layoffs put pressure on everyone. So, too, did modest changes in the legislation (called sweeteners) and a warning letter from leaders of the U.S. Chamber of Chamber of Commerce that "Americans will not tolerate those who stood by and let the calamity happen." Chamber of Commerce leaders had routinely espoused private market solutions to America's problems, but now they urged decisive federal action.[54] On October 3, chastened House members voted, 263–171, to fund Paulson's bank restoration program. Two days before, Senate members had voted in favor, 74–25. Within hours, President Bush signed legislation to create the $700 billion Troubled Asset Relief Program (TARP). Journalists quickly identified the fund by its shorter and more memorable acronym.

TARP provided Paulson with funds to recapitalize the nation's banks. Paulson summoned nine leading bankers to the U.S. Treasury. On October 13, in a dramatic meeting, Paulson, Geithner, Bernanke, and Sheila Bair, the FDIC chair, told the assembled bankers that they would each accept a large injection of TARP funds for their banks. The regulators had agreed to place $25 billion each in Citigroup, Wells Fargo, and JPMorgan Chase and another $15 billion in Bank of America. New York Fed officials described Citi and Bank of America as "financial death stars." Paulson had also penciled in Goldman Sachs and Morgan Stanley each for $10 billion plus an additional $10 billion for Merrill Lynch. The two remaining bankers at the meeting received more limited sums, mostly on the grounds that their banks cleared transactions for every other bank, which meant that every banker had to trust them. The assembled bankers only had to sign the forms that regulators had prepared for them. Eventually, 945 financial firms participated in TARP.[55] Supermarket banks were safe again. And, for that moment at least, government authority and prestige were in the ascendance.

Many Americans detested the idea that well-paid bankers who, by common agreement, had fostered the crisis were now at the receiving end of immense government generosity. During the next months, however, federal officials rescued banks and insurance companies of every size. By February 2009, Federal Reserve, Treasury, and FDIC officers had loaned, injected, or promised to guarantee an astonishing $9.7 trillion. The financial system's integration from top to bottom meant that to leave any one firm unprotected would inevitably lead to another series of panicked withdrawals. As a result, federal officials "backstopped" investment bankers, money market funds, Fannie and Freddie, the largest insurance company, commercial banks, and, by extension, every client to whom those firms owed money.[56]

That backstopping was, however, difficult to explain in a few words. The financial crisis lacked historians and a historical narrative that was accessible to citizens. Nor could the story be reduced to a few heroes and a gang of villainous bankers and boodling politicians. The opaque networks among investment banks and their links to commercial bank subsidiaries did not compose a likely made-for-TV program. Instead, the $700 billion TARP fund, easily the most visible part of bank rescue politics, turned into the subject of comment and complaint that continued for years. Ordinary Americans as well as many of their leaders in Congress spoke about TARP as if it represented a fundamental break in American history. Americans had always helped themselves, they repeated again and again, ignoring the federal government's annual subsidies to homeowners, farmers, and motorists, to name only the most obvious recipients. By October, plummeting stock prices and rising unemployment pushed anti-TARP fury to new heights. Where are our bailouts? many who suffered and others who were offended now demanded, and why had the government not provided mortgage assistance to "good people" and to "underdogs" like us? Paulson detested the term "bailout," but it stuck. TARP, an economist later observed, "was wounded on arrival."[57]

In 1999, President Clinton and leading bankers had ushered supermarket banks into existence. By late 2008, the most powerful, successful, and well-funded banks like Citi and Bank of America resided as desiccated wards of government. Their once-celebrated CEOs, including Chuck Prince, had been forced to take early (and extremely comfortable) retirements. "Free market" and other such terms carried a nasty, out-of-fashion ring, at least among academics and those who wrote op-ed pieces for national magazines and newspapers.[58]

Such was the troubled state of the political economy handed off to Barack Obama, the newly elected president, and to Timothy F. Geithner, his treasury secretary. Like every president and treasury secretary, Obama and Geithner accepted their responsibility to restart economic growth; and again like every president and treasury secretary since the 1960s, they put supermarket banks at the center of their plans. Unlike their predecessors, Obama and Geithner would require those supermarket bankers to operate in a more constrained fashion to avoid another financial meltdown.

Opponents were quick to mount a counterattack. In short order, those who were infuriated by TARP, by Geithner and Obama's centralizing plans, and by government's ascendance mounted challenges aimed at retaking the driver's seat. That period of government's authority and prestige in American culture and politics was short-lived. Geithner, the president's chief strategist, enjoyed only a short period in which to work. Geithner had also inherited the politics of delay, litigation, and hard politicking that had characterized bank politics since Saxon's term as comptroller.

CHAPTER 7

Reregulating the Regulators:
Barack Obama and Timothy Geithner

On January 20, 2009, President Barack H. Obama took the oath of office and gave his inaugural address. Obama spoke as unemployment reached 7.5 percent and 4.8 million Americans drew unemployment insurance, the highest number in forty years. The new president launched his term by talking about markets. "The question before us," he said, is not "whether the market is a force for good or ill." Its ability "to generate wealth and expand freedom is unmatched," Obama asserted. Yet "this crisis has reminded us that without a watchful eye, the market can spin out of control."[1] Banks and other parts of the private sector produce wealth, Obama seemed to say. Government's job, in contrast, is to keep those wealth producers honest and also to prevent their avarice and shortsightedness from damaging the economy. In decades past, however, Americans had heard countless assertions about how the unhindered market was certain to foster an accelerating prosperity, if only government bureaucrats abolished legal barriers and permitted that market to come fully into being.

On April 29, the president struck a revised theme at an evening news conference. Obama turned journalists' attention to failing banks and insurance companies. The context for the president's remarks was changed from only two years earlier, when bank executives, including Ken Lewis and Chuck Prince, had lauded their firms as paragons of scrupulous investment analysis and capitalist wealth production. Now, the federal government owned nearly 80 percent of the insurance company American International Group and held preferred shares in Bank of America and Citigroup. Banks, the president argued, had been "over-leveraged" and "outdated regulations . . . [had] allow[ed] recklessness among a few to threaten the prosperity of all."

Still, Obama contended, "I don't want to run banks," and "I want to disabuse people of this notion that somehow we enjoy meddling in the private sector."[2] Like his predecessors in the Oval Office since the 1970s, Obama hearkened to the conventional theme of government as an outside force that hesitantly "intervened" in business affairs when bank executives' misbehavior undermined economic growth.

The policy implications of Obama's inaugural and press conference remarks were purposely ambiguous. The federal government that had framed bank operations in detail, that only recently injected TARP funds into banks, and that now even guaranteed bank debt was to remain out of sight. Government, in Obama's public remarks, would in principle only protect Americans against the market's occasional excesses, akin to a night watch police officer. Obama's cop, in this iteration, did not flush out the robbers gathering in the bushes but instead acted only once the crooks pointed guns at victims. Obama intended his rhetoric of limited government to hold at bay the many who detested the Troubled Asset Relief Program and government financial aid activities of any kind.[3] The president's rhetoric set up political space for his program of stiffer financial service regulation. Obama's cop on the beat, with Congress's approval, would identify financial miscreants as they gathered, planned, and lurked.

Geithner Before the Crisis

Obama's move toward government regulation was under way prior to his inauguration. Early in January 2009, a business writer identified a "shift away from New York's plutocrats and to Washington's politicians."[4] Timothy F. Geithner, Obama's treasury secretary, emerged as the chief actor among those Washington politicians.

Geithner lacked his predecessors' formal credentials. Since 1961, treasury secretaries such as C. Douglas Dillon, Donald T. Regan, Robert E. Rubin, and Henry M. Paulson enjoyed years of experience at top-ranked financial firms, including Merrill Lynch and Goldman Sachs. Lawrence H. Summers, Clinton's treasury secretary after Rubin, never led a financial corporation. Summers, however, held a PhD in economics and served for five years as the World Bank's chief economist. Summers was a professor of economics at Harvard University. Either through advanced college training or years of executive responsibilities at large corporations, treasury secretaries had answers, seemingly at hand, for presidents as they sought to guide the econo-my's future course.

Geithner, in contrast, held a master's degree in international economics and East Asian studies. And he had never led or been employed at a financial corporation of any size. Before 2000, Geithner worked as a civil servant in the Reagan, Bush, and then Clinton Treasury Departments. He described him-self as "a seriously late bloomer." During the Clinton years, Rubin and Sum-mers, having spotted a talented young man still in his thirties, moved Geithner into more responsible posts. Despite his promotion, Geithner never played a top role in the passionate finance-related debates such as those that surrounded interstate banking in 1994 and Gramm-Leach-Bliley in 1999. Geithner had, however, acquired firsthand experience in dealing with parts of the international bank crises of the late 1990s that Summers, Greenspan, and Rubin helped extinguish. Following the Lehman bankruptcy, with many (inaccurately) blaming Gramm-Leach-Bliley's authors for establishing a straight line to the financial crisis, Geithner's lack of involvement with ear-lier legislation proved an advantage in dealing with insistent journalists and clamorous lawmakers.[5]

Starting in 2003, the still youthful-appearing Geithner served as presi-dent of the Federal Reserve Bank of New York. By law and custom, New York Fed presidents carried more prestige, visibility, and clout than their counter-parts at the other eleven district banks. Geithner was no exception. Most of the largest commercial and investment banks, including Citigroup, JPMor-gan Chase, Lehman Brothers, and Goldman Sachs, remained headquartered in New York City, near Geithner's office. Key bankers, including Jamie Dimon, served on the New York Fed's board of directors. Geithner described board members as "an elite roster of the local financial establishment." From his lofty position at the New York Fed, Geithner spoke and dined with business journalists and with U.S. and international bank executives and regulators on a daily basis.[6]

Geithner's time as the New York Fed's president and his regular contact with the heads of major banks conferred no special ability to forecast the fi-nancial crisis that began around August 2007. Geithner, like most econo-mists, top bank strategists, financial journalists, and even Bernanke and Paulson, was only partly alert to the piling up of risky securities taking place at Citigroup, AIG, and at Lehman and Bear Stearns. As early as 2004, Geithner had expressed concern about the way modern risk management strategies could also "amplify large moves in asset prices." Yet, Geithner sought not to alarm bankers with scary warnings, he later reported. In spring 2007, as additional bad news about subprime mortgages appeared in print, Geithner told an audience gathered at the Federal Reserve Bank of Richmond that regulators lacked the ability to oversee the buildup of risk outside commercial banks, in places like hedge funds and money market funds. To be fair, the authors of Gramm-Leach-Bliley had not authorized Geithner to rein in Bank of America and Citigroup's risky dealings through their investment bank subsidiaries. Nor for that matter had Congress authorized the New York Fed to moderate the high-stakes borrowing and investing taking place at Bear Stearns, Lehman Brothers, money market funds, and other financial firms that were not also commercial banks.[7]

Still, Geithner learned a great deal during his time at the Treasury and the New York Fed. The economic swings Geithner observed in earlier years encouraged him to draw conclusions about bankers' potentially dangerous practices. Financial executives, he concluded, took on risks without anticipating the consequences of those decisions for the American and worldwide financial systems. Risky strategies set by executives like Chuck Prince at Citigroup and by AIG executives, for example, severely damaged their firms. Dick Fuld's Lehman entered bankruptcy. Prince, Fuld, and those less-visible AIG executives also inflicted great damage on countless Americans' earnings and on distant bankers that extended around the world and endured for years. Geithner (and others) described the resulting contagion as "systemic risk," the risk that one or several deeply linked banks and insurance firms imposed on U.S. and world financial institutions and economies as a whole, as Lehman's and Citi's dealings had done.[8] Geithner's international experience encouraged him to link singular catastrophes into big picture views of the relationship among politics, banks, and the economy.

Geithner, now forty-seven years of age, also brought a valuable set of observations to his early months at the Treasury Department. Obama surely identified Geithner's way of thinking at their first meeting. During 2008's last months, amid TARP's political fireworks and the forced recapitalization of Merrill Lynch, Fannie, Freddie, AIG, and commercial banks such as Citi, Geithner worked with several guiding ideas that partly emancipated him from the day's "push or get pushed" politics. Geithner, for example, determined that leaders in the Obama administration possessed few "good options." In one of Geithner's favored phrases, he and the president would select among "the least-bad ones." Where Geithner encountered obstacles, he laced his conversations with other favored phrases such as "Life is about alternatives."[9] In other words, Geithner's thoughts about the politics of finance sometimes arrived in the form of aphorisms through which he determined a way to clear the path ahead.

Geithner's expressions also had a short, pithy quality that made his thoughts accessible to the president and work associates. "You have been the sort of person anyone would want alongside them in the financial crisis foxhole," Bernanke told Geithner at his going-away dinner from the New York Fed. Few at that dinner likely noticed a subtle difference between Bernanke's and Geithner's method of problem solving. Bernanke, a scholar of the Great Depression and a former college professor, created ideas based on deep study and writing in history and economics. Bernanke's interest in long trends perhaps led him to misjudge the degree to which the American financial system—with its money market funds, asset-backed securities, and short-term, leveraged bank borrowing—had changed since 2000. Geithner's record in predicting the downturn was no better than Bernanke's. Geithner, however, the longtime treasury employee and New York Fed president, rested his judgments on conversations with bankers, on streetwise sensibilities about the way bankers operated, and on a series of ad hoc frameworks that also included "Hope is not a strategy," "Plan beats no plan," and simply, "No fucking way."[10]

Geithner relied on another phrase, the "Old Testament view," to describe the outlooks of many Americans who objected to federal bank rescues starting with Bear Stearns. Those Old Testament thinkers, according to Geithner, sought punishment for bankers who had created the crisis. Old Testament thinkers preferred bankruptcy for those who had failed to run their firms' properly, regardless of economic consequences for the U.S. economy and innocent bystanders. Geithner, however, judged action to keep banks functioning as regrettable but fundamentally necessary for the nation's prosperity. Failure of one or several interconnected banks, Geithner worried, would drag jobs, mortgage-backed securities, money market funds, and retirement accounts over the edge of a sharp and steep precipice. As early as June 2008, Geithner published a five-point program to head off future bank crises. He placed a strong Federal Reserve at the program's center. Geithner also regularly announced the importance of requiring banks and other financial firms to hold additional capital, which he described as "shock absorbers."[11] Geithner did not lack for judgments about his opponents or recommendations to guide bankers and the economy toward safer ways of conducting business.

In January 2009, at his confirmation hearing before members of the Senate Finance Committee, Geithner promised to shape "new rules of the road." With those rules, he intended to remodel the regulatory agencies that had governed banking since 2000. Geithner would not seek to dismantle large banks. Nor would he advocate in favor of government ownership of those big banks, an idea that the briefly radicalized Larry Summers and Alan Greenspan recommended at that time. "The most prudent course is the most forceful course," Geithner informed senators, suggesting his willingness to employ his considerable authority to shape a Federal Reserve–centered regulatory regime equipped to take prompt action when risks accumulated at financial institutions.[12] Geithner (and Obama) emphasized establishment of a regulatory regime that left bank management in private hands and that promoted fast economic recovery led by supermarket banks. Geithner was a natural successor to James Saxon, Don Regan, Gene Ludwig, and Bob Rubin. Geithner also inherited their determination to avoid talking about the federal government's role as a market maker.

History Mattered

Despite Geithner's stated boldness, history played an important part in limiting his freedom of action. No one, it seemed, had produced a widely accepted account of the crisis of 2008. That narrative would have to include an occasional hero like Hank Paulson, a no-nonsense banker and free-market advocate who, after Lehman, turned leader of the government's rescue effort. The author of that same narrative would also foreground long-term trends such as the credit rating firms that awarded AAA ratings to asset-backed securities backed by subprime mortgages, the deep connectedness of shadow and regulated banking, and the deeply fractured nature of bank supervision. The author of this salutary account would also have to take account of invisible factors such as the use of short-term loans at once-great financial houses like Bear Stearns to finance the packaging and sale of asset-backed securities loaded with subprime mortgages. Authors of that missing historical account would have to demonstrate to 2009 lawmakers that Gramm-Leach-Bliley's many innovations had played no direct role in fomenting the many problems confronting national leaders.

Such a historical account, even the most meticulously constructed, would no doubt have encountered tough headwinds in winning converts. Most

Americans as well as many lawmakers failed to understand subprime mortgages and asset-backed securities. Those critics remained adamant in their
conviction that authors of Gramm-Leach-Bliley's many innovations had
committed a grievous act. Less than a decade later, by this reasoning,
Gramm-Leach-Bliley's easy terms for bankers led directly and almost pre-
dictably to the terrible calamity that befell millions of innocent victims in
the United States and around the world.

Curiously, few lawmakers or bankers from the great fights of the 1960s
to the 1990s remained active in policy circles. Longevity, to be sure, did not
equate with wisdom or understanding. Old-timers might have illuminated
trends over time, or, just as easily, those long-serving policy actors might have
chosen to weigh down discussions with dull recitations about how bankers
once operated. Senator Christopher J. "Chris" Dodd, who had worked so
hard up to 1994 to protect Connecticut's insurance companies, was among
the few holdovers. Rep. Barney Frank, who first won election to the House of
Representatives in 1981, was another holdover. In 2009, Frank chaired the
House Financial Services Committee while Dodd chaired the Senate Banking
Committee, both influential posts. Yet, Frank, by his own admission, had
not thought carefully about financial regulation before 2002, when he moved
to a senior position on the Financial Services Committee. Members of a
new generation of bankers and lawmakers were and remained creatures of
history. And yet, this new generation's leaders lacked an informed contact
with the past and a shared narrative about how they had arrived at the crisis
of 2008. They substituted the passions of the day.[13]

Lacking a compelling narrative about bankers and lawmakers, the policy debates Geithner inherited repeated the ritualized and brutalized themes
of the past, even though a new cast of characters was in charge. Key members of this fresh-faced group included the Fed chair Ben Bernanke, FDIC
chair Sheila Bair, treasury secretary Geithner, and key members of Congress
such as Dodd and Frank. Like their predecessors, Bernanke and the others
argued about freighted questions such as which federal bank agency ought
to be anointed the supreme regulator, the appropriateness of "bailing out"
risk-taking bankers, and whether federal officials should authorize bankers
to trade risky products. As before, binary ideas about markets and regulation and of course about the government's size ran through discussions about
methods to prevent another meltdown. Lawmakers readily cited government
regulation, the Federal Reserve, President Obama, and TARP's billions
awarded to failed bankers as reason enough to oppose all or any part of

proposals that Geithner had not yet even offered. History surely never repeated itself, but the crisis of 2008 only heightened the self-seeking, anger,
posturing, and antagonism that had characterized bank politics since the
1960s. Geithner, not much interested in another round of fiery debates—
and often petulant and antagonistic toward those who opposed him and the
president—intended to reorganize bank regulators and impose new rules on
bankers. Had Geithner possessed a history of bank politics since the 1960s,
he might have realized that even the smallest changes came only after acid
debate, extended litigation, and hard arm-twisting in Congress. In March
2009, a *New York Times* writer described the situation in front of Geithner
as "a marathon battle."[14]

New Rules for Regulators

The legislative struggle began in earnest on March 26, with Geithner's testimony before members of the House Committee on Financial Services. "Market discipline failed to constrain dangerous levels of risk-taking throughout
the system," Geithner told committee members. In a similar way, he contended, "supervision and regulations had not constrained the buildup in leverage and risk." During 2007 and 2008, when the crisis appeared in daily
headlines, regulators lacked "good options for managing the failure of . . .
important, large, financial institutions." According to Geithner, advocates of
risk management through market discipline (such as Greenspan) had failed
just as much as Rubin and Summers, who had fashioned the loose-fitting
Gramm-Leach-Bliley legislation in 1999. Undercapitalized bankers, for example, did not comprehend the potential economic damage contained in the
securitized mortgages they sold around the world. Financial services, in
other words, required "new rules of the game."[15] Geithner started with the
rule makers.

One of Geithner's key ideas was to reduce the number of bank regulators
and focus authority in one set of hands. He slated the Federal Reserve to
emerge as the undisputed regulator. In the previous decade, Rubin had described the constellation of regulators as part of the nation's financial architecture. Not even Alan Greenspan, at the peak of his authority and popularity
earlier in the decade, had dared confront the proponents of that multiheaded
financial architecture.[16] To reduce that architecture to a single point, Geithner
headed into a politics that possessed momentum and steadfast defenders.

Several generations of regulators, presidents, and lawmakers starting with Kennedy and Saxon had demonstrated that a quest to remodel that regulatory architecture was to venture toward a dark and deep pit.

For decades, multiple regulators had checked bankers' dealings in a decentralized fashion. Supervision of Bank of America and Citigroup provide a case in point. Under Gramm-Leach-Bliley, the comptroller's examiners oversaw Lewis's and Prince's banking operations and how those banks worked with their investment bank businesses that packaged mortgages. Often at the same moment, employees of the U.S. Securities and Exchange Commission (SEC) reviewed the two banks' securities dealers. Yet, federal law and SEC practice had never directed its supervisory officials to check on the large number of subprime mortgages bundled into asset-backed securities that Citi and other firms assembled daily. Sheila Bair's FDIC officials also reviewed Lewis's and Prince's books but sought to understand their dealings relative to protecting depositors. Meanwhile, Federal Reserve officials supervised the holding companies (like Citigroup, Bank of America, and JPMorgan Chase) that actually owned the operating banks and their many investment bank subsidiaries. According to Geithner, however, bank supervisors including the comptroller, the SEC, and his New York Fed had failed to recognize Citi's "dramatic exposure to an increase in mortgage defaults and even more dramatic declines in the price of mortgage securities."[17]

These confusing supervisory methods composed only one part of a fragmented system. Federal Reserve examiners worked out of the twelve district banks. As a result, examiners at the Richmond Federal Reserve Bank reviewed Bank of America's holding company in Charlotte; and examiners at distant Federal Reserve Banks in San Francisco and New York looked at Wells Fargo's and Citi's holding companies. At any moment, assiduous examiners employed by the Federal Reserve district bank, the FDIC, and the comptroller's office scrutinized Bank of America's multiple dealings, but those examiners had no obligation to work together with a goal of comprehending long-term trends in the banking system and how those trends meshed as a whole in the United States and around the world. Americans learned in 2010 that once in a while even Geithner's New York Fed supervisors had failed to perform every mandated review. Still more, employees at the little-known Office of Thrift Supervision oversaw AIG's fast-growing business of insuring asset-backed securities. That department of AIG operated out of offices in London, England, and Paris, France, creating a geographic barrier that even the most assiduous examiners located in the

United States would have a hard time penetrating. Regardless of the regulatory agency, bank examiners, with Congress's approval, worked at cross-purposes. They permitted large gaps in coverage to mature; and, they failed to communicate findings to each other. All in all, no one person or agency was in charge of bank supervision; and, as a result, no person or agency, including the treasury secretary and the Federal Reserve chair, possessed the capacity to produce a big picture view of American finance.[18] No larger gap in regulation existed than the one that separated regulated commercial banks and many other financial businesses like hedge funds that resided almost entirely outside of anyone's sight or reach.

Decades earlier, Citi's Wriston had made an identical point about how his bank faced more rigorous and costly regulations than less rule-bound firms like Sears, which issued credit cards and sold insurance. Wriston and McColl among others moved into investment banking to avoid the regulator's heavy hand. By 2008, as one result, investment banking occupied a larger place in the nation's financial economy than a decade earlier—and their activities remained unreported to bank supervisors. In fact, no one at the comptroller's office, the Federal Reserve, or the Treasury Department oversaw the buildup of risk at Merrill Lynch, Lehman, and Bear Stearns. In August 2007, as the crisis started, economist Paul A. McCulley characterized money market funds and investment banks such as Lehman, Merrill Lynch, and Bear Stearns as parts of a shadow banking system. Bank of America's and Citi's investment bank subsidiaries that dealt in securitized mortgages and credit card debt also composed part of the shadow system.[19]

Executives and employees at those shadow banks did not operate in darkened corners, outside business hours, or in an illicit fashion. They arrived at work handsomely attired and conducted business in well-appointed quarters located in their city's highest profile buildings. Joseph M. Gregory, a top Lehman executive, regularly commuted to work from his Long Island home in a helicopter. On any weekday morning, thousands of street-bound New Yorkers might glimpse Gregory's descent from the sky to the West Side Heliport, where a limousine and driver stood ready to chauffer him to Lehman's thirty-eight-story, glass-sheathed headquarters in Times Square.[20] Each year, millions passed by Lehman's headquarters and its multiple signs featuring the company's name.

Public visibility characterized shadow bankers' relationship with ordinary Americans. Lehman's well-educated and well-paid executives, such as Joseph Gregory and CEO Richard Fuld, cooperated with journalists who in turn wrote approving stories with titles like "Richard Fuld: Lehman's He-Man." By encouraging regular and friendly contact with business reporters, Fuld and others sought to tout their market know-how, spotlight higher earnings, motivate subordinates, attract new business, and place additional lift under their firm's stock price.[21] Fuld's apparent market savvy and Lehman's financial might composed vital parts of the lore and legend that surrounded the nation's largest investment banking firms and their top officials.

Yet, Lehman's and other shadow bankers' business dealings remained invisible to the government's many regulators. Unlike the offices at the regulated commercial banks that took deposits, cashed checks, financed appliance dealers' inventories, and wrote auto loans, the shadow banks operated far from the regulators' gaze. As long as Fuld did not register Lehman as a bank financial holding company and offer FDIC-insured deposits, he and other shadow bankers remained at liberty to finance issues of mortgage and other types of asset-backed securities at leverage ratios of $29 in debt to $1 in capital, and higher if creditors went along. They were engaged in a fabulously lucrative and fabulously risky business. And the financial crisis, as Geithner and others now recognized, had started in the shadow banking system, among money market funds, investment banks, firms like Bear Stearns and Lehman, and in Bank of America's and Citigroup's (equally unsupervised) securities dealers. Traders at those firms dealt in the overnight loans backed by mortgages and other asset-based securities that had fallen far and fast in value. Insurance company dealings, by one account, had also "led to an amplification of downward pressures" during the run-up to the financial crisis of 2008.[22] To that point, however, fifty state agencies supervised insurance firms.

Congressional and presidential authors of this dispersed and fragmented system had never determined to secure detailed information about shadow banking firms and their daily or annual operations. Remarkably, at the beginning of the crisis, neither Sheila Bair's FDIC nor any other federal regulator possessed information regarding the extent of mortgage securitizations taking place among shadow (and regulated) banking firms. Bair later reported having to purchase that information from vendors. During past decades, members of Congress, comptrollers, treasury secretaries, and Federal Reserve chairs had revisited the idea of assigning bank regulation to one agency, but negotiations to change the rules and reorganize agencies always broke down. In 1999, Gramm-Leach-Bliley's authors described their handiwork as "functional regulation." Several years after the crisis, Geithner characterized bank regulation as "riddled with gaps and turf battles." Bank supervision, he added, "was a ludicrously balkanized mess." In a similar vein, anthropologist and *Financial Times* writer Gillian Tett in 2015, looking back on the crisis, determined "that tunnel vision and tribalism had contributed to the disaster."[23]

Geithner was alert to the self-interested dealings that had characterized bankers' politics for decades. Still, nearly a year on the job, Geithner remained optimistic about his ability to write legislation that imposed common standards on commercial banks like Citigroup, on shadow banks like Wells Fargo's investment banking subsidiaries, and of course on the gigantic insurance firms such as AIG. "The largest, most interconnected firms must be subject to one uniform, consistent set of standards," Geithner told members of the Joint Economic Committee in November 2009.[24] McColl had made an identical claim when he urged that shadow banks be subject to the same Community Reinvestment Act standards as his NationsBank. Bankers' capital standards were another topic with a record of tortured debate.

Increasing Bankers' Capital and Making Their Trades More Visible

Anyone with experience in bank regulation or in senior bank management would have heard about the central place that capital standards occupied in arguments about bank supervision. At its most basic, the capital standard Geithner and others talked about focused on the amount of money that a bank would have left over after paying its debts. Like any important topic in the financial services area, the capital standard to which regulators held bankers did not materialize on the basis of a neutral formula created and applied by a panel of impartial, expert economists. Capital standards had a history and bankers held determined opinions about them. Older bankers perhaps recalled Wriston's urging that Federal Reserve officials not hold his Citibank, with its far-flung businesses, to the same capital standards as smaller and less diversified banks. As Geithner and others remembered, Lehman and Citigroup borrowed heavily to finance their operations, a risky but lucrative business model when it was humming. Bankers described that system of using borrowed funds as one of levering up, as for instance those overnight (repo) loans based on leverage ratios $1 in capital to $29 dollars in borrowed funds. Again, shadow bankers like Lehman's Fuld had operated successfully on borrowed money for years, as had executives at Citigroup's investment banking units. And yet, as Geithner and others observed, those miniscule capital levels and vastly larger sums of borrowed money exposed each bank and the entire financial system to increased risk in the event of a run that started anywhere. Geithner described higher capital standards as similar to shock absorbers—abundant capital allowed banks to "take hits" and still not frighten creditors into starting a run.[25]

Boosting capital levels constituted an important and widely reported part of government action to control the financial crisis. In October 2008, Paulson, Bair, Bernanke, and Geithner had injected TARP funds into Bank of America and the other eight banks to bolster cash on hand, restore confidence, and restart lending. In June 2009, Geithner's Treasury Department issued a proposal to impose higher capital levels. Geithner's aim was to cut off risky dealings before they accumulated. To add to the document's political heft and reach, Obama offered remarks at a press conference and Geithner coauthored an op-ed in the *Washington Post* (with presidential adviser and former treasury secretary Lawrence Summers). Obama, Summers, and Geithner wanted to "rais[e] capital and liquidity requirements . . . with more stringent requirements for the largest and most interconnected firms."[26] Here was a strike at one of the arteries of the supermarket bank that Wriston and others thought should operate with reduced capital requirements.

Geithner's argument for increased capital levels started its political life with plenty of opposition. In November 2009, only five months after Geithner rolled out his plan and a mere thirteen months after Paulson and others injected TARP funds, a writer for *American Banker* reported that "today's [capital] reserves could be tomorrow's profits" at JPMorgan Chase, Wells Fargo & Co., and Bank of America.[27] Bankers were making the case for lower capital requirements once again. Geithner also wanted to bring visibility to bankers' trading practices.

As yet another shopworn proposal, Geithner urged Congress to require bankers to relocate their riskiest trades in a central clearinghouse. Here was an idea that was both more than a decade old and still loaded with political fireworks. In 1998, Brooksley E. Born, chair of the U.S. Commodity Futures Trading Commission, recommended the use of a clearinghouse for over-the-counter trading in volatile financial instruments. Born sought to make it possible for regulators to watch that part of the financial system in its variety and volatility. Summers, Rubin, and Greenspan speedily killed Born's proposals with Congress. As a result, by 2008, AIG's insurance on bankers' asset-backed securities increased in value to more than $3 trillion without federal supervision or knowledge. AIG's near collapse in turn added to the nervousness that followed Lehman's bankruptcy and helped convert a large bank run into a full-blown financial crisis. By 2009, Geithner later recalled, after the financial crisis destroyed firms, jobs, and savings, Born's proposals "ha[d] been boiled down to a morality play, pitting a heroic . . . [regulator] against nefarious financial Goliaths."[28]

By June 2009, however, Geithner was a convert to the central clearing-house idea. Geithner's central clearinghouse plan, if it came to pass, included higher capital requirements and other rules that Born had not considered. Still, Geithner sounded a lot like Born, even as he recalled that the argument between Born and her powerful detractors was "less black-and-white" and "more about turf and interests than substance and ideology."[29] Turf and interests had blocked presidential efforts to create a single bank regulator for decades.

Geithner, Congress, and the Hard Politics of Making the Federal Reserve the Key Regulator

Early in his term, Geithner resurrected the idea of the single bank regulator. He planned to merge the comptroller, the FDIC, and the Office of Thrift Supervision, that nearly unknown agency that regulated savings and loans as well as AIG's financial products division. In Geithner's plan, Bernanke's Federal Reserve examiners would in turn review every division of the largest firms such as Bank of America, JPMorgan Chase, and AIG. That Bank of America was a commercial bank and AIG a large insurance firm would not matter for regulatory purposes. Federal Reserve officials would advise the treasury or the FDIC, if it survived as a stand alone agency, to place troubled banks and insurance firms into a conservatorship before their problems extended out to other firms, as had happened with Lehman and AIG. To concentrate knowledge and authority in one place, Geithner liked to argue, would eliminate the "blind-men-and-the elephant problems," such as when no regulator possessed a big picture view of each bank's interconnectedness and took no responsibility to check. Again, the absence of that big picture view and the inability of any one person or agency to connect each bank to the whole of the nation's financial workings had characterized bank regulation for decades. "Vast swaths of the financial system had no one in charge," Geithner later complained, while "others . . . swarm[ed] with regulators in tribal warfare."[30] Presidents in the past had proposed to consolidate regulators, only to have those plans land on dusty shelves at the Library of Congress.

Turf and tribal interest remained in the ascendance. Geithner urged members of Congress to endow the Federal Reserve with authority to designate the largest financial firms such as AIG and JPMorgan Chase as systemically important. By that term, Geithner and others meant that the largest firms, with their habit of relying on borrowed funds rather than their own capital, had threated the financial system as a whole. But many in and out of Congress blamed Bernanke's Federal Reserve for the bank crisis, Congressman Frank told Geithner. As a result, any proposal to make the Federal Reserve the sole regulator "was dead on arrival."[31]

Turf protection morphed quickly into turf expansion. The FDIC's Bair carried her fight to directly to Frank, Dodd, and even to the president's chief of staff. If Bair's FDIC officials were to take responsibility for closing troubled banks, then they would require an enhanced role in supervising those banks. Bair, meanwhile, was not the only regulator in the fray. "The Fed and . . . [the comptroller] were fighting us and each other," Bair later reported. Bair was also a vocal advocate for the idea of forming an interagency group to watch for systemic risk in American banking, another idea she brought directly to Frank. Geithner was adamantly opposed to that idea. "You can't convene a committee to put out a fire," Geithner had told a Senate committee. But he was blunter in making that same point in a meeting with financial executives. "There isn't going to be any fucking council," he boldly announced.[32]

Geithner remained furious about the turf-oriented politicking that was taking place. In late July 2009, he called a meeting at the Treasury Department with the FDIC's Bair, the comptroller, the head of the SEC, and others to express his disgust at their lobbying efforts. Not only had Bair and others sought to create a council of regulators, an idea Geithner detested, but top officials at the Federal Reserve and the comptroller resented their potential loss of authority to a consumer protection agency that Geithner and Obama sought to create. "You're having a lot of fun right now, fucking with us," he shouted. At some time in the near future, Geithner added, "we're going to be in the room and you're not." Bair described Geithner's remarks as a "rant" and characterized his behavior toward other regulators as "arrogan[t] and disdainful."[33]

And yet, contrary to Geithner's stern warning, members of Congress chose only to eliminate the Office of Thrift Supervision, AIG's forlorn regulator. Otherwise, the remaining regulatory agencies, including Bair's FDIC, actually ended up comfortably ensconced in the final legislation. And, as a key part of the bill, congressional leaders created an interagency committee composed of fifteen regulators (ten voting), including the chair of the Federal Reserve and the comptroller of the currency, and charged them to serve as a full-time watchdog for systemic risk. Congressional leaders named this new body the Financial Stability Oversight Council (FSOC) and designated the treasury secretary as the chair. Geithner, as he later admitted, had "spoke[n] too soon" about never accepting a committee to oversee federal bank regulation.[34]

The Federal Reserve's Bernanke also succeeded in protecting his turf. Geithner had planned to limit the Federal Reserve to supervision of the thirty-five financial holding companies valued at more than $50 billion. Federal Reserve officials were frightened and furious at this threat to their prestige and authority. Presidents of the twelve district banks, Bernanke reported, perceived the stripping of smaller banks from their supervision "as an existential threat" and a potential "blind spot" in their ability to identify financial problems. In 2007–2008, however, Federal Reserve officials had not identified the emerging crisis, a point that diminished their credibility with lawmakers and ordinary Americans. But as Bernanke and reserve bank presidents telephoned and met with members of Congress through May 2010, they invoked an older image of service and commitment to ask "who knows more about the local economy than the community banker?" Given this heightened engagement with local bankers and lawmakers, one senator scolded Bernanke for his lobbyist-like behavior. Indeed, Bernanke's Federal Reserve officials relied on Linda L. Robertson, a seasoned operative, to handle their congressional liaison. Even with Robertson's able advice, Bernanke judged the venerable Federal Reserve at a moment of "great political peril."[35]

Congressional leaders ultimately permitted Bernanke and his frenetic reserve presidents to retain their authority. Senators favorable to the Fed joined with community bankers to strip a proposal to audit the Federal Reserve, a piece of legislation aimed at diminishing Bernanke's authority through increased review at the hands of the U.S. General Accountability Office. Bernanke attributed their success to the intensive lobbying undertaken by members of each of the reserve bank's boards and advisory groups.

They composed "the Fed family," Bernanke related. Prior to the financial crisis, Bernanke had spoken several times at community bankers' conventions, and he also visited reserve bank offices, where he cultivated good will with the bankers and businesspeople who populated their boards. Regional bankers, like insurance agents in every city and town, had long built their prestige and political power through such local and national coalitions. Bernanke, the Harvard PhD and Princeton economist, had grown up in Dillon, South Carolina, a town of some six thousand residents in the rural South. Bernanke retained a sensitive feel for bankers' striving and coalition building, and for the softer but still insistent small-town idioms that had long guided their portion of American bank politics.[36]

Bernanke could not retain the Federal Reserve's consumer protection responsibilities. Geithner and Obama insisted on putting those activities in a new agency. Elizabeth Warren, a member of the Harvard law faculty, led a nationwide effort to create a consumer financial protection agency. Such an agency was Warren's answer to the predatory bankers and other financial executives who had misled and swindled hapless homebuyers. "The Fed had not done enough to prevent abuses in mortgage lending before the crisis," Bernanke later admitted. Warren's proposed agency to protect consumers engendered solid but silent opposition among larger bankers, who preferred to remain out of public view on this popular legislation. In a nimble maneuver, moreover, community bankers split from their big-bank counterparts to support the agency's creation. In return, those community bankers, led by Camden R. Fine, insisted that Barney Frank exempt banks holding less than $10 billion in assets from the new agency's rule enforcement. As a result of Fine's efforts, nearly all of his community bank members remained exempt from scrutiny.[37] In turn, Obama, Warren, and Geithner had their Consumer Financial Protection Bureau.

Fine's energized small bankers rang up another legislative victory. The FDIC maintained an insurance fund to pay depositors if a bank failed. FDIC officials, as before, would unwind the failed bank's assets and liabilities, a process that bankers called resolution. Banks paid the insurance premiums in the event a resolution took place, and those premiums were set to increase under pending legislation. Once again, Fine sought to exempt his community bankers by shifting those higher costs to the big banks. Heads of those larger firms such as Bank of America and Citigroup resided in a politically toxic situation and again preferred to stay clear of the fray.

But it was not only a matter of the larger bankers' having lost their swagger in favor of Fine's small-town upstarts. Starting in the 1970s, several factors, including Wright Patman's death, the virtual disappearance of antitrust enforcement, and the consolidation of financial services into supermarket banks, had come together to diminish the ability of Fine's community bankers to cut dramatic figures in national politics. But community bankers remained important actors in small towns and in many suburban districts, and Fine had retained his Washington, D.C., office and his visibility among lawmakers. In the post-crisis circumstances of 2009 and 2010, Fine's smaller bankers, with their ability to celebrate the farm economy as well as small-town and suburban neighborliness, once again mustered sufficient clout to wrest exemption from costly and complicated rules. In 2009, the rhetorically adept Fine talked about the fairness of having "the systemic risk firms [such as Citigroup and Bank of America] pay for any resolution."[38] Fine, a sophisticated lobbyist, adopted popular hostility to the Federal Reserve, TARP, and bigness in general to his own purposes. Angry Americans also had a say about how federal officials would deal with a future bank crisis.

Tea Party Anger and the Dodd-Frank Act

During 2009–2010, the popular rage that had exploded around bank bailouts, TARP, home foreclosures, and the Great Recession coalesced into a political movement aimed at stopping Geithner's bank legislation. Opponents called themselves the Tea Party, after the colonists who had dumped British tea into Boston Harbor more than two centuries earlier. Many among those colorful Tea Party activists disliked federal safety net programs such as food stamps, and still others disliked the federal government's very existence. Tea Partiers attended noisy gatherings, carried American flags, brandished guns, and talked candidly about "tak[ing] our country back" from the nation's first African American president. Even senators such as Richard C. Shelby (R-AL), who were at first inclined to cooperate with Geithner to create a central clearinghouse for volatile financial products and force higher capital levels on bankers, quickly pulled back from any appearance of cooperating with the president. As a next step, Republican leaders such as Rep. John A. Boehner (R-OH) and Senator Mitchell "Mitch" McConnell, Jr., (R-KY) sought to redirect the Tea Party leaders' sharply antigovernment views into a strategy of denying Obama any legislative victories.[39]

This racialized and angry rhetoric quickly emerged as another regular feature of bank politics. In the fall of 2009, members of Frank's Financial Services Committee needed seven weeks rather than the customary several hours to "mark up" financial legislation. In January 2010, Scott P. Brown, a Republican and self-styled Tea Party candidate, won a special election in Massachusetts to replace Senator Edward M. Kennedy, who had died in August 2009. Brown's election also deprived majority Democrats of the sixty votes required to close Senate debate. In May 2010, delegates to the Republican Party's Utah state convention shouted "TARP, TARP, TARP" as they voted not to renominate Robert F. Bennett to his U.S. Senate seat. Bennett, first elected in 1992, had made the mistake of voting for TARP. Bennett's loss sent a message to Republicans about the political danger of supporting both big banks and President Obama, although in fact Secretary Paulson had proposed the TARP legislation and President Bush had signed it. Instead, Republican leaders and avid Tea Party members, Geithner argued sarcastically, had determined to "rebel against any compromise with a tyrannical socialist President."[40]

The Tea Party's heated rhetoric and Republicans' anti-Obama calculations influenced both the way lawmakers voted on Geithner's proposed legislation and the way they described it. On June 30, 2010, the Democratic majority in the House approved pending legislation by a vote of 237–192. Three Republican members joined the majority. On July 15, senators voted 60–39 in favor, including the newly elected Senator Brown and two other Republicans. The price for Brown's vote was to permit bankers to allocate up to 3 percent of their capital to riskier undertakings like trading securities. At virtually the same moment, the Senate majority leader, Harry M. Reid (D-NV), described Wall Street bankers who had "rigged the game," lost money, and then "came crying to the taxpayers for help." McConnell, the minority leader, talked about "the American people [who] don't like this government-driven solution to the financial crisis." Arguments in favor of this legislation ranged from the global to the local. As one example, Senator Dodd spoke about the United States emerging as a world leader in bank regulation. As another, Rep. Gregory Meeks (D-NY) wanted to make certain that the pending legislation did not harm banks' dealing in exotic securities, threatening his Queens constituents' jobs at those banks. Lawmakers, in short, repeated favored tropes about greedy bankers, unhindered markets, American leadership, arbitrary government, and their unceasing efforts to protect ordinary citizens.[41] Perhaps the lack of a widely accepted historical narrative made it easier to do so.

On July 21, 2010, President Obama signed the Dodd-Frank Wall Street Reform and Consumer Protection Act. Two among Geithner's key recommendations had survived, but in modified form. Members of Congress authorized the Financial Stability Oversight Council (the committee Geithner did not want created) to require financial corporations with assets of more than $50 billion to eliminate risky businesses. And second, Congress allowed regulators to subject especially interconnected firms to even more stringent regulation. Under Dodd-Frank, systemically important insurance firms like AIG and Prudential and banks like Citigroup now sat in the same regulatory boat. Nowhere was that common treatment more central to Geithner's aims than the creation of a uniform set of requirements to supervise trading in risky financial products and also to judge whether those large risk-prone firms possessed adequate capitalization to cushion a future downturn. "There will be no more tax-funded bailouts, period," Obama promised dignitaries at the signing ceremony, making a politically mandated promise that no one (including the president) knew with certainty he would be able to carry out.[42]

But the president and Geithner had not placed bankers in the hands of hostile regulators bent on pell-mell reorganization of banks and banking practice. The truth was quite the reverse. Obama, in setting the direction for Geithner's bank legislation that matured as the Dodd-Frank Act, carried forward a longtime effort by presidents to build larger banks that fostered economic growth. "The fact is," Obama told listeners as part of the signing ceremony, "the financial industry is central to our Nation's ability to grow, to prosper, to compete, and to innovate."[43] In 1961, President Kennedy had delivered a nearly identical message to Comptroller Saxon. Kennedy had only Saxon to push such a jarring idea forward against fierce opposition; and the cautious Kennedy sent that message quietly. Obama, in contrast, broadcast his commitment to big banks leading the economy forward clearly and in public. The large supermarket banks Saxon first envisioned and that others brought to fruition across five decades of tumultuous politics had emerged as a central feature of the American financial system.

And yet, no president since 1961 had managed to diminish the infighting that characterized each feature of bank regulation and legislation. Bank regulation, to be sure, remained nearly as unwieldy as before the crisis. Obama appointed each of the fifteen members who sat on the Financial Stability Oversight Council. Several years later, Geithner, still smarting from his inability to make the Federal Reserve the principal regulator, described the new arrangement as "bureaucratic balkanization." In practice, the fifteen-member council opened many spaces for bankers, members of Congress, and regulators to weigh in on deliberations. As in years past, arguments in and out of the council revolved around such vital questions as how to emancipate bankers from seemingly stringent federal controls and how to accelerate economic growth. Only the day after Obama signed Dodd-Frank into law, an industry analyst warned that its adverse "scope and depth" would "likely suppress . . . [bank growth] for an extended period." Tim Geithner remained at the center of these disputes, which a Harvard University political scientist characterized up to that point as the politics of "institutional strangulation."[44] Every president from Kennedy to Obama could probably have characterized bank politics in similar terms.

Dodd-Frank's approval encouraged a new cast of aggrieved actors to organize against federal officials and federal government's newfound hand in bankers' affairs. Between 2010 and 2017, Rep. Thomas Jeb Hensarling (R-TX) took the lead in an effort to dismantle the Dodd-Frank Act. Hensarling brought a special animus toward the Volcker Rule contained in the Dodd-Frank Act. The Volcker Rule, which an Obama official named after the former Federal Reserve chair Paul A. Volcker, limited the amount of money that bankers could use to trade securities for their firm's accounts. In 2016, as part of his campaign for president, Donald J. Trump emerged as an equally fervent opponent of the Dodd-Frank Act and the Volcker Rule. Like each president prior to Obama, Trump, once elected, sought to alter bank regulations and hasten economic growth.

EPILOGUE

Another Round of Bank Politics

In July 2010, President Obama signed the Dodd-Frank Act. The act ran more than 840 pages in length. Major legislation was often lengthy. Obama and congressional authors also left parts of bank regulation unfinished, which was a customary feature of congressional action in banking and in other areas. To complete Dodd-Frank, lawmakers directed the comptroller's office, the Federal Reserve, and other bank regulatory agencies to prepare nearly four hundred detailed rules. Rule making was not the stuff of newspaper headlines, Facebook entries, and lead stories on TV news. At quick glance, topics like appropriate measures of a bank's capital adequacy or the leadership of the Consumer Financial Protection Bureau could never enlist and hold a large audience's attention.

The Dodd-Frank Act of 2010 still fostered passion. The bank crisis of 2008 and the job losses and home foreclosures that followed remained vital topics for lawmakers and elicited painful memories that extended into the next decade for millions of Americans. All of a sudden, the dull process of Dodd-Frank rule making opened another opportunity for regulators and lawmakers to restrain bankers' speculation, argue for more bank lending, and offer community bankers a helping hand against the supermarket banks. The mind-numbing business of writing bank rules carried practical consequences for bankers, lawmakers' careers, regulators' authority, and bank customers that did not require a lengthy explanation to anyone involved in the process.

Dodd-Frank's authors, including Tim Geithner, sought to head off the next bank crisis and to maintain supermarket banks at the center of the American financial economy. Between 2010 and 2017, however, Rep. Thomas Jeb Hensarling (R-TX) led a growing opposition to the Dodd-Frank Act. Hensarling's ideas, if Congress approved them, held out the possibility that community bankers would once again achieve a privileged place in banking's hierarchy, reversing decades of decline at the hands of lawmakers and super-market bankers. In this volatile setting, the Volcker Rule was tailor-made for Hensarling and other Dodd-Frank critics during Obama's presidency.

The Volcker Rule

In mid-2010, Paul A. Volcker was in the news again. In 1979, President Carter appointed Volcker to chair the Federal Reserve Board of Governors. Volcker's principle concern was to reduce inflation, which in May–June 1980 spiked as high as 14.4 percent. By 1983, Volcker's harsh medicine of interest rate increases and a recession brought inflation down to 3.4 percent for the year. A few years later, a business writer described Volcker's "reputation as the person who had, almost singlehandedly, killed inflation in the United States."[1] In 1983, President Reagan appointed Volcker to a second term.

In 1987, Reagan declined to offer a third term. Volcker's success in man-aging the economy had made him "the second most powerful man in the country," an encomium that undermined the president's credibility as mas-termind of the economic recovery. As well, Reagan and several bankers, per-haps including Hugh McColl, wanted Volcker to change the Fed's rules to make it easier for banks to merge and enter new and exciting financial areas such as underwriting corporate bond and stock issues. Federal Reserve lead-ers, if Reagan had his way, would foster creation of the supermarket banks that each president starting with Kennedy had craved as a device to improve the economy's pace. The independent-minded Volcker resisted those propos-als and argued instead that U.S. bankers needed to add capital. Additional capital made banks safer, ran his argument. Volcker was one of the key reg-ulators who had resisted Walter Wriston's insistence that large and diverse banks like his Citicorp did not require high capital levels. Years later, former Federal Reserve chair Alan Greenspan described Volcker as "the most impor-tant [Fed] Chairman ever."[2]

Following the financial crisis of 2008, Volcker, by then retired, was equally adamant about urging limits on bankers' speculative instincts. Vol-cker, at age eighty-two, was not another sclerotic former regulator bent on promoting a pet idea in the spring of 2010, as Dodd and Frank ushered pend-ing legislation toward a close; Volcker wanted lawmakers to prohibit bank executives from using the bank's funds to buy and sell securities that the bank would own.[3] Bankers used the term "proprietary trading" to describe speculative activity undertaken for their firms alone rather than as another customer service.

Proprietary trading was hardly a neutral term. According to MIT economist Simon H. Johnson, bad bets by bankers could undermine their firms, project losses on trading partners, and once more lead federal officials to inject funds to put those banks upright. Proprietary trading, in other words, threatened to bring a repeat of the crisis of 2008. Johnson also alerted non-specialists to the dangers to the financial system that resided nearby in the event Congress failed to pass the Volcker Rule. He appeared on Bloomberg Television and published muckraking articles in the *New York Times* and elsewhere deftly linking the Volcker Rule's heralded protections against greedy bankers, gigantic banks, and impenetrable bank rules to vivid memories of job losses and sheriff's sales of foreclosed homes. Johnson urged the Federal Reserve and other regulators to shrink the nation's largest banks to their mid-1990s size. In 2013, Camden Fine's Independent Community Bankers of America (ICBA) named Johnson a Main Street hero.[4] Fine and his ICBA member bankers still recognized the political value contained in a resonant phrase like "Main Street."

Treasury Secretary Geithner never shared Johnson's disdain for larger banks or his positive view of Volcker's proposal. Proprietary trading had not contributed to the bank runs of 2008, Geithner contended. Bankers' proprietary trading was actually advantageous to their firms and to the economy, Geithner determined, allowing buyers and sellers to consummate deals quickly. By this reasoning, bankers, through their buying, selling, and matching activities, helped markets work in a more efficient and smoother fashion. Propriety trading and the bankers who engaged in it were "market making," Geithner added.[5] Investment bankers had always made markets in the stocks and other commodities they bought and sold for clients. "Market making" was another resonant term that carried political heft, at least among the regulators and the small number of lawmakers who set the rules by which bankers made those markets.

Volcker refused to allow objections brought by Geithner or economists like Johnson to get in the way of promoting his ban on proprietary trading. During his time at the Federal Reserve, Volcker had tangled with two U.S. presidents. In 2010, Volcker, long removed from the Fed, still brought resources to this dispute. Volcker remained "a well-regarded lion of the regulatory world," a business writer reported in July. Volcker, as part of maintaining his influence and reputation, possessed a knack for generating favorable publicity to support ideas about bank rules and the national economy. Starting in 2009, Volcker chaired the President's Economic Recovery Advisory Board. In that capacity, he enjoyed occasional contact with Obama and Geithner and improved access to members of Congress. And, after years in public service, Volcker recognized the value of granting access to journalists who sought his peppery observations to add to a story with an approaching deadline. As part of his campaign to ban proprietary trading, Volcker visited congressional offices and "worked the phone" from his home in Manhattan.[6]

Volcker's proposal, if Congress approved it in full, would return commercial bankers to a regime closer to the 1933 Glass-Steagall ban on risky investment deals. Proprietary trading, to be certain, was not an idea that plainspoken Americans understood or had heard reports about. Geithner, however, feared creating the more general impression that Obama administration leaders "were soft on [bank] reform." In December 2009, Geithner assembled a proposal to "get Volcker on board" and at the same time "minimize the potential damage to useful financial activity." David M. Axelrod, a top Obama aide, dubbed Volcker's idea as the "Volcker Rule," which the president unveiled on January 21, 2010, at a gathering that included Volcker. The Volcker Rule, if it came to pass, applied only to banks supervised by the FDIC and the Federal Reserve, once again replicating the distinction between commercial and shadow banks. Meanwhile, by May, Geithner needed the vote of Senator Brown of Massachusetts to pass the Dodd-Frank Act. Brown, eager to protect two financial firms in his state, demanded that the Volcker Rule permit bankers to invest as much as 3 percent of their capital in proprietary trading activities.[7] Two months later, President Obama signed the Dodd-Frank Act, including the Volcker Rule's 3 percent exclusion.

In the short run, the Volcker Rule led to conflicting outcomes. New executive teams at Citigroup and Bank of America shuttered their proprietary trading desks. Still other bank leaders maintained their proprietary operations and chafed at the 3 percent limit. And, at the same time, Geithner lamented, five officials at regulatory agencies including the Federal Reserve, the comptroller, and the FDIC would have to supervise bankers' Volcker Rule compliance.[8] Geithner still disliked interagency committees.

By February 2012, leaders at those agencies had failed to prepare the Volcker Rule's ultimate version—the one that would specify bankers' proprietary trading behavior in detail. Newly invigorated bankers brought sharp lawyering to block, modify, or delay the Volcker Rule's implementation. In one such tactic, bankers' lawyers, responding to a regulator's request for comment on pending rules, submitted a 530-page document. Well-organized bankers still feared a loss of their market-making business. As a practical matter, only the largest banks, like Goldman Sachs, maintained proprietary trading desks and made markets. Finally, in December 2013, MIT economist Johnson, who kept tabs on the Volcker Rule's development, announced that "big banks" had "lost . . . the conceptual fight." In January 2014, regulators published the Volcker Rule in the Federal Register. More than three years had gone by since Congress approved the Dodd-Frank Act. Volcker described "legions of lobbyists" and others who had fostered "a long and arduous process."[9]

The Volcker Rule, in its final form, ran seventy-one pages in length plus a regulators' preamble that required nearly nine hundred pages. Proprietary trading remained legal, including the 3 percent limit, but regulators added rules to render bankers less freewheeling than before 2010. Market making, as Geithner had contended, still justified bankers' right to engage in proprietary trades. To get that far, President Obama and his new treasury secretary had, by several accounts, brought "heavy pressure" on regulators to stop arguing and produce a final rule. Those regulators in turn had undergone "contortions" to reach agreement, one writer reported.[10] Lawsuits lay ahead.

In December 2013, the Volcker Rule had not yet appeared in the Federal Register. Small bankers and their lawyers at major law firms filed a lawsuit. They were prepared to "pounce," a business writer reported. Executives of 275 small banks in particular feared losses on risky investments made before 2008. "The intent of the Volcker Rule was to prohibit proprietary trading by the large banks," argued Camden Fine, the ICBA's inexhaustible president and CEO. Fine asked, "How did this intent ever evolve into including the divestiture of legitimate portfolio holdings of community banks?" In February 2014, bank leaders withdrew the suit. Regulators had modified the Volcker Rule to "minimize . . . the compliance burden," announced the head of the American Bankers Association. Fine and his community bankers, still successfully blaming larger bankers like Chuck Prince's Citigroup for the nation's financial problems, managed to carve out an exemption from part of the Volcker Rule.[11]

Lawsuits and recitation of words such as "burden" could not have surprised observers. Between the 1960s and the 1990s, securities dealers, insurance agents, and small-town bankers had sought the protection of courts and

Congress against bankers such as Walter Wriston and Hugh McColl and against aggressive comptrollers like James Saxon, William Camp, and Eugene Ludwig. Contemporary lawmakers, however, rarely expressed an interest in political, social, or financial history dating to the previous decades. Among disgruntled members of Congress and bankers intent on reducing apparent and real burdens, the next step was to seek the Dodd-Frank Act's repeal.

Jeb Hensarling and Dodd-Frank

In November 2012, President Obama won a second term. With Obama in office until January 2017, congressional opponents, Republicans mostly, stood no chance of returning bank legislation to its pre-crisis state. The Dodd-Frank Act, however, offered Republican leaders a large and irresistible topic to recruit adherents among bankers seeking additional exemptions and voters already hostile to anything that smacked of President Obama and government rules—or hostile, at least, to rules that failed to deliver measurable benefits on the spot. Anger about TARP and now Dodd-Frank had political use as Republican leaders prepared for succeeding rounds of congressional and presidential elections. Rep. Thomas Jeb Hensarling (R-TX) seized the rhetorical and congressional lead in this undertaking.

From the start, Hensarling brought valuable credentials to the gathering effort to seek Dodd-Frank's dismemberment. Hensarling was not a sophisticated economic thinker. His ideas about how the business system worked consisted of notions and nostrums about supply and demand taught in undergraduate economics courses. Hensarling, like millions of Americans, thought that markets appeared as a result of a natural human proclivity. Markets, among those who held this view, existed on the basis of an invisible ordination and consecration. It followed that bank rules, or almost any federal regulation, diverted useful economic activity to politically contrived causes like controlling proprietary trading. Heads of the largest commercial and investment banks like Hugh McColl and Robert Rubin had known better.

Hensarling, however, moved in political circles that conferred legitimacy on these ideas and on his negative views about the government's bank regulations. Senator Phil Gramm was Hensarling's mentor. During the late 1970s, Hensarling, a Texas native, attended Texas A&M University, where he heard then Professor Gramm's classroom accounts about the stated links between lower taxes, fewer government rules, and improved economic growth. In 1982, Hensarling graduated from the University of Texas Law School and joined a law firm. Years later, he reported "hat[ing] the work."[12] A job with Gramm offered a path into more interesting and influential activity.

In 1985, Gramm hired Hensarling as a top aide in his Texas office. During the next decade, Hensarling immersed himself in promoting Gramm's career and ideas. In 1990, Hensarling directed Gramm's reelection campaign. In turn, Gramm, as director of the National Republican Senatorial Committee, made Hensarling his executive director, a post that included meeting candidates and helping them raise election funds. During Gramm's final term, Hensarling worked for an energy firm and at Maverick Capital, a hedge fund owned by one of Gramm's major supporters.[13] Members of Congress had permitted hedge funds to reside in that vast area of shadow banking located beyond the federal government's purview. Hedge fund operators in turn often perceived themselves as financial buccaneers unconstrained by institutions.

Two themes informed Hensarling's politics from childhood up to the point at which he secured a visible place in Congress. First, Hensarling grew up in a household suffused with antigovernment rhetoric. In 1964, when Hensarling was seven years old, his parents supported Barry Goldwater for president. Goldwater championed ideas such as diminished federal spending and a sharp reduction in the number of federal rules. Hensarling's mother cried when Goldwater lost, he reported. Hensarling credited Gramm with having exerted the deepest influence on his antigovernment thinking. As a student in Gramm's courses, Hensarling told a writer in 2009, I "suddenly saw how free-market economics provided the maximum good for the maximum number." Gramm was also the author of the second theme that informed the young Hensarling. Gramm, according to Hensarling, demonstrated the meaning of being a Republican.[14] Hensarling never defined that term for journalists or his fellow lawmakers. Most likely, it had to do with Hensarling's acquisition of Gramm's well-honed ability to translate marketplace abstractions into pithy sayings about pocketbook issues.

In November 2002, Hensarling won election to Congress. His large district, composed mostly of small towns and farms, ran southeasterly from Dallas. During that decade, Hensarling's constituents earned slightly less than other Americans. In his district 10 percent of the residents resided in poverty and another 21 percent earned less than $25,000 a year. Those figures approximated the national average.[15] Now Hensarling sought to rewrite laws to permit trusted businessmen and women rather than government to increase his least well-off constituents' wages.

Hensarling took these ideas about government and the economy to Washington, D.C. In his first term, he voiced distrust for federal agencies. In September 2003, for example, the Congressional Budget Office (CBO) estimated the expenses of a proposed federal prescription drug program. Hensarling dismissed the CBO's projection as having "less predictive value than a Ouija board." Hensarling quickly developed a reputation as a strong advocate for reduced taxes and a diminished number of federal programs. In March 2004, a *New York Times* writer recognized Hensarling as a leader among Republicans who planned to shrink federal spending. "I didn't come to Congress to grow government," Hensarling told a journalist in March 2004. Late in 2005, former senator Gramm, long a favorite figure among federal government critics, told a political writer, "I hope people will remember Jeb long after they've forgotten me."[16] In only three years, Hensarling had emerged as one of the go-to figures among lawmakers and the many Americans who favored sharp tax cuts and a diminished federal hand in managing the nation's economy.

In subsequent years, Hensarling's antigovernment rhetoric assumed a harder, more insistent edge. Hensarling, as before, advocated for a federal government that was smaller, less intrusive, and not as costly. Not even Lehman's bankruptcy and the unraveling of the nation's financial arrangements moved Hensarling to change his mind about government spending. In October 2008, he voted against the $700 billion TARP, refusing the urgings of President Bush and congressional leaders from both parties. Starting in 2009, Hensarling adopted the Tea Party's anti-TARP views. TARP's cash injections and loans to banks amounted to "the opposite of the dynamic of entrepreneurial capitalism," Hensarling told an interviewer in April 2009. The Obama administration and congressional Democrats, Hensarling added, used TARP funds to "advance their social and political agenda." Hensarling expressed fear regarding what they "are attempting to do to my country." Obama and Democrats, Hensarling judged, "fostered suspect undertakings." In June, with Tea Party activists enjoying greater prominence and clout among Republicans, Hensarling introduced legislation to terminate TARP by year's end. Obama and House Democrats would never approve such a dramatic change, Hensarling recognized. In November 2009, a popular writer characterized Hensarling as "the GOP's most powerful Nobody."[17] Around that time, Hensarling committed to a long-term strategy of delegitimizing and repealing Obama's major legislation. The Dodd-Frank Act and the Volcker Rule resided at the top of his list.

In 2014, Republicans held the majority of House seats and Hensarling assumed the chair of the Committee on Financial Services. Angry Tea Party voters and a slow-moving economic recovery contributed to Republicans' electoral success. In January, Hensarling held hearings titled "The Impact of the Volcker Rule on Job Creators." Again, the Volcker Rule capped bankers' proprietary trading at 3 percent of capital. Many or most Americans still lacked familiarity with its onerous limitations. As well, members of a House committee could not simply repeal a rule by majority vote. Instead, Hensarling used hearings to focus journalists' and supporters' attention on government regulations that hit "Main Street, and regrettably the poor and downtrodden amongst us become collateral damage." MIT professor Simon Johnson also testified at the hearing. Johnson's sober concerns about dealing with bankers and "systemic risk" and "how [regulatory] agencies will work together" could never match Hensarling's more quotable assertion that the Volcker Rule would "take $800 billion out of the economy . . . the equivalent of taking more than $6,900 out of every American household's paycheck." Hensarling was canny in his ability to link remote federal bank regulations to constituents' anger about TARP, federal "bailouts," and an overriding interest in maintaining both hands and feet on a wobbly economic and social ladder.[18]

During 2016, as the presidential election drew near, Hensarling relied on his sharp wit to skewer bank regulators and their regulations. In mid-March, American Banking Association leaders held a "summit" in Washington, D.C. In past decades, bankers like Hugh McColl and Walter Wriston turned to federal lawmakers and regulators to advance favored causes such as the right to sell insurance and underwrite bonds. Politically self-protective bankers would have invited Hensarling or any chair of the House Financial Services Committee to their gathering. The Dodd-Frank Act, Hensarling told audience members, "should be called the Obama Financial Control Law." By whatever name, that legislation imposed "incomprehensible complexity and more government control." "Working families," Hensarling warned his prosperous listeners, "have seen their paychecks shrink by more than $1,600." Hensarling was equally adept at linking obscure bank regulations to the growing perception among voters that the federal government awarded favors to the undeserving and failed to help decent Americans like them.[19]

In that talk to the bankers' summit, Hensarling brought a special message to heads of smaller banks. "Washington's regulatory waterboarding is drowning community banks and small businesses," he asserted. "I will not rest until Dodd-Frank is ripped out by its roots and tossed on the trash-heap of history," Hensarling assured audience members. "Never let it be said that Jeb Hensarling doesn't know how to work a crowd," a blog post writer remarked afterward, noting that Hensarling sought to make clear that "his heart is with the banks." Audience members, always attuned to any committee chair's views, would have heard and read toned-down versions of these remarks many times. But now, as the next election approached, Hensarling needed to build enthusiasm among bankers and other likely supporters.[20] Hensarling's remarks constituted one of the ritualized features of recruiting and motivating heads of large and small banks in advance of a major legislative effort like repealing Dodd-Frank. Republicans still had to elect the next president. In June 2016, Hensarling met with Donald J. Trump, the Republican Party's certain nominee.

Donald J. Trump and American Bank Politics

Trump and Hensarling spoke at Trump Tower in New York, where they discovered a common and deep animosity toward the Dodd-Frank Act. In campaign stops and interviews, Trump had made Dodd-Frank's many rules a regular target. In January 2016, interviewed on Fox TV, he described Dodd-Frank as "a disaster in so many different ways." The nation's banks were "totally regulated to a point where no banker . . . is controlling their [sic] own bank." The net result of those regulations, Trump asserted in another dramatic overstatement, was that bankers had stopped making loans to small business people. In October, at a campaign stop in Charlotte, North Carolina, Trump also blamed Democratic Party nominee Hillary Clinton for "lifting Glass-Steagall [and] pushing subprime lending," an act that in turn had "brought us the financial recession."[21] (More accurately, Hillary Clinton's husband, President Bill Clinton, had promoted passage of the Gramm-Leach-Bliley Act in 1999.) Perhaps Trump did not realize, or did not care, that Hensarling's mentor, Phil Gramm, played a key part with President Clinton in the act of ushering supermarket banks to legal completion. Nor did Trump seem to recognize that Gramm-Leach-Bliley's complex rules had played little or no role in bringing about the financial crisis of 2008. In great measure, however, Trump sounded like Hensarling, who since 2010 had decried regulations that reportedly harmed banker and borrower alike.

Hensarling did not offer an immediate embrace of Trump's candidacy. But Dodd-Frank certainly presented them with a common legislative enemy. "Here's something we both agree with," Hensarling told a television audience after the meeting with Trump. The Dodd-Frank Act fostered "poverty," contributed to "middle income people [remaining] trapped," and its "mind-numbing . . . regulations [kept] capital on the sidelines."[22] Every president starting with Ford had made similar points in public about the federal government's countless rules and their supposed connection to slowed growth. Phil Gramm had advanced his career in Congress based on an identical argument. Opposition to the federal government and its rules that derailed the markets' automatic and beneficent workings enjoyed a lengthy history in American political maneuvering, even if inaccurate. In this latest iteration, Hensarling brought fresh zeal and keen rhetorical skills to the formidable tasks of eliminating the Volcker Rule and the Dodd-Frank Act.

In September 2016, Hensarling filed his Financial Choice Act. That title evoked an image of sovereign consumers who conducted business with financial supermarkets that would, at long last, operate with fewer legal and institutional constraints. In truth, Hensarling's proposed legislation included phrases like "risk-weighted assets" that only financial specialists could understand. Hensarling "ask[ed] for the moon in Dodd-Frank revamp," a writer for *American Banker* determined. Naturally, Hensarling aimed to eliminate the Volcker Rule and to increase congressional oversight of the Federal Reserve, the comptroller, and the Consumer Financial Protection Bureau, another group of favorite Republican targets. "It's time for economic growth for all, bank bailouts for none," Hensarling announced in one of his crisp talking points.[23] With the hyperbole of campaign season at full throttle, no one apparently asked Hensarling or Trump how the Dodd-Frank Act had foisted so many nefarious outcomes at one time onto American business or how Hensarling's equally complex Financial Choice Act would relieve those evils. Unlike Trump, however, Hensarling was articulate, rhetorically disciplined, and always insistent about the economic benefits certain to follow when market-oriented bankers replaced federal regulators in the allocation of capital.

On November 8, 2016, Donald J. Trump was elected president. That same month, a *Fortune* writer described Hensarling as "Washington's newest power player." For a day or two, journalists reported that Trump's top officials were considering Hensarling for the post of treasury secretary. Trump's aides, according to a news report, liked Hensarling's "free-market background and deep GOP ties."[24] Hensarling and Trump were allies and competitors in the business of denouncing the Dodd-Frank Act and the Volcker Rule and promising faster economic growth.

Trump took the oath of office on January 20. By late January, the steam behind Trump's plans to eviscerate the Dodd-Frank Act had begun to run out. "I do support the Volcker Rule," Trump's nominee for treasury secretary Steven T. Mnuchin told members of the Senate Finance Committee on January 19. Mnuchin at the same time sought to redefine the Volcker Rule to permit bankers "to provide the necessary function of liquidity in customer markets." Mnuchin sounded like Geithner several years earlier. And Mnuchin, like Geithner and other federal bank regulators across several decades, planned to make those changes based on his administrative authority rather than through lengthy and unpredictable negotiations with members of Congress. Presidential appointees like Saxon, Rubin, and Ludwig had shown presidents what regulators could accomplish without taking the arduous path of legislative enactment. At the same time, Mnuchin talked about reorganizing the multiple federal bank regulatory agencies such as the Fed, the FDIC, and the comptroller. The idea of regulatory simplification harked back to every presidential administration since Kennedy's.[25]

Trump also began to revise his earlier, grandiose statements. On January 30, Trump, always a hyperactive phrasemaker, promised to do "a big number on Dodd-Frank." But on February 3, he hosted a meeting at the White House for business leaders, including Jamie Dimon, JPMorgan Chase's chairman, president, and CEO. "There's nobody better to tell me about Dodd-Frank than Jamie," Trump announced. Now, however, Trump emphasized "cutting a lot out of Dodd-Frank" rather than its overturn.[26]

Trump was never a coherent, nuanced, or even a partly informed financial thinker.[27] In past decades, he had worked with city, county, state, and federal officials as well as foreign leaders to develop large hotels and prestige golf courses. Trump's experience as a business executive had taught him that government rules and maintenance of close financial and personal connections with lawmakers and regulators produced winners and losers. And now, Trump wanted banks to make loans to his supporters; and he sought to protect the largest supermarket banks such as Dimon's JPMorgan Chase as the nation's financial mainstays.

With those two ideas in mind, Trump introduced subtle changes in his approach to bank politics. First, Dimon emerged as the president's banker, an informal position held in the past by executives such as Walter Wriston and Hugh McColl. Since the mid-1980s, Dimon had served as a top officer in Sandy Weill's worldwide financial empire and then as president of the gigantic JPMorgan Chase. In 2017, Dimon was the only top bank executive who remained active from the era when building supermarket banks was in vogue. Nothing in Dimon's background and contemporary responsibilities suggested anything as dramatic as a vast remodeling of the rules that framed the American financial architecture. Bankers including Dimon had already spent billions to adapt their operations to conform to Dodd-Frank's rules. Rather than the abolition or radical diminution of regulation, heads of the largest banks such as Dimon and Bank of America's CEO Brian T. Moynihan sought to bring European and U.S. bank rules into closer alignment on questions such as how to measure capital adequacy.[28]

Trump's second change regarding bank politics was still more understated. Trump appointed Gary D. Cohn to head the National Economic Council. In 1993, President Clinton had created that post and appointed Robert Rubin to head it. Like Rubin, Cohn was a former top official at Goldman Sachs, where he directed financial operations around the world. Given their backgrounds and Trump's priorities, Cohn (along with Dimon and Mnuchin) planned to modify regulations in a way that increased lending and maintained the dominance of the largest U.S. banks in the world financial system. "The United States has a huge competitive advantage," Cohn told a TV interviewer on February 3, "and . . . we want to preserve that advantage."[29] Alan Greenspan and Robert Rubin had also sought to maintain that international advantage, as for instance by derailing Brooksley Born's plans to make over-the-counter trading of super-risky derivatives more visible to regulators. Heightened visibility, Greenspan and Rubin asserted, would encourage traders to decamp for London. The idea of American banks as major players in the world economy dominated financial policy makers' agendas in every administration from Reagan to Trump.

Trump also needed rules and legislation that permitted bankers to make additional loans to businesses that employed his white, working-class constituents located in declining towns and cities. Trump's supporters expected pay raises and a spot near the front of the line for hometown jobs. Trump's voters also sought to regain their fellow citizens' respect for remaining at hard and dirty jobs. Trump enthusiasts found meaning in building products with their hands and recognized that most other Americans no longer valued handworkers. In a curious way, Hensarling's pithy remarks about the federal government's size, spending, and remote rules appealed to Trump's supporters who, accurately or not, no longer trusted federal officials to look out for them. In 1999, Clinton experienced a similar dilemma. He and his key aides favored the growth of supermarket banks but did not want to leave their small-town and central-city constituents lagging still farther behind. Clinton insisted on including the Community Reinvestment Act in the Gramm-Leach-Bliley bill to reduce the gap. To be evenhanded, for decades manufacturing executives as well as federal and local officials had failed to bolster education and job-training systems to create paths for a limited number of Trump's supporters to earn higher wages and reclaim their self-respect.[30] Whether Trump and his White House staff possessed the know-how, clout, commitment, and deft touch to blend legislation that advanced global supermarket banks and also increased community bank lending to the modest, low-tech firms that hired Trump's supporters remained to be seen.

By mid-February 2017, only a month after Trump's inauguration, long-time observers of bank politics dismissed Hensarling and Trump's prospects for eliminating the Dodd-Frank Act. Those observers used terms like "long hard slog" to describe the substantial effort that any president and treasury secretary would face in seeking a large overhaul of bank legislation. "Dodd-Frank's tentacles go deep [and] won't be easily cut," a writer for an insurance-oriented publication noted that month. The supermarket bank continued to reside at the center of a presidential project nearly five decades old. And yet, if any one lesson emerges from supermarket bankers' halting ascent in American politics, it is that no outcome is certain or inevitable. The market rules for American banking remain a matter of grinding politics.[31] History governed banking institutions, but few recognize its presence in their daily lives. Disconnection is part of the American style of politics, except when it is time to apportion blame or gain an advantage. Hensarling's moment to gain that advantage was evanescent.

Connections

On May 23, 2017, for half an hour or so, bank politics achieved a momentary linkage between past and present. Jeb Hensarling sat for an interview and audience questions at the American Enterprise Institute (AEI), a market-oriented think tank located in Washington, D.C. The AEI's Peter J. Wallison conducted the interview, no doubt by design. Between 1981 and 1985, Wallison had served as general counsel to the Treasury Department. In that position, he advised Treasury Secretary Donald Regan about legal and legislative strategies to win congressional authorization for Hugh Mc-Coll, Walter Wriston, and other executives of that decade to create super-market banks. Wallison and Regan had failed to bring most of those plans to fruition.[32] Hensarling and Wallison, as everyone in that room had to rec-ognize, represented two generations of federal officials who had dedicated their professional lives to the idea that government regulations created more problems than they solved and that reduced taxes and fewer bank rules would inevitably hasten the pace of economic growth. During the interview, Hensarling lamented the "weight, volume, and complexity of the Dodd-Frank regulatory burden."[33] During President Obama's time in office, that joyous day when bankers would experience fewer rules had resided in the future. With Trump in the White House and Republican majorities in both houses, Hensarling had a window to pass the Financial Choice Act.

Market talk was the language Hensarling used to build a legislative co-alition. Starting in 2010, Hensarling's job, as he defined it, had been to mo-bilize bankers and fellow lawmakers behind the effort to eliminate the detested Dodd-Frank Act and its Volcker Rule. Hensarling's appearance at the AEI was another stop in that lengthy effort. Hensarling, as audience members expected, referred often to the market's dynamism and transfor-mative powers. "Freedom" was one of Hensarling's favored concepts and "market discipline" was another. That market discipline, Hensarling re-ported, "prevents me from having to pay $50 for a hamburger instead of $5."[34] Years in office had not diminished Hensarling's skill at articulating well-rehearsed, down-home phrases that suggested the uselessness of most government programs. In Hensarling's capable hands, market talk always found a ready audience among contemporary Americans. Senator Gramm, Hensarling's mentor, achieved national recognition and a modest national following with that same rhetorical skill. Phil Gramm, Comptroller James Saxon, President Ronald Reagan, and Citicorp president Walter Wriston had an invisible presence in front of the camera and microphone that morning.

Hensarling liked the idea of a nation built around markets, at least in the abstract. As a seasoned legislator, however, he treated market talk as a device to gain tangible legislative goals, emulating Gramm. Hensarling sought not to eliminate financial rules but to rewrite them in a way that favored small and regional banks and credit unions. Hensarling also sought to rein in the Federal Reserve's bank supervision authority. It was an "open question," Hensarling told his AEI audience, "whether [the Federal Reserve] ought to have a role in prudential regulation."[35] During the years between the 1930s and the 1970s, Wright Patman had also denounced Federal Reserve policies as part of a passionate commitment to protecting the markets of his small-town bankers.

Market talk was about practical politics. During the long run-up to Gramm-Leach-Bliley, market talk, at least among most bankers, comptrollers, and each president, was never about eliminating government but about creating a legal and politically safe place for supermarket banks offering new financial products. Those big banks would take their place alongside the Tennessee Valley Authority, the interstate highway program, the GI Bill, and the space program as government programs that fostered technological innovation and added directly to productivity increases, more jobs, and wage growth. Programs like interstate highway construction were large, expensive, and difficult to bring into being, but the economic payoffs were vast— as were the costs imposed on central-city residents.[36]

Bank politics promised a way out of expensive and politically exhausting government projects. Equally tangled and jumbled, bank politics consisted of an effort by members of competing coalitions assembled in each decade to use the federal government to create an unseen, automatic path toward rising prosperity. No one's taxes had to be increased! No new bureaucracy would have to supervise this growth; and no group of federal bureaucrats would make determinations about interest rates and what disgusted critics like Gramm and Hensarling described as the political allocation of loans— as for instance the Community Reinvestment Act. Prosperity through changes in bank rules promised a political economy that would eliminate the need for political economy.

Market talk also blinded participants to one of the reasons they rarely succeeded in changing bank rules. Sovereign markets were fair and rational in allocating resources, or so ran the reasoning taught in every first-year economics course. But American institutions were not built and managed by economists or by market talk. Exactly who would prosper—and whose business model, lifestyle, region, occupation, and hard-earned prestige would falter—was one of the perennial questions that got in the way of promulgating that next set of bank rules and the prosperity to follow. The markets that government made, including bankers' markets, governed American life in ways large and small, but also in unseen ways. That lack of visibility contributed to the idea that markets rather than government mattered. Bank politics was an exercise in economic acceleration through private firms rather than through another federal department and program. Here was an idea around which bankers like Sandy Weill and Hugh McColl and presidents as different as Lyndon Johnson, Bill Clinton, and Donald Trump could rally. And perhaps, as productivity increases slowed in the 1970s and as partisan divides widened starting in the 1980s, bank politics remained among the handful of areas where presidents, comptrollers, and bankers stood a running chance at fostering prosperity.[37]

Not everyone had signed on to this half-century-long experiment in government-guided prosperity through the financial sector. Paul Volcker was not present at the AEI that May morning for Hensarling's remarks. Volcker was as voluble as Hensarling; and he was a crystal clear thinker about bank policy. Maybe it was just as well Volcker chose not to attend. Volcker, it seems, had little faith in mortgage securitization and other types of "financial engineering" that bankers and lawmakers had embraced and celebrated.[38] Nor was he persuaded that new bank rules promulgated each decade brought that elusive prosperity into being. Volcker's experience taught different lessons. Volcker worked at the Treasury Department in 1963, when Patman conducted the "Saxon hearings." He left the Federal Reserve chair in 1987, a short time before Bill Seidman permitted McColl to expand operations to Texas. Volcker had observed and presided over bankers' dealings in a period of monumental change.

In December 2009, months before Congress approved the Dodd-Frank Act, Volcker spoke to economists, financial executives, and lawmakers including the British prime minister and Treasury Secretary Geithner. This distinguished group had gathered for the Wall Street Journal Future of Finance Initiative held at the luxurious South Lodge Hotel in the United Kingdom. The commercial bank remained at the center of the American economy, he reminded audience members. Otherwise, Volcker judged that financial innovations like insurance that AIG provided for asset-backed securities had brought "us right to the brink of disaster." In contrast, Volcker told surely astonished audience members, "the most important financial innovation I have seen the past 20 years is the automatic teller machine."[39] Historians, myself included, urge our students and fellow citizens to avoid speculation about paths not taken. But Volcker's admonitions alert us to the choices about the organization of bankers' markets that federal officials made.

NOTES

Introduction

1. Erik M. Erlandson, "A Technocratic Free Market: How Courts Paved the Way for Administered Deregulation in the American Financial Sector, 1977–1988," *Journal of Policy History* 29, no. 3 (July 2017): 350. Robert M. Collins, *More: The Politics of Economic Growth in Postwar America* (New York: Oxford University Press, 2000), 235, determines that postwar lawmakers "pursued [growth] as a goal in its own right."

The supermarket bank concept lacks historical treatment. One reason for this scholarly gap is that bankers never settled on a term to describe banks that took deposits and made loans and also underwrote insurance and dealt in stocks and bonds. During the 1920s, J. P. Morgan was a supermarket bank, but no one described it that way. In 1933, members of Congress and President Franklin D. Roosevelt approved the Glass-Steagall Act, which required banks like J. P. Morgan to abandon its riskier dealings such as underwriting stock issues. In the 1970s, Donald T. Regan began to describe his Merrill Lynch, with its stock sales and checking accounts and nationwide offices, as a supermarket bank. Most likely, members of a presidential commission acquired the term as part of the publicity Regan created. I describe these developments in Chapter 2. Yet, the "supermarket" term never achieved widespread currency. Business writers sometimes described these multiservice operations as "universal banks," but that term also floundered in popular usage. Instead, Americans simply described banks as larger and offering additional services. Federal regulators and lawmakers characterized these enlarged firms as bank holding companies and assigned the Federal Reserve to regulate them. I adopted "supermarket" throughout this book in order to create a common term and to remind nonspecialists about the consistent and intense politics that surrounded efforts to advance and retard the growth of multipurpose banks. Thomas P. Fitch, *Dictionary of Banking Terms*, 4th ed. (Hauppauge, NY: Barron's, 2000), 190, correctly identifies supermarket banking as a political goal.

2. Brian Balogh and Bruce J. Schulman, eds., *Recapturing the Oval Office: New Historical Approaches to the American Presidency* (Ithaca, NY: Cornell University Press, 2015); Ellis W. Hawley, *The New Deal and the Problem of Monopoly: A Study in Economic Ambivalence* (Princeton, NJ: Princeton University Press, 1966); Iwan Morgan, "Presidents, the Federal Budget, and Economic Good, 1946–2008," in *The President and American Capitalism Since 1945*, ed. Mark H. Rose and Roger Biles (Gainesville: University Press of Florida, 2017), 81–98.

3. Pamela Walker Laird demonstrates the important role played by mentorships in determining who succeeded to the top ranks of business in her aptly titled *Pull: Networking and Success Since Benjamin Franklin* (Cambridge, MA: Harvard University Press, 2006).

4. See especially Richard A. Posner, *A Failure of Capitalism: The Crisis of '08 and the Descent into Depression* (Cambridge, MA: Harvard University Press, 2009); Posner, a federal

appellate judge appointed to the bench in 1981 by President Reagan, asserts that "there is nothing irrational about stretching to buy a house in a neighborhood with good schools so that your kids can get a better education" (102).

5. As in earlier decades, bankers continued to write contracts to guarantee payment of debt, large or small. In dealing with these newer types of overnight and short-term loans, however, bankers treated the loan and the collateral as a sale and purchase. They described these sales and return sales as repurchase agreements, or repos. As one hypothetical example of a repo, a trader at Lehman sold asset-backed securities (backed perhaps by mortgages or credit card debt) to a trader at JPMorgan Chase, who in turn sent the money to pay for those securities. In a day or in a few days, Lehman repurchased those securities, less a small sum that served as interest payment. On each transaction, bankers at JPMorgan Chase and elsewhere had to size up the quality of the mortgages that undergirded the securities that Lehman was offering to sell. JPMorgan, or any would-be lender, could insist on a higher rate of interest— or stop purchasing those securities on the spot. In mid-September 2008, bankers at JPMorgan Chase and other large firms determined that Lehman's collateral (the asset-backed securities) had fallen sharply in value and that, in fact, the entire firm was in jeopardy.

Bankers, according to economist Gary Gorton, "began to worry about [mortgages underlying] their loans and refused to renew" them. Trust had been lost. See Gary Gorton, "The Development of Opacity in U.S. Banking," *Yale Journal on Regulation* 31, no. 3 (2014): 825–851. Charles M. Calomiris and Stephen H. Haber, *Fragile by Design: The Political Origins of Banking Crises and Scarce Credit* (Princeton, NJ: Princeton University Press, 2014), 28–33, provide a fine overview of banking basics, including the risks inherent in taking deposits and making loans. Anat Admati and Martin Hellwig, *The Bankers' New Clothes: What's Wrong with Banking and What to Do About It* (Princeton, NJ: Princeton University Press, 2013), 164, explain the way in which bankers treated those overnight loans as sales and purchases. Jerry W. Markham, *A Financial History of the United States*, vol. 3, *From the Age of Derivatives into the New Millennium (1970–2001)* (Armonk, NY: M.E. Sharpe, 2002), 103–107, highlights the institutional development of the repurchase business during the 1980s and 1990s. See also Douglas W. Allen, *The Institutional Revolution: Measurement and the Economic Emergence of the Modern World* (Chicago: University of Chicago Press, 2012), 56–61, for a superb rendering of the methods aristocratic and bourgeois Europeans relied on in the early modern era to gain and retain trust.

6. Lily Geismer, "Agents of Change: The Clintons and the Long History of Microfinance in the United States and the World," a paper presented at the Charles Warren Center, Harvard University, March 2016. Professor Geismer's paper reminded me that market talk obviated the need to talk about redistribution. My thanks to Professor Geismer for kindly sharing this paper with me. I borrowed "grinding politics" from Michael R. Fein, *Paving the Way: New York Road Building and the American State, 1880–1956* (Lawrence: University Press of Kansas, 2008). Professor Fein contends that he borrowed the term from me. Michael had it in print first, and so I'm pleased to award authorship to him.

7. "As a generalization," political scientist Marc Allen Eisner observes, "there are no markets without the state." See his "Markets in the Shadow of the State: An Appraisal of Deregulation and Implications for Future Research," in *Government and Markets: Toward a New Theory of Regulation*, ed. Edward J. Balleisen and David A. Moss (New York: Cambridge University Press, 2010), 519. See also Christy Ford Chapin, "The Politics of Corporate Social Responsibility in American Health Care and Home Loans," *Business History Review* 90, no. 4

(Winter 2016): 648, for the perceptive observation that "commercial bankers created products in a manner designed to satisfy . . . political objectives."

Historians have long studied government and business in the United States. We often describe these studies with the term "political economy." Whatever the exact phrase, authors of these studies make clear that government regulation of rates and service levels were a normal and an expected part of conducting business. As an example, lawmakers and regulators helped create the great railroad firms of the nineteenth and twentieth centuries; and those same lawmakers even determined railroad routes. By so doing, government officials created railroads' hinterlands and stations. The presence of a trunk line or a repair depot might set a town on the road to prosperity. See, for example, Albert J. Churella's magisterial *The Pennsylvania Railroad*, vol. 1, *Building an Empire, 1846–1917* (Philadelphia: University of Pennsylvania Press, 2011); and also see Richard R. John, *Network Nation: Inventing American Telecommunications* (Cambridge, MA: Belknap Press of Harvard University Press, 2010), for an authoritative and deeply researched study of government's role in promoting American telecommunications. The University of Pennsylvania Press has published prize-winning books in its series American Business, Politics, and Society.

8. Professional historians will recognize my use of concepts such as the "associational state"; and historians will also recognize the central role I assign to lawmakers and others who raised important symbols such as economic growth. These themes have enjoyed a deep and lengthy development at the hands of top-tier historians, including Hawley, *The New Deal and the Problem of Monopoly*; K. Austin Kerr, *American Railroad Politics, 1914–1920: Rates, Wages, and Efficiency* (Pittsburgh: University of Pittsburgh Press, 1968); and Louis Galambos, "The Emerging Organizational Synthesis in Modern American History," *Business History Review* 44, no. 3 (Autumn 1970): 279–290. Brian Balogh, *The Associational State: American Governance in the Twentieth Century* (Philadelphia: University of Pennsylvania Press, 2015); and William J. Novak, "The Myth of the 'Weak' American State," *American Historical Review* 113, no. 3 (June 2008): 752–772, bring state-oriented actors and their networks front and center. Thomas J. Sugrue, *The Origins of the Urban Crisis: Race and Inequality in Postwar Detroit* (Princeton, NJ: Princeton University Press, 1996), places those state actors and business leaders in the local and urban scene. Pamela Walker Laird's *Pull* alerted me to the smaller networks through which business executives recruited, socialized, and promoted the next generation of top executives. Susie Pak, *Gentleman Bankers: The World of J. P. Morgan* (Cambridge, MA: Harvard University Press, 2013), provides a rich and deep story about leading bankers and their extended and intensive relationships with government officials and other bankers who resided in their group or in another one. Several decades ago, Richard H. K. Vietor, *Contrived Competition: Regulation and Deregulation in America* (Cambridge, MA: Belknap Press of Harvard University Press, 1994), drew my sustained attention to the way that government rules framed the business of banking. Thomas K. McCraw, *Prophets of Regulation: Charles Francis Adams, Louis D. Brandeis, James M. Landis, Alfred E. Kahn* (Cambridge, MA: Belknap Press of Harvard University Press, 1984); and Walter A. Friedman, *Fortune Tellers: The Story of America's First Economic Forecasters* (Princeton, NJ: Princeton University Press, 2014), offer insight into how to treat individual business leaders and thinkers as institutional actors.

Still other scholars have influenced my thinking on these issues in profound ways. Alfred D. Chandler, Jr., *The Visible Hand: The Managerial Revolution in American Business* (Cambridge, MA: Belknap Press of Harvard University Press, 1977); and Thomas Parke

Hughes, *Networks of Power: Electrification in Western Society, 1880–1930* (Baltimore: Johns Hopkins University Press, 1983), reminded me that complex organizations and innovative managers were and remain central actors in American history. I continue to relish the ecological ideas of Chicago School sociologists, including Louis Wirth and Roderick D. McKenzie. As well, I have found great relevance in the writings of economic sociologists, including Neil Fligstein, Mark Granovetter, and Karl P. Polanyi. K. Austin Kerr and Louis P. Galambos first brought business and professional associations and trade publications to my attention as authors and curated repositories for institutionalized behaviors.

For several decades, historians have awarded precedence to the study of social change in American life. I concur with this emphasis. Starting in 1979 with my book on the origins of the Interstate Highway System, I have also identified presidents and key lawmakers as crucial agents of change in the American political economy. In recent years, Stephen Skowronek's publications reinforced my predilection to study presidential actions. Books by (and memorable conversations with) Ellis W. Hawley, Austin Kerr, Donald R. McCoy, and David M. Welborn no doubt guided my thinking about presidents, economic growth, and the institutional office of the president. Julian Zelizer's many publications were also valuable as I pondered how presidents maneuvered to shape economic regulation and legislation. Early drafts of Brian Balogh, "Consumer in Chief: Presidential Leadership in America's 'Consumer Republic'"; and Morgan, "Presidents, the Federal Budget, and Economic Good," both in Rose and Biles, eds., *The President and American Capitalism Since 1945*, arrived at the right moment.

Chapter 1

1. John F. Kennedy, "Speech by Senator John F. Kennedy in Seattle, WA, at the Civic Auditorium (Advance Release Text)," September 6, 1960, *The American Presidency Project*, hosted by the University of California, Santa Barbara, www.presidency.ucsb.edu. Mark H. Rose, Bruce E. Seely, and Paul F. Barrett, *The Best Transportation System in the World: Railroads, Trucks, Airlines, and American Public Policy in the Twentieth Century* (Philadelphia: University of Pennsylvania Press, 2010), 100–101, 136–137; Ross M. Robertson, *The Comptroller and Bank Supervision: A Historical Appraisal* (Washington, DC: Office of the Comptroller of the Currency, 1968), 146. See also American Bankers Association, *The Commercial Banking Industry: A Monograph Prepared for the Commission on Money and Credit* (Englewood Cliffs, NJ: Prentice-Hall, 1962), 62.

2. American Bankers Association, *The Commercial Banking Industry*, 48, 54–55. On the origins of the Glass-Steagall Act, see Edwin J. Perkins, "The Divorce of Commercial and Investment Banking: A History," *Banking Law Journal* 88, no. 6 (June 1971): 483; and also see Eugene N. White, "Before the Glass-Steagall Act: An Analysis of the Investment Banking Activities of National Banks," *Explorations in Economic History* 23 (1986): 33–55, where the author explains the act's origins and also contends that its strictures on bankers' activities were not needed to enhance financial safety. On J. P. Morgan's breakup, I turned to Susie J. Pak's superbly crafted *Gentlemen Bankers: The World of J. P. Morgan* (Cambridge, MA: Harvard University Press, 2013), 192–193.

3. "Counterfeit Crusade," *Barron's National Business and Financial Weekly*, May 14, 1956, p. 1; "The Real Story Behind Landing Citibank in S.D," *Argus Leader*, April 5, 2015.

4. "Pugnacious Bank Chief James Joseph Saxon," *New York Times*, April 14, 1966; and for Kennedy's commitment to the idea that regulatory agencies required improvements in procedures and personnel and that changes in those agencies could lead to economic improvements,

see John F. Kennedy, "Address of Senator John F. Kennedy Accepting the Democratic Party Nomination for the Presidency of the United States—Memorial Coliseum, Los Angeles," July 15, 1960; and John F. Kennedy, "Special Message to the Congress on the Regulatory Agencies," April 13, 1961; both in *The American Presidency Project*, University of California at Santa Barbara. For a distinguished business historian's account of Kennedy's desire to overhaul the regulatory agencies, see Thomas K. McCraw, *Prophets of Regulation: Charles Francis Adams, Louis D. Brandeis, James M. Landis, Alfred E. Kahn* (Cambridge, MA.: Belknap Press of Harvard University Press, 1984), 206. Iwan Morgan explores the president's legal responsibility for economic growth and the Congress's failure to provide the tools to bring that growth into being in his "Presidents, the Federal Budget, and Economic Good, 1946–2008," in *The President and American Capitalism Since 1945*, ed. Mark H. Rose and Roger Biles (Gainesville: University Press of Florida, 2017), 81–98.

5. "Banking: At It Again," *Time* 87, no. 16 (April 22, 1966).

6. "Kennedy Picks Chicago Lawyer J. J. Saxon as Comptroller After Announcement Snarl," *Wall Street Journal*, September 21, 1961; Edward T. O'Toole, "Views of New U.S. Comptroller on Bank Mergers Are Awaited," *New York Times*, September 22, 1961; Robertson, *The Comptroller and Bank Supervision*, 148. Saxon's ideas about mergers and branching enjoyed wide circulation among leaders at organizations at which he had worked, including Chicago's First National Bank and the American Bankers Association. See Commission on Money and Credit, *Money and Credit: Their Influence on Jobs, Prices, and Growth* (Englewood Cliffs, NJ: Prentice-Hall, 1961), unpaginated introductory materials, 161–166. Sean Vanatta brought this report to my attention.

7. U.S. Office of the Comptroller of the Currency, *Ninety-Ninth Annual Report of the Comptroller of the Currency, 1961* (Washington, DC: U.S. Government Printing Office, 1962), 21; "Comptroller of the Currency: Organization Chart (Mid-August 1962)," *Banking: Journal of the American Bankers Association* 55 (September 1962): 172; Edward T. O'Toole, "New Controller of the Currency Sees Office's Freedom Assured," *New York Times*, November 17, 1961; Herbert Bratter, "Fresh Air in the Comptroller's Office," *Banking: Journal of the American Bankers Association* 55 (September 1962): 45; Sam Dolnick, "A Job Title That Adds Confusion," *New York Times*, September 28, 2010. See also Paul A. Samuelson, *Economics: An Introductory Analysis* (New York: McGraw-Hill, 1961), where the author of a widely assigned textbook describes the work of the Federal Reserve and the Federal Deposit Insurance Corporation, but not the Office of the Comptroller of the Currency.

8. O'Toole, "New Controller of the Currency Sees Office's Freedom Assured"; "Two Agencies to Give Objections to New York Bank Merger at Hearing: Comptroller Sets Dec. 4 for Airing Of Views on First National City and Westchester Bank Merger," *Wall Street Journal*, November 22, 1961.

9. James J. Saxon to the Board of Governors of the Federal Reserve System, January 22, 1962, in *Nomination of James J. Saxon: Hearing Before the Committee on Banking and Currency, United States Senate*, 87th Congress, 2d Session, February 6, 1962 (Washington, DC: U.S. Government Printing Office, 1962), 5–6; "Comptroller Bars First National City Merger Proposal," *Wall Street Journal*, December 20, 1961. See also Harold van B. Cleveland and Thomas F. Huertas, *Citibank, 1812–1970* (Cambridge, MA.: Harvard University Press, 1985), 249–250.

10. U.S. Office of the Comptroller of the Currency, *Ninety-Ninth Annual Report*, 15; U.S. Treasury, Office of the Comptroller of the Currency, *Years of Reform: A Prelude to Progress, 101st Annual Report, 1963* (Washington, DC: U.S. Government Printing Office, 1964), 42, 44.

11. "Bank Branch War Opens in Chicago: Financial Community Split on the Issue of Allowing Units to Be Set Up," *New York Times*, January 11, 1959; "Currency Comptroller Sees No 'Conflict' with Justice Agency," *Wall Street Journal*, February 7, 1962; Elizabeth Tandy Shermer, *Sunbelt Capitalism: Phoenix and the Transformation of American Politics* (Philadelphia: University of Pennsylvania Press, 2013), 9.

12. "Saxon Approves Merger of 2 California Banks; Justice Agency May Act, 1963," *Wall Street Journal*, September 20, 1963; U.S. Office of the Comptroller of the Currency, *Ninety-Ninth Annual Report*, 15.

13. U.S. Treasury, Office of the Comptroller of the Currency, *Years of Reform*; U.S. Treasury, Office of the Comptroller of the Currency, *The Banking Structure in Evolution: A Response to Public Demand, 102nd Annual Report, 1964* (Washington, DC: U.S. Government Printing Office, 1965), 3.

14. Nancy Beck Young, *Wright Patman: Populism, Liberalism, and the American Dream* (Dallas: Southern Methodist University Press, 2000), 23.

15. Ibid., 73–81, including quotations on 74, 79. Young determines that Patman's legislation failed to protect small business owners. See also Daniel Scroop, "The Anti-Chain Store Movement and the Politics of Consumption," *American Quarterly* 60, No. 4 (December 2008): 928.

16. Young, *Wright Patman*, 204–206, including Rayburn quotation, 7.

17. S. E. Babington to Lyndon B. Johnson, May 13, 1964, Box 154, Folder: FG 110-5 1/25/66–, Lyndon B. Johnson Library, Austin, TX (cited hereafter as LBJL).

18. Edward T. O'Toole, "State-Federal Friction Expected at House Hearings on Banking," *New York Times*, April 2, 1963; *Conflict of Federal and State Banking Laws: Hearings Before the Committee on Banking and Currency, House of Representatives*, 88th Congress, 1st Session, April 30, May 1, 2, 3, and 6, 1963 (Washington, DC: U.S. Government Printing Office, 1963).

19. *Conflict of Federal and State Banking Laws*, 3.

20. *Conflict of Federal and State Banking Laws*, 2–3, 9–10, 48. Benjamin Haggott Beckhart, *Business Loans of American Commercial Banks* (New York: Ronald Press, 1959), 121–122, describes bankers' loans to tobacco dealers. Loring C. Farwell, ed., et al., *Financial Institutions*, 4th ed. (Homewood, IL: R. D. Irwin, 1966), 370–371, reports that "banks held non-real estate loans to farmers of $7 billion" and notes that the total of bank loans to farmers had increased since World War II.

21. *Conflict of Federal and State Banking Laws*, 6; "State Banks Suggest Comptroller Saxon Be Ousted; Fight National Bank Branches," *Wall Street Journal*, May 1, 1963; Young, *Wright Patman*, 228; C. Herschel Schooley to President Lyndon B. Johnson, October 3, 1966, Box 83, Office Files of John Macy, Folder: Camp, William B., LBJL.

Antitrust law was a contested affair. See Laura Phillips Sawyer, "California Fair Trade: Antitrust and the Politics of 'Fairness' in U.S. Competition Policy," *Business History Review* 90, no. 1 (Spring 2016): 31–56. Sean Vanatta reminded me to connect my findings to Sawyer's fine essay. Finally, see economist Richard Sylla's "United States Banks and Europe: Strategy and Attitudes," in *European Banks and the American Challenge: Competition and Cooperation in International Banking Under Bretton Woods*, ed. Stefano Battilossi and Youssef Cassis (New York: Oxford University Press, 2002), 59, for the observation that state bank regulators protect[ed] the local positions of the numerous smaller yet politically powerful banks that feared an invasion by the money-center banks." In turn, Sylla adds, those state regulators, "gained from an absence of bank failures in the sheltered local cartels."

22. Robert H. Bremner, *Chairman of the Fed: William McChesney Martin Jr. and the Creation of the Modern American Financial System* (New Haven, CT: Yale University Press, 2004), 81, 90, 95, 174; Young, *Wright Patman*, 168, and Martin as quoted in Young, 228; Peter Conti-Brown, *The Power and Independence of the Federal Reserve* (Princeton, NJ: Princeton University Press, 2016), 51; Iwan Morgan, "Monetary Metamorphosis: The Volcker Fed and Inflation," *Journal of Policy History* 24, no. 4 (2012): 546–547; Bernard D. Nossiter, "He's Rocking Financial Boats," *Los Angeles Times*, July 7, 1963.

23. John F. Kennedy, Memorandum to the Chairman of the Council of Economic Advisers [et al.], March 29, 1962; Walter W. Heller, Memorandum for Mr. [Myer] Feldman, April 11, 1963, both in Council of Economic Advisers, Committee on Financial Institutions, Folder: 11 April 1963, Papers of John F. Kennedy, President's Office Files, Presidential Library and Museum, Boston, MA.

24. "Martin, Saxon Clash on Bank Control Plan," *Los Angeles Times*, June 25, 1963; "Saxon Urges Banks to Challenge SEC Bid to Regulate Any Pooled Investment Funds," *Wall Street Journal*, March 13, 1963.

25. "FRB-Saxon Dispute May Be Arbitrated," *Los Angeles Times*, September 25, 1963; "Saxon Denounces FRB For Decision on Bonds of Washington State," *Wall Street Journal*, September 9, 1963; H. J. Maidenberg, "Bond Men Vexed by Plan of Saxon," *New York Times*, June 22, 1963; Eileen Shanahan, "Bitter Banking Battle Looms On Issue of Bond Underwriting," *New York Times*, August 26, 1963; Eileen Shanahan, "Investment Bankers Criticize Official's Underwriting Bid," *New York Times*, October 8, 1963; "Saxon Claims Monopoly by Investment Bankers in Municipals Dealings," *Wall Street Journal*, October 25, 2011.

26. "Saxon Denounces FRB for Decision on Bonds of Washington State," *Wall Street Journal*, September 9, 1963.

27. Walter Heller, Memorandum for the President, February 28, 1964, Box 13, EX FI 2, Folder: FI 2 Banks–Banking 11/23/63–4/24/64, LBJL.

28. Myer Feldman, Memorandum for the President, March 26, 1964, Papers of Lyndon B. Johnson, Box 154, EX FG 110-4/A, Folder: FG 110-5 Comptroller of the Currency, 11/23/63–12/21/65, LBJL; "Reserve Governor Lays Failure of Regulators' Liaison Group to Saxon," *Wall Street Journal*, March 12, 1964; "U.S. Comptroller Says FRB 'Fixes Prices' on Bank Interest Rates," *Wall Street Journal*, March 11, 1964.

29. Recorded conversation with John T. Jones, December 23, 1963, University of Virginia Miller Center; Joseph A. Pratt and Christopher J. Castaneda, *Builders: Herman and George R. Brown* (College Station: Texas A&M University Press, 1999), 188; Walter L. Buenger and Joseph A. Pratt, *But Also Good Business: Texas Commerce Banks and the Financing of Houston and Texas, 1886–1986* (College Station: Texas A&M University Press, 1986), 202. Well-informed Houston business leaders such as Jones would have been alert to the presence of New York banks in Houston-area lending.

30. George Brown, January 2 and 13, 1964, recordings lbj_wh6401_03_1143 and lbj_wh6401_13_1350, both in LBJL; "Saxon Approves Merger of Banks," *New York Times*, January 14, 1964; Buenger and Pratt, *But Also Good Business*; Robert Dallek, *Flawed Giant: Lyndon Johnson and His Times* (New York: Oxford University Press, 1998), 94; see also Dallek's perceptive observations regarding Johnson's hyperbolic style of speech as "self-aggrandizement"

and also as part of a desire for recognition as the nation's greatest "presidential legislator" (231); and Pratt and Castaneda, *Builders*, 162–163.

31. H. Erich Heinemann, "Justice Department Fighting a Merger of Houston Banks," *New York Times*, October 19, 1966; "Saxon Approves Merger of Banks," *New York Times*, January 14, 1964; "Merger of 2 Houston Banks Wins Approval; Court Fight Expected," *Wall Street Journal*, January 14, 1964; Buenger and Pratt, *But Also Good Business*, 175. As Buenger and Pratt point out, merged banks in Texas still had to operate from one location.

32. Recorded conversation with Ramsey Clark, no. 11052, November 23, 1966, University of Virginia Miller Center; "Justice Agency Asks High Court to Bar Houston Bank Merger for Test of New Law," *Wall Street Journal*, December 22, 1966. In March 1967, the Supreme Court returned *United States v. First City National Bank of Houston et al.* to the district court for trial. See U.S. Treasury, Comptroller of the Currency, *Annual Report 1967* (Washington, DC: U.S. Government Printing Office, 1968), 15–16.

33. "Bank Merger Hit by Supreme Court," *Los Angeles Times*, June 18, 1963; "Court Reverses Merger of Two Big N.Y. Banks," *Los Angeles Times*, March 11, 1965; "Antitrust Law: Supreme Court Develops Presumption of Illegality in Applying Section 7 of the Clayton Act to Bank Merger," *Duke Law Journal* 1964, no. 1 (Winter 1964): 146.

34. "Fed. Reserve Approves Bank Merger," *Los Angeles Times*, September 7, 1961; Benjamin J. Klebaner, "The Bank Merger Act: Background of the 1966 Version," *Southern Economic Journal* 34, no. 2 (October 1967): 253–254.

35. Edward G. Guy, "The Applicability of the Federal Antitrust Laws to Bank Mergers," *Federal Reserve Bank of New York Monthly Review*, March 1966, 80–83.

36. Recorded conversation with Dwight Eisenhower, citation no. 8303, July 2, 1965, University of Virginia Miller Center; Klebaner, "The Bank Merger Act," 250, 256; Richard D. Hylton, "The Bank Merger; 'Manny Hanny': A Name for History Books," *New York Times*, July 16, 1991; "Banking Circles Wondering Can Egg Be Unscrambled?" *Los Angeles Times*, March 12, 1965; "President Signs Bill Setting New Bank Merger Standards," *Los Angeles Times*, February 23, 1966.

37. "President Signs Bill Setting New Bank Merger Standards"; Young, *Wright Patman*, 226–235; Eileen Shanahan, "Bank Bid Scored by Katzenbach," *New York Times*, August 19, 1965; Joe Califano, Memorandum for the President, September 25, 1965, and Lee C. White to the President, both in Box 13, Folder: FI 2 8/7/65–4/12/66, LBJL; Klebaner, "The Bank Merger Act," 254; recorded conversation with George Brown, citation no. 10815, September 21, 1966, University of Virginia Miller Center.

38. Kenneth O' Donnell, Memorandum for Walter Jenkins, February 10, 1964, Box 154, Folder: FG 110-5 1/25/66; C. Herschel Schooley to Billy D. Moyers, February 2, 1965, Box 85, Office Files of John Macy, Folder: Saxon, James J.; Marvin Watson to Mr. President, January 24, 1966, and Nicholas deB. Katzenbach, February 7, 1965, both in Box 154, Folder: FG 110-5 12/22/65–1/24/66; all in LBJL.

39. Thomas J. Foley, "Banking Donnybrook: Saxon-Barr Feud Warmer," *Los Angeles Times*, February 7, 1965. See also, "Banking: The Saxon Crusade," *Time*, October 18, 1963, 101, which was perhaps Moore's source for the crusader term.

40. George S. Moore to Jack J. Valenti, April 21, 1965; Jack Valenti to George S. Moore, April 24, 1965; Jack Valenti, Memorandum for the President, April 23, 1965, all in Folder: FG 110-5, 11/23/63–12/21/65; Harry McPherson to Marvin Watson, January 24, 1966; Marvin

Watson to the President, January 24, 1966, both in FG 110-5, 12/22/65–1/24/66, all in Box 154, LBJL.

41. "At It Again," *Time*, April 22, 1966; Office Files of John Macy, Box 516, Folder: Saxon, John J., LBJL; David L. Mason, *From Buildings and Loans to Bail-Outs: A History of the American Savings and Loan Industry, 1831–1995* (New York: Cambridge University Press, 2004), 160.

42. John J. Macy, Memorandum for the Record, November 4, 1966, Box 83, Office Files of John Macy, Folder: Camp, William B., LBJL.

43. William B. Camp to the President, November 9, 1966, Box 154, Folder: FG 110-5 5/26/64–, LBJL; Marvin Watson to the President, August 30, 1967, Box 35, Folder: William B. Camp, LBJL.

44. Marvin Watson to the President; Joseph D. Hutnyan, "Camp's First Year as Comptroller: Smooth, Orderly and Respectable," *American Banker*, January 25, 1968, in Box 154, Folder: FG 110-5 1/25/66–, LBJL; J. Carlisle Rogers to William B. Camp, May 30, 1967, Box 14, FI 2 5/24/67–6/21/67, LBJL. Camp often asserted that Congress and regulators should not place limits on bankers' operating authority except "where bank solvency and liquidity are threatened"; see his remarks before the West Virginia Bankers Association, Homestead, West Virginia, July 29, 1967, in U.S. Treasury, Comptroller of the Currency, *Annual Report 1967* (Washington, DC: U.S. Government Printing Office, 1968), 228; and before the Texas Bankers Association, San Antonio, Texas, May 14, 1968, in U.S. Treasury, Comptroller of the Currency, *Annual Report 1968* (Washington, DC: U.S. Government Printing Office, 1969), 244.

45. U.S. Treasury, Comptroller of the Currency, *Annual Report 1968*, 156–157.

46. "Citizens-Southern Bank Is Barred from Acting as an Insurance Agent," *Wall Street Journal*, April 4, 1967.

47. U.S. Treasury, Comptroller of the Currency, *Annual Report 1969* (Washington, DC: U.S. Government Printing Office, 1969), 14.

48. John H. Allan, "97 Investment Bankers Suing Saxon over Bonds," *New York Times*, January 15, 1966; "National Banks Can't Underwrite or Deal in Tax-Exempt Revenue Bonds, Court Decides," *Wall Street Journal*, December 16, 1966.

49. "How Have the Comptroller's Rulings Fared?" *Banking* 60 (August 1967): 132, 134.

50. U.S. Treasury, Comptroller of the Currency, *Annual Report 1968*, 18.

51. Sylla, "United States Banks and Europe," 61, notes that during the 1960s "ambitious business-school students viewed banking as a rather stodgy, old-fashioned, and over-regulated business."

52. "Comptroller of the Currency: Organization Chart," *Banking* 55 (September 1962): 172; U.S. Treasury, Comptroller of the Currency, *Annual Report 1968*, 173; and *Annual Report 1969*, 23; Robertson, *The Comptroller and Bank Supervision*, 173.

53. Saxon and Camp's actions at the comptroller's office hold up reasonably well against political scientist Daniel P. Carpenter's nicely conceived effort to identify the characteristics of federal agencies where leading officials enjoyed the ability to initiate rules, recommend legislation, and adjudicate among business claimants seeking a leg up on competitors; see Carpenter, *The Forging of Bureaucratic Autonomy: Reputations, Networks, and Policy Innovations in Executive Agencies, 1862–1928* (Princeton, NJ: Princeton University Press, 2001), 354–355.

54. Economists Charles W. Calomiris and Stephen H. Haber, *Fragile by Design: The Political Origins of Banking Crises and Scarce Credit* (Princeton, NJ: Princeton University Press, 2014), 195–198, contend that the populist-small banker coalition held sway up to around

1970, when demographic and technological change, inflation, and other factors that resided outside the formal political arena began to undermine that long-standing connection. In an identical fashion, economist Peter S. Rose, *The Changing Structure of American Banking* (New York: Columbia University Press, 1987), 351, also locates the first changes in bank rules taking place during the 1970s. And yet, Presidents Kennedy and Johnson supported the efforts of the comptrollers Saxon and Camp to authorize creation of large, multipurpose banks throughout the 1960s, before the appearance of inflation and other factors. Also see economist Ross Levine's "Finance and Growth: Theory and Evidence," in *Handbook of Economic Growth*, vol. 1A, ed. Philippe Aghion and Steven N. Durlauf (New York: Elsevier, 2005), 923, for the contention "that political, legal, cultural, and even geographical factors influence the financial system." Put another way, lawmakers and others relied on courts, regulators, and legislation to shape bankers' operations across decades, and from head to toe.

Chapter 2

1. Donald T. Regan, *A View from the Street* (New York: New American Library, 1972), 143.

2. "Historic Inflation United States—CPI Inflation," http://www.inflation.eu/inflation-rates/united-states/historic-inflation/cpi-inflation-united-states.aspx; Terry Robards, "The Day Wall St. Met the President," *New York Times*, May 31, 1970; Terry Robards, "War and Economy Spur Stock Drops," *New York Times*, May 5, 1970; Mark H. Rose, Bruce E. Seely, and Paul F. Barrett, *The Best Transportation System in the World: Railroads, Trucks, Airlines and American Public Policy in the Twentieth Century* (Philadelphia: University of Pennsylvania Press, 2010), 152.

3. Robert D. Hershey, Jr., "Drain on Savings Banks," *New York Times*, November 8, 1970; A. Sederberg, "Prime Mortgage Rate in Area Boosted to 9%,"*Los Angeles Times*, December 12, 1969; Matthew P. Fink, *The Rise of Mutual Funds: An Insider's View* (New York: Oxford University Press, 2008), 81.

4. Samuel H. Williamson, "Daily Closing Value of the Dow Jones Average, 1885 to Present," MeasuringWorth 2018, http://www.measuringworth.com/DJA/; Robards, "The Day Wall St. Met the President"; Regan, A *View from the Street*, 142–143. Walter A. Friedman, *Fortune Tellers: The Story of America's First Economic Forecasters* (Princeton, NJ: Princeton University Press, 2014), explains the factors that attracted so many Americans to market indexes.

5. Regan, A *View from the Street*, 27.

6. Robards, "War and Economy Spur Stock Drops."

7. U.S. President, *Economic Report of the President Transmitted to the Congress February 1970 Together with the Annual Report of the Council of Economic Advisers* (Washington, DC: U.S. Government Printing Office, 1970), 102–104; John M. Meyer, Jr., "Commission on Private Financial Institutions: Prospects and Problems," *Bankers Magazine* 153 (Winter 1970): 9–11.

After the 1970s, economist and historian Michael A. Bernstein perceptively reports, political realignments created a situation in which "no American president would have the opportunity to intervene in and manage macro-economic performance in the dramatic fashion that had emerged right after World War II." See his "American Presidential Authority and Economic Expertise Since World War II," in *Recapturing the Oval Office: New Historical Approaches to the American Presidency*, ed. Brian Balogh and Bruce J. Schulman (Ithaca, NY: Cornell University Press, 2015), 213. As a consequence of that politically limiting realignment, faster bank growth emerged as one of the few tools available to presidents anxious for devices to accelerate economic growth. But presidents still had to expend vast sums of political capital to change bank rules. No wonder those presidents supported the actions of comptrollers like Saxon in one period or Eugene A. Ludwig in a later period, who altered bank rules by administrative actions.

8. U.S. Senate Committee on Banking, Housing and Urban Affairs, *The Report of the President's Commission on Financial Structure and Regulation (December 1972), Including Recommendations of Department of the Treasury* (Washington, DC: U.S. Government Printing Office, 1973), 1; Jennifer Burns, *Goddess of the Market: Ayn Rand and the American Right* (New York: Oxford University Press, 2009), 2–3, 149–150.

9. U.S. Senate Committee on Banking, Housing, and Urban Affairs, *Report of the President's Commission on Financial Structure and Regulation (December 1972)*, 2.

10. Charles Gardner, "Hunt Commission Near Agreement on Program Designed for Action," *Banking* 64 (December 1970): 10; Records of the President's Commission on Financial Structure and Regulation, Minutes of Meeting of October 28, 1970, Box 6, National Archives, College Park, MD (cited hereafter as Hunt Commission, Minutes, NA-2).

11. R. Alton Gilbert, "Requiem for Regulation Q: What It Did and Why It Passed Away," *Federal Reserve Bank of St. Louis Review* 68, no. 2 (February 1986): 22–26; David L. Mason, *From Buildings and Loans to Bail-Outs: A History of the American Savings and Loan Industry, 1831–1995* (New York: Cambridge University Press, 2004), 185.

12. Hunt Commission, Minutes, NA-2.

13. Ibid.

14. Ibid.; H. Erich Heinemann, "Savings Banks' Survival," *New York Times*, November 9, 1970.

15. Hunt Commission, Minutes, NA-2.

16. Ibid. Sam Peltzman, an economist and leader in efforts to reduce government regulation, determined that "recommendations for reduced legal barriers to entry by one type of financial intermediary into another's market pervade the Hunt Commission Report," in "The Costs of Competition: An Appraisal of the Hunt Commission Report; A Comment," *Journal of Money, Credit and Banking* 4, no. 4 (November 1972), 1001.

17. H. Erich Heinemann, "Revamping Urged for Bank System," *New York Times*, December 17, 1971; U.S. Senate Committee on Banking, Housing, and Urban Affairs, *Report of the President's Commission on Financial Structure and Regulation (December 1972)*, 8–9, 59–62; Mason, *From Buildings and Loans to Bail-Outs*, 207.

18. U.S. Senate Committee on Banking, Housing, and Urban Affairs, *Report of the President's Commission on Financial Structure and Regulation (December 1972)*, 8–9; "Hunt Commission Theme: Let Freedom Ring," *Banking* 72 (January 1972): 15.

19. Gardner, "Hunt Commission Near Agreement," 10; Roland Robinson, "The Hunt Commission Report: A Search for Politically Feasible Solutions to the Problems of Financial Structure," *Journal of Finance* 27, no. 4 (September 1972): 768.

20. H. Erich Heinemann, "A Tree Falls, but Who Hears? Hunt Study Produces Almost No Reaction," *New York Times*, January 16, 1972; J. Betz, "Variable Rate Mortgage Backed," *Los Angeles Times*, July 9, 1972; "Reaction to Hunt Commission Report," *United States Investor/Eastern Banker* 83, no. 3 (January 1972): 7–8.

21. "The New York Fed's Chief Objected to Some Hunt Commission Proposals," *Los Angeles Times*, January 25, 1972; "Branch Banking—The Most Controversial of the Hunt Commission's Recommendations," *United States Investor/Eastern Banker* 83 no. 8 (1972):

9–10; "The Squeezing of the Small Bank," *United States Investor/Eastern Banker* 83, no. 41 (October 1972): 7. Wyatt C. Wells documents Arthur Burns's efforts to protect the Federal Reserve's preeminence in *Economist in an Uncertain World: Arthur F. Burns and the Federal Reserve, 1970–78* (New York: Columbia University Press, 1994), 178–186.

22. Richard M. Nixon, "Special Message to the Congress Proposing Changes in the Nation's Financial System," August 3, 1973, *The American Presidency Project*, University of California at Santa Barbara; Edwin L. Dale, "Nixon Proposes Major Changes in Bank System," *New York Times*, August 3, 1973; "Nixon Wants Lid Off Bank Interest," *Los Angeles Times*, August 3, 1973; Mason, *From Buildings and Loans to Bail-Outs*, 207; Greta R. Krippner, *Capitalizing on Crisis: The Political Origins of the Rise of Finance* (Cambridge, MA: Harvard University Press, 2011), 74; Judith Stein, *Pivotal Decade: How the United States Traded Factories for Finance in the Seventies* (New Haven, CT: Yale University Press, 2010), 92.

23. Dale, "Nixon Proposes Major Changes in Bank System"; Mason, *From Buildings and Loans to Bail-Outs*, 208; Heinemann, "A Tree Falls, but Who Hears?"; Arthur F. Burns to Charles E. Walker, August 17, 1972, Box B45, Folder: Hunt Commission, Meeting re Proposals, May 4, 1973, Gerald R. Ford Library, Ann Arbor, MI (cited hereafter as GRFL). See also Donald P. Jacobs and Almarin Phillips, "Overview of the Commission's Philosophy and Recommendations," in *Policies for a More Competitive Financial System: A Review of the Report of the President's Commission on Financial Structure and Regulation; Proceedings of a Conference Held at Nantucket, Massachusetts, June 1972* (Boston: Federal Reserve Bank of Boston, 1972), 9–20. Jacobs and Phillips, co-directors of research for the commission, contended that "the most vocal objection to the *Report*" was that "the flow of funds to housing would be adversely affected, and . . . national housing goals would not be met" (14).

24. Richard M. M. McConnell, "Treasury Officials Assess the Reaction to Structure 'Package,'" *Banking* 66 (October 1973): 100, 103–104; Mason, *From Buildings and Loans to Bail-Outs*, 208; Krippner, *Capitalizing on Crisis*, 73–74. For Nixon as a policy politician, see Joan Hoff's superbly argued *Nixon Reconsidered* (New York: Basic Books, 1994).

25. Mason, *From Buildings and Loans to Bail-Outs*, 208.

26. Ibid., 211.

27. *Financial Institutions Act of 1975: Hearings Before the Subcommittee on Financial Institutions of the Committee on Banking, Housing, and Urban Affairs, United States Senate, 94th Congress, 1st Session, on S. 1267 and S. 1475, May 14, 15, 16, and June 11, 1975* (Washington, DC: U.S. Government Printing Office, 1975), 2.

28. Rose, Seely, and Barrett, *The Best Transportation System in the World*, 166–170; and also see Thomas Borstelmann, *The 1970s: A New Global History from Civil Rights to Economic Inequality* (Princeton, NJ: Princeton University Press, 2012), 151, who finds that after changes in airline rules, "deregulation rolled through other industries as well." In contrast, I find that the effort to modify bank rules took place over the course of decades and that rules never disappeared.

29. "Ford Requests Rate Freedom for Truckers," *Los Angeles Times*, November 13, 1975; *President Ford's Economic Proposals: Hearings Before the Joint Economic Committee, Congress of the United States, 93rd Congress, 2nd Session, October 11, 16, and 18, 1974* (Washington, DC: U.S. Government Printing Office, 1974), 12; Rose, Seely, and Barrett, *The Best Transportation System in the World*, 170.

30. Deputy Secretary of the Treasury, Memorandum for the Economic Policy Board, March 16, 1974, Box 58, Folder: EPB: Task Force on Bank Regulatory Reform (1), GRFL; Rose, Seely, and Barrett, *The Best Transportation System in the World*, 166–184.

31. Rose, Seely, and Barrett, *The Best Transportation System in the World*, 186–189. "Deregulation was a radical project before it became a conservative one," historian Daniel T. Rogers contends. See his *Age of Fracture* (Cambridge, MA: Belknap Press of Harvard University Press, 2011), 8.

32. Mason, *From Buildings and Loans to Bail-Outs*, 208–211; "The Legislative Outlook: Time to Wrap Up the 1970s (Hunt) and Turn to the 1980s (McFadden)," *United States Banker* 91, no. 2 (1980): 52; Grover W. Ensley to Charles L. Schultze and Lyle Gramley, March 28, 1977; Grover W. Ensley to Charles L. Schultze, March 18, 1977, plus undated attachment, Charles L. Schultze files, all in Box 141, Folder: National Association of Mutual Savings Banks meeting, Jimmy Carter Presidential Library, Atlanta, GA (cited hereafter as JCPL).

33. Mason, *From Buildings and Loans to Bail-Outs*, 146–147, 200–203; Nina Cornell to Stan Morris, March 25, 1977, Charles L. Schultze files, Box 75, Folder: Regulatory Reform [5]; Stu Eizenstat and Jim McIntyre to the President, January 22, 1979; Rick Hutcheson to Stu Eizenstat and Jim McIntyre, January 26, 1979, both in Box: Office of the Staff Secretary, Folder: 1/26/79; Charles L. Schultze and W. Michael Blumenthal to the President, May 25, 1979, Box: Schultze 107, Folder: EPG Anti-Inflation [3]; Stu Eizenstat to the President, Office of the Staff Secretary, Box 214, Folder: 11/26/80, all in JCPL.

34. Mason, *From Buildings and Loans to Bail-Outs*, 214–215; Judith Miller, "Banks' Automatic Shift of Savings to Checking Accounts Held Illegal," *New York Times*, April 21, 1979.

35. Jimmy Carter, "Financial Reform Legislation Message to the Congress Proposing the Legislation," May 22, 1979, *The American Presidency Project*, University of California at Santa Barbara; Stu Eizenstat to the President, November 25, 1980, Office of the Staff Secretary, Box 214, Folder: 11/26/80, JCPL. For Carter's commitment to the development of full-service banking, see also U.S. Department of the Treasury, "Transition Briefing Book: Treasury Initiatives and Issues, November 15, 1980," Donald T. Regan Papers, Box 183, Folder: 1 [1], JCPL.

36. Mason, *From Buildings and Loans to Bail-Outs*, 216; Depository Institutions Deregulation and Monetary Control Act of 1980, Public Law 96-221, 94 Stat. 132.

37. "Mr. Carter's Clear Economic Success," *New York Times*, November 29, 1980.

38. "Donald Regan of Merrill Lynch: An Interest in Everything," *Nation's Business* 60, no. 4 (April 1972).

39. "Merrill's Bold Success Story: After Regan, Gains May Be Consolidated," *New York Times*, December 12, 1980; Edwin J. Perkins, *Wall Street to Main Street: Charles Merrill and Middle-Class Investors* (New York: Cambridge University Press, 1999), 222; Linda Grant, "It Looks Like Bank, Acts Like Bank, but Its Name Is Merrill Lynch," *Los Angeles Times*, March 15, 1981.

40. "Donald Regan of Merrill Lynch: An Interest in Everything," *Nation's Business* 60, no. 4 (April 1972); Thomas Parke Hughes, *Networks of Power: Electrification in Western Society, 1880–1930* (Baltimore: Johns Hopkins University Press, 1983).

41. Grant, "It Looks Like Bank, Acts Like Bank."

42. Donald T. Regan, "The Changing Marketplace," 1, 11–13, unpublished typescript, Donald T. Regan Papers, Box 223, Folder 4, Library of Congress, Washington, DC (cited hereafter as LC). Regan employed an outside researcher to prepare background materials and then recorded his observations on cassette tapes. A Merrill Lynch employee transcribed his spoken words, and Regan corrected them in pencil. Donald T. Regan to Annette De Lorenzo, March 18, 1977; Gary A. Monteforte to Donald T. Regan, August 12, 1977, both in Regan

Papers, Box 223, Folder 7, LC. See also Peter Z. Grossman, "New Waves at Merrill Lynch: Will They Create a Wall Street Tide Again," *Financial World* 148 (April 15, 1979): 24–28.

43. "Pratt Wants to Let S&Ls Get into New Fields," *Los Angeles Times*, September 11, 1981; Leslie Wayne, "Savings Institutions Reshaping Operations in Face of Big Losses," *New York Times*, May 25, 1981; Charles P. Alexander, "Will Reagan's Plan Work?" *Time* 117, no. 8 (February 23, 1981); Stephen M. Aug, "Special Report: The Financial Revolution Radical Change Is Under Way in an Industry Through Which Millions of Us Borrow and Invest," *Nation's Business* 70, no. 4 (April 1982).

44. Paul A. Volcker to Donald T. Regan, April 9, 1981; Roger Mehle to Secretary Regan, August 14, 1981; Donald T. Regan to Jake Garn, n.d., plus attachment, "Questions and Answers Relating to Senator Garn's Letter of June 23," August 12, 1981, all in Box 179, Folder 8; and Donald T. Regan to the President, April 24, 1982, Box 180, Folder 1, all in Regan Papers, LC; Clyde H. Farnsworth, "Treasury Backs Change in Savings Bank Aid," *New York Times*, October 20, 1981.

45. "Chairman St. Germain Approaches His New Job Cautiously," *ABA Banking Journal* 73 (April 1, 1981): 85. See also Christy Ford Chapin, "The Politics of Corporate Social Responsibility in American Health Care and Home Loans," *Business History Review* 90, no. 4 (Winter 2016): 16. Professor Chapin kindly shared this impressive article in draft form.

46. Donald T. Regan to Fernand J. St. Germain, May 29, 1981, Box 179, Folder 8; Donald T. Regan (and Cabinet Committee on Economic Affairs) to the President, April 24, 1981, Box 180, Folder 1; R.T. McNamar to Fernand J. St. Germain, August 3, 1981, Box 179, Folder 8; William B. O'Connell, October 29, 1982, typescript, attached to Office of the Secretary to Secretary Regan, November 3, 1982, Box 38, Folder 2, all in Regan Papers, LC.

47. Mason, *From Buildings and Loans to Bail-Outs*, 218–220; Roger W. Mehle to Secretary Regan, October 2, 1981, Box 148, Folder 4, Regan Papers, LC.

48. Kenneth B. Noble, "Amid Debate, U.S. Panel Asks Wider Powers for Thrift Units," *New York Times*, February 26, 1982; Julian Walmsley, "A Tough Year for US Bankers," *The Banker* 133 (February 1983): 91; O'Connell, October 29, 1982, typescript, attached to Office of the Secretary to Secretary Regan, November 3, 1982.

49. Roger W. Mehle, Jr., to Secretary Regan (through McNamar and Sprinkel), February 23, 1982; E. George Cross II to Secretary Regan, February 26, 1982, both in Box 180, Folder 1; O'Connell, October 29, 1982, typescript, attached to Office of the Secretary to Secretary Regan, November 3, 1982, all in Regan Papers, LC; Carol Loomis, "The Fight for Financial Turf," *Fortune* 104, no. 13 (December 28, 1981): 54–55; Mason, *From Buildings and Loans to Bail-Outs*, 218–219; Ronald Reagan, "Remarks on Signing the Garn–St. Germain Depository Institutions Act of 1982," October 15, 1982, *The American Presidency Project*, University of California at Santa Barbara. See also Gary Gerstle, *Liberty and Coercion: The Paradox of American Government from the Founding to the Present* (Princeton, NJ: Princeton University Press, 2015), 319, where Regan appears as a radical figure bent on loosening the rules that governed savings and loan associations.

50. "Depository Institution Holding Company Deregulation Act of 1983," July 1, 1983, Box 103, Folder 8, Regan Papers, LC.

51. "Bankers Press for Decontrol," *New York Times*, February 22, 1984.

52. *Competitive Equity in the Financial Services: Hearings Before the Committee on Banking, Housing, and Urban Affairs, United States Senate*, 98th Congress, 2nd Session, part 3,

March 6, 7, 13, 27 and 28, 1984 (Washington, DC: U.S. Government Printing Office, 1984), 624–625, 815–816, 1721.

53. Robert A. Bennett, "Chilling Specter at Continental," *New York Times*, May 20, 1984; Kenneth B. Noble, "House Panel Approves New Limits on Banking," *New York Times*, June 27, 1984. Compare my findings about Regan's ability to foster change in bank rules with political economist Martijn Konings, *The Development of American Finance* (New York: Cambridge University Press, 2011), 133, who contends that the "Reagan administration . . . reformed financial institutions in such a way as to multiply the options available to financial capital." See as well Rodgers, *Age of Fracture*, 62, where historian Rodgers argues that "like all legislative fads, deregulation eventually ran out of steam." The urge among lawmakers and bankers to remodel bank rules persisted into the late 1990s, reappeared in 2008, and remained intact at least until 2017.

54. Peter T. Kilborn, "Trading Jobs at the Top: Donald Thomas Regan," *New York Times*, January 9, 1985.

55. For an account of bank deregulation as fewer rules, see Peter S. Rose, "What, How, Why and Whither of U.S. Bank Deregulation," *Canadian Banker* 91 (February 1984): 38–39. In contrast, see Jane D'Arista, *The Evolution of U.S. Finance*, vol. 2, *Restructuring Institutions and Markets* (Armonk, NY: M. E. Sharpe, 1994), who determines that "financial deregulation in the 1980s and early 1990s primarily meant knocking down the walls that had separated financial functions." D'Arista also determines "that the market's scope is limited by the pervasiveness of the government's role in financial regulation compared to the past" (55). D'Arista, like most economists, is prescriptive in her judgments. Compare these ideas with the perceptive observation of Rodgers, *Age of Fracture*, 76, that many understood the market, itself only a metaphor, as in fact "a socially detached array of economic actors, free to choose and optimize."

Chapter 3

1. Leslie Wayne, "Citi's Soaring Ambition," *New York Times*, June 24, 1984; see also Marc Levinson, *An Extraordinary Time: The End of the Postwar Boom and the Return of the Ordinary Economy* (New York: Basic Books, 2016), 96.

2. Joseph J. Schroeder, *They Made Banking History: The Association of Reserve City Bankers, 1911–1960* (New York: Rand McNally, 1962), vii, xvii–xviii; Jean E. Smith to Paul A. Volcker, March 3, 1980, Box 97653, Folder: Reserve City Bankers, Boca Raton, Florida 3/30–31/80, Paul A. Volcker files, Federal Reserve Bank of New York (cited hereafter as FRBNY).

3. Walter B. Wriston, "Looking Backward at the Nineteen-Eighties," remarks to the Reserve City Bankers, Boca Raton, Florida, March 31, 1980, Volcker files; Walter B. Wriston to Paul A. Volcker, July 17, 1981, Anthony M. Solomon Files, Box 114541, Folder: Bank Holding Company Acquisitions, both in FRBNY.

During the 1970s, critics, including Wriston, highlighted federal rules in fostering railroad bankruptcies. See Walter Wriston, introduction to *Competition in Financial Services*, by Cleveland A. Christophe (New York: First National City Corp., 1974). Louis Hyman, *Debtor Nation: The History of America in Red Ink* (Princeton, NJ: Princeton University Press, 2011), 163–164, traces the path by which executives at Sears Roebuck Acceptance Corporation created a large financial firm. See also Sean H. Vanatta, "Citibank, Credit Cards, and the Local Politics of National Consumer Finance, 1968–1991," *Business History Review* 90, no. 1 (Spring 2016): 60, who highlights the determination among corporate officials as early as the 1960s to remove funds from banks in order to boost earnings on their cash and lower interest costs. Jane D'Arista, *The Evolution of U.S. Finance*, vol. 2, *Restructuring Institutions and Markets* (Armonk, NY: M. E. Sharpe, 1994), 414, determines that in 1980, "banks held 39.1 percent of total credit market debt owed by nonfinancial borrowers," but only 26.5 percent in 1992. Wriston could not foresee the future, but he had identified an important and challenging development for commercial bankers.

4. Wriston, "Looking Backward at the Nineteen-Eighties"; Missouri banker, as cited in Phillip L. Zweig, *Wriston: Walter Wriston, Citibank, and the Rise and Fall of American Financial Supremacy* (New York: Crown Publishers, 1995), 695. Richard R. John, *Network Nation: Inventing American Telecommunications* (Cambridge, MA: Belknap Press of Harvard University Press, 2012), 90, determines that laissez-faire "denoted a political economy in which a promoter no longer needed to obtain a special charter to enter a business." Starting in the 1840s, state lawmakers began to approve general incorporation, or laissez faire, laws. Between 1889 and 1993, *Wall Street Journal* writers employed laissez faire 538 times, including 185 uses during the 1980s. Similarly, between 1923 and 1998, *Wall Street Journal* writers used "free enterprise" 3,962 times, including 848 mentions during the 1970s.

5. Zweig, *Wriston*, 18–20.

6. Ibid., 5, 18–21.

7. Ibid., 24–26.

8. Ibid., 29, 46, 58, 61, 82.

9. Ibid., 66. See also Harold van B. Cleveland and Thomas F. Huertas, *Citibank, 1812–1970* (Cambridge, MA.: Harvard University Press, 1985), 254–256; Richard Sylla, "United States Banks and Europe: Strategy and Attitudes," in *European Banks and the American Challenge: Competition and Cooperation in International Banking Under Bretton Woods*, ed. Stefano Battilossi and Youssef Cassis (New York: Oxford University Press, 2002), 61; Douglas Martin, "Walter B. Wriston, Banking Innovator as Chairman of Citicorp, Dies at 85," *New York Times*, January 21, 2005; Office of the Comptroller of the Currency, U.S. Department of the Treasury, "The Negotiable CD: National Bank Innovation in the 1960s," https://www.occ.treas.gov /about/what-we-do/history/150th-negotiable-cd-article.html; Parker B. Willis, "The Secondary Market for Negotiable Certificates of Deposit," report prepared for the Steering Committee for the Fundamental Reappraisal of the Discount Mechanism appointed by the Board of Governors of the Federal Reserve System, February 23, 1967, https://fraser.stlouisfed.org/files /docs/historical/federal%20reserve%20history/discountmech/secmark_willis.pdf.

10. Edward Cowan, "Personality: Young Banker in Foreign Service," *New York Times*, November 24, 1963; Zweig, *Wriston*, 92–93; Cleveland and Huertas, *Citibank*, 264, 275.

11. Zweig, *Wriston*, 149–150.

12. Ibid.; Eileen Shanahan, "Investment Bankers Criticize Official's Underwriting Bid," *New York Times*, October 8, 1963; H. Erich Heinemann, "City Bank Plans Automation Center on Wall St.," *New York Times*, November 17, 1966.

13. Cleveland and Huertas, *Citibank*, 259; Zweig, *Wriston*, 198, 205.

14. Claudia H. Deutsch, "Harry J. Volk, 94, a Bank Executive Known for Innovations," *New York Times*, May 18, 2000; "First National City Bank," *Wall Street Journal*, October 1, 1968; Cleveland and Huertas, *Citibank*, 295–297. As early as 1958, Federal Reserve officials had identified the apparent loophole that permitted one-bank holding companies to engage in nonbank businesses such as insurance. See U.S. Senate Committee on Banking and Cur-

rency, *Bank Holding Company Act: Report of the Board of Governors of the Federal Reserve System* (Washington, DC: U.S. Government Printing Office, 1958), 8–9.

15. George S. Moore, *The Banker's Life: The Memoirs of a Feisty Missourian Who Built the Biggest Bank in the World* (New York: W. W. Norton, 1987), 121; Deutsch, "Harry J. Volk." In 1933, authors of the Glass-Steagall Act designated the Federal Reserve as the holding company regulator, but that authority was "indirect," writes historian Peter Conti-Brown. In 1956, members of Congress made the Fed the holding company's sole and direct regulator and continued that authority in the 1970 legislation. During the 1970s, however, Federal Reserve officials remained conservative in their interpretation of the types of activities heads of the new, one-bank holding companies might undertake. On both counts, see Peter Conti-Brown, *The Power and Independence of the Federal Reserve* (Princeton, NJ: Princeton University Press, 2016), 160–161; and Peter S. Rose, *The Changing Structure of American Banking* (New York: Columbia University Press, 1987), 355, 363.

16. "Holding Concerns Set Merger; Plan Tops $376 Million," *Wall Street Journal*, January 20, 1969; Zweig, *Wriston*, 256.

17. Zweig, *Wriston*, 258–259; "Citibank Subsidiary Set to Buy Minority Share of Ramada Inns' Unit," *Wall Street Journal*, July 28, 1970; "Chase and City Bank Plan Units on Coast," *New York Times*, August 24, 1970.

18. Zweig, *Wriston*, 237, 260–261; "Bank Drops Merger as U.S. Opposes It," *New York Times*, June 14, 1969.

19. Zweig, *Wriston*, 324.

20. "Citibank Indirectly Enters Life Insurance Business," *Wall Street Journal*, April 28, 1971; "First National City's Insurance Plan Cleared," *Wall Street Journal*, October 25, 1971.

21. Matthew P. Fink, *The Rise of Mutual Funds: An Insider's View* (New York: Oxford University Press, 2008), 139–140; the observation regarding Justice Stewart is cited in Zweig, *Wriston*, 325.

22. B. H. Erich, "Closed-End Investing Unit Is Sponsored by City Bank," *New York Times*, June 16, 1972; "Citicorp Plans Unit to Aid Investors in San Francisco," *Wall Street Journal*, December 21, 1972; for Wriston's remark on entrepreneurial spirit, see Zweig, *Wriston*, 325.

23. "City Bank to Erect a 54-Story Tower at East 53d Street," *New York Times*, July 22, 1973; Paul Goldberger, "Citicorp's Center Reflects Synthesis of Architecture," *New York Times*, October 12, 1977. Architectural and planning historian Benjamin Flowers determines that "the skyscraper continues to serve as a global barometer of urbanization and the accumulation of wealth and power." See his *Skyscraper: The Politics and Power of Building New York City in the Twentieth Century* (Philadelphia: University of Pennsylvania Press, 2009), 192.

24. Zweig, *Wriston*, 540; "The Glory Days Are Over at Citicorp," *Business Week*, November 7, 1977, 65, Box 35573, binder titled "Citibank," Volcker files, FRBNY.

25. Zweig, *Wriston*, 552–553; Vanatta, "Citibank, Credit Cards, and the Local Politics of National Consumer Finance," 70–72. Edward Boyer, "Citicorp After Wriston," *Fortune*, July 9, 1984, 148, cites a figure of twenty-six million cards mailed and five million acceptances. Citicorp officials kept the details of the mailing secret.

26. Vanatta, "Citibank, Credit Cards, and the Local Politics of National Consumer Finance," 68, 72–75; "The Real Story Behind Landing Citibank in S.D.," *Argus Leader*, April 5, 2015.

27. "The Glory Days Are Over at Citicorp."

28. Zweig, *Wriston*, 353; report prepared by the Federal Reserve Bank of New York, January 16, 1978, Box 35573, binder titled "Citibank"; Chester B. Feldberg to Files, June 7, 1977, Box 142572, Folder: President's Office Citibank, 1964–1977; Chester B. Feldberg to the Files, April 14, 1977, Box 142572, Folder: President's Office, Bankers Trust Company 1961–1977, all in Volcker files, FRBNY; Paul W. Boltz to Chairman Burns, January 21, 1976, Burns Papers, Box B3, Folder: Bank Earnings & Losses, GRFL; Vanatta, "Citibank, Credit Cards, and the Local Politics of National Consumer Finance," 77.

29. John M. Crewdson, "2 Big Banks Shun a House Inquiry," *New York Times*, January 17, 1976; Zweig, *Wriston*, 352–357, 540; Walter B. Wriston, foreword to *Evolving Concepts in Bank Capital Management*, by Donald S. Howard and Gail M. Hoffman (New York: Citicorp, 1980); F. C. Schadrack to the Files, March 11, 1975, Box 142572, Folder: President's Office Chase Manhattan Bank, 1961–1977, Volcker files, FRBNY; Levinson, *An Extraordinary Time*, 96. In March 1977, analysts with Moody's Investors Service awarded a Triple-A rating, their highest, to Citicorp's debts. They based their decision on Citicorp's diversity, size, earnings, and worldwide operations; see "Citicorp's Debt Gets Rating of Triple-A From Moody's," *Wall Street Journal*, March 11, 1977.

30. A. Crittenden, "Citicorp's Conservative Rebel," *New York Times*, December 22, 1980.

31. Wyatt C. Wells, *Economist in an Uncertain World: Arthur F. Burns and the Federal Reserve, 1970–1978* (New York: Columbia University Press, 1994), 232–233; Walter B. Wriston to Anthony M. Solomon, July 17, 1981, Box 11451, Folder: Bank Holding Company Acquisitions, Solomon files, FRBNY; Zweig, *Wriston*, 785.

32. Wriston, as cited in Robert A. Bennett, "Wriston Ponders Idea of a Bankless Citicorp," *New York Times*, July 31, 1981.

33. During the next two years, Wriston purchased failing S&Ls in Illinois and Florida. See John Morris, "Citicorp Savings Makes Its Debut in Illinois With Mortgage Deal," *American Banker*, April 3, 1984, 3; Geoff Brouillette, "Citicorp Has Had Talks with Thrift: Regulators Try to Work Out Deal for California S&L Firm," *American Banker*, March 2, 1982; Wriston, as quoted in Zweig, *Wriston*, 753.

34. Martin, "Walter B. Wriston, Banking Innovator."

35. William Ollard, "Banker of the Year, 1984," *Euromoney*, October 1, 1984, 262.

36. I am grateful to Pamela W. Laird for a decades-long conversation about the importance of mentors in facilitating and hastening corporate and government promotions. See her valuable *Pull: Networking and Success Since Benjamin Franklin* (Cambridge, MA.: Harvard University Press, 2006).

37. Ernest T. Patrikis to Messrs. Volcker, Timlen, Guy, Piderit and Oltman, November 1, 1977. As of late 1976, a New York Fed official determined that Citicorp had advanced $1.6 billion to nonbanking subsidiaries, out of which 37 percent did not include interest payments on the loans; see "Suggested Topics for Discussion with Citicorp Management," ca. April 1977. Both items are in Box 142572, Folder: President's Office, Citibank, 1964–1977, Volcker files, FRBNY.

38. Joseph D. Hutnyan, "Why Citicorp Hates Nationwide Banking," *Bottomline* 1, no. 7 (May 1984): 9, described Wriston as a "tycoon unfettered by the traditional biases of his peers, who doesn't quake at the sight of Congress and who has lots of muscle and loves to use it." The National Council of Savings Institutions published *Bottomline*. See also Stephen B. Adams, *Mr. Kaiser Goes to Washington: The Rise of a Government Entrepreneur* (Chapel Hill: University of North Carolina Press, 1997), for his development of the concept of business leaders who

built their firms around government contracts. Bill Childs kindly brought Adams's smart book to my attention.

39. Wriston to Volcker, July 17, 1981.

40. Robert A. Bennett, "Inside Citicorp," *New York Times*, May 29, 1983.

Chapter 4

1. "Business People; NCNB's Chief Sees Big Regional Banks," *New York Times*, July 8, 1985.

2. John Helyar, "Regional Trend: In the Merger Mania of Interstate Banking, Style and Ego Are Key—NCNB's Assertiveness Repels Some Targets, but Rivals in South Are Better Liked—Vicious Huns vs. Good Guys," *Wall Street Journal*, December 18, 1986. See also Howard A. Covington, Jr., and Marion A. Ellis, *The Story of NationsBank* (Chapel Hill: University of North Carolina Press, 1993), 202–205, where I located the *Wall Street Journal* article.

3. Pete Endardio, "Hugh MColl: Just a Good Ol' Dog-Eat-Dog Banker," *Business Week*, April 7, 1986, 62.

4. Covington and Ellis, *The Story of NationsBank*, 9–11, including quotation on p. 10.

5. Ross Yockey, *McColl: The Man with America's Money* (Atlanta: Longstreet, 1999), 14–17, 20–21, 30–31.

6. Covington and Ellis, *The Story of NationsBank*, 24, 38.

7. Yockey, *McColl*, 32.

8. Ibid., 36.

9. Covington and Ellis, *The Story of, NationsBank*, 61; Yockey, *McColl*, 36–40, 44–45.

10. Covington and Ellis, *The Story of NationsBank*, 62–63.

11. Yockey, *McColl*, 48, 109.

12. Ibid., 112, 116–121.

13. Ibid., 157–158; "North Carolina National Bank," *Wall Street Journal*, November 13, 1969; "American Commercial Agency," *Wall Street Journal*, January 14, 1969; "NCNB Agrees to Acquire Mortgage Banking Concern," *Wall Street Journal*, September 9, 1971; "NCNB Plan to Acquire Two Firms Is Cleared by the Federal Reserve," *Wall Street Journal*, August 3, 1972.

14. Yockey, *McColl*, 124, 127, 134; Covington and Ellis, *The Story of NationsBank*, 94; "Net of Banking Industry Will Rise 5%–7% in 1971, NCNB Corp. Predicts," *Wall Street Journal*, May 6, 1971.

15. Yockey, *McColl*, 136–137; Hugh L. McColl, Jr., "New Capital for Small Banks: How Best to Raise It?" *Banking* 65 (November 1972): 50, 54; Covington and Ellis, *The Story of NationsBank*, 95.

16. Yockey, *McColl*, 193; Covington and Ellis, *The Story of NationsBank*, 113; John H. Allan, "NCNB—the Southeast's Bank Giant," *New York Times*, May 5, 1974.

17. Yockey, *McColl*, 130–135, 216–217, 249; "Fed Denies a Request by NCNB to Retain TranSouth Financial," *Wall Street Journal*, May 15, 1978.

18. Yockey, *McColl*, 249; "Fed Denies a Request by NCNB to Retain TranSouth Financial"; "NCNB Sells 25 TranSouth Offices," *New York Times*, July 3, 1979.

19. "Comptroller Clears NCNB Acquisition," *New York Times*, November 25, 1982; "NCNB Names McColl Chairman and Chief," *Wall Street Journal*, April 28, 1983; Ronald J. Kudla, "The Current Practice of Bank Long-Range Planning," *Long Range Planning* 15, no. 3 (June 1982): 132–138; Robert A. Bennett, "A Guide to Banking's Hottest Market," *New York Times*, May 23, 1982.

20. "NCNB Corp. Is Cleared by Fed to Buy Control of Lake City, Fla., Bank," *Wall Street Journal*, December 10, 1981; "NCNB Bank Looks to Fill Its Expansion Needs," *New York Times*, June 29, 1981; Susan Harrigan, "NCNB Is Seeking Entry to Florida Banking Market," *Wall Street Journal*, June 23, 1981; "NCNB Gains Approval for 2 Acquisitions," *Wall Street Journal*, December 2, 1982; "Gulfstream Banks in NCNB Link," *New York Times*, August 26, 1982; George G. C. Parker, "Now Management Will Make or Break the Bank," *Harvard Business Review* 59, no. 6 (November/December 1981): 140–148.

21. Anthony M. Solomon to Paul A. Volcker, July 28, 1981, Anthony M. Solomon Files, Box 114541, Folder: Bank Holding Company Acquisitions, FRBNY; "Details Trip up Florida Interstate Banking Group," *American Banker*, January 27, 1984, 2.

22. Peter Field, "Why Deregulation May Turn Out to Be a Damp Squib," *Euromoney* (1981), 85–91; Marshall Puckett to Mr. Solomon, October 3, 1984, Solomon Files, Box 95631, Folder: [illegible], FRBNY; Martha Brannigan and Scott Killman, "More Merger Proposals Are Expected Under Southeast Region Banking Laws," *Wall Street Journal*, July 3, 1984; Yockey *McColl*, 194.

23. Covington and Ellis, *The Story of NationsBank*, 193–195; Stephanie Stokes, "Bankers Face Rapid Change," *Boca Raton News*, November 16, 1983; "There's a Tough New Kid on the Block in Florida: Who? Just Call Him Hugh 'NCNB' McColl, Please," *American Banker*, April 12, 1984, 24.

24. Robert A. Hamilton, "Mergers Seen at Area Banks," *New York Times*, June 16, 1985; Kenneth Michael, "Court Upholds Regional Bank Zones Ruling Clear Sun Banks, Landmark Out-of-State Mergers," *Orlando Sentinel*, June 11, 1985. Charles W. Calomiris and Stephen H. Haber count thirty-eight states involved in interstate banking compacts by 1988. See their *Fragile by Design: The Political Origins of Banking Crises and Scarce Credit* (Princeton, NJ: Princeton University Press, 2014), 202.

25. L. Michael Cacace, "1984 Was Year of Consolidation: The Result: Deposits Acquired Through Mergers Soared," *American Banker*, March 22, 1985; "Testimony of Governor Laurence H. Meyer: Mergers and Acquisitions in Banking and Other Financial Services; Before the Committee on the Judiciary, U.S. House of Representatives, June 3, 1998," at https://www.federalreserve.gov/boarddocs/testimony/1998/19980603.htm; "Record Set for Mergers," *New York Times*, November 1, 1988.

26. Ronald Smothers, "NCNB Chairman's Southern Empire: 'We Won't Have to Worry About the Other Guy Acquiring Us,'" *New York Times*, April 4, 1989; Endardio, "Hugh MColl."

27. Cacace, "1984 Was Year of Consolidation"; Andrea Bennett, "Theobold: Turf Protection Is Reason for Regional Pacts," *American Banker*, May 1, 1984.

28. Peter S. Goodman, "L. William Seidman, Who Led F.D.I.C. During Savings and Loan Crisis, Dies at 88," *New York Times*, May 13, 2009.

29. Bill Bancroft, "Texas Bank Bailouts Merge with Sorrow," *Chicago Tribune*, December 28, 1986.

30. Leonard Sloane, "Shifts at Dallas Republic Bank," *New York Times*, January 10, 1980; Robert A. Bennett, "Texas Banks Riding Oil Boom," *New York Times*, May 14, 1980.

31. "Economic Woes Force Texas Banks into Sweeping Changes," *Oklahoma City Journal Record*, April 22, 1986; Bancroft, "Texas Bank Bailouts Merge with Sorrow."

32. Bill Atkinson, "The Whys of Texas," *American Banker*, October 17, 1990; David La-Gesse, "First RepublicBank Corp. Opens Doors; Pink Slips Go Out as Dallas Banking Firms Complete Merger," *American Banker*, June 8, 1987.

33. "First Republicbank, as Expected, Posts $1.5 Billion Net Loss," *Wall Street Journal*, April 27, 1988.

34. L. William Seidman, *Full Faith and Credit: The Great S&L Debacle and Other Washington Sagas* (New York: Times Books, 1993), 80–81, 126–129, 153–154; Yockey, *McColl*, 340–341; "Texas Bank Expected to Post Another Big Quarterly Loss: Citicorp Looking at Books of Troubled First RepublicBank," *Los Angeles Times*, June 29, 1988.

35. Yockey, *McColl*, 321.

36. Seidman, *Full Faith and Credit*, 151–152.

37. Yockey, *McColl*, 341, 343, 349; Leonard M. Apcar, "First RepublicBank Bailout May Damage Capital-Raising Efforts by Other Banks—Takeover by NCNB, Aided by $4 Billion from U.S., Doesn't Protect Holders," *Wall Street Journal*, August 1, 1988.

38. Apcar, "First RepublicBank Bailout May Damage Capital-Raising Efforts by Other Banks"; Yockey, *McColl*, 322.

39. Nathaniel C. Nash, "U.S. Will Provide Billions to Rescue Ailing Texas Bank," *New York Times*, July 30, 1998; Richard I. Stillinger, "NCNB Strikes Gold in Texas," *Bankers Monthly* 106, no. 8 (August 1989): 73.

40. Seidman, *Full Faith and Credit*, 153–159; Philip Shabecoff, "L. William Seidman, Chief Clarifier," *New York Times*, December 15, 1974.

41. "Bank of America Corporation—Company Profile, Information, Business Description, History, Background Information on Bank of America Corporation," *Reference for Business*, http://www.referenceforbusiness.com/history2/18/Bank-of-America-Corporation .html; Yockey, *McColl*, 453–454, quote on p. 454.

42. Hugh McColl, "Commercial Banks Need More Freedom to Compete Effectively," *American Banker*, June 29, 1989. In 1982, Sears executives purchased Dean Witter, a securities dealer. According to Jane D'Arista, *The Evolution of U.S. Finance*, vol. 2, *Restructuring Institutions and Markets* (Armonk, NY: M. E. Sharpe, 1994), 76, Sears emerged as "the first full-service financial 'supermarket.'"

43. McColl, "Commercial Banks Need More Freedom to Compete Effectively."

Chapter 5

1. "Williamson Herds Hogs to Final," *Telegram & Gazette* (Worcester, MA), April 3, 1994; "President Takes Break from Whitewater Talk," *Las Vegas Review-Journal*, April 3, 1994.

2. Peter Applebome, "What's Doing in Charlotte," *New York Times*, February 27, 1994; "The 25 Largest Banks," *Financial World* 163, no. 4 (February 15, 1994): 58; "McColl Candidacy for U.S. Job Denied," *American Banker*, November 10, 1992.

3. David L. Mason, *From Buildings and Loans to Bail-Outs: A History of the American Savings and Loan Industry, 1831–1995* (New York: Cambridge University Press, 2004), 239; Robert M. Garsson, "Clinton: Lending Is Key to Reviving the Economy," *American Banker*, December 16, 2013; "Labor Force Statistics From the Current Population Survey," https://data .bls.gov/pdq/SurveyOutputServlet; Stephen Davis, "The FOB at the OCC," *Institutional Investor* 28, no. 3 (March 1994).

4. Al From and Bruce Reed, Memorandum to the President-Elect and the Vice President Elect, December 19, 1992, https://clinton.presidentiallibraries.us/items/show/4577, William J. Clinton Presidential Library, Little Rock, AR; Kenneth Cline, "NationsBank Pressing for Changes in CRA Enforcement," *American Banker*, March 22, 1993; William J. Clinton, "Remarks to the National Urban League," August 4, 1993, *The American Presidency Project*,

University of California at Barbara; Kenneth Cline, "Banker of the Year: Hugh L. Mc-Coll Jr.," *American Banker*, January 24, 1994, 6.

5. Steve Cocheo, "An Early Reading of the Clinton/Gore Administration," *ABA Banking Journal* 85, no. 1 (January 1993); "After the Nafta Victory," *New York Times*, November 19, 1993; Jim McTague, "Front Row on Washington: The Unmitigated Gall of NationsBank's Mc-Coll," *American Banker*, August 2, 1993; Gene Sperling, Bruce Reed, Memorandum for the President, July 14, 1993, WCPL.

6. Stephen Davis, "The FOB at the OCC," *Institutional Investor* 28, no. 3 (March 1994).

7. Norbert McCrady, "Comment: Push for Interstate Branching Demonstrates That Regulators Are Ignoring Banks' Best Interests," *American Banker*, December 8, 1993.

8. Barbara A. Rehm, "Ludwig Backs Insurance Sales, Interstate Branching for Banks," *American Banker*, September 14, 1993; Davis, "The FOB at the OCC"; "Statement of Eugene A. Ludwig, Comptroller of the Currency, Washington, DC," in *Interstate Banking and Insurance Activities of National Banks: Hearings Before the Committee on Banking, Housing, and Urban Affairs, United States Senate*, 103rd Congress, 1st Session, on nationwide banking and branching and the insurance activities of national banks, October 5 and November 3, 1993 (Washington, DC: U.S. Government Printing Office, 1994), 7–9.

9. Michael Quint, "Court Backs Banks' Sales of Insurance," *New York Times*, July 11, 1991. Historian Erik M. Erlandson, "A Technocratic Free Market: How Courts Paved the Way for Administered Deregulation in the American Financial Sector, 1977–1988," *Journal of Policy History* 29, no. 3 (July 2017): 350–377, describes judges and regulators starting in the early 1980s who were engaged in a process of "administered deregulation." Regulators in that period, however, never modified the rules under which bankers and insurance agents operated.

10. Linda Greenhouse, "Law Upheld on Bank Insurance Sales," *New York Times*, June 8, 1993.

11. "Response to Written Questions of Senator Sasser from Eugene A. Ludwig," in *Interstate Banking and Insurance Activities of National Banks*, 252–253.

12. John F. Fitzgerald, "Dodd Hailed for Role in Keeping Big Banks Out of Insurance Sales," *Hartford Courant* (1984); Stephen Labaton, "Votes Seen for House Banking Bill," *New York Times*, November 21, 1991; George Judson, "Campaign Trail Appeals to Dodd," *New York Times*, October 27, 1992; Keith Bradsher, "Bill Gains to End Interstate Banking Curbs," *New York Times*, February 4, 1994; Kenneth Silverstein, "Banks Target States in Battle to Bring Interstate Branching," *Corporate Cash Flow Magazine* 14, no. 12 (November 1993).

13. Jerry Knight, "Interstate Banking Gets Unexpected Boost in Congress; Dodd Drops Long-Held Objection, Making Passage This Year Likely," *Washington Post*, February 4, 1994.

14. Steven F. Sullivan, "Don't Bank on Insurance," *Life Association News* 88, no. 7 (July 1993): 60.

15. Steven Brostoff, "Dodd Halts Move to Limit Bank Activity," *National Underwriter* 98, no. 7 (February 14, 1994).

16. Harry A. Jacobs, Jr., to Donald W. Riegle, November 23, 1987; James Tozer, Jr., to Donald W. Riegle, February 26, 1987, both in Folder: Banking Correspondence, 1987; and John W. Ennest to Donald W. Riegle, Jr., February 10, 1988, Folder: Banking Correspondence, 1988; all in Box 82, Donald W. Riegle, Jr., Papers, University of Michigan–Flint Archives (cited hereafter as Riegle Papers, UMI-F).

17. Donald W. Riegle, handwritten memo, undated, ca. 1987 (handwriting confirmed by the archivist), Box 82, Folder: Community Reinvestment Act, 1988, Riegle Papers, UMI-F;

Lisa Servon, *The Unbanking of America: How the New Middle Class Survives* (New York: Houghton Mifflin Harcourt, 2017), 8. Rebecca Marchiel, "Neighborhoods First: The Urban Reinvestment Movement in the Era of Financial Deregulation, 1966–1989" (PhD diss., Northwestern University, 2014), explains the Community Reinvestment Act's local and urban origins.

18. Donald W. Riegle, Jr., "Statement on the Financial Modernization Act," draft, undated, ca. mid-1988; Donald W. Riegle, "Washington's Outlook for Banking," typescript prepared for delivery to the Michigan Bankers Association Management Conference, Dearborn, MI, December 11, 1987; and "Bank1494 for Realtors," undated, ca. April 1988; all in Box 82, Folder: Financial Services Modernization Act (S. 1886), 1988, Riegle Papers, UMI-Flint; and John B. Albright, "Riegle Seeks Banking Unity," *Lansing State Journal*, October 13, 1987, in Box 83, Folder: Financial, Banking Reform, Nonbank Banks, 1985–1989, Riegle Papers, UMI-Flint.

19. "McColl Calls," *Bankers Monthly* 110, no. 1 (January 1993); "Speaking His Mind," *Institutional Investor* 27 no. 3 (March 1993): 40; Cline, "NationsBank Pressing for Changes in CRA Enforcement"; Gail Russell Chaddock, "What It Took to Enact Banking Reform: Contributions, Compromise, and Having Powerful Friends in High Places," *Christian Science Monitor*, October 21, 1994.

20. Justin Fox, "Ludwig, Once Viewed as Threat, Thrives as Bankers' Champion," *American Banker*, July 25, 1995; Barbara A. Rehm, "News Analysis: Policymakers Renewing the Call for Overhaul of Bank Regulations," *American Banker*, February 17, 1994; Norbert McCrady, "Comment: Branching Will Help Fat Cats Feed Clinton's War Chest," *American Banker*, April 27, 1994.

21. Chaddock, "What It Took to Enact Banking Reform."

22. *Congressional Record*—Senate, September 13, 1994, 103rd Congress, 2nd Session, vol. 140, part 17, no. 127, in Box 84, Folder: Committee, Banking 1993–1994, 2 of 2, Riegle Papers, UMI-Flint; "The Nation's New Interstate Banking Law," *Business Review–Federal Reserve Bank of Philadelphia* (November/December 1994): 21.

23. *Congressional Record*—Senate, September 13, 1994, in Riegle Papers, UMI-Flint; "The Nation's New Interstate Banking Law." See also Charles W. Calomiris and Stephen H. Haber, *Fragile by Design: The Political Origins of Banking Crises and Scarce Credit* (Princeton, NJ: Princeton University Press, 2014), 202, who identify a "final blow to the [small] banks" in the 1994 legislation.

24. William J. Clinton, "Remarks on Signing the Riegle-Neal Interstate Banking and Branching Efficiency Act of 1994," September 29, 1994, *The American Presidency Project*, University of California at Santa Barbara.

25. "Banking Bill Spells Regulatory Relief," *Savings & Community Banker* 3, no. 9 (September 1994): 8; Dave Skidmore, "Interstate Bank Pact Reached; Compromise Would Dismantle Laws Dating to the 1920s," *Austin American Statesman*, July 26, 1994; Barbara Rehm, "Victory Seems Near for Champion of Interstate," *American Banker*, August 10, 1994; Clinton, "Remarks on Signing the Riegle-Neal Interstate Banking and Branching Efficiency Act of 1994."

26. Steven Greenhouse, "When Robert Rubin Talks . . . ," *New York Times*, July 25, 2013.

27. Kim Phillips-Fein, *Fear City: New York's Fiscal Crisis and the Rise of Austerity Politics* (New York: Metropolitan Books, 2017), 1–9; Rubin, as cited in Steven Greenhouse, "When Robert Rubin Talks." See also Benjamin C. Waterhouse, "Mobilizing for the Market: Organized Business, Wage-Price Controls, and the Politics of Inflation, 1971–1974," *Journal of American History* 100, no. 2 (September 2013): 478, for the perceptive observation that "the

politics of inflation served as a boot camp for groups such as . . . the Chamber of Commerce . . . and ultimately helped guarantee that market capitalism trumped economic planning in America's policy arsenal."

28. Thomas J. Sugrue, *The Origins of the Urban Crisis: Race and Inequality in Postwar Detroit* (Princeton, NJ.: Princeton University Press, 1996); Judith Stein, *Pivotal Decade: How the United States Traded Factories for Finance in the Seventies* (New Haven, CT: Yale University Press, 2010); Tracy Neumann, *Remaking the Rust Belt: The Postindustrial Transformation of North America* (Philadelphia: University of Pennsylvania Press, 2016).

Bankers like Wriston and regulators like Donald Regan and Robert Rubin did not seek something so simple and unlikely as tossing regulations overboard. Instead, they sought to shape rules that advanced commercial banking as part of a prospering U.S. economy. During the 1970s and 1980s, a few scholars, lawmakers, and regulators described these one-industry programs with terms like "industrial policy. See Otis L. Graham, Jr., *Losing Time: The Industrial Policy Debate* (Cambridge, MA.: Harvard University Press, 1992).

29. Mark P. Jacobsen and Julie L. Williams, "The Business of Banking: Looking into the Future," *Business Lawyer* 50, no. 3 (May 1995): 783–785; Barbara Rehm, "Policymakers Renewing the Call for Overhaul of Bank Regulations," *American Banker*, February 17, 1994, 2; Eugene N. White and Naomi R. Lamoreaux, "Were Banks Special Intermediaries in Late Nineteenth Century America? Commentary," *Review–Federal Reserve Bank of St. Louis* 80, no. 3 (May/June 1998), 13–36; Thomas Stanton, as quoted in Peter David, "From Niche to Death Trap," *The Economist*, April 30, 1994.

Wriston and others bankers often blamed excessive regulation for their firms' lower-than-expected earnings. Yet, see also Eli M. Remolona and Kurt C. Wulfekuhler, "Finance Companies, Bank Competition, and Markets," *Federal Reserve Bank of New York Quarterly Review* 17 (Summer 1992), for the argument that during the period 1985–1990, banks actually outperformed finance companies in factoring and other areas.

On new types of credit, see Louis Hyman, *Debtor Nation: The History of America in Red Ink* (Princeton, NJ: Princeton University Press, 2011), 220–280; and Hyman, *Borrow: The American Way of Debt* (New York: Vintage Books, 2012), 217–247.

30. "Rubin Calls for Modernization Through Reform of Glass-Steagall Act," *Journal of Accountancy* 179 no. 5 (May 1995): 12; "Clinton Backs Merging Bank, Insurance Firms," *Chicago Tribune*, February 27, 1995.

31. Keith Bradsher, "House G.O.P. Plans Vote on Bank-Securities Law," *New York Times*, September 28, 1995; Bradsher, "No New Deal for Banking; Efforts to Drop Depression-Era Barriers Stall, Again," *New York Times*, November 2, 2013; "Statement of Bob Fulwider, Independent Insurance Agents of America; Accompanied by Ann Kappler," in *H.R. 1062, the Financial Services Competitiveness Act of 1995, Glass-Steagall Reform, and Related Issues (Revised H.R. 18): Hearings Before the Committee on Banking and Financial Services, House of Representatives*, Part 4, 104th Congress, 1st Session (Washington, DC: U.S. Government Printing Office, 1995), 17.

32. Keith Bradsher, 'Insurance Agents Win Again on Bank Bill," *New York Times*, June 14, 1995; Idem, "House G.O.P. Plans Vote on Bank-Securities Law," *New York Times*, September 28, 1995; Idem, "Rubin Renews Call for Bank-Insurer Mergers," *New York Times*, September 23, 1995; "No New Deal for Banking."

33. Nick Gilbert, "Better Leach Than Ludwig," *Financial World* 164, no. 10 (April 25, 1995).

34. Jim McTague, "Regulation 'L,'" *Barron's* 75, no. 1 (January 2, 1995); Gilbert, "Better Leach Than Ludwig"; Fox, "Ludwig, Once Viewed as Threat, Thrives as Bankers' Champion."

35. "Ludwig Lifts Restrictions on US Banks," *Balance Sheet* 5, no. 4 (Winter 1996): 3.

36. Ibid.; Phil Britt, "Lessening Burdens," *America's Community Banker* 5, no. 7 (July 1996): 43; "OCC Revises Part 5 Applications Process," *ABA Bank Compliance* 17, no. 12 (December 1996): 4–5.

37. *Office of the Comptroller of the Currency's Recent Regulatory Actions: Hearing Before the Subcommittee on Financial Institutions and Regulatory Relief of the Committee on Banking, Housing, and Urban Affairs, United States Senate,* 105th Congress, 1st Session (Washington, DC: U.S. Government Printing Office, 1997), 2, 4–6; Robert M. Garsson, "Dismantling Glass-Steagall: Glass-Steagall Repeal: Is It in the Stars for Banks at Last?" *American Banker,* March 20, 1995; Gilbert, "Better Leach Than Ludwig"; Michelle Celarier, "Chipping at the Firewalls," *Euromoney,* December 1996, 52–56.

38. Leslie Eaton with Laura M. Holson, "Travelers Chief, at 65, Lands 'The Deal' of a Life of Deals," *New York Times,* April 11, 1998; Stephen E. Frank, Anita Raghavan, and Leslie Scism, "The Big Umbrella: Travelers/Citicorp Merger—How Can Racehorse CEOs Learn to Run in Tandem?" *Wall Street Journal,* April 7, 1998; Laura Sachar, "Sandy Weill's Expansion Team," *Financial World* 156, no. 16 (August 11, 1987).

39. Floyd Norris, "In the Weill Empire, Some Mixed Results," *New York Times,* March 1, 1990.

40. Monica Langley, *Tearing Down Walls: How Sandy Weill Fought His Way to the Top of the Financial World . . . and Then Nearly Lost It All* (New York: Wall Street Journal Books/Free Press, 2003), 272–274; Mitchell Martin, "A New No. 1: Financial Giants Unite; Citicorp and Travelers Plan to Merge in Record $70 Billion Deal," *International Herald Tribune,* April 7, 1998.

41. Greg Burns, "A Mammoth Money Match: Citicorp, Travelers Deal Worth $85 Billion; Some Question if 'Supermarket' Concept Can Work," *Chicago Tribune,* April 7, 1998; Mitchell Martin, "Citicorp and Travelers Plan to Merge in Record $70 Billion Deal: A New No. 1; Financial Giants Unite," *New York Times,* April 7, 1998; Langley, *Tearing Down Walls,* 289; Carol J. Loomis, James Aley, and Lixandra Urresta, "Citigroup: 'One Helluva Candy Store!'" *Fortune,* May 11, 1998, 72–78.

42. "OCC's Ludwig Urges Insurers, Agents to Stop Fighting and Welcome Banks," *Best's Review* 97, no. 10 (February 1997): 18; Andrew Osterland, "Shatterproof Glass," *Financial World* 166, no. 6 (June 17, 1997): 32–36; George F. Williams, "Who Will Curb the Comptroller?" *American Agent & Broker* 69, no. 1 (January 1997): 22; "Washington People: Leach Letter Calls Ludwig Push Against Reform Bill 'Unseemly,'" *American Banker,* July 28, 1997; "Legislative Update," *American Banker,* November 13, 1997; Philip Maher, "Washington Catches Up," *Investment Dealers' Digest: IDD* 63, no. 21 (May 26, 1997): 2.

43. "Fed Issues Citi Blueprint," *CFO Alert* 5, no. 37 (September 28, 1998): 1; "In Brief: White House Threatens to Veto Reform Bill," *American Banker,* August 10, 1998; Leslie Wayne, "Politics Again Leaves U.S. Financial Overhaul in Limbo," *New York Times,* October 5, 1998; Leslie Wayne, "The Comptroller for the Moment; Banking Lawyer May Have Trod on Some Senatorial Toes," *New York Times,* December 8, 1998; Robert Rubin to Erskine Bowles and Gene Sperling, September 22, 1998, National Economic Council, Financial Modernization, WCPL; see also Gene Sperling, Memorandum to the President, July 9, 1998, National Economic Council, Financial Modernization, WCPL.

44. Peter Pae, "Bank Lobby Opposes Reform Bill; ABA Stance Another Setback for GOP Plan to Revamp Finance Laws," *Washington Post*, March 26, 1998; Steven Brostoff, "H.R. 10 Agreement Reached," *National Underwriter* 102, no. 40 (October 5, 1998): 1, 65; Leslie Wayne, "Prospect of Gramm Reign Worries Wall St.," *New York Times*, November 5, 1998.

45. Brian Collins, "Senate Committee Approves H.R. 10," *National Mortgage News*, September 21, 1998, 34; Jeffrey Marshall, "Taking Another Road into Banking," *U.S Banker* 108, no. 12 (December 1998): 38–52.

46. Brian Garrity and Jeffrey Keegan, "Citigroup's Turf Wars Could Hurt Bank Legislation," *Investment Dealers' Digest*, November 16, 1998, 1–8; "Financial-Services Reform Is Dead for This Year," *Best's Review* 99, no. 7 (November 1998); Collins, "Senate Committee Approves H.R. 10," 34.

47. Robert E. Harris, "The Banking Business Will Miss Gene Ludwig," *Texas Banking* 87 no. 3 (March 1998): 7; Wayne, "Prospect of Gramm Reign Worries Wall St."

48. "Treasury Secretary Robert E. Rubin, Senate Banking Committee," text as prepared for delivery June 17, 1998, https://clinton.presidentiallibraries.us/items/show/4864,WCPL.

49. "Operating Sub Issue Returns to Haunt HR 10," *Bank Investment Services Report* 7, no. 19 (May 10, 1999): 1; Alan Greenspan, "Statements to the Congress: Alan Greenspan," *Federal Reserve Bulletin* 85, no. 6 (June 1999): 419–423; "Statement by Alan Greenspan, Chairman, Board of Governors of the Federal Reserve System, Before the Committee on Banking, Housing, and Urban Affairs, U.S. Senate, June 17, 1999," p. 9, WCPL.

50. Walter A. Friedman, *Fortune Tellers: The Story of America's First Economic Forecasters* (Princeton, NJ: Princeton University Press, 2014), 211, describes Greenspan as "the most powerful [economic] forecaster in the world during his tenure at the helm of the Federal Reserve between 1987 and 2006"; David B. Sicilia and Jeffrey L. Cruikshank, *The Greenspan Effect: Words That Move the World's Markets* (New York: McGraw-Hill, 2000), xi; Robert J. Samuelson, "The Idolizing of Greenspan," *Newsweek*, November 27, 2000, 59. In contrast, economist Martin H. Wolfson, "An Institutional Theory of Financial Crises," in *The Handbook of the Political Economy of Financial Crises*, ed. Martin H. Wolfson and Gerald A. Epstein (New York: Oxford University Press, 2013), 185, contends that Greenspan "implemented his free-market philosophy during his tenure at the Federal Reserve."

51. Sperling, Memorandum to the President, July 9, 1998; Stephen Labaton, "Senate Votes to Drop Barriers Between Nation's Financial Industries," *New York Times*, May 7, 1999. In the mid-1990s, historian Peter Conti-Brown reports, Clinton administration officials appointed economist Laurence Meyer to the Federal Reserve with the understanding that he would promote the Community Reinvestment Act; see Conti-Brown, *The Power and Independence of the Federal Reserve* (Princeton, NJ: Princeton University Press, 2016), 245.

52. "Treasury Secretary Robert E. Rubin, Senate Banking Committee."

53. Kirk Victor, "Loan Star Phil," *National Journal* 31, no. 44 (October 30, 1999): 3122; Rob Wells and John Rega, "Banking Laws Braced for Sweeping Reforms: Depression-Era Roots: Treasury and Fed Finally Reach Accord over Bank Legislation," *National Post*, October 15, 1999; Michael Schroeder, "Fed, Treasury Agree on Framework for Regulation of Financial Services," *Wall Street Journal*, October 15, 1999.

54. Stephen Labaton, "Republicans Propose a Deal on Financial Services," *New York Times*, October 13, 1999; "Banking Law Overhaul Clears a Major Hurdle: Treasury, Fed Agree to Share Oversight," *Chicago Tribune*, October 15, 1999; Stephen Labaton, "Deal on Bank Bill Was Helped Along by Midnight Talks," *New York Times*, October 24, 1999; "US Banking Re-

form Lex Column," *Financial Times*, October 19, 1999; David L. Glass, "The Gramm-Leach-Bliley Act: Overview of the Key Provisions; Presentation Before the State of New York Banking Department," *New York Law School Journal of Human Rights* 17, no. 1 (2000): 1–38.

55. "The New American Universal Bank," *Harvard Law Review* 110, no. 6 (April 1997): 1321; William J. Clinton, "Statement on Signing the Gramm-Leach-Bliley Act," November 12, 1999, *The American Presidency Project*, University of California at Santa Barbara. See also Monica Prasad, *The Land of Too Much: American Abundance and the Paradox of Poverty* (Cambridge, MA: Harvard University Press, 2012), for her contention that there was no natural constituency for regulation. Prasad overlooks the unending battles among leaders of business groups such as insurance agents who relied on their home-state legislators to protect them from distant competitors through regulations. As one additional example, the main actors in this book—commercial bankers and insurance executives—united in their efforts to prevent nonbanks such as Wal-Mart from purchasing thrifts. Regulation mattered deeply, it appears. In this area, Prasad notices perfectly the tendency in the United States to use "the power of the state against the power of capital" (263). Finally, see Prasad's equally valuable observation that "the United States is not a laissez-faire or liberal political economy at all, and it never has been" (263).

56. "The Making of a Law: Q & A with Edward Yingling," *ABA Banking Journal* 91 no. 12 (December 1999): 20–24. Bankers had funded a large portion of the growth that took place among their less regulated competitors, Jane D'Arista reports, in *The Evolution of U.S. Finance*, vol. 2, *Restructuring Institutions and Markets* (Armonk, NY: M. E. Sharpe, 1994), 426–433.

57. Gregory L. Miller, "'New' Economy Masks Lethargy in 'Old,'" *ABA Banking Journal* 91, no. 12 (December 1999). See also Carmen M. Reinhart and Kenneth S. Rogoff, *This Time Is Different: Eight Centuries of Financial Folly* (Princeton, NJ: Princeton University Press, 2009), 290–292, for their account of the widespread conviction among bankers and lawmakers that they had constructed a financial system that was unlikely to undergo a severe contraction.

58. Joseph E. Stiglitz, *Free Fall: America, Free Markets, and the Sinking of the World Economy* (New York: W. W. Norton, 2010), xvi.

Chapter 6

1. "Kenneth D. Lewis, President and Chief Operating Officer, Bank of America, Speaks to the Greater Miami Chamber of Commerce on 'The New Gold Rush: High Tech in the Old Economy,'" *PR Newswire*, May 03, 2000; David Boraks, "In Big Integration Job, B of A's Lewis Stresses the Little Things," *American Banker*, December 5, 2002, 2A.

2. Patrick Dalton, "A Look at Banking's Legal Landscape," *ABA Bankers News* 10, no. 16 (August 6, 2002): 5.

3. Landon Thomas, Jr., and Jennifer Bayot, "Changing the Guard: The Titan; A Hands-On Boss Will Try to Let an Old Friend Lead," *New York Times*, July 17, 2003; Bethany McLean, "Is This Guy the Best Banker in America?" *Fortune*, July 6, 1998, 126–128; Charles W. Thurston, "World's Best Banks 2001," *Global Finance* 15, no. 11 (October 2001): 32–69; Bob Kapler, "Living Richly at Citibank Means There's More to Life Than Money," *Financial Services Marketing* 3, no. 2 (March 1, 2001): 12.

4. Duff McDonald, *Last Man Standing: The Ascent of Jamie Dimon and JPMorgan Chase* (New York: Simon & Schuster, 2009), 122–124; Gary Silverman and David Wells, "JP Morgan to Acquire Bank One for Dollars 58bn: Biggest US Bank Merger in Five Years Highlights Push to Favour Retail over Corporate Sector," *Financial Times*, January 15, 2004; Patricia Crisafulli,

The House of Dimon: How JPMorgan's Jamie Dimon Rose to the Top of the Financial World (Hoboken, NJ: John Wiley & Sons, 2009), 15, 144–145, 148.

5. Kapler, "Living Richly at Citibank Means There's More to Life Than Money"; 2004 annual reports of Bank of America, Citigroup, JPMorgan Chase, and Wells Fargo.

6. Shawn Tully, "The Jamie Dimon Show," *Fortune*, July 22, 2002, 88–96; Samuel Theodore, "The Crisis That Never Was: Banks Have Responded Well to the Difficulties of the Past Year, Not Least Because They Have Applied Hard-won Lessons About Diversification of Earnings and Risk Control," *Euromoney* 34, no. 410 (June 2003).

7. Monica Langley, Mitchell Pacelle, and Jathon Sapsford, "People Power: Two Financiers' Careers Trace a Bank Strategy That's Now Hot; Weill and Dimon Built a Titan by Focusing on Consumers; Today They're Arch-Rivals; A Risk: Higher Interest Rates," *Wall Street Journal*, January 16, 2004; Boraks, "In Big Integration Job, B of A's Lewis Stresses the Little Things"; David Boraks, "Branch Plan to Put B of A Branding Push to the Test," *American Banker*, December 31, 2002, 1.

8. Riva D. Atlas, "Bank of America and FleetBoston Agree to $48 Billion Merger," *New York Times*, October 28, 2014; Damian Paletta, "Some Now Back B of A–Fleet Deal; Others Want Conditions," *American Banker*, January 15, 2004; Gene Marcial, "FleetBoston: Bait?" *Business Week*, September 17, 2001, 125; "Can BofA's Ken Lewis Really Make His Maths Add Up?" *Euroweek*, December 15, 2003; "Big Move by Bank of America," *Bank News* 103, no. 12 (December 2003): 24; Boraks, "Branch Plan to Put B of A Branding Push to the Test"; "2003 Deals of the Year: Return of the Bubbly," *Institutional Investor*, January 2004, 80–93.

9. Kenneth D. Jones and Chau Nguyen, "Increased Concentration in Banking: Megabanks and Their Implications for Deposit Insurance," *Financial Markets, Institutions & Instruments* 14, no. 1 (February 2005); Ieva M. Augstums, "Latest Mergers Widen Gap Between Texas's Larger, Smaller Banks," *Knight Ridder Tribune Business News*, June 28, 2004.

10. John C. Soper, "What's Next for Consolidation in Banking?" *Business Economics* 36, no. 2 (April 2001): 39–43; Jones and Nguyen, "Increased Concentration in Banking"; Theodore, "The Crisis That Never Was"; Charles W. Calomiris and Stephen H. Haber, *Fragile by Design: The Political Origins of Banking Crises and Scarce Credit* (Princeton, NJ: Princeton University Press, 2014), 215.

11. "Wachovia, Lennar Win Servicing Rankings," *Commercial Mortgage Alert*, January 30, 2004.

12. Jones and Nguyen, "Increased Concentration in Banking"; Kenneth H. Thomas, "A Safety Net to Cover the Big Umbrella," *Christian Science Monitor*, May 1, 1998; Maria Fabiana Penas, "Bank Mergers and Too-Big-to-Fail Policy" (PhD diss., University of Maryland, 2001), 65–66.

13. Riva D. Atlas, "Credit Card Merger: The Deal Maker; Against Expectations, Bank Resumes Its Buying Ways," *New York Times*, July 1, 2005.

14. "BofA Buys Credit Card Bank MBNA in Acquisition Spree," *Euroweek*, July 1, 2005; Atlas, "Credit Card Merger"; "Bank of America to Acquire MBNA," *Teller Vision* 1337 (September 2005): 7.

15. "BofA Buys Credit Card Bank MBNA in Acquisition Spree"; Kathryn M. Welling, "On the Bubble Economy," *Traders*, May 1, 2002. Starting in 1986, reports historian Rowena Olegario, Bank One securitized credit card debt. See her *The Engine of Enterprise: Credit in America* (Cambridge, MA: Harvard University Press, 2016), 186. On the process by which bankers converted credit card balances into asset-based securities, see Louis Hyman, *Debtor Nation:*

The History of America in Red Ink (Princeton, NJ: Princeton University Press, 2011), 253–257; and Hyman, *Borrow: The American Way of Debt* (New York: Vintage Books, 2012), 231–234.

16. Louis Hyman, "American Debt, Global Capital: The Policy Origins of Securitization," in *The Shock of the Global: The 1970s in Perspective*, ed. Niall Ferguson et al. (Cambridge, MA.: Harvard University Press, 2010), 135; Fred R. Bleakley, "'Hot New Game' in Financing," *New York Times*, June 4, 1985; Brian Collins, "RTC Closes Its Doors After Resolving 747 Failed Thrifts in 6 Years," *National Mortgage News*, January 2, 1996, 6; O. Emre Ergungor, "Securitization," *Economic Commentary* [Federal Reserve Bank of Cleveland], August 15, 2003. Jerry W. Markham, *A Financial History of the United States*, vol. 3, *From the Age of Derivatives into the New Millennium (1970–2001)* (Armonk, NY: M. E. Sharpe, 2002), 144, characterizes as "blindingly complex" the efforts of bankers during the 1980s to figure out how to make securitization work. Only two decades later, in 2003, economist and future Federal Reserve Board member Frederic S. Mishkin, *The Economics of Money, Banking, and Financial Markets* (New York: Addison Wesley, 2003), 269, described securitization as "one of the most important financial innovations in the past two decades." Business writer Andrew Ross Sorkin, *Too Big to Fail: The Inside Story of How Wall Street and Washington Fought to Save the Financial System—and Themselves* (New York: Viking, 2009), 90, reports that even after asset-backed securities had achieved a standard place in bankers' dealings, Federal Reserve chair Alan Greenspan could still report only an incomplete understanding about "some of the complexities of some of the instruments."

17. Christopher O'Leary, "The New Supremo in ABS: Rivals Scramble to Find Ways to Compete with ABS' New Kingpin: Salomon SB/Citibank," *Investment Dealers' Digest*, August 2, 1999, 1–21; Michael D. McNickle, "Credit Cards Can Create Profits, Not Just Debts," *New York Times*, July 30, 1994; Karina Robinson, "Rare Flora in Securities Bouquet," *New York Times*, October 17, 1992.

18. John Ginovsky, "Rules Catching Up with the Law," *Bankers News* 8, no. 6 (March 21, 2000); Sara Sager, "Preemption Rights of National Bank Operating Subsidiaries: The Fight for Visitorial Power," *Journal of Corporation Law* 30, no. 1 (Fall, 2004): 181–198. See also Olegario, *The Engine of Enterprise*, 172–181, for a fine overview of the way securitization worked.

19. Sager, "Preemption Rights of National Bank Operating Subsidiaries," 181–198.

20. Frederick Feldkamp, "Asset Securitization: The Alchemist's Dream," in *Securitization Yearbook 2000*, supplement to *International Financial Law Review*, October 2000, 5; "Federal Reserve Board Approves the Banc Corporation as Financial Holding Company," *PR Newswire*, March 14, 2000.

21. Robert E. Litan with Jonathan Rauch, *American Finance for the 21st Century* (Washington, DC: Brookings Institution Press, 1998), 7, 17; Joshua Cooper Ramo, "The Three Marketeers," *Time*, February 15, 1999. Rubin never specified the relationships among elements in his version of market architecture. Sociologist Neil Fligstein's *The Architecture of Markets: An Economic Sociology of Twenty-First-Century Capitalist Societies* (Princeton, NJ: Princeton University Press, 2001) is an excellent place to begin to study the concept and its uses. Fligstein seeks to set aside economists' models in favor of sociologists' questions such as the rules that are prerequisite to the functioning of markets. Politics and culture loom large in framing market architecture, Fligstein contends.

22. "The Chosen Ones?" *Financial Times*, April 5, 2004.

23. Timothy L. O'Brien, "First Union to Acquire Money Store for $2.1 Billion," *New York Times*, March 5, 1998; "OCC Rips Subprime Credit Reporting," *National Mortgage News*,

May 10, 1999, 3. Journalist Scott Patterson, *The Quants: How a New Breed of Math Whizzes Conquered Wall Street and Nearly Destroyed It* (New York: Crown Publishing Group, 2010), explains in accessible prose the work of mathematical specialists in evaluating and packaging asset-backed securities.

24. Gary Silverman, "Big Lenders Forced to Bank on 'Untouchables,'" *Financial Times*, April 3, 2003.

25. Karen Thomas, "'Secret' Credit Scores Hurting Consumers," *Origination News* 8, no. 11 (August 1999): 3; "OCC Rips Subprime Credit Reporting," 3; Atif Mian and Amir Sufi, *House of Debt: How They (and You) Caused the Great Recession, and How We Can Prevent It from Happening Again* (Chicago: University of Chicago Press, 2014), 102; Lisa Servon, *The Unbanking of America: How the New Middle Class Survives* (New York: Houghton Mifflin Harcourt, 2017), xvii.

26. George W. Bush, "President Calls for Expanding Opportunities to Home Ownership," June 17, 2002, http://georgewbush-whitehouse.archives.gov/news/releases/2002/06/20020617 -2.html.

27. "President Hosts Conference on Minority Homeownership," October 15, 2002, http:// georgewbush-whitehouse.archives.gov/news/releases/2002/10/20021015.html; Brian Balogh, "Consumer in Chief: Presidential Leadership in America's 'Consumer's Republic,'" in *The President and American Capitalism Since 1945*, ed. Mark H. Rose and Roger Biles, 21–35 (Gainesville: University Press of Florida, 2017).

28. Darryl Hicks, "Norwest Mortgage Plans to Make Low-Mod a 21st Century Priority," *National Mortgage News*, November 23, 1998, 12; Mian and Sufi, *House of Debt*, 102; "Citicorp Buys Source One Mortgage, Other Deals Still Pending," *Origination News* 8, no. 7 (April 1999): 20; "Residential Loan Production," *National Mortgage News*, December 31, 2001, 1.

29. "Citicorp Buys Source One Mortgage, Other Deals Still Pending," 20.

30. "Citi's Associates Deal Makes It a Contender in Retail and Subprime," *Credit Card News*, September 15, 2000; Paul Muolo, "Citigroup Now Poised to Dominate Subprime: Is Countrywide Next on List?" *National Mortgage News*, September 11, 2000, 1, 36; O'Leary, "The New Supremo in ABS"; Joan Ogden, "Using Derivatives to Manage Risk: The Banks' Best Solutions," *Global Finance* 12, no. 3 (March 1998): 48–62.

31. Mark Johnson, "The World's Best Banks 2002," *Global Finance* 16, no. 10 (October 2002): 24–62.

32. "Top 20 Residential Originators in 2001," *National Mortgage News*, March 25, 2002, 1; "Lehman Buys Mortgage M&A Specialist CRSI," *National Mortgage News*, January 28, 2002: 2; Jennifer Bayot, "Ripple Effect of Turmoil Seen in Financial Markets," *New York Times*, June 10, 2003.

33. Mark Fogarty and Michael Muckian, "Wells Fargo Tops Local Minority Lending," *Business Journal* 20, no. 10 (November 29, 2002); "Subprime Originators by No. of Loans Originated in 4Q-02," *National Mortgage News*, April 7, 2003, 37; Paul Muolo, "Subprime Market as Hot as Prime," *National Mortgage News*, December 9, 2002, 1.

34. Laura Mandaro, "How Kovacevich Kept Wells Ahead," *American Banker*, December 4, 2003, 2A; "ACORN to Protest Predatory Lending at Wells Fargo Annual Meeting; ACORN Members Will Also Speak at Meeting in Support of Anti-Predatory Lending Resolution," *Business Wire*, April 22, 2004.

35. Robert J. Shiller, *The Subprime Solution: How Today's Global Financial Crisis Happened, and What to Do About It* (Princeton, NJ: Princeton University Press, 2008), 5; Sheila

Bair, *Bull by the Horns: Fighting to Save Main Street from Wall Street and Wall Street from It-self* (New York: Free Press, 2012), 44; Matthew Desmond, *Evicted: Poverty and Profit in the American City* (New York: Crown Publishers, 2016), 125, 150–151; Financial Crisis Inquiry Commission, *The Final Crisis Inquiry Report: Final Report of the National Commission on the Causes of the Financial and Economic Crisis in the United States* (New York: Public Affairs, 2011), xv–xvi; Raghuram G. Rajan, *Fault Lines: How Hidden Fractures Still Threaten the World Economy* (Princeton, NJ: Princeton University Press, 2010), 40. Historian Walter Licht drew my attention to health-care employees, postal workers, and others who earned modest wages and began to experience problems making mortgage payments as early as 2005. In 2006, historian Rowena Olegario reports, 25 percent of new mortgages were subprime. See her *The Engine of Enterprise*, 218.

36. George A. Akerlof and Robert J. Shiller, *Animal Spirits: How Human Psychology Drives the Economy, and Why It Matters for Global Capitalism* (Princeton, NJ: Princeton University Press, 2009), 36–37.

37. Bethany McLean and Joe Nocera, *All The Devils Are Here: The Hidden History of the Financial Crisis* (New York: Penguin, 2010), 302, 305; Timothy F. Geithner, *Stress Test: Reflections on Financial Crises* (New York: Crown Publishers, 2014), 136–137.

38. Arthur E. Wilmarth, Jr., "Citigroup's Unfortunate History of Managerial and Regulatory Failures," *Journal of Banking Regulation* 15, nos. 3–4 (2014): 245–246; Ben S. Bernanke, *The Courage to Act: A Memoir of a Crisis and Its Aftermath* (New York: W. W. Norton, 2015), 177–178, 368–369; David Luttrell, Harvey Rosenblum, and Jackson Thies, "Understanding the Risks Inherent in Shadow Banking: A Primer and Practical Lesson Learned," *Federal Reserve Bank of Dallas Staff Papers* 18 (November 2012): 11; Hyun Song Shin, "Financial Intermediation and the Post-Crisis Financial System," paper prepared for the 8th BIS Annual Conference, June 25–26, 2009, 3, http://www.bis.org/events/conf090625/hyunshinpaper .pdf; Robin Sidel, David Reilly, and David Enrich, "Citigroup Alters Course, Bails Out Affiliated Funds; Taking on $49 Billion of Assets Further Dents Banking Giant's Capital," *Wall Street Journal*, December 14, 2007; Jenny Anderson and Eric Dash, "Citigroup Loss Raises Anxiety over Economy," *New York Times*, January 16, 2008; "Citigroup: Chucking in the Towel," *The Economist*, November 5, 2007, 1; Matthew Richardson, Roy C. Smith, and Ingo Walter, "Large Banks and the Volcker Rule," in *Regulating Wall Street: The Dodd-Frank Act and the New Architecture of Global Finance*, ed. Viral V. Acharya et al. (New York: John Wiley & Sons, 2011), 181. See Jeffrey Friedman and Wladimir Kraus, *Engineering the Financial Crisis: Systemic Risk and the Failure of Regulation* (Philadelphia: University of Pennsylvania Press, 2011), 128–129, for a smart discussion of "radical ignorance," a condition the authors characterize as one of not being alert to the "unknown unknown." In this instance, they report, bankers "were not ignoring risk that they knew about. Rather, they were ignorant of the fact that triple-A securities might be much riskier than advertised."

39. Jeff Kearns and Yalman Onaran, "Bear Stearns Shares Fall on Liquidity Speculation (Update6)," Bloomberg.com, March 10, 2008; John H. Cochrane, "Toward a Run-Free Financial System," in *Across the Great Divide: New Perspectives on the Financial Crisis*, ed. Martin Neil Baily and John B. Taylor (Stanford, CA: Hoover Institution Press, 2014), 198; Jennifer Taub, "Time to Reduce Repo Risk," *New York Times*, April 4, 2014; Gary Gorton and Andrew Metrick, "Securitized Banking and the Run on Repo," *Journal of Financial Economics* 104, no. 3 (June 2012); Gary Shorter, "Bear Stearns: Crisis and 'Rescue' for a Major Provider of Mortgage-Related Product," *Congressional Research Service Report*, March 26 2008; Landon

Thomas, Jr., "JPMorgan and Fed Move to Bail Out Bear Stearns," *New York Times*, March 14, 2008.

40. "Bear Stearns Alarm Gives CDO Markets Rollercoaster Ride," *Euroweek*, June 22, 2007, 1; Paul J. Davies, "Leveraged Funds Rush to Sell Debt," *Financial Times*, February 28, 2008; "Professionally Gloomy," *The Economist*, May 17, 2008, 12; Gorton and Metrick, "Securitized Banking and the Run on Repo"; Randall Dodd and Paul Mills, "Outbreak: U.S. Subprime Contagion." *Finance & Development* 45, no. 2 (June 2008): 14–18; Viral V. Acharya and T. Sabri Oncu, "The Repurchase Agreement (Repo) Market," in Acharya et al., *Regulating Wall Street*, 332; Geithner, *Stress Test*, 136.

41. Gary B. Gorton, *Slapped by the Invisible Hand: The Panic of 2007* (New York: Oxford University Press, 2010), 3; Gary B. Gorton, *Misunderstanding Financial Crises: Why We Don't See Them Coming* (New York: Oxford University Press, 2012), 194; Financial Crisis Inquiry Commission, *The Final Crisis Inquiry Report*, xx–xxi; Frederic S. Mishkin, "Over the Cliff: From the Subprime to the Global Financial Crisis, *Journal of Economic Perspectives* 25, no. 1 (2011): 51.

42. McLean and Nocera, *All The Devils Are Here*, 346; Martin Wolf, *The Shifts and the Shocks: What We've Learned—and Have Still to Learn—from the Financial Crisis* (New York: Penguin Press, 2014), 21; Philip A. Wallach, *To the Edge: Legality, Legitimacy, and the Responses to the 2008 Financial Crisis* (Washington, DC: Brookings Institution Press, 2015), 56–58; Sorkin, *Too Big to Fail*, 229; United States Financial Crisis Inquiry Commission, *The Financial Crisis Inquiry Report: Final Report of the National Commission on the Causes of the Financial and Economic Crisis in the United States* (New York: Public Affairs, 2011), 309.

43. Sorkin, *Too Big to Fail*, 143–145.

44. Ibid., 262, 359–61, 370–371, 531; Bernanke, *The Courage to Act*, 262; Henry M. Paulson, Jr., *On the Brink: Inside the Race to Stop the Collapse of the Global Financial System* (New York: Business Plus, 2010), 203.

45. Bernanke, *The Courage to Act*, 248–249; Michael J. De La Merced and Julia Werdigier, "The Origins of Lehman's 'Repo 105,'" *New York Times*, March 12, 2010; Shiller, *The Subprime Solution*, 45; Richard Berner, "Lessons from the Financial Crisis—Eight Years Later," Office of Financial Research (OFR), U.S. Department of the Treasury, January 24, 2017, Financial-Research.gov; "Legal Entity Identifier (LEI)," OFR, Financial Research.gov; Shin, "Financial Intermediation and the Post-Crisis Financial System," 17, 19.

46. Paulson, *On the Brink*, 191; Sorkin, *Too Big to Fail*, 311.

47. Sorkin, *Too Big to Fail*, 291, 303, 305; Paulson, *On the Brink*, 192; Eric Dash, "U.S. Gives Banks Urgent Warning to Solve Crisis," *New York Times*, September 12, 2008. Barry Eichengreen, *Hall of Mirrors: The Great Depression, the Great Recession, and the Uses—and Misuses—of History* (New York: Oxford University Press, 2015), 201, identifies "a failure of the Treasury, Fed, and Congress to prepare for the worst."

48. Sorkin, *Too Big to Fail*, 291, 303, 305; Paulson, *On the Brink*, 216.

49. Sorkin, *Too Big to Fail*, 390, 413; Luttrell, Rosenblum, and Thies, "Understanding the Risks Inherent in Shadow Banking," 25; Bernanke, *The Courage to Act*, 269; Wolf, *The Shifts and the Shocks*, 21; Walter A. Friedman, *Fortune Tellers: The Story of America's First Economic Forecasters* (Princeton, NJ: Princeton University Press, 2014).

50. Hugh Son and Erik Holm, "Fed Takes Control of AIG With $85 Billion Bailout (Update4)," Bloomberg.com, September 17, 2015; Sorkin, *Too Big to Fail*, 236–237, 397, 417; Paulson, *On the Brink*, 218, 229; Thomas Ferguson and Robert Johnson, "Too Big to Bail: The

'Paulson Put,' Presidential Politics, and the Global Financial Meltdown, Part I: From Shadow Financial System to Shadow Bailout," *International Journal of Political Economy* 38, no. 1 (Spring 2009): 4; Bernanke, *The Courage to Act*, 281–282, 286–287; Wolf, *The Shifts and the Shocks*, 21; Eichengreen, *Hall of Mirrors*, 209; Board of Governors of the Federal Reserve System, "Press Release," September 16, 2008.

51. Wallach, *To the Edge*, 43–78; Sorkin, *Too Big to Fail*, 536; Geithner, *Stress Test*, 223, 294; Paulson, *On the Brink*, 243.

52. Sorkin, *Too Big to Fail*, 439; Wallach, *To the Edge*, 81; "King Henry," *Newsweek* (cover), September 29, 2008; Bernanke, *The Courage to Act*, 304–306; "From Crisis, 'King Henry' Rises," *New York Times*, September 22, 2008; Daniel Gross, "How Paulson Became the New Face of Capitalism," *Newsweek*, September 19, 2008.

53. Bernanke, *The Courage to Act*, 304.

54. Carl Hulse and David M. Herszenhorn, "Defiant House Rejects Huge Bailout; Next Step Is Uncertain," *New York Times*, September 29, 2008.

55. Geithner, *Stress Test*, 5; Sorkin, *Too Big to Fail*, 524–525; Olegario, *The Engine of Enterprise*, 219.

56. Mark Pittman and Bob Ivry, "U.S. Taxpayers Risk $9.7 Trillion on Bailout Programs (Update1)," Bloomberg.com, February 9, 2009; "Citigroup Receives Bailout Investment, Asset Guarantee," *Banking & Financial Services Policy Report* 28, no. 1 (January 2009). See Calomiris and Haber, *Fragile by Design*, 204–205, for an accessible overview of the multiple government programs that backstopped banks and the economy as a whole. See also Zoltan Pozsar et al., "Shadow Banking," Federal Reserve Bank of New York Staff Report No. 458, July 2010, revised February 2012, 5–6, 13,15–17, 34–35. Pozsar and his colleagues determine that supermarket banks were not made more stable through diversification into securities dealings. In their language as economists, the supermarket banks' "broker-dealer and asset management activities . . . [were] not parallel, but serial and complementary to the . . . [financial holding company's] banking activities" (17). As such, a shortfall anywhere along the chain rippled into the bank (17, 34–35).

57. Bernanke, *The Courage to Act*, 370–371, 375; Eichengreen, *Hall of Mirrors*, 211.

58. Angus Burgin, *The Great Persuasion: Reinventing Free Markets Since the Depression* (Cambridge, MA.: Harvard University Press, 2012), 214–216; Joseph E. Stiglitz, *Free Fall: America, Free Markets, and the Sinking of the World Economy* (New York: W. W. Norton, 2010), xi–xiv. See also Richard A. Posner, *A Failure of Capitalism: The Crisis of '08 and the Descent into Depression* (Cambridge, MA.: Harvard University Press, 2009); Posner, one of President Reagan's federal appellate bench appointees, judged the depression "a failure of capitalism, or more precisely of a certain kind of capitalism ('laissez-faire' in a loose sense, 'American' versus 'European' in a popular sense), and of capitalism's biggest boosters" (260). The idea that a high level of risk had to accompany innovation and economic growth never lost well-placed advocates among policy makers. Between 2006 and 2011, Kevin M. Warsh served as a member of the Federal Reserve Board of Governors. "To achieve long run stability," he warned in 2014, "we must be accepting of considerable turbulence along the way." See his "Rethinking Macro: Reassessing Micro-Foundations," in Baily and Taylor, *Across the Great Divide*, 72–73.

Chapter 7

1. Barack Obama, "Inaugural Address," January 20, 2009, *The American Presidency Project*, University of California at Santa Barbara.

2. Barack Obama, "The President's News Conference," April 29, 2009, *The American Presidency Project*, University of California at Santa Barbara.

3. I formulated this paragraph based on impressions gained from essays contained in *The President and American Capitalism Since 1945*, ed. Mark H. Rose and Roger Biles (Gainesville: University Press of Florida, 2017).

4. "Obama Takeover Augurs Financial Regulator Shakeup," *New York Times*, January 5, 2009.

5. Timothy F. Geithner, *Stress Test: Reflections on Financial Crises* (New York: Crown Publishers, 2014), 36; "Treasury Is Redoing Team Working on Global Crises," *Wall Street Journal*, August 17, 1998. Economists Matthew Richardson, Roy C. Smith, and Ingo Walter, "Large Banks and the Volcker Rule," in *Regulating Wall Street: The Dodd-Frank Act and the New Architecture of Global Finance*, ed. Viral V. Acharya et al. (New York: John Wiley & Sons, 2011), 209, determine that "the commingling of commercial banking with investment banking . . . did not contribute to the recent financial crisis."

6. Geithner, *Stress Test*, 89; "Geithner's Calendar at the New York Fed," http://documents .nytimes.com/geithner-schedule-new-york-fed.

7. David Wighton, "Citigroup Riding a Trend and Not a Blip," *Financial Times*, July 19, 2007; Alex Chambers, "Is the Banking Boom Sustainable?" *Euromoney*, February 2007; "Bank of America; Bank of America CEO Lewis Sees Growth Initiatives in 2008," *Business & Finance Week*, May 5, 2008, 552; Gillian Tett and James Drummond, "NY Fed President Warns of Risk to Structured Credit," *Financial Times*, May 11, 2005; Geithner, *Stress Test*, 94–95, 99–104; "Fed's Geithner on Daunting Task of Risk Management in Derivatives," *Hedge Funds and Private Equity* 1, no. 2 (May 2007); David Wessel, "The Economy; CAPITAL: Financial Markets Can Look to Economy as Model of Stability," *Wall Street Journal*, April 15, 2004.

8. Geithner, *Stress Test*, 79–80, 90–93, 426.

9. Ibid., 247, 490.

10. Ben S. Bernanke, *The Courage to Act: A Memoir of a Crisis and Its Aftermath* (New York: W. W. Norton, 2015), 380; Barry Eichengreen, *Hall of Mirrors: The Great Depression, the Great Recession, and the Uses—and Misuses—of History* (New York: Oxford University Press, 2015), 5, 212; Per H. Hansen, "Review Essay," review of Eichengreen's *Hall of Mirrors*, *Business History Review* 89, no. 3 (Autumn 2015): 559; Geithner, *Stress Test*, 490.

11. Geithner, *Stress Test*, 9; "Fed's Geithner on Daunting Task of Risk Management in Derivatives"; Steven Sloan, "Geithner on Bear Rescue: No Regrets," *American Banker*, June 10, 2008, 1; Timothy F. Geithner, "We Can Reduce Risk in the Financial System," *Financial Times*, June 8, 2008.

12. Cheyenne Hopkins, "Geithner Urges Fast, Bold Financial System Rescue," *American Banker*, January 22, 2009, 1; Geithner, *Stress Test*, 247, 251, 490; "Live-Blogging the Geithner Confirmation Hearing," *New York Times*, January 21, 2009; Edmund L. Andrews, "Battles over Reform Plan Lie Ahead," *New York Times*, March 26, 2009; Bernanke, *The Courage to Act*, 394–395; Cheyenne Hopkins, "Geithner: Systemic Risk a Fed Job," *American Banker*, March 12, 2009, 3.

13. Per H. Hansen, "Business History: A Cultural and Narrative Approach," *Business History Review* 86, no. 4 (2012): 698–699; Barney Frank, *Frank: A Life in Politics from the Great Society to Same-Sex Marriage* (New York: Farrar, Straus and Giroux, 2015), 257, 285. See Henry Kaufman, *Tectonic Shifts in Financial Market: People, Policies, and Institutions* (New York: Palgrave Macmillan, 2016). Kaufman had a lengthy and successful career with the Fed-

eral Reserve Bank of New York and then with Salomon Brothers, Inc., an investment bank. Contemporary bankers, Kaufman observed in 2016, have not experienced an education that equipped them "to understand change over time or how broad political, social, and economic developments impinge on financial markets, and vice versa"; history, for those bankers, he adds, amounted to "an unnecessary luxury or a frivolous . . . pursuit" (116). For the recruitment and socialization of investment bankers before and after 2008, compare Karen Ho, *Liquidated: An Ethnography of Wall Street* (Durham, NC: Duke University Press, 2009); and Kevin Roose, *Young Money: Inside the Hidden World of Wall Street's Post-Crash Recruits* (New York: Grand Central Publishing, 2014). Anthropologist Ho's pre-2008 bankers were immersed in a "shareholder value ideology" with profoundly negative consequences for the American and world economy (*Liquidated*, 324). Journalist Roose's new recruits had begun "to talk about the world in a transactional, economized way. Their universes started to look like giant balance sheets" (*Young Money*, 278).

14. Rose Marie Kushmeider, "U.S. Federal Financial Regulatory System: Restructuring Federal Bank Regulation," *FDIC Banking Review*, January 19, 2006; Frank, *Frank*, 261–262, 306–307; Cheyenne Hopkins, "Extraordinary Measures: Tarp's Toll Expected to Be Felt for Years," *American Banker*, September 22, 2009, 1; "The Coming Battle over Wall Street Reform," *New York Times*, March 27, 2009. And see Charles W. Calomiris and Stephen Haber, *Fragile by Design: The Political Origins of Banking Crises and Scarce Credit* (Princeton, NJ: Princeton University Press, 2014), x, for the valuable observation that banks served as "an institutional embodiment—a mirror of sorts—of the political system that is a product of a society's deep history."

15. *Addressing the Need for Comprehensive Regulatory Reform: Hearing Before the Committee on Financial Services, U.S. House of Representatives*, March 26, 2009, 111th Congress, 1st Session (Washington, DC: U.S. Government Printing Office, 2009), 7.

16. Sebastian Mallaby, *The Man Who Knew: The Life and Times of Alan Greenspan* (New York: Penguin Press, 2016), 469–470, 567, 679.

17. Mark Jickling and Edward V. Murphy. "Who regulates Whom? An Overview of U.S. Financial Supervision," Congressional Research Service (CRS) Reports and Issue Briefs. (Washington, DC: Congressional Research Service, 2009); Geithner, *Stress Test*, 137. See Richard H. K. Vietor, *Contrived Competition: Regulation and Deregulation in America* (Cambridge, MA.: Belknap Press of Harvard University Press, 1994), 256, for a valuable figure showing the complex web of state and federal regulatory agencies and the kinds of firms they regulated. Christy Ford Chapin's paper at the 2017 Business History Conference reminded me of Vietor's figure.

18. Kushmeider, "U.S. Federal Financial Regulatory System"; Jon Hilsenrath and Fawn Johnson, "Fed Faults New York Office's Oversight of Big Banks," *Wall Street Journal*, May 6, 2010; Geithner, *Stress Test*, 96–97, 122–123, 400. See especially Chicago Booth, IGM Forum, "Factors Contributing to the 2008 Global Financial Crisis," IGMChicago.org, October 17, 2017, for a report of a survey conducted among thirty-seven economists at leading universities such as Stanford, MIT, Harvard, and Chicago regarding the origins of the financial crisis of 2008. Almost all the polled economists cited "flawed financial sector regulation and supervision," "underestimated risks (financial engineering)," and fraudulent mortgages as among the most important factors. I completed research for this book in June 2017. Nonetheless, my findings about the crisis's origins in the underestimated risks of subprime lending, the interconnectedness of investment banks such as Bear Stearns and Lehman with Citigroup and

other commercial banks' investment units, the difficulty of discerning that interconnectedness, a repo run, and fragmented bank regulation are consistent with the results announced in this poll. Compare my findings alongside the determinations of surveyed economists with Calomiris and Haber, *Fragile by Design*, 210–213, who find that federal officials joined with inner-city activists and heads of those large government-sponsored enterprises to lower mortgage underwriting standards for subprime and prime borrowers. That coalition emerged under the auspices of the Community Reinvestment Act. Calomiris and Haber describe this arrangement as the "Game of Bank Bargains," a memorable framing but inaccurate in its assessment.

19. Paul A. McCulley, "The Shadow Banking System and Hyman Minsky's Economic Journey," Pimco.com, May 2009.

20. Andrew Ross Sorkin, *Too Big to Fail: The Inside Story of How Wall Street and Washington Fought to Save the Financial System—and Themselves* (New York: Viking, 2009), 11.

21. Ibid., 96–100. Emily Thornton, "Richard Fuld: Lehman's He-Man," *Business Week*, March 29, 2004; Justin Schack, "Restoring the House of Lehman: How Tough-as-Nails CEO Dick Fuld Defied the Conventional Wisdom about Lehman Brothers—and Himself—to Recapture the Investment Bank's Lost Glory," *Institutional Investor International Edition* (May 2005). Ho, *Liquidated*, informs my sketch of the habits and attire among Wall Street's leading investment bankers.

22. McCulley, "The Shadow Banking System and Hyman Minsky's Economic Journey"; Tobias Adrian and Hyun Song Shin, "The Shadow Banking System: Implications for Financial Regulation," Federal Reserve Bank of New York Staff Report No. 382, July 2009; John Gapper, "Banks Must Relearn Their Trade," *Financial Times*, July 29, 2007, 1.

23. Sheila Bair, *Bull by the Horns: Fighting to Save Main Street from Wall Street and Wall Street from Itself* (New York: Free Press, 2012), 49; Kushmeider, "U.S. Federal Financial Regulatory System"; Geithner, *Stress Test*, 96, 400; Gillian Tett, *The Silo Effect: the Peril of Expertise and the Promise of Breaking Down Barriers* (New York: Simon & Schuster, 2015), x.

24. "Geithner Testimony on Financial Regulatory Reform," *Financial Times*, November 19, 2009.

25. Geithner, *Stress Test*, 91–93.

26. U.S. Department of the Treasury, *Financial Regulatory Reform: A New Foundation* (Washington, DC: U.S. Department of the Treasury, 2009), 31; Timothy Geithner and Lawrence Summers, "The Case for Financial Regulatory Reform," *Washington Post*, June 15, 2009; Barack Obama, "Remarks on Financial Regulatory Reform," June 17, 2009, *The American Presidency Project*, University of California at Santa Barbara.

27. Matthew Monks, "Big Banks' Reserves: Tomorrow's Big Profits?" *American Banker*, November 2, 2009, 1; "Reshaping US Regulations," *Fund Strategy*, April 13, 2009; "Bailed Out Banks Chafe Against Government Controls," *Euromoney*, May 2009.

28. *Addressing the Need for Comprehensive Regulatory Reform*, 9; Simon Johnson and James Kwak, *13 Bankers: The Wall Street Takeover and the Next Financial Meltdown* (New York: Pantheon Books, 2010), 10; Geithner, *Stress Test*, 86–87; Mallaby, *The Man Who Knew*, 531–535.

29. U.S. Department of the Treasury, *Financial Regulatory Reform*, 47–48; "Geithner Seeks Clampdown on Derivatives Dealers," *Reuters Hedgeworld*, July 10, 2009; Geithner, *Stress Test*, 87.

30. *Addressing the Need for Comprehensive Regulatory Reform*, 55, 57, 59; Geithner, *Stress Test*, 396, 401.

31. Geithner, *Stress Test*, 401–402.

32. Bair, *Bull by the Horns*, 184, 186; Geithner, *Stress Test*, 402–403.

33. Damian Paletta and Deborah Solomon. "U.S. News: Geithner Vents at Regulators as Overhaul Stumbles," *Wall Street Journal*, August 4, 2009; Geithner, *Stress Test*, 404–405; Bair, *Bull by the Horns*, 191.

34. Geithner, *Stress Test*, 403.

35. Bernanke, *The Courage to Act*, 458–460. See Sarah Binder and Mark Spindel, *The Myth of Independence: How Congress Governs the Federal Reserve* (Princeton, NJ: Princeton University Press, 2017); Binder, a political scientist, and Spindel, an investment adviser, conclude that "Congress and the Federal Reserve are interdependent institutions—the inevitable consequence of reelection-seeking, blame-avoiding politicians who hold the power to make and remake political institutions" (232).

36. Bernanke, *The Courage to Act*, 5–6, 11–18, 448–449, 460–461.

37. Ibid., 445–448.

38. Joe Adler, "ABA: Create New Resolution Agency," *American Banker*, April 16, 2009, 5. See also Victoria Finkle, "Is Dodd-Frank Really Killing Community Banks?" *American Banker*, August 19, 2015. I located this article in Lisa Servon, *The Unbanking of America: How the New Middle Class Survives* (New York: Houghton Mifflin Harcourt, 2017), 27–28, 195.

39. Theda Skocpol and Vanessa Williamson, *The Tea Party and the Remaking of Republican Conservatism* (New York: Oxford University Press, 2012), 7, 160; Geithner, *Stress Test*, 417; Daniel Carpenter, "Institutional Strangulation: Bureaucratic Politics and Financial Reform in the Obama Administration," *Perspectives on Politics* 8, no. 3 (Summer 2010): 831.

40. Geithner, *Stress Test*, 407, 417; Michael Cooper, "G.O.P. Senate Victory Stuns Democrats," *New York Times*, January 19, 2010; Carl Hulse and David M. Herszenhorn, "Bank Bailout Is Potent Issue for Fall Elections," *New York Times*, July 10, 2010; Kirk Johnson, "Utah Delegates Oust Three-Term G.O.P. Senator from Race," *New York Times*, May 8, 2010; Carpenter, "Institutional Strangulation," 825.

41. Geithner, *Stress Test*, 424; "Congress Sends Financial Bill to Obama," *New York Times*, July 15, 2010; Edward Wyatt and David M. Herszenhorn, "In Deal, New Authority over Wall Street," *New York Times*, June 25, 2010.

42. Barack Obama, "Remarks on Signing the Dodd-Frank Wall Street Reform and Consumer Protection Act," July 21, 2010, *The American Presidency Project*, University of California at Santa Barbara; Chris V. Nicholson, "The Dodd-Frank Bill Up Close," *New York Times*, June 28, 2010.

43. Obama, "Remarks on Signing the Dodd-Frank Wall Street Reform and Consumer Protection Act."

44. Geithner, *Stress Test*, 434; Alistair Barr, "Big Banks Face 'Jarring Shake-up' from New Regulations," *MarketWatch*, June 26, 2010; Carpenter, "Institutional Strangulation," 825.

Epilogue

1. "Historical Inflation Rates: 1914–2017," http://www.usinflationcalculator.com/inflation/historical-inflation-rates/; Leonard Silk, "At Fed, Change and Continuity," Economic Scene, *New York Times*, June 3, 1987. Peter Conti-Brown, *The Power and Independence of the Federal*

Reserve (Princeton, NJ: Princeton University Press, 2016), 51–58, connects Volcker's legendary image as a strong-willed central banker to the idea of the Fed's independence from day-to-day politics. And also see Sarah Binder and Mark Spindel, *The Myth of Independence: How Congress Governs the Federal Reserve* (Princeton, NJ: Princeton University Press, 2017), 192, in which the authors contend that "Volcker's capacity to sustain a vigorous anti-inflation campaign rested directly on . . . [Federal Reserve Open Market Committee] members' perceptions of support from the president and his administration."

2. Silk, "At Fed, Change and Continuity"; Board of Governors of the Federal Reserve System, "Paul A. Volcker: Chairman, Board of Governors, 1979–1987," Federal Reserve History, http://www.federalreservehistory.org/People/DetailView/82; Alan Greenspan as quoted in Sebastian Mallaby, *The Man Who Knew: The Life and Times of Alan Greenspan* (New York: Penguin Press, 2016), 233; Roger E. Alcaly, "The Man Who Knew Better," *New York Review of Books*, February 23, 2017, 24, guided me to this quotation.

3. Timothy F. Geithner, *Stress Test: Reflections on Financial Crises* (New York: Crown Publishers, 2014), 414.

4. Simon Johnson, "Will There Be a Meaningful Volcker Rule?" *New York Times*, June 7, 2012; "MIT Professor Simon Johnson Talks Big Banks on Bloomberg TV," *Surveillance Show*, October 18, 2012; Simon H. Johnson, "Keynote Address: The Continuing Problem of 'Too Big to Fail,'" *North Carolina Banking Institute* 18, no. 1 (2013); "Newsmaker Interview: Through Another Lens," *Independent Banker*, January 6, 2014.

5. Geithner, *Stress Test*, 414.

6. Louis Uchitelle, "Volcker Pushes for Reform, Regretting Past Silence," *New York Times*, July 10, 2010.

7. Geithner, *Stress Test*, 414–415, 421; Jack Bao, Maureen O'Hara, and Alex Zhou, *The Volcker Rule and Market-Making in Times of Stress*, Finance and Economics Discussion Series 2016-102 (Washington, DC: Board of Governors of the Federal Reserve System, 2016).

8. Geithner, *Stress Test*, 427–428, 434.

9. Jesse Eisinger, "The Volcker Rule, Made Bloated and Weak," *New York Times*, February 23, 2012; Simon Johnson, "Making the Volcker Rule Work," *New York Times*, December 10, 2013; Peter Eavis, "'Long and Arduous Process' to Ban a Single Wall Street Activity," *New York Times*, December 10, 2013.

10. Ben Protess and Peter Eavis, "At the Finish Line on the Volcker Rule," *New York Times*, December 10, 2013; Evan Weinberger, "US Financial Regulators Approve Volcker Rule," *Law360*, December 10, 2013; Commodity Futures Trading Commission, 17 CFR Part 75, *Federal Register* 79, no. 21 (January 31, 2014): 6007; Evan Weinberger, "Volcker Rule's Next Stop: The Courtroom," *Law360*, December 6, 2013.

11. Weinberger, "Volcker Rule's Next Stop"; Andy Peters, "Volcker Rule a Threat to Small Banks, Industry Says," *American Banker*, December 20, 2013; Rachel Abrams, "After Changes, Banking Group Drops Suit Against Volcker Rule," *New York Times*, February 12, 2014.

12. Joseph Guinto, "Jeb Hensarling: The GOP's Most Powerful Nobody," *D Magazine*, November 2009. I never uncovered evidence that Jamie Dimon, Sandy Weill, Don Regan, and Jeb Hensarling actually read or discussed in any detail the ideas of free-market economic thinkers such as Milton Friedman. Late in 1999, as members of the U.S. Senate, the U.S. House, and the president's top officials undertook the final push in Congress toward Gramm-Leach-Bliley's approval, no one in a position of banking, regulatory, or legislative authority, including Alan Greenspan or Phil Gramm, advocated for the abolition of bank rules. As historian

Daniel T. Rogers, *Age of Fracture* (Cambridge, MA: Belknap Press of Harvard University Press, 2011), 5–7, 9, 43–44, confirms, however, market talk had slipped into nearly everyone's vocabulary during the 1970s, but such talk was hardly determinative in the exhausting legislative negotiations that led up to the approval of such major legislation as the Gramm-Leach-Bliley Act of 1999. My other sources for the concept of market talk include regular reading in the *New York Times*, *Wall Street Journal*, *The Economist*, presidential addresses, conversations with colleagues, friends, and family, and Karen Ho, *Liquidated: An Ethnography of Wall Street* (Durham, NC: Duke University Press, 2009). Ultimately, I decided that the talk and actions of my key figures such as Phil Gramm, Sandy Weill, Jeb Hensarling, and others would have to stand in for a chapter focused on free-market thinkers' influence beyond similarly inclined intellectual circles and a portion of the literate public. Scholarly treatments of market advocates in politics and in corporate boardrooms include Kevin M. Kruse, *One Nation Under God: How Corporate America Invented Christian America* (New York: Basic Books, 2015); Lisa McGirr, *Suburban Warriors: The Origins of the New American Right* (Princeton, NJ: Princeton University Press, 2001); Bethany Moreton, *To Serve God and Wal-Mart: The Making of Christian Free Enterprise* (Cambridge, MA: Harvard University Press, 2009); and Kim Phillips-Fein, *Invisible Hands: The Making of the Conservative Movement from the New Deal to Reagan* (New York: W. W. Norton, 2009). Finally, in this regard, see Luigi Zingales, *A Capitalism for the People: Recapturing the Lost Genius of American* Prosperity (New York: Basic Books, 2012), in which the author, a University of Chicago economist, contends that "the real effect of Gramm-Leach-Bliley was political, not economic" (51).

13. Guinto, "Jeb Hensarling."

14. Ibid.; Charles Mohr, "Goldwater—His Personality and His Beliefs: Senator's Conservative Philosophy Is Uniquely Individualistic but Many of His Views Often Seem Contradictory," *New York Times*, July 19, 1964. See as well Elizabeth Tandy Shermer, *Sunbelt Capitalism: Phoenix and the Transformation of American Politics* (Philadelphia: University of Pennsylvania Press, 2013), for a masterful account of Goldwater's ideas in the context of Phoenix politics starting in the 1930s.

15. "Texas 5th District Profile," *New York Times*, December 10, 2010.

16. Guinto, "Jeb Hensarling"; Robert Pear, "House Conservatives Issue a Make-or-Break Medicare List," *New York Times*, September 18, 2003; Richard A. Oppel, Jr., "Senate Approves Budget Intended to Curb Deficit," *New York Times*, March 13, 2004; John J. Miller, "Rep. Budget Reform: Jeb Hensarling (R., Tex.) Is Doing Vital Work," *National Review* 57, no. 24 (December 31, 2005): 26.

17. "Rep. Jeb Hensarling Proposes Bill to End the TARP Program," *National Mortgage Professional Magazine*, June 15, 2009; Guinto, "Jeb Hensarling."

18. "Rep. Jeb Hensarling Holds a Hearing on Volcker Rule Impact on Job Creators," *Financial Markets Regulation Wire*, January 15, 2014; Katherine J. Cramer, *The Politics of Resentment: Rural Consciousness in Wisconsin and the Rise of Scott Walker* (Chicago: University of Chicago Press, 2016).

19. "Hensarling Remarks at American Bankers Association Summit [2]," *Federal Information & News Dispatch*, March 15, 2016; Eduardo Porter, "Trump Budget Proposal Reflects Working-Class Resentment of the Poor," *New York Times*, March 7, 2017; Arlie Russell Hochschild, *Strangers in Their Own Land* (New York: New Press, 2016), 5–8, 147–151.

20. "Deal Breaker: Congressman Apologizes to Banks for Waterboarding Them with Dodd-Frank . . . Literally," *Newstex Finance & Accounting Blogs*, March 15, 2016; "Hensarling

Remarks at American Bankers Association Summit [2]"; "Panel Backs Two Bills That Would Undo Parts of Dodd-Frank," *CQ Roll Call*, April 13, 2016.

21. "Donald Trump, Republican Presidential Candidate, Is Interviewed on Fox News," *Financial Markets Regulation Wire*, January 26, 2016; "Donald Trump, Republican Presidential Candidate, Delivers Remarks at a Campaign Event," *Financial Markets Regulation Wire*, October 26, 2016.

22. Donna Borak, "Donald Trump, Jeb Hensarling Meet on Dodd-Frank Alternative; Texas Congressman Detailed His Proposal to Replace the Regulatory-Overhaul Law in Speech in New York," *Wall Street Journal*, June 7, 2016; Brent Cebul, "The Antigovernment Impulse: The Presidency, the 'Market,' and the Splintering Common Good," in *The President and American Capitalism Since 1945*, ed. Mark H. Rose and Roger Biles (Gainesville: University Press of Florida, 2017), 99–122.

23. Financial CHOICE Act of 2016, H.R. 5983, 114th Congress (2015–2016); Ian McKendry, "Cheat Sheet: Hensarling Asks for the Moon in Dodd-Frank Revamp," *American Banker*, June 8, 2016; "Hensarling Opening Statement at Financial CHOICE Act Markup," *Federal Information & News Dispatch*, September 13, 2016.

24. Geoff Colvin, "Meet Washington's Newest Power Player, Jeb Hensarling," *Fortune*, November 17, 2016; Elise Viebeck, "Jeb Hensarling Seeks to Tamp Down Trump Cabinet Talk," *Washington Post*, November 10, 2016.

25. "Sen. Orrin G. Hatch Holds a Hearing on the Nomination of Steve Mnuchin to Be Secretary of the Treasury, Morning Session," *Political/Congressional Transcript Wire*, January 19, 2017; George Yacik, "Mnuchin on the Hill; FHA Mortgage Loan Volume Rises as Risk Grows," *American Banker*, January 23, 2017; Joe Adler, "Cheat Sheet: What Trump Can—and Can't—Do to Dodd-Frank," *American Banker*, February 6, 2017. See also Sidney M. Milkis and Nicholas Jacobs, "'I Alone Can Fix It': Donald Trump, the Administrative Presidency, and Hazards of Executive-Centered Partisanship," *The Forum* 15, no. 3 (2017), in which the authors determine that Trump's executive actions are best understood not as efforts to increase or reduce the size of government, but as the use of "national administrative power aggressively to change the trajectory of policy."

26. Donald J. Trump: "Remarks in a Strategy and Policy Forum," February 3, 2017, *The American Presidency Project*, University of California at Santa Barbara.

27. Douglas Blackmon, "Did They See the Trump White House Coming," interview with Michael Kranish and Marc Fisher, Miller Center, *American Forum*, Miller Center.org, April 9, 2017.

28. Kate Kelly, "Trump's Economic Cabinet Is Mostly Bare: This Man Fills the Void," *New York Times*, February 11, 2017; Charles Duhigg, "Do You Need to Worry About Trump's Reforms? It Depends," *New York Times*, February 9, 2017; Peter Conti-Brown, "The Presidency, Congressional Republicans, and the Future of Financial Reform," Penn Wharton Public Policy Initiative, Issue Brief 5, no. 2 (February 2017); "A Conversation with Brian Moynihan," Council on Foreign Relations, CFR.org, January 25, 2017; Andy Peters, "Stress Tests, Living Wills Are Good for Industry, Dimon Says," *American Banker*, December 8, 2017.

29. Kelly, "Trump's Economic Cabinet Is Mostly Bare"; "Jamie Dimon, Chairman, President, and CEO, JPMorgan Chase, Is Interviewed on Bloomberg Television," *Financial Markets Regulation Wire*, January 18, 2017; Rachel Augustine Potter, "Why Trump Can't Undo the Regulatory State so Easily," Brookings.edu, February 6, 2017; Robert C. Pozen, "What Will Happen to Dodd-Frank Under Trump's Executive Order," Brookings.edu, February 6, 2017;

"Gary Cohn, Chief Economic Advisor to President Donald Trump, on Bloomberg TV Regarding Financial Regulations and Government Policies," *Financial Markets Regulation Wire*, February 3, 2017.

30. Porter, "Trump Budget Proposal Reflects Working-Class Resentment of the Poor"; Guy Molyneux, "Mapping the White Working Class," *American Prospect*, December 20, 2016; Mark Muro and Sifan Liu, "Tech in Metros: The Strong Are Getting Stronger," Brookings.edu, March 8, 2017; Joan C. Williams, "What So Many People Don't Get About the U.S. Working Class," *Harvard Business Review*, November 10, 2016; Joseph Parilla and Mark Muro, "Where Global Trade Has the Biggest Impact on Workers," Brookings.edu, December 14, 2016; Noam Scheiber, "Trump Move on Job Training Brings 'Skills Gap' Debate to the Fore," *New York Times*, June 15, 2017. See Carlo Rotella, *Good with Their Hands: Boxers, Bluesmen, and Other Characters from the Rustbelt* (Berkeley: University of California Press, 2002), for a firsthand and moving account of the men and women who believed "that strong hands doing skilled work had built particular ways of life infused with value" (3).

31. Ian McKendry, "Four Takeaways from Mnuchin's Capitol Hill Grilling," *American Banker*, January 20, 2017; and Ian McKendry, "Trump Administration Aiming for Two-Tiered Regulatory System," *American Banker*, May 2, 2017; Michael Barr and Peter Conti-Brown, "Repealing Dodd-Frank: What's the Likely Fallout," Knowledge@Wharton, Apple Podcast, February 10, 2017; "Dodd-Frank's Tentacles Go Deep, Won't Be Easily Cut," *National Underwriter Life & Health Breaking News*, February 6, 2017; Renae Merle, "GOP Preparing Plan to Gut Consumer Finance Protection Bureau, Roll Back Wall Street Regulations," *Washington Post*, February 9, 2017; David Dayen, "Dismantling Dodd-Frank—and More," *American Prospect*, February 6, 2017; Sapna Agarwal and Aparna Piramal Raje, "We Are in a Deglobalizaton Period: Business Historian Geoffrey G. Jones," Livemint.com, March 20, 2017.

32. Claudia Cummins, "Former Reagan Official Still Fighting for Banks," *American Banker*, August 14, 1992.

33. "Assessing the CHOICE Act: A Conversation with House Committee on Financial Service Chairman Jeb Hensarling (R-TX)," American Enterprise Institute, AEI.org, May 23, 2017.

34. Ibid.

35. Ibid.

36. Marc Levinson, *An Extraordinary Time: The End of the Postwar Boom and the Return of the Ordinary Economy* (New York: Basic Books, 2016), 257–270; Robert J. Gordon, *The Rise and Fall of American Growth: The U.S. Standard of Living Since the Civil War* (Princeton, NJ: Princeton University Press, 2016), 389–393; Mark H. Rose and Raymond A. Mohl, *Interstate: Highway Politics and Policy Since 1939*, 3rd ed. (Knoxville: University Press of Tennessee, 2012).

37. Brian Balogh, *The Associational State: American Governance in the Twentieth Century* (Philadelphia: University of Pennsylvania Press, 2015), 200–202, 218–219; David M. P. Freund, "Marketing the Free Market: State Intervention and the Politics of Prosperity in Metropolitan America," in *The New Suburban History*, ed. Kevin M. Kruse and Thomas J. Sugrue (Chicago: University of Chicago Press, 2006), 11–32.

38. Alan Murray, "Paul Volcker: Think More Boldly; The Former Fed Chairman Says the Conference Proposals Don't Go Nearly Far Enough to Accomplish What Needs to Be Accomplished," in "Future of Finance," special report, *Wall Street Journal*, December 14, 2009.

39. Ibid.

INDEX

Acharya, Viral V., 230n5
Adams, Stephen B., 214n38
adjustable rate mortgages, 7, 149
Admati, Anat, 198n5
Advance Investors Corporation, 75
African Americans: economic dislocations of, 149; homeownership and, 146; subprime mortgages and, 148
AIG. *See* American International Group (AIG)
airline deregulation, 54, 208n28
Allen, Douglas W., 198n5
American Bankers Association (ABA), 18, 20, 30, 113, 125, 184, 188
American Commercial Bank, 4, 86–87
American Dream Downpayment Act, 146
American Enterprise Institute (AEI), 193–96
American Express, 5, 43–44
American International Group (AIG), 155, 159, 162, 167, 172, 196
American Telephone and Telegraph (AT&T), 39
antitrust actions: bank mergers and, 3, 21–22, 28–30; Congress and exclusions to, 31; contestation of, 202n21; Justice Department and, 30–31; Patman and, 22; presidents and, 36; Saxon and, 19
asset-backed securities: American International Group and, 155; credit cards and, 140, 224n15; federal regulations and, 140–41; mortgages and, 6, 8; risk and, 143–44; supermarket banks and, 5; understanding of, 225n16
Associates First Capital, 147

Association of Reserve City Bankers, 67
automated teller machines (ATMs): consumer business and, 76; development of, xi, 7, 196
Axelrod, David M., 183

Babington, S. E., 23–24
bail-outs: anti-TARP views and, 157–58; bank regulations and, 188, 190; FDIC and, 62; Obama opposition to, 178; Paulson and, 131; popular anger over, 176; risk-taking and, 165; savings and loan associations (S&Ls), 59–61
Bair, Sheila, 156, 165, 167, 169, 173–74
Balogh, Brian, 200n8
BankAmerica, 5, 106, 132
BankAmericard, 90
bank deregulation, 6, 211n55
bank executives: bank regulations and, 13, 15, 83; competition and, 138; connections between, 134–35; credit cards and, 37; future of banking and, 68; Great Recession and, 2; mentorship of, 7, 71–72, 83, 85, 88–89, 135, 214n36; new lines of business and, 33–35; Old Testament thinkers and, 163; politics of, 38; predatory behavior of, 85; protection of, 137; reserve city, 67–68; risky strategies of, 162; securitization and, 140–41; shadow banking system and, 168–69; small-town, 2, 16, 24, 30, 34, 47, 49–50, 82, 88–89, 93, 108, 113–14, 125; state-chartered, 31; strategic friendships of, 147; subprime mortgages and, 144–46; trading practices, 171; understanding of bank operations by, 7
bank failures, 97–98, 138, 163
Bank Holding Company Act, 58, 73

Banking Act of 1933, 2
Bank Merger Act of 1960, 31
bank mergers: acceleration of, 20; antitrust
    actions and, 3, 21–22, 28–31, 36;
    competition and, 31; concentration of
    wealth and, 137; impact on small banks,
    37; increase in, 94; insurance companies
    and, 123–25; interstate bank compacts
    and, 94; Johnson and, 28; Lewis and, 137;
    lobbying for, 30–31; modest income
    housing promises in, 136; profitability of,
    94; Saxon and, 18–20, 23, 28–31; Texas,
    28–29, 96–98
Bank of America: commercial loans and,
    138; creation of, 2, 5, 132; credit cards
    and, 139–40; federal regulations and, 15,
    167; financial crisis of 2007–2008 and,
    136, 153; financial strength of, 132–33,
    135, 137, 139; government ownership in,
    159; growth and, 137; Merrill Lynch and,
    153; operation of, 7; proprietary trading
    and, 183; securities dealers in, 7, 169;
    TARP funds for, 157, 171
Bank of Chapel Hill, 88
Bank One, 134–35, 139, 224n15
bank politics: economic growth and, 69,
    114, 196, 206n7–207n7; litigation and, 38;
    lobbying and, 38; market talk and, 2, 38,
    194–96; narrative of, xi, xii; presidents
    and, 1, 6, 38, 206n7–207n7; Trump and,
    192
bank regulations: bank stock and, 26;
    branch offices and, 2–5, 7, 9, 15, 20, 25, 47;
    business practices and, 15; capital
    standards in, 170; Clinton and, 3–6, 106,
    124, 127, 129–30; commercial banks, 46;
    Congress and, 16, 50–52, 55, 120–21,
    123–26, 129, 165–66, 174; consolidation
    of, 55; council of, 173; divided, 134;
    Federal Reserve System and, 166–67;
    financial modernization of, 129–30; Ford
    and, 51–52; Glass-Steagall Act, 15–16;
    growth and, 14, 99–100; holding
    companies and, 63, 73, 123, 127–28; Hunt
    Commission and, 46–47; interagency
    committee for, 174; interpretations of,
    100; interstate banking and, 57, 92–93;
    Kennedy and, 2–3, 5–6, 13; legislative
    action and, 16, 30–31, 50–52, 55, 112,
    120–21, 123–26, 129; Ludwig and, 6;
    market talk and, 194–96; McColl and, 6,
    83, 91; narrative of, 177; Nixon and,
    41–44, 50–51; non-bank competitors and,
    80; Obama and, 160, 173, 176; politics of,
    9–10, 47, 111, 131, 170–79; predictability
    and security of, 44; presidents and, 1–3,
    5–6, 9, 14, 124, 173; reform and, 114;
    Regan and, 59, 63–64; Regulation Q, 45,
    47–48, 50–51, 53; regulatory reform of,
    53–54; regulatory relief and, 61; revenue
    bonds and, 26; rhetoric of, 47–48; Rubin
    and, 6; savings and loan associations
    (S&Ls), 46; Saxon and, 2–4; securitization
    and, 140–41; simplification of, 191; single
    regulator in, 172, 176; state-federal, 49;
    state regulations and, 141; Summers and,
    6; supermarket banks and, 2–4, 143;
    supervisory methods of, 167–68; turf
    protection and, 62, 172–73; Volcker Rule
    and, 9; Wriston and, 14, 72, 91
bank restoration programs, 156
banks: capital ratios, 78–79; computers and,
    72; credit cards and, 76–77; Depression
    and, 2; disinvestment in, 40; economic
    prosperity and, 1, 7; expansion of
    financial services and, 27, 33–35, 62, 64,
    120; full-service, 35; injections of funds
    into, 156–57; insurance sales and, 34–35,
    108–10, 113, 118–20; interstate compacts
    and, 92–93; proprietary trading and,
    181–82; recapitalization of, 156–57;
    underfunding of, 88. See also commercial
    banks; small-town banking; supermarket
    banks
bank stock, 26
bank subsidiaries: comptroller's office and,
    142–43; securitization and, 141; state
    regulations and, 142; supermarket banks
    and, 141–42
Bear Stearns, 150–52, 168–69
Bennett, Robert F., 125, 177
Bernanke, Ben: AIG bail-out, 155;
    community banks and, 175; financial
    crisis of 2007–2008 and, 151–53, 155–56,
    163, 173; problem-solving style of, 163;
    recovery plans, 156, 171; regulatory
    authority and, 165, 171; securitization
    and, 161; turf protection, 174
Bernstein, Michael A., 206n7
Binder, Sarah, 233n35, 234n1

Bliley, Thomas J., Jr., 118
BNP Paribas, 151
Boehner, John A., 176
Born, Brooksley E., 171–72, 192
Borstelmann, Thomas, 208n28
Bowery Savings Bank, 40, 43, 59
Boyer Edward, 213n25
Brennan, William J., 29
bridge bank, 98–99
Brookhaven Bank and Trust Company, 23
Brouillette, Geoff, 214n33
Brown, George R., 28–29, 31
Brown, Scott P., 177, 183
Burns, Arthur M., 39, 49–50, 78–79, 208n21
Bush, George W.: bank restoration programs, 156; expansion of financial services and, 146; on minority homeownership, 145–46, 148
Business Council, 122
business loans: commercial banks and, 47; savings and loan associations and, 49, 60–61, 117; supermarket banks and, 138; wealthy clients and, 144–45
business mortgages, 138

C&S/Sovran Corp, 106
California Federal Savings and Loan Association, 43, 48–49, 59
Calomiris, Charles M., 198n5, 205n54–206n54, 216n24, 219n23, 229n56, 231n14, 232n18
Camp, William B.: bank growth and, 33–36; bank regulations and, 33–34, 205n44; as comptroller of the currency, 33, 36–37; dual banking system and, 33–34; holding companies and, 73; loyalty to Saxon by, 33; mergers and, 34; mutual funds and, 75
Campbell, Gordon W., 93
capitalism: anti-regulation and, 79; bankers and, 14; financial crisis of 2007–2008 and, 154; laissez faire, 229n58; loans and, 14; risk and, 229n58
capital standards: development of, 170; raising, 171; risk and, 170–71; U.S. and European rules for, 192; Wriston and, 78–79, 170
Carpenter, Daniel P., 205n53
Carter, Jimmy: bank regulations and, 55–56; deregulation and, 54; inflation

and, 181; regulatory reform and, 54; on small savers, 55–56; Volcker and, 181
C. Douglas Wilson & Co., 89
certificate of deposit (CD), 71
chain stores, 21–22
Chandler, Alfred D., 199n8
Chapin, Christy Ford, 198n7, 231n17
Charlotte, NC: bank growth in, 85–88, 105–6; McColl and, 83; NationsBank in, 105; North Carolina National Bank headquarters in, 84–85
Chase Manhattan Bank: bank regulations and, 15; capital ratios and, 79; Glass-Steagall Act and, 2; impact on small banks, 3; mergers and, 134; mortgage originations, 147; revenue bonds and, 26–27, 37; subprime mortgages and, 144
Chemical Banking Corporation, 106
Chubb Ltd., 74
Churella, Albert J., 199n7
CIT Bank, 43
Citibank: capital ratios and, 78–79; credit cards and, 76–77; expansion of financial services and, 69, 76–78, 81–82; future of banking and, 68; international banking and, 77; threats to sell, 80; Wriston and, 67, 76, 81
Citicorp: bank regulations and, 82; First RepublicBank Corporation bid, 97; growth and, 106, 138; insurance sales and, 109; interstate banking and, 94; overleveraging of, 78; reserve levels and, 140; Travelers Group merger and, 5, 122–24; Triple-A rating, 214n29; Wriston and, 4, 76, 82
Citicorp Investment Management, Inc., 75
CitiFinancial, 147
Citigroup: borrowed funds and, 170–71; creation of, 2, 5, 123, 126; federal regulations and, 167; financial crisis of 2007–2008 and, 136, 149–50, 162; financial strength of, 135, 137; government ownership in, 159; internal control and, 139; legislative action and, 121; operation of, 7, 127; proprietary trading and, 183; securities dealers in, 7, 169; securitization and, 141; subprime mortgages and, 146–47, 149; TARP funds for, 157
Citizens & Southern National Bank (C&S), 34–35, 37

Citizens National Bank (Los Angeles), 20
Clark, Ramsey, 29, 204n32
Clinton, Bill: bank regulations and, 3–6,
  106, 124, 127, 129–30; bank subsidiaries
  and, 141–42; economic growth and, 106,
  115, 124–25, 128; economic recovery and,
  193; increased trade and, 107, 114;
  inner-city and rural lending efforts, 115;
  interstate banking and, 108, 114, 126;
  Ludwig and, 108; McColl and, 106, 112,
  115, 136; supermarket banks and, 101,
  127–28, 158, 193; Travelers-Citi merger
  and, 123
Clinton, Hillary, 189
Cohn, Gary D., 192
commercial banks: competition and, 117;
  decline of, 68, 113; economic growth and,
  135–36, 220n28; expansion of financial
  services, 120, 129; federal regulations
  and, 4, 14–15, 46, 54, 58; fortress
  mentality of, 68, 92; Glass-Steagall Act
  and, 2; growth of, 108, 116; home
  mortgages and, 46, 48; interest rates, 47;
  limits on, 56; loans and, 13–14; opposition to, 42; politics of, 37; postwar
  changes in, 117; revenue bonds, 26–27;
  securities, 35; securitization and, 140–41;
  short-term loans, 150; state regulations
  and, 15, 46; TARP funds for, 157; threats
  to, 64, 68; Volcker Rule and, 183
Commercial Credit Corporation, 146–47
commercial loans, 13–14, 61, 138
Committee on Financial Institutions, 25–26
community banks, 174–76, 193. See also
  small-town banking
Community Reinvestment Act (CRA):
  banker compliance with, 129, 136; bank
  holding companies and, 128; bank
  regulations and, 124, 126; Democratic
  protection of, 118; economic recovery
  and, 111–12, 125, 193; opposition to, 115,
  125; politics of, 195; Riegle and, 111–12
Comptroller of the Currency: authority of,
  142; bank regulations and, 7, 17, 120, 134;
  Camp as, 33; commercial banks and, 108;
  development of, 36–37; independence of,
  17; Ludwig as, 6, 108, 119–20; mergers
  and, 18–20, 23–24; office of, 17; Saxon as,
  2, 18; state insurance regulations and,
  124; supermarket bank regulation, 120

computers, xi, 72
Congress: asset-backed securities and, 141;
  bank regulations and, 16, 50–52, 55,
  120–21, 123–26, 129, 165–66, 174;
  commercial banks and, 129; CRA rules
  and, 126; divided regulatory scheme of,
  134; interstate banking and, 110–15
Congressional Budget Office (CBO), 187
Connecticut: banks and insurance in, 62,
  109–10; interstate bank compacts and, 94
Connecticut General Life Insurance
  Company, 74–75
construction industry, 40
consumer banks, 80–81
consumer business: ATMs and, 76; bank
  insurance sales, 108, 113; banks for, 80,
  137; credit cards and, 76–77; loans and, 49
Consumer Financial Protection Bureau,
  175, 180, 190
Conti-Brown, Peter, 213n15, 222n51,
  233n1–234n1
Continental Illinois National Bank and
  Trust Company, 35, 37, 62, 99, 138
Council of Economic Advisers (CEA), 25,
  27, 43
Council of Insurance Agents and Brokers,
  110
Cox, Christopher C., 154
CRA. See Community Reinvestment Act
  (CRA)
Crawford, Morris D., Jr., 43, 54, 59
credit cards: banks and, 37, 90, 139–40;
  expansion of, 76–77; as a growth
  opportunity, 139; politics of, xi;
  securitization and, 140, 224n15; Visa
  cards, 76
Crocker-Anglo National Bank, 20
Crocker-Citizens National Bank, 20–21, 36
cross-selling, 7, 135, 148
Crown Zellerbach Corporation, 43

Dallek, Robert, 203n30–204n30
D'Amato, Alfonse M., 120–21, 124–25
D'Arista, Jane, 211n55, 212n3, 217n42,
  223n56
Daschle, Thomas A., 114
Democrats: bank regulations and, 177;
  Community Reinvestment Act and, 118;
  TARP and, 187
Department of the Treasury, 17

Depository Institutions Deregulation and
  Monetary Control Act (DIDMCA), 56
deregulation: airline, 54, 208n28; banks, 6,
  211n55; Carter and, 54; Ford and, 52–53
Dillon, C. Douglas, 18, 160
Dimon, Jamie: as bank executive, 134–35,
  192; Bear Stearns and, 150–51, 154;
  Federal Reserve Bank of New York and,
  161; financial crisis of 2007–2008 and,
  155; Geithner and, 154; mergers and, 134,
  139; supermarket banks and, 135; Trump
  and, 191–92; Weill and, 121
Dodd, Christopher J.: bank regulation and,
  177; interstate banking support, 110, 113;
  opposition to bank sales of insurance, 62,
  109–10, 113, 165
Dodd-Frank Act: efforts to dismantle, xii,
  179–81, 185, 188–91, 193–94; origins of, 9;
  proprietary trading and, 183; regulatory
  authority of, 178–80
Dodd-Frank Wall Street Reform and
  Consumer Protection Act. See Dodd-
  Frank Act
Donaldson, Lufkin and Jenrette, 62
Dow Jones Industrial Average, 40, 154
dual banking system, 23, 33–34

economic growth: American understanding
  of, 52–53; bank growth and, 2–3, 21, 36,
  69, 115; bank-led, 130, 196; banks and, 7,
  220n28; Clinton and, 107, 114, 124–25,
  128; commercial banks and, 135–36;
  Fannie Mae/Freddie Mac and, 152;
  historical treatment of, 199n8; interstate
  banking and, 114; markets and, 1, 130;
  mortgage-backed securities and, 9;
  politics of, 10, 28; presidents and, xiii, 1,
  5–6, 13, 41, 178; regulatory reform and,
  54; risk and, 143; supermarket banks and,
  38, 128; trade and, 107, 114; underperformance and, 116
Economic Recovery Advisory Board, 183
Edge Act, 74
Edgerton, J. Howard, 43, 45–46, 48–49,
  51, 59
Eichengreen, Barry, 228n47
Eisenhower, Dwight D., 31
Eisner, Marc Allen, 198n7
Epstein, Gerald A., 222n50
Equal Credit Opportunity Act, x

Erlandson, Erik M., 218n9
Exchange Bancorporation of Tampa, 93

Faircloth, Duncan, 114
Fannie Mae, 152–53, 157
Farwell, Loring C., 202n20
Federal Deposit Insurance Corporation
  (FDIC): bank failures and, 98, 138; bank
  regulations and, 17, 19, 172; customer
  protection and, 58, 95; injections of
  funds, 62, 97–99, 156–57; insurance
  premiums, 175; overextended banks and,
  95; prohibition on bond underwriting, 58;
  securitization and, 169; tightening of
  credit and, 106
Federal Home Loan Bank Board, 55
Federal Reserve Bank of New York, 15, 49,
  78–79, 161–62
Federal Reserve System: bank holding
  companies and, 6, 120, 127, 129, 213n15;
  bank regulations and, 17, 22, 49, 124, 195;
  consumer protection and, 175; financial
  crisis of 2007–2008 and, 155, 173–74;
  financial holding companies and, 6, 143,
  174; financial services and, 5; Greenspan
  and, 112, 133; interest rates and, 133;
  interstate banking and, 92; lobbying by,
  174; mergers and, 19; presidents and, 49;
  reserve city bankers, 67–68; Saxon and,
  25, 27; securitization and, 142–43; as sole
  regulator, 166–68, 172–73; supermarket
  bank campaign and, 4; supervisory
  methods of, 167–68; Volcker and, 59,
  181–82
Federal Savings and Loan Insurance
  Corporation (FSLIC), 59–60, 80
Fein, Michael R., 198n6
Fidelity Savings & Loan, 80
Financial Choice Act, 190, 194
financial crisis of 2007–2008: American
  International Group and, 155; bank
  executives and, 2, 152–54, 157, 159, 163;
  bank-led economy and, 130–31; bank
  runs and, 151, 154; Bear Stearns and,
  150–51; capital standards and, 171;
  Citigroup and, 136, 149–50; Fannie Mae/
  Freddie Mac and, 152; Federal Reserve
  and, 173–74; Geithner and, 161–62;
  government bail-outs, 155–58; investment banking and, 136; Lehman Brothers

financial crisis of 2007–2008 (continued)
and, 153–54; loss of homes in, 136, 149;
low-income borrowers and, 149; Merrill
Lynch and, 152–54; narrative of, 164–66;
origins of, 231n18–232n18; overnight
loans and, 150–51; political movements
and, 176; recapitalization of banks,
156–57; recovery plans, 156; risk-taking
and, 166; shadow banking system and,
168–69; Volcker on, 181
financial holding companies: creation of,
130; Federal Reserve System and, 6, 143,
174; supervision of, 174
financial services business: commercial
banks and, 24, 62–64, 68; competition
and, 47; cross-selling, 7, 135; development
of, 58; Nixon and, 42–43; politics of, 10;
regulatory relief and, 61; reorganization
of, 50, 53, 56, 63
Financial Stability Oversight Council
(FSOC), 174, 178
Fine, Camden R., 175–76, 182, 184
First Atlanta Corporation, 84
First City National Bank of Houston, 29
First National Bank of Chicago, 15, 18
First National Bank of Lake City, Florida, 92
First National Bank of New York, 70
First National City Bank (N.Y.): ATMs in,
76; bank growth and, 71–76; change of
name to Citibank, 76; expansion of
financial services and, 72, 74–76; federal
regulations and, 15; international
banking and, 71–72, 74; merger
applications of, 18–19; push for fewer
restrictions, 13–14; revenue bonds and,
35; Wriston and, 38, 70–71
First National City Overseas Investment
Corporation, 74
First RepublicBank Corporation, 96–99,
106, 136
First Union Corporation, 105, 144
First Wachovia Corporation, 105. See also
Wachovia Corporation
Fitch, Thomas P., 197n1
FleetBoston Financial Corporation, 136, 139
Fligstein, Neil, 200n8, 225n21
Florida: bank expansion into, 84, 89, 92–94;
interstate compacts and, 93–94;
population growth in, 92
Florida Bankers Association, 92–93

FNC Credit, 74
Ford, Gerald R.: bank regulations and,
51–52; deregulation and, 52–53; Equal
Credit Opportunity Act and, x; freedom
rhetoric of, 53; rate freedom and, 53;
regulatory reform and, 53–54
foreclosures, 9, 149, 176, 180
Frank, Barney, 165, 173, 175, 177
Freddie Mac, 148, 152–53, 157
freedom rhetoric: bank politics and, xiii;
Ford and, 53; Hensarling and, 194
Friedman, Jeffrey, 227n38
Friedman, Walter A., 199n8, 206n4, 222n50
Fuld, Richard S., 153, 162, 168–69, 171
full-service banks: insurance sales and, 35,
118; mutual funds and, 60; revenue bonds
and, 60; Travelers Group as, 122. See also
supermarket banks

Galambos, Louis P, 200n8
Garn, Jacob, 61–62
Garn-St. Germain Depository Institutions
Act, 61, 81, 99
GE Capital Mortgage Services, 148
Geismer, Lily, 198n6
Geithner, Timothy F.: bank legislation,
176–80; on bank supervision, 170; capital
standards and, 170–71; consumer
protection and, 175; Dodd-Frank Act and,
9; education and career of, 161; financial
crisis of 2007–2008 and, 153–56, 161–62;
market making and, 182, 184; Obama and,
158, 162; politics of finance and, 162–63,
165–66; proprietary trading and, 182–83;
regulatory regime of, 163–64, 166–67; on
risk, 161–62; as Secretary of the Treasury,
158, 160; on single bank regulator, 172–74,
176; supermarket banks and, 10, 158, 180;
trading practices and, 171–72
Georgia: bank expansion into, 84, 93–94;
interstate compacts and, 93–94
Gerstle, Gary, 210n49
Gilbert, Richard G., 48
Gingrich, Newton L., 118
Glass-Steagall Act: abolition of, 120–21;
attempts to revoke, 117–18; bank practices
and, 2, 46; comptroller's office and, 17;
holding company regulation and, 213n15;
mutual funds and, 75; Regulation Q and,
45; revenue bonds and, 26; revisions to

rule 5, 120; separation of commercial
and investment banking in, 15–16, 35,
37, 58, 100
GMAC Commercial Mortgage Corporation,
138
Goldman Sachs, 157, 184
Goldwater, Barry, 186
Gorton, Gary, 198n5
Graham, Otis L., Jr., 220n28
Graham, Robert, 93
Gramm, William Philip: anti-regulation
and, 125–26, 190; asset-backed securities
and, 143; bank politics and, 6; bank
subsidiaries and, 128; dislike of the CRA,
115, 125–26; federal regulations and, 129;
Hensarling and, 185–87; influence of,
185–86; market talk and, 194; securitization and, 144; supermarket banks and, 6,
124–25; thrift charters and, 125
Gramm-Leach-Bliley Financial Services
Modernization Act of 1999: bank
regulations and, 167, 169; blame for
financial crisis, 161, 164–65, 189–90;
Congress and, 132; economic growth and,
130; financial architecture of, 9, 129;
securitization and, 141, 143–44;
supermarket banks and, 6, 130
Granovetter, Mark, 200n8
Great Recession: banks and, 2, 130–31;
impact on housing and jobs, 136;
investment banking and, 136. See also
financial crisis of 2007–2008
Great Western Savings & Loan, 40, 42
Greenspan, Alan: asset-backed securities
and, 143; bank holding companies and,
123, 127, 129; bank regulations and, 134; as
Federal Reserve Chair, 112, 133, 222n50;
financial holding companies and, 130;
Hunt Commission and, 43–44, 79; interest
rates and, 133; libertarian views of, 44;
regulatory authority of, 123–24; securitization and, 142–43, 225n16; Travelers-Citi
merger and, 123–24; U.S. competitive
advantage and, 192; on Volcker, 181
Gregory, Joseph M., 168
Guinto, Joseph, 234n12

Haber, Stephen H., 198n5, 205n54–206n54,
216n24, 219n23, 229n56, 231n14, 232n18
Hanover Bank, 30

Hansen, Horace R., 23–24
Hawke, John D., Jr.: as comptroller of the
currency, 134; protection of supermarket
banks by, 142–43; securitization and, 142;
subprime mortgages and, 145
Hawley, Ellis W., 200n8
Hayes, Alfred, 49
hedge funds, 162, 168, 186
Heller, Walter W., 25–27
Hellwig, Martin, 198n5
Hensarling, Thomas Jeb: antigovernment
views of, 186–90, 193; anti-TARP views,
187; bank politics and, 193, 196; beliefs
about markets, 185, 194; economic
growth and, 10; efforts to dismantle the
Dodd-Frank Act, xii, 179–81, 185, 188–91,
194; efforts to dismantle the Volcker
Rule, 188, 190–91, 194; influence of Gramm on,
185–87; legislative action and, 9–10,
194–95; market talk and, 194–95;
opposition to Obama by, 187–88; Trump
and, xii, 189–91
Hispanics: economic dislocations of, 149;
subprime mortgages and, 148
Ho, Karen, 231n13, 232n21, 235n12
Hoff, Joan, 208n24
holding companies: bank regulations and,
63, 73, 123, 127–28, 212n14; banks and,
73; Federal Reserve System and, 6, 120,
127, 129; international banking and, 74;
interstate banking and, 81, 114; nonbank
subsidiaries and, 128. See also financial
holding companies
home mortgages: comptroller's office and,
142; defaulted, 7–8; first-time homebuyers
and, 146; foreclosures, 9, 149, 176, 180;
interest rates, 40, 45, 59–60; market
shares, 147; minorities and, 145–46, 148;
no-money-down, 61; savings and loan
associations and, 40, 42, 45–46, 48,
59–61; securitization and, 142; subprime,
144–47; tax incentives for, 50. See also
subprime mortgages
housing industry: bank investments in, 136;
falling home prices in, 149; legislation for,
52; mortgage rates and, 40; residential
production and, 146; savings and loan
associations and, 42, 45; subprime
mortgages and, 144; tax incentives for, 50
Hughes, Thomas Parke, 200n8

Hunt, Reed O., 43–50
Hunt Commission, 42–51, 53, 56–57, 60
Hutnyan, Joseph D., 214n38
Hyman, Louis, 211n3, 220n29, 224n15

Independent Bankers Association of
America, 61, 81
Independent Community Bankers
Association (ICBA), 22–24, 125, 182, 184
Independent Insurance Agents of America,
109
Industrial Bank of Fayetteville, 90
inflation, 39, 48, 51, 220n27
inner-city lending, 111–13, 115
insurance: bank sales of, 34–35, 108–10, 113,
118–20; state regulations and, 120–21,
124, 169
insurance companies: banking business
and, 68, 74–75, 100; bank mergers and,
123–25; defense of, 62, 109–10, 113, 165;
federal regulations and, 74; independent
agents in, 110; opposition to commercial
banks by, 42; opposition to supermarket
banks by, 118–19, 121; state regulations
and, 169; TARP funds for, 157; thrift
charters and, 125
Interest Rate Control Act, 45, 48
interest rates: federal regulations and, 15,
43; home mortgages, 40, 45, 59–60; home
state determination of, 77; impact on
consumers, 51; money market funds and,
40; Regulation Q and, 45, 47–48, 54–55;
savings and loan associations (S&Ls), 40,
43–46, 51; small savers and, 50, 55–56
InterFirst Corporation, 96
international banking: Citibank, 77; holding
companies and, 74; North Carolina
National Bank (NCNB), 89; Wriston and,
71–72, 74
interstate banking: Clinton and, 108, 114,
126; competition for, 93; Congress and,
110–15; credit cards and, 77; development
of, 74, 84, 92; Dodd and, 110; federal
prohibition on, 57, 92; McColl and,
88–89, 92–94, 112–15, 126; North
Carolina National Bank, 90; politics of,
111–13, 115; small-town banking
opposition to, 113–14; state prohibitions
on, 92; state regulations and, 113; Texas
approval of, 96

interstate compacts, 92–94
Investment Bankers Association, 72
investment banking: financial crisis of
2007–2008 and, 136; opposition to
commercial banks by, 42; revenue bonds
and, 35; securities firms as, 6–7; as
shadow banking system, 168–69;
short-term loans, 150–51; supermarket
banks and, 128; TARP funds for, 157
Investment Company Institute, 75

Jacobs, Donald P., 208n23
Jacobs, Nicholas, 236n25
Jenrette, Richard R., 62
John, Richard R., 199n7
Johnson, Lyndon B.: bank growth and, 14,
31, 36; bank mergers and, 28–29, 31; bank
regulations and, 2–3; Camp and, 32;
economic growth and, 28; Interest Rate
Control Act, 45; Saxon and, 27, 31–32;
style of speech, 203n30–204n30; Texas
banks and, 27–28, 137
Johnson, Simon H., 182, 184, 188
Jones, John T., 28, 203n29
J. P. Morgan & Co., 15
JPMorgan Chase & Co.: Bear Stearns and,
150; mergers and, 134; profitability of,
135, 137; TARP funds for, 157; Trump
and, 191
Justice Department: antitrust actions and,
30–31, 74, 95; bank mergers and, 28–31

Katzenbach, Nicholas, 31
Kaufman, Henry, 230n13–231n13
Kennedy, Edward M., 177
Kennedy, Jacqueline, 71
Kennedy, John F.: appointment of Saxon,
2–3, 13, 16–18; assassination of, 27; bank
growth and, 14, 26, 31, 36; bank
regulations and, 2–3, 5–6, 13, 16, 25;
economic growth and, 13, 16
Kennedy, Robert F.: antitrust actions and, 3,
21, 29; mergers and, 19–20, 28; opposition
to Saxon by, 31
Kerr, K. Austin, 200n8
Konings, Martijn, 211n53
Kovacevich, Richard M.: employee
motivation, 148; recognition of, 134;
securitization and, 142–43; strategic
friendships of, 147; subprime mortgages

and, 147–48; supermarket banking and, 133, 135
Kraus, Wladimir, 227n38
Kruse, Kevin M., 235n12

Laird, Pamela Walker, 197n3, 199n8, 214n36
laissez faire laws, 212n4
Lasker, Bernard J., 40
Leach, James A., 118
Lehman Brothers: bankruptcy of, 8–9, 153–54, 162, 172; borrowed funds and, 170–71; domestic and worldwide business and, 138; investment banking and, 6; as shadow banking system, 168–69
Levine, Ross, 206n54
Lewis, Kenneth D.: acquisitions of, 136–39; admiration for, 135; bank growth and, 138; Bank of America and, 132–33, 137; financial crisis of 2007-2008 and, 2, 159; mentorship of, 7; mergers and, 137; Merrill Lynch and, 153; securitization and, 140–41, 143; supermarket banks and, 136, 138
libertarians, 44
Licht, Walter, 227n35
loans: capitalism and, 14; commercial banks and, 13–14, 61, 138; manufacturing, 89; ship, 71; short-term, 7–8, 150–52
Long-Term Capital Management, 143, 154
low-income lending: subprime mortgages and, 144–46; in underinvested city and rural areas, 111
Ludwig, Eugene A.: banker autonomy and, 142; bank holding companies and, 123; bank regulations and, 9, 117; Clinton and, 108; commercial bank advocacy, 108–10, 118, 120; as comptroller of the currency, 6, 108, 119–20; insurance companies and, 120–21, 123; interstate banking and, 112–15; rule 5 and, 119–21; on Saxon, 113; subsidiaries and, 143; supermarket banks and, 119–20, 136

MacDonald, Thomas H., 37
Manufacturers Hanover Trust Company, 30–31
Manufacturers Trust Company, 30
Marchiel, Rebecca, 219n17
Marion Bank & Trust Company, 90
market discipline, 166, 194

market making, x, 182, 184
markets: banks and, 1; beliefs about, 185; Obama on, 159–60; presidents and, 1, 10; risk management and, 166; state and, 198n7
market talk: in American life, 1, 8, 194; bank politics and, 38; bank regulations and, 194–96; concept of, 235n12; economic growth and, 130; expanded trade and, 107; Great Recession and, 131; interstate banking and, 114; legislative action and, 194–96; supermarket banks and, 195
Markham, Jerry W., 198n5, 225n16
Martin, William McChesney: independence of, 25; regulation of bank stock and, 26; revenue bonds and, 26–27; Saxon dispute, 25–27, 31–32
Massachusetts: interstate bank compacts and, 94; negotiable order of withdrawal (NOW) accounts in, 49
MBNA Corporation, 139
McColl, Hugh L., Jr.: bank growth and, 84, 88, 91–95, 99–101, 107–8, 132, 136–37; bank operations and, 7; bank regulations and, 6, 100; Clinton and, 106, 112, 115; as "Clinton's banker," 4, 112, 136; commercial bank acquisition, 90; early years of, 85; education and career of, 85–91; entrepreneurship of, 85; Florida acquisitions, 92–94; Georgia acquisitions, 93–94; inner-city and rural lending efforts, 113; interstate banking and, 88–89, 92–94, 112–15, 126; Marine Corps and, 4–5, 84–85; mentorship of, 83, 85, 88–89, 135; mergers and, 94; personality of, 84–85, 91; political accomplishments of, 100, 107, 115; recognition of, 90, 106–7; regulator relationships and, 83, 91, 95, 97–99; securitization and, 141; Seidman and, 97–98; supermarket banks and, 5, 136; Texas acquisitions, 95, 97–99
McConnell, Mitchell, Jr., 176–77
McCoy, Donald R., 200n8
McCraw, Thomas K., 199n8
McCulley, Paul A., 168
McGirr, Lisa, 235n12
McIntyre, Thomas J., 52
McKenzie, Roderick D., 200n8
McLaren, Richard W., 74

Meeks, Gregory, 177
mentorship: Lewis and, 7; McColl and, 83,
    85, 88–89, 135; Weill and, 135; Wriston
    and, 71–72
mergers. *See* bank mergers
Merrill Lynch: banks and, 3; federal
    regulations and, 58, 113; financial crisis of
    2007–2008 and, 136, 152–53; financial
    services of, 46–47, 108, 117; flexibility of,
    63, 68, 81–82; investment banking and, 6,
    35, 56–57; market making, x; mutual
    funds and, 57; Regan and, 4–5, 56–58; as
    shadow banking system, 168; TARP
    funds for, 157
Meyer, Laurence, 222n51
Milkis, Sidney M., 236n25
minority homeownership, 145–46, 148
Mishkin, Frederic S., 225n16
Mnuchin, Steven T., 191–92
money market funds: federal regulations
    and, 100; interest rates, 40, 68; movement
    to, 117; as shadow banking system,
    168–69; TARP funds for, 157; withdraw-
    als from, 151, 154
Money Store, 144–45
Moore, George S.: expansion of financial
    services and, 72; holding companies and,
    74; Saxon and, 31–32; Wriston and,
    71–72, 83
Moreton, Bethany, 235n12
Morgan, Iwan, 200n8, 201n4
Morgan Stanley & Co., 15, 157
Morris, John, 214n33
mortgage-backed securities, 8–9, 150
Moynihan, Brian T., 192
mutual funds: banks and, 60, 62, 75, 112;
    holding companies and, 63; interest
    rates, x; Merrill Lynch and, 57–58;
    regulation of, 4, 47, 50; savings and loan
    associations and, 60; supermarket banks
    and, 137–38; Travelers Group and, 5,
    121–22

NAFTA. *See* North American Free Trade
    Agreement (NAFTA)
National Association of Realtors, 62
National Bank of Commerce, 28
National Bank of Westchester, 19
National City Bank of New York, 70
National Economic Council, 192

NationsBank: growth and, 99, 106–7, 137;
    lobbying by, 113; McColl and, 4; purchase
    of BankAmerica, 132. *See also* North
    Carolina National Bank (NCNB)
Nationwide Financial Services, 78
Native Americans, 148
NCNB Corporation, 89, 91
NCNB National Bank of Florida, 93
negotiable order of withdrawal (NOW)
    accounts, 49
New Hampshire, 49
Nixon, Richard M.: bank growth and, 38;
    bank regulations and, 41–44, 50–51;
    Cambodian invasion and, 39, 41;
    economic growth and, 41; financial
    executives and, 4, 39–41; Hunt Commis-
    sion and, 42–51; impeachment of, 51; on
    small savers, 50; supermarket banks and,
    5, 41; Vietnam War and, 39–41
North American Free Trade Agreement
    (NAFTA), 107
North Carolina: bank expansion in, 84,
    90–91; bank mergers in, 87; capital poor
    residents of, 86; manufacturing loans in,
    89; in-state branching, 15, 87. *See also*
    Charlotte, NC
North Carolina National Bank (NCNB):
    branch offices and, 87–88, 91; commercial
    banks and, 90; credit cards and, 90;
    expansion into Florida, 92–94; expansion
    into Georgia, 93–94; expansion into
    Texas, 95, 97–99; expansion of financial
    services and, 89–91; growth and, 87–92,
    99; international banking, 89; interstate
    banking and, 88–90, 92–94; McColl and,
    83–84; mergers and, 87–88; name change
    to NationsBank, 99; National Division,
    88–89; underfunded clients, 88. *See also*
    NationsBank
Northeast: full-service banks and, 137;
    investment in, 69; savings and loan
    associations in, 60
Northeast Bancorp, 94
Norwest Bank, 134

Obama, Barack H.: bank regulations and, 9,
    160, 173, 176, 185; capital standards and,
    171; consumer protection and, 173, 175;
    Dodd-Frank Act and, 178, 180, 185;
    economic growth and, 158; Geithner and,

158, 162; on markets, 159–60; supermarket banks and, 158, 178; Tea Party opposition to, 176; Volcker and, 183
Office of Thrift Supervision, 167, 172, 174
Olegario, Rowena, 224n15, 225n18, 227n35
Onassis, Aristotle, 71
O'Neal, E. Stanley, 152
overnight loans, 8, 150–51, 169–70

Pak, Susie, 199n8
Patman, Wright: bank regulations and, 22, 30, 36, 94; chain stores and, 21–22; Glass-Steagall Act and, 16; opposition to Saxon by, 2, 9, 17, 21–23, 31; as a populist, 21; small-town banking and, 9, 16, 22–24, 37, 50, 94
Patrikis, Ernest T., 214n37
Patterson, Scott, 226n23
Paulson, Henry M.: Fannie Mae/Freddie Mac conservatorship, 152; financial crisis of 2007–2008 and, 151–56, 164; injections of funds into banks by, 131, 152–54; Lehman Brothers and, 153–54; as Secretary of the Treasury, 160
Peltzman, Sam, 207n16
Penn Central Railroad, 39–40, 45
Perot, H. Ross, 97
Phillips, Almarin, 208n23
Phillips-Fein, Kim, 235n12
Pistor, Charles H., Jr., 96
Polanyi, Karl P., 200n8
political economy: Citicorp growth and, 82–83; commercial banks and, 24; federal regulations and, 114, 195, 199n7; finance and, 45, 63; financial risk in, 136; impact of presidents in, 200n8; laissez faire, 212n4, 223n55; Obama inheritance of, 158; turf protection in, 42
Posner, Richard A., 229n58
Pozsar, Zoltan, 229n56
Prasad, Monica, 223n55
presidents: antitrust actions and, 36; bank regulations and, 1–3, 5–6, 9, 14, 173, 206n7–207n7; economic prosperity and, xiii, 5–6, 13, 41, 178; markets and, 1, 10
President's Commission on Financial Structure and Regulation. See Hunt Commission
President's Economic Policy Advisory Board, 79

Prince, Charles O.: bank acquisitions and, 121, 139; domestic and worldwide business and, 138; financial crisis of 2007–2008 and, 2, 159; resignation from Citigroup, 150; risky strategies of, 162; securitization and, 141, 143–44; subprime mortgages and, 146–47, 150; supermarket banks and, 135; Weill and, 134
proprietary trading, 181–84, 188
Prudential Insurance Company, 43–44

race: homeownership and, 145–46; subprime mortgages and, 8, 144–45, 148
radical ignorance, 227n38
Ramada Worldwide, 74
Rand, Ayn, 44
rate freedom, 53
Reagan, Ronald W.: asset-backed securities and, 141; bank growth and, 38; bank regulations and, 6, 56, 79; financial executives and, 4; regulatory relief and, 56, 61–62; savings and loan infusions and, 61; Volcker and, 181
Reed, John S., 122–24
Reese, Addison H., 86–90
Regan, Donald T.: bank growth and, 38; bank regulations and, 4, 59, 63–64, 211n53; future of banking and, 58; holding companies and, 73; Merrill Lynch and, 56–58, 68; as Reagan's chief of staff, 63; regulatory relief and, 61–62; savings and loan infusions and, 59–61; as Secretary of the Treasury, 56, 59, 79, 160; supermarket banks and, 47, 57–58, 126
Regulation Q: American understanding of, 52; attempts to revoke, 45, 47–48, 50–51, 53, 55–56, 61; Hunt Commission and, 46–48, 50; regulatory reform and, 53; savings and loan defense of, 45, 48, 51, 54; savings interest rates and, 45; small savers and, 55
regulatory reform: Carter and, 54–55; expansion of financial services in, 114; Ford and, 53–54; presidents and, 38. See also bank regulations
regulatory relief, 56, 61
Reid, Harry M., 177
Reinhart, Carmen M., 223n57

Remolona, Eli M., 220n29
Republican Party: anti-TARP views, 177;
    bank controls and, 118; campaign
    promises, 118; Dodd-Frank Act and, 185;
    on federal spending, 187; House and
    Senate majorities, 117–18, 194; opposition
    to Obama by, 176–77, 185; Tea Party and,
    187–88; Trump and, 189
Republic National Bank of Dallas, 96
repurchase agreements, 8, 198n5
reserve city bankers, 67–68
Resolution Trust Corporation, 141
revenue bonds: bank expansion into, 33, 37,
    64; bank underwriting of, 2, 35, 47, 60;
    commercial banks and, 56, 58; savings
    and loan associations underwriting of,
    60; Saxon-Martin dispute, 26–27
Richardson, Matthew, 230n5
Riegle, Donald W., Jr.: bank regulations
    and, 111; inner-city and rural lending
    efforts, 111–12, 125; interstate banking
    and, 112–15; political accomplishments
    of, 112, 115
Riegle-Neal Interstate Banking and
    Branching Efficiency Act, 114
risk: bank regulations and, 162; borrowed
    funds and, 170–71; Geithner on, 161–62,
    166; regulatory regime and, 164–65;
    securitization and, 143–44, 150, 161;
    shadow banking system and, 168–69;
    subprime mortgages and, 145; systemic,
    162, 173, 188
Robertson, Linda L., 174
Robinson-Patman Act, 21
Rockefeller, David, 2–3, 15, 37, 79
Rodgers, Daniel T., 209n31, 211n53, 235n12
Rogoff, Kenneth S., 223n57
Roosa, Robert V., 18
Roose, Kevin, 231n13
Roosevelt, Franklin D., 15, 21
Rose, Peter S., 206n54, 211n55
Rotella, Carlo, 237n30
Rubin, Robert E.: bank holding companies
    and, 123, 128; business-first investment,
    116; education and career of, 115; federal
    regulations and, 9, 116–17; legislative
    action and, 119; media and, 118–19;
    National Economic Council and, 192; as
    Secretary of the Treasury, 115–16, 160;
    supermarket banks and, 6, 126; Travelers-

    Citi merger and, 123; U.S. competitive
    advantage and, 192
rule 5, 119–21
rural lending, 111–13, 115
Ruth, Jack, 87–88

Salinger, Pierre, 28
Salomon Smith Barney, 127
Saunders, Stuart T., 39
savings and loan associations (S&Ls):
    bankruptcy of, 106; branch offices and,
    47; business loans and, 61; disinvestment
    in, 40; federal regulations and, 46, 54;
    financial health of, 59–60; financial
    services and, 43–44, 46–50, 56; home
    mortgages and, 40, 42, 45–46, 48, 54,
    59–60; "hot money" flows in, 59; housing
    industry and, 42, 45, 50; interest rates, 40,
    43–48, 51, 54; interstate banking and, 81;
    lobbying by, 51, 54, 60; negotiable order
    of withdrawal (NOW) accounts, 49;
    no-money-down mortgages, 61;
    opposition to commercial banks by, 42;
    rescue of, 59–61; securitization and, 141;
    state regulations and, 46; tax incentives
    for, 50; underfunding of, 59
Sawyer, Laura Phillips, 202n21
Saxon, James J.: bank growth and, 2–5, 10,
    19–21, 23–24, 26–28, 36; changes in bank
    regulations and, 2, 13–14, 21, 31–33, 36,
    38, 72; as comptroller of the currency, 2,
    4–5, 9, 13, 16–18, 36–37; departure of, 32;
    education and career of, 16–18;
    expansion of financial services and, 27,
    33, 35, 64, 72; lawsuits against, 35;
    Martin dispute, 25–27, 31–32; mergers
    and, 18–20, 23, 28–31; mutual funds and,
    75; opposition to, 2–3, 9, 21–25, 27, 31–32;
    Patman and, 2, 9, 17, 19, 21–22; regula-
    tion of bank stock and, 26; revenue bonds
    and, 26–27
Schooley, C. Herschel, 22, 31, 36–37
Sears, Roebuck: credit cards and, 4; federal
    regulations and, 100, 113; as holding
    company, 73; insurance sales and, x, 4, 68;
    as supermarket bank, 217n42
Secretary of the Treasury: Dillon as, 18, 160;
    Geithner as, 158, 160; Paulson as, 160;
    Regan as, 56, 59, 79, 160; Rubin as,
    115–16, 160

Securities and Exchange Commission (SEC), 26
securities firms: doing "God's work," 144; as investment bankers, 6–7; regulation of, 6; securitization and, 141
Securities Industries Association, 62
securitization: credit cards and, 140; economic growth and, 144; Federal Reserve System and, 142–43; government-led, 141; growth of, 141; regulator awareness of, 169; risk and, 143–44, 150; savings and loan associations and, 141; short-term loans and, 152; subprime mortgages and, 144–45, 150–52; subsidiaries and, 141–42; understanding of, 225n16
Security National Bank, 87
Seidman, William, 95, 97–100, 156, 196
Senate Banking Committee: bank regulations and, 112, 124, 128; Riegle and, 111–12; Saxon and, 27
shadow banking system: financial crisis of 2007–2008 and, 168–69; hedge funds and, 186; regulation of, 168–69; risk and, 168–69; Volcker Rule and, 183
Shearson Lehman Hutton, 94, 100
Shelby, Richard C., 176
Shermer, Elizabeth Tandy, 235n14
ship loans, 71
short-term loans, 7–8, 150–52
Simon, William E., 50–53
Skowronek, Stephen, 200n8
small savers, 50, 55–56
small-town banking: exemption from regulations, 175; federal regulations and, 114; Federal Reserve and, 174–75; impact of Saxon's rules on, 2, 16, 22–24, 37; interstate banking opposition, 113–14; large banks and, 2–3, 21; lobbying by, 176; protection of, 16, 114; state regulations and, 113
Smith, Roy C., 230n5
social change, 200n8
Solomon, Anthony, 79
Solomon, Emmet G., 20
Source One Mortgage, 147
South Dakota: credit card business in, 77; interest rates in, 77; investment in, 69
Southern National Bank, 29
Spencer, William I., 78

Spindel, Mark, 233n35, 234n1
state-chartered bankers, 31
Stewart, Potter, 75
St. Germain, Fernand J., 59–62
stock market, 40, 42, 127, 156
Storrs, Thomas I., 89–93
strategic friendships, 147
subprime mortgages: adjustable rate, 149; asset-backed securities and, 164–65, 167; borrower characteristics, 8, 145; cross-selling and, 148; defaulted, 149; Fannie Mae/Freddie Mac purchases of, 152; financial crisis of 2007–2008 and, 8, 150–51, 162, 164–65; foreclosures and, 149; growth of, 146–48; increased volume of, 147–48; Kovacevich and, 147–48; neighborhoods for, 145; overnight loans and, 151; race and, 8, 145, 148; residential production and, 146; risk and, 145; securitization and, 144–47; valuations and, 149–50; Weill and, 146–47
Sugrue, Thomas J., 199n8
Summers, Lawrence H., 6, 128, 143, 160, 171
supermarket banks: bank subsidiaries and, 141–43; Clinton and, 101, 127–28, 158; community banks and, 176; competition and, 20, 138; concentration of wealth in, 137; cross-selling and, 137; defining, 197n1; development of, 3–5, 46, 54, 73, 136; economic growth and, 3, 38, 128, 135; fear of, 100–101; federal regulations and, 5, 120, 126; government bail-outs, 158; holding companies and, 73; impact on small-town banks, 2–3; investment decisions in, 128; leadership of, 7; legalization of, 6; Ludwig and, 119–20; market talk and, 8; mortgage-backed securities and, 8–9; Nixon and, 41; Obama and, 158, 178; operation of, 7; opposition to, 51, 118–19, 121; as a political goal, 197n1; politics of, 10, 107–8, 194; protection of top executives in, 137; push for, 101; Regan and, 47, 57–58, 126; Rubin and, 6, 126; rule 5 revision, 119–21; securitization and, 143; short-term loans, 7–8; single regulator of, 172–73; TARP funds for, 157
Sylla, Richard, 202n21–203n21, 205n51
systemic risk, 162, 173, 188

TARP. *See* Troubled Asset Relief Program
   (TARP)
Tea Party: antigovernment views of, 176–77;
   anti-TARP views, 187; Republican Party
   and, 187–88
Tett, Gillian, 170
Texas: bank growth in, 96; banking losses
   in, 96–97; bank mergers in, 28–29, 96–98;
   economy and, 95–96, 99; interstate
   banking and, 96
Texas National Bank of Commerce, 28
Texas National Bank of Houston, 28
thrift charters, 125
"too big to fail" (TBTF), 138
trade barriers, 107
trading clearinghouse, 171–72
TranSouth Financial Corporation, 91
Travelers Group: Citicorp merger and,
   5, 122–24; Weill and, 121–23
Troubled Asset Relief Program (TARP),
   156–58, 160, 171, 185, 187
Trump, Donald J.: antigovernment
   supporters of, 192–93; bank growth
   and, 14; bank politics and, 192–93;
   bank regulations and, 6, 179; Dodd-
   Frank Act and, 189–91; Hensarling and,
   xii, 189–91
Trust Company of Florida, 89, 92

underperformance, economic, 116
Union Bancorp, Inc., 73
Union Bank of California, 73
U.S. Bureau of Public Roads, 37
U.S. Chamber of Commerce, 156
U.S. Commodity Futures Trading
   Commission, 171
U.S. Securities and Exchange Commission,
   5–6, 58, 167

Valenti, Jack J., 28, 31–32
Vanatta, Sean, 211n3–212n3
Vietnam War: economy and, 40–41; Nixon
   and, 39–41; student protests against, 39
Vietor, Richard H. K., 199n8, 231n17
Visa cards, 76
Volcker, Paul A.: bank policy and, 196,
   234n1; capital standards and, 181; on
   Citibank, 78; inflation and, 181; influence
   of, 182–83; proprietary trading and,
   181–84; savings and loan associations

and, 59–60; security trading and, 9;
   Wriston and, 80
Volcker Rule, 9, 179, 181–84, 188, 190–91,
   194
Volk, Harry J., 73

Wachovia Corporation: financial strength
   of, 88, 90–91; First Wachovia Corporation, 105; MBNA and, 139; purchase of
   First Atlanta Corporation, 84; regional
   strength of, 87, 105; regulator relationships and, 87; servicing of business
   mortgages, 138
Wallison, Peter J., 194
Walter, Ingo, 230n5
Warren, Elizabeth, 175
Warsh, Kevin M., 229n58
Waterhouse, Benjamin C., 219n27–220n27
Weill, Sanford I.: bank operations and, 7;
   bank regulations and, 6, 121; as chair of
   Travelers Group, 121–22; Citicorp merger
   and, 122–24; cross-selling and, 148;
   mentorship of, 135; personality of, 121;
   Prince and, 134; securitization and, 141;
   strategic vision of, 122; subprime
   mortgages and, 146–47; supermarket
   banks and, 5; undercapitalized firms and,
   144
Welborn, David M., 200n8
Wells, Wyatt C., 208n21
Wells Fargo & Company: commercial loans
   and, 138; merger bids, 97–98, 136;
   mortgage originations, 147–48; profitability of, 135; securitization and, 142;
   subprime mortgages and, 147; supermarket banking and, 133–34; TARP funds
   for, 157
Wells Fargo Home Mortgage, Inc., 142,
   147–48
White, Eugene N., 200n2
Wirth, Louis, 200n8
Wolfson, Martin H., 222n50
Wriston, Walter B.: anti-regulation and, 70,
   79, 126; bank growth and, 67, 71–78,
   80–83, 100, 138, 214n33; bank politics
   and, 38; bank regulations and, 6, 14, 64,
   72, 79–80, 91, 168; on capital standards,
   78–79, 170; certificate of deposit and, 71;
   commercial banks and, 212n3; consumer
   banks and, 80–81; credit cards and,

76–77; early years of, 69–70; education and career of, 70–72, 81; future of banking and, 67–69; holding companies and, 73–74, 78; insurance industry and, 74–75; international banking and, 71–72, 74; laissez faire laws and, 212n4; mentorship of, 71–72; mutual funds and, 75; personality of, 214n38; political accomplishments of, 81–83; on railroad bankruptcies, 211n3; recognition of,

80–81; reserve levels and, 140; ship loans and, 71; supermarket bank campaign and, 4; threats to sell Citibank by, 80
Wulfekuhler, Kurt C., 220n29

Yingling, Edward L., 129
Young, Nancy Beck, 202n15

Zelizer, Julian, 200n8
Zingales, Luigi, 235n12

ACKNOWLEDGMENTS

During 2008–2009, I had the honor to serve as president of the Business History Conference. I needed to prepare a presidential address for the meeting in June 2009. Around that time, I was also paying keen attention to news reports about drastic losses taking place among stressed homeowners and at the nation's leading commercial and investment banks, such as Citigroup and Bear Stearns. During the weekend of September 12–14, 2008, political and bank leaders met at the Federal Reserve Bank of New York. JPMorgan Chase's Jamie Dimon and Treasury Secretary Henry Paulson were among those who spent all or part of the weekend at the New York Fed. They sought to resolve the financial problems that had accumulated at Lehman Brothers Holdings, but failed to do so. The next day, September 15, Lehman's attorneys filed for bankruptcy.

I started research for this book on September 15. I had a few ideas in mind. I had the good fortune to have studied with John Burnham, Ellis Hawley, and Austin Kerr. Austin and John's friendship and wisdom sustained my early years as a historian in ways too difficult to enumerate or explain. Books and articles by Lou Galambos, Sam Hays, and Robert Wiebe focused members of my generation on the institutional arrangements that governed American politics and business organizations. Years later, Bill Childs brought to my attention Brian Balogh's sophisticated work on federal officials who wrote legislation and shaped regulations that informed American life in theme and detail, often silently. In June 2009, I gave my presidential address, later published in *Enterprise & Society* (*E&S*). Phil Scranton, *E&S*'s talented editor, applied his well-honed skills to getting ideas front and center. The book was under way.

Much of the pleasurable work of historical scholarship remains invisible to outsiders. During these years of research and writing, I enjoyed warm conversations and helpful correspondence with economists and historians about the main elements in American financial development. Most likely, Michele Alacevich, Dan Amsterdam, Joe Arena, Jack Bauman, Gavin Benke,

Albert Churella, Alexander Sayf Cummings, Colleen Dunlavy, Jeff Fear, Michael Fein, Jeffrey Fine, David Freund, Walter Friedman, David Gold-field, Tom Hanchett, Per Hansen, Daniel Holt, Roger Horowitz, Vicki Howard, Louis Hyman, Richard John, Arnie Kanov, Desmond Lachman, Walter Licht, Christina Lubinski, David Mason, Andrew McGee, Stephen Mihm, Paul Miranti, Ted Muller, Laura Phillips Sawyer, David Schuyler, Phil Scranton, Kelly Shannon, Ellie Shermer, Dick Sylla, Kristin Szylvian, Joel Tarr, Dan Wadhwani, Ben Waterhouse, and Mark Wilson never realized the degree to which I absorbed their keen observations about the location of primary sources, about the politics of urban and industrial change, about the way businesses and banks hired, promoted, and worked in practice, and about the origins of the financial crisis. Sometimes we just talked.

Librarians at Florida Atlantic University (FAU) proved especially helpful at each stage in this project's development. The FAU library already maintained subscriptions to publications like *American Banker* and *Institutional Investor* that bankers read daily. I overloaded FAU's interlibrary loan staff with requests for books and articles by economists, bankers, insurance company officials, homebuilders, and financial analysts. Holly Hargett, Melanie Poloff, April Porterfield, and other hardworking librarians hunted down obscure documents. They fulfilled each request cheerfully, sometimes within a day or two. I am in their debt.

Historical research depends on talented and unheralded librarians and archivists located around the United States. Allen Fisher at the Lyndon B. Johnson Library and Guian McKee, a faculty member at the University of Virginia's Miller Center, provided a crash course on how to access the treasures that resided in Johnson's taped telephone conversations. Julie Sager at the Federal Reserve Bank of New York went far out of her way to identify valuable and long-buried files. I am pleased for the opportunity to thank the wonderful staffs at the Jimmy Carter, Bill Clinton, and Gerald Ford Presidential Libraries. My special thanks to Jason Kaplan at the Clinton Library. I enjoyed equally helpful advice at the Briscoe Center for American History at the University of Texas, the Library of Congress, the Minnesota Historical Society, National Archives II, Texas A&M University Library and Archives, and the Genesee Historical Collections Center at the University of Michigan–Flint.

I presented early results of my research at scholarly conferences and at research forums. To prepare for these important gatherings, authors deliver short papers in advance to commentators. Those commentators in turn pro-